A Kodansha Comics Trade Paperback Original
Attack on Titan volume 5 copyright © 2011 Hajime Isayama
English translation copyright © 2013 Hajime Isayama

Published in the United States by Kodansha Comics, an imprint of Kodansha USA Publishing, LLC, New York.

Publication rights for this English edition arranged through Kodansha Ltd, Tokyo.

First published in Japan in 2011 by Kodansha Ltd., Tokyo as Shingeki no Kyojin, volume 5.

ISBN 978-1-61262-254-5

Original cover design by Takashi Shimoyama (Red Rooster)

Printed in the United States of America.

www.kodanshacomics.com

9 8 7 6 5
Translator: Sheldon Drzka
Lettering: Steve Wands

ATTACK ON TITAN

5

HAJIME ISAYAMA

"Attack on Titan" Character Introductions

104th TRAINING CORPS

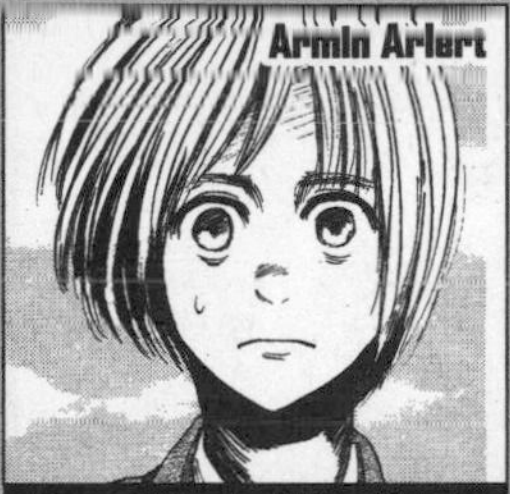
Armin Arlert

Eren and Mikasa's childhood friend. Though Armin isn't athletic in the least, he is an excellent thinker and can produce unique ideas.

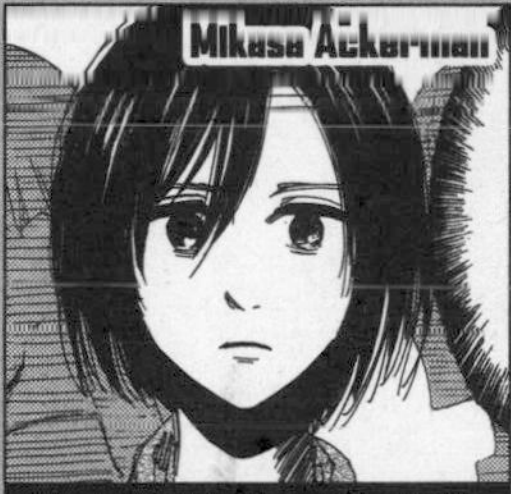
Mikasa Ackerman

Mikasa graduated at the top of her training corps. Her parents were murdered before her eyes when she was a child. After that, she was raised alongside Eren, whom she tenaciously tries to protect.

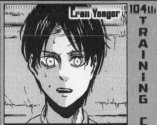

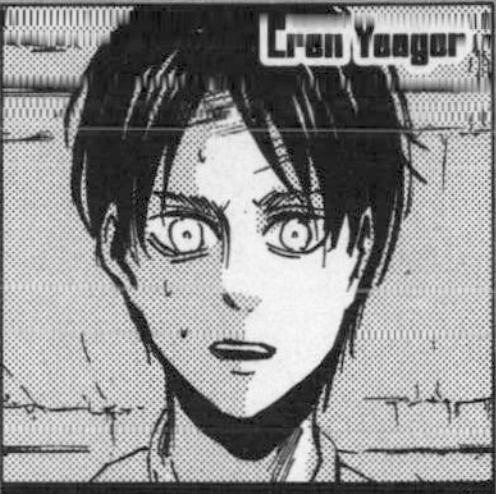
Eren Yeager

Longing for the world outside the wall, Eren aims to join the Survey Corps. He can turn himself into a Titan.

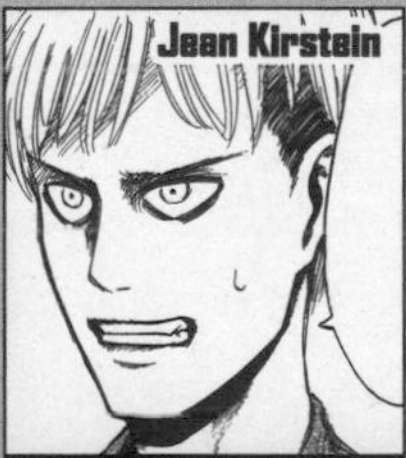
Jean Kirstein

Superior at vertical maneuvering. Jean is honest to a fault, which often puts him at odds with other people.

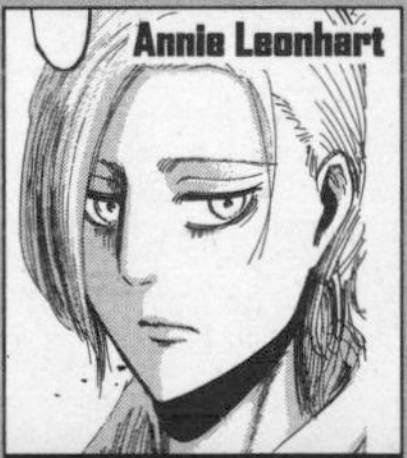
Annie Leonhart

Annie's small stature belies her great skill in the art of hand-to-hand combat. She's a realist through and through, and tends to be a loner.

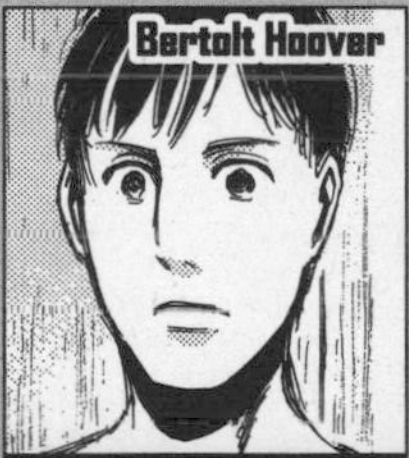
Bertolt Hoover

Has a high degree of skill in everything he's been taught, but is indecisive and lacks initiative.

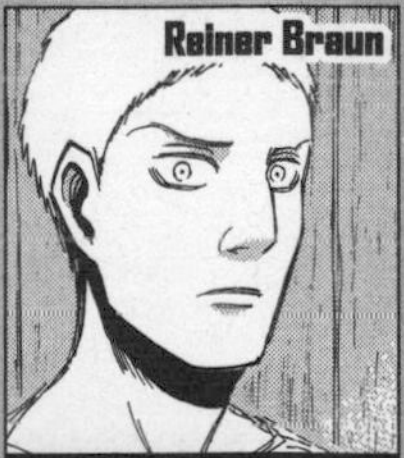
Reiner Braun

Graduated second in his training corps. Reiner is as strong as an ox and has the will to match. His comrades have a great deal of trust in him.

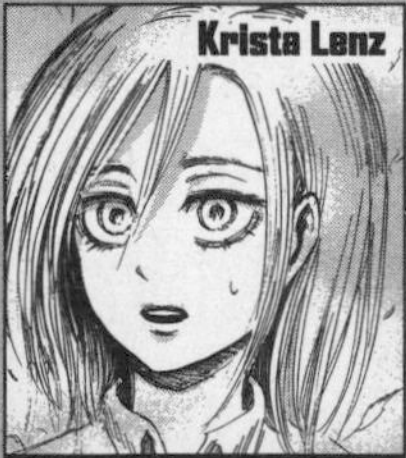
Krista Lenz

Extremely short, with a friendly, warm-hearted personality.

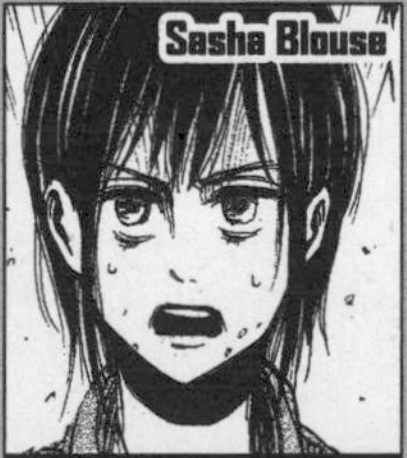
Sasha Blouse

Sasha is very agile and has remarkable instincts. Owing to her unconventionality, she isn't suited for organized activity.

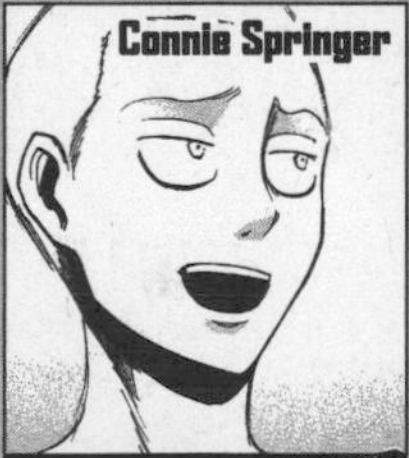
Connie Springer

Effective at vertical maneuvering, but slow on the uptake, so his comprehension of tactics is less than stellar.

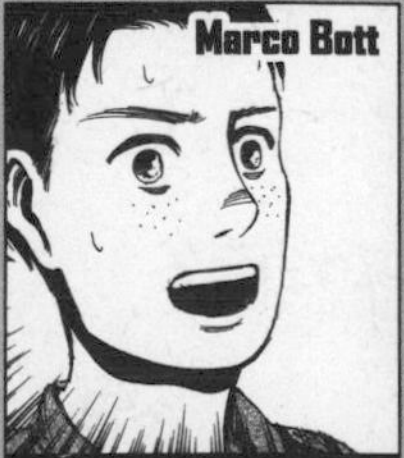
Marco Bott

Yearned to join the Military Police Brigade so he could serve the king. Marco died during the Titan mop-up operation.

A doctor and Eren's father. He went missing after the Titan attack five years ago.

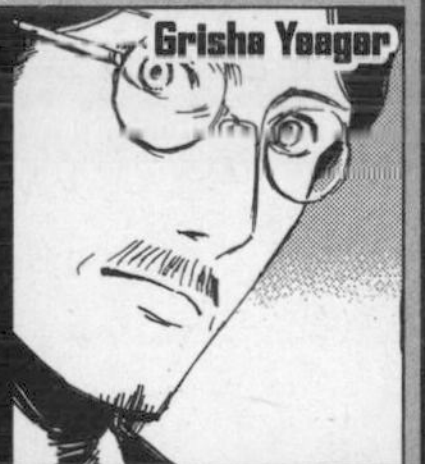
Grisha Yeager

Captain of the Survey Corps said to be the strongest human alive.

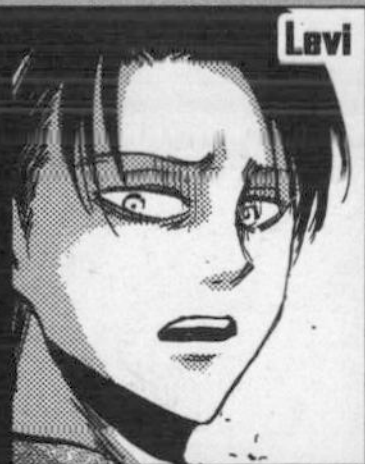
Levi

Commander of the Survey Corps.

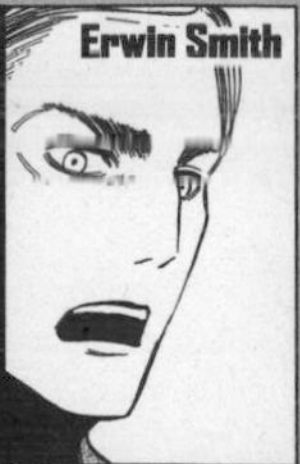
Erwin Smith

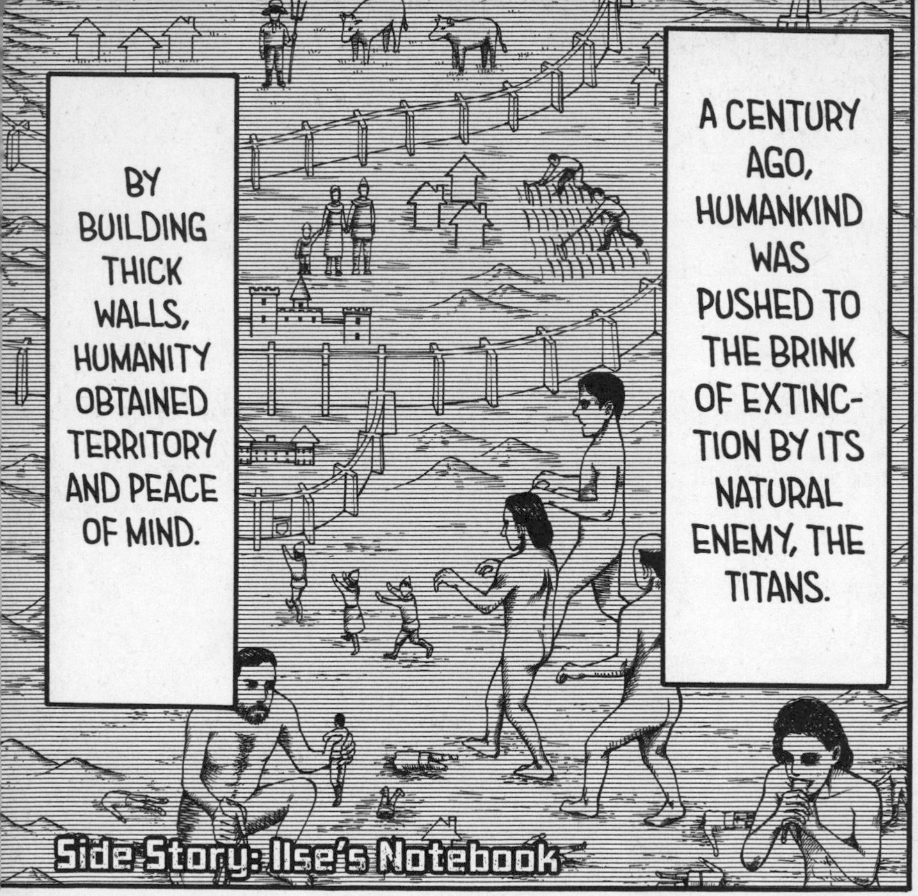
A CENTURY AGO, HUMANKIND WAS PUSHED TO THE BRINK OF EXTINCTION BY ITS NATURAL ENEMY, THE TITANS.
BY BUILDING THICK WALLS, HUMANITY OBTAINED TERRITORY AND PEACE OF MIND.
Side Story: Ilse's Notebook
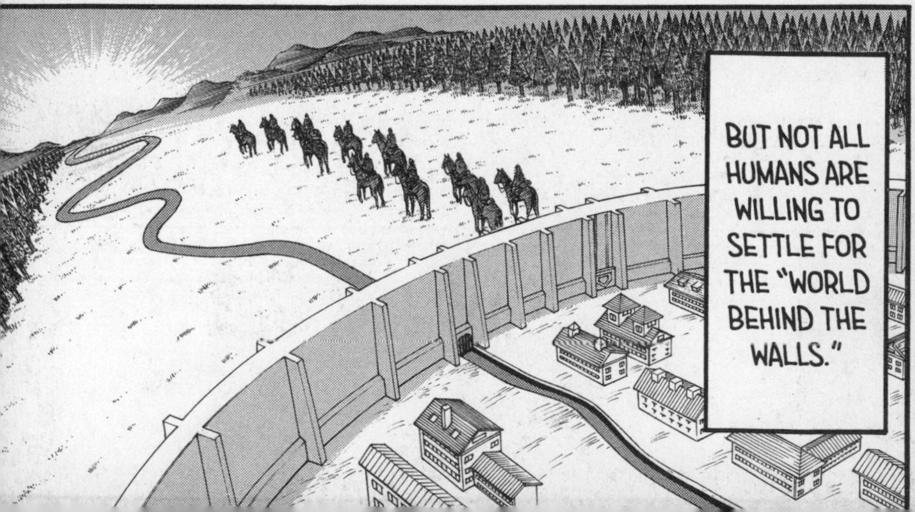
BUT NOT ALL HUMANS ARE WILLING TO SETTLE FOR THE "WORLD BEHIND THE WALLS."

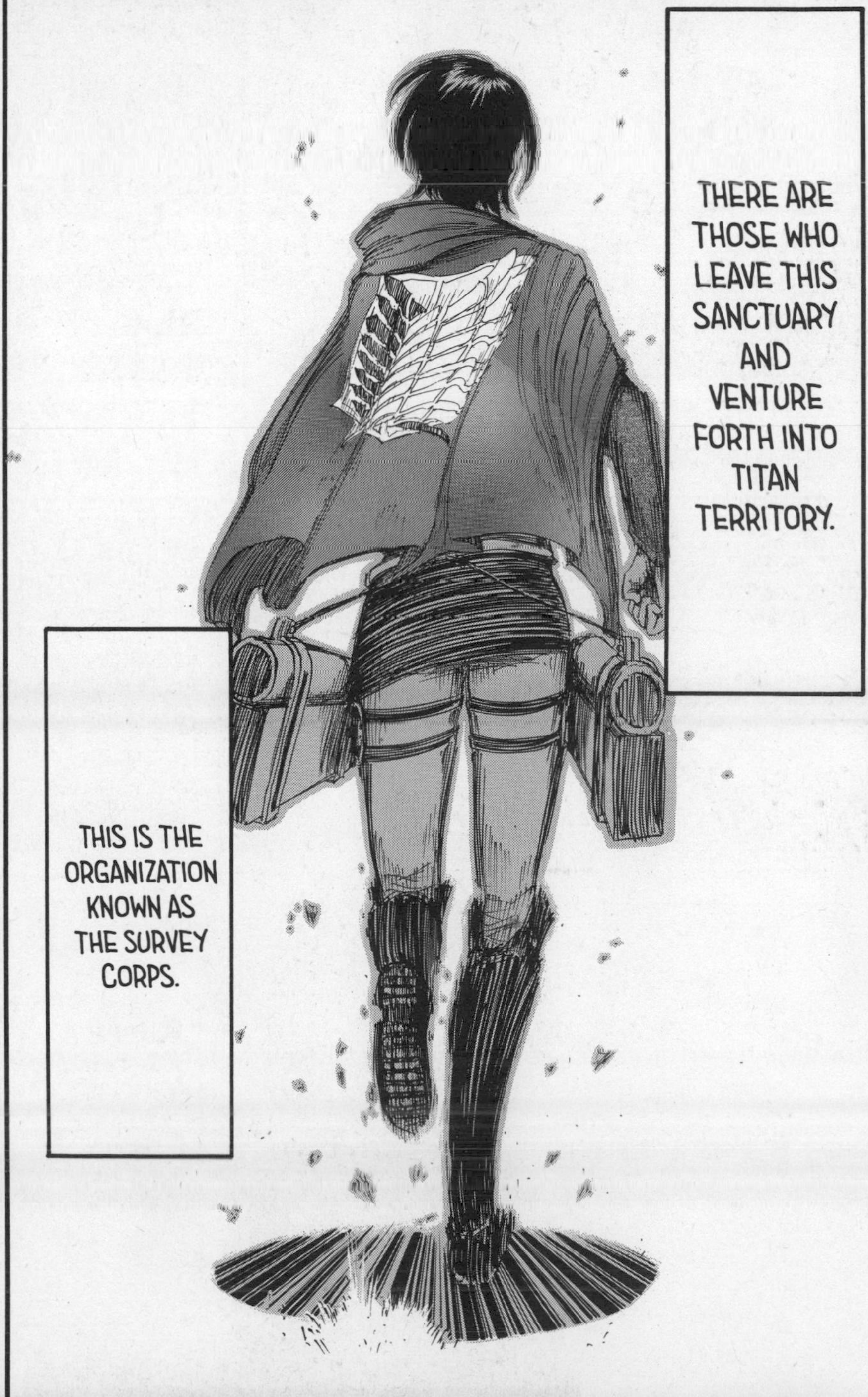
THERE ARE THOSE WHO LEAVE THIS SANCTUARY AND VENTURE FORTH INTO TITAN TERRITORY.
THIS IS THE ORGANIZATION KNOWN AS THE SURVEY CORPS.

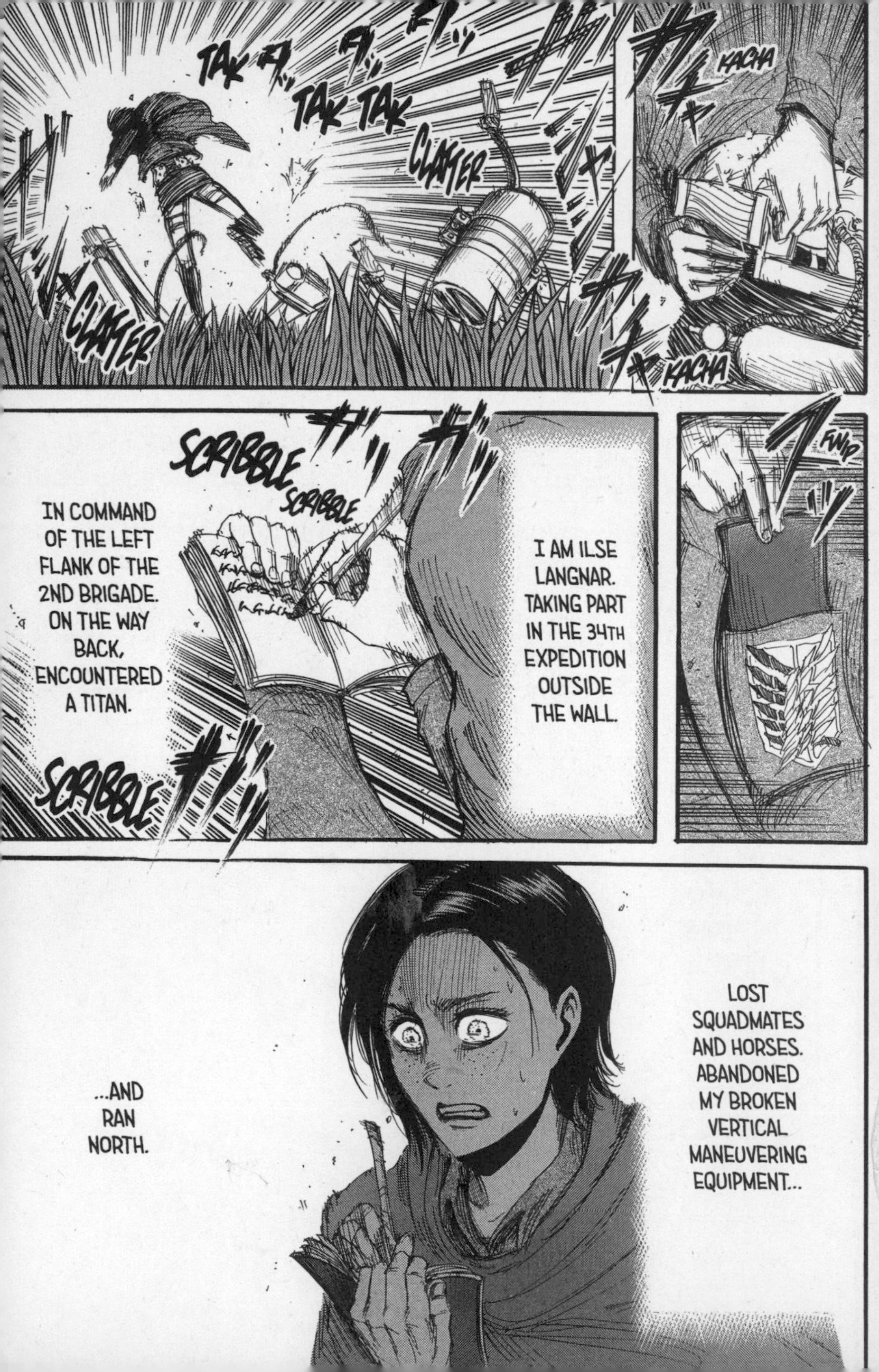
KACHA
KACHA
TAK
TAK TAK
CLATTER
CLATTER
FWIP
I AM ILSE LANGNAR. TAKING PART IN THE 34TH EXPEDITION OUTSIDE THE WALL.
SCRIBBLE
SCRIBBLE
IN COMMAND OF THE LEFT FLANK OF THE 2ND BRIGADE. ON THE WAY BACK, ENCOUNTERED A TITAN.
SCRIBBLE
LOST SQUADMATES AND HORSES. ABANDONED MY BROKEN VERTICAL MANEUVERING EQUIPMENT...
...AND RAN NORTH.

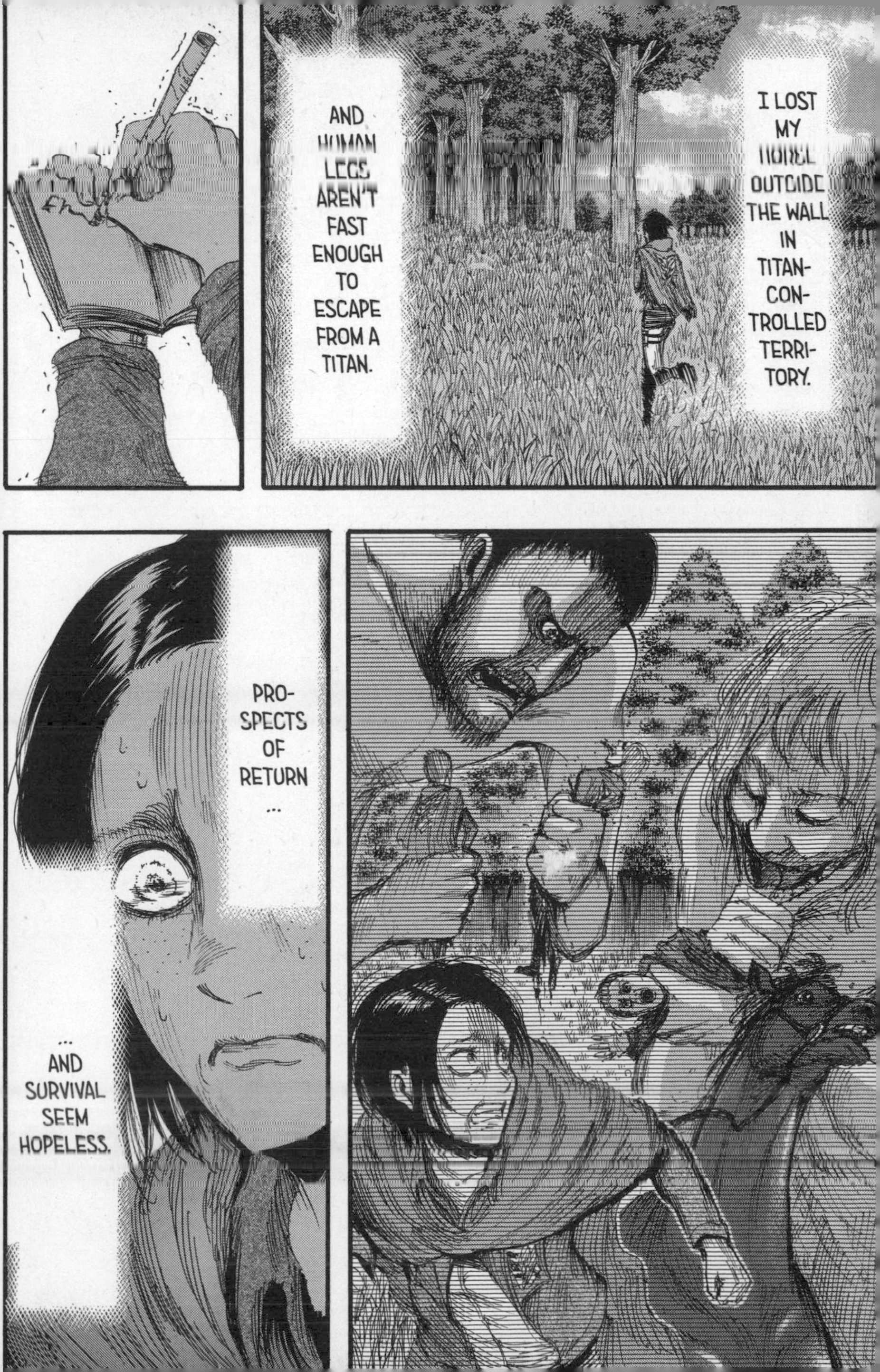
I LOST MY HORSE OUTSIDE THE WALL IN TITAN-CONTROLLED TERRITORY.
AND HUMAN LEGS AREN'T FAST ENOUGH TO ESCAPE FROM A TITAN.
PROSPECTS OF RETURN ...
... AND SURVIVAL SEEM HOPELESS.

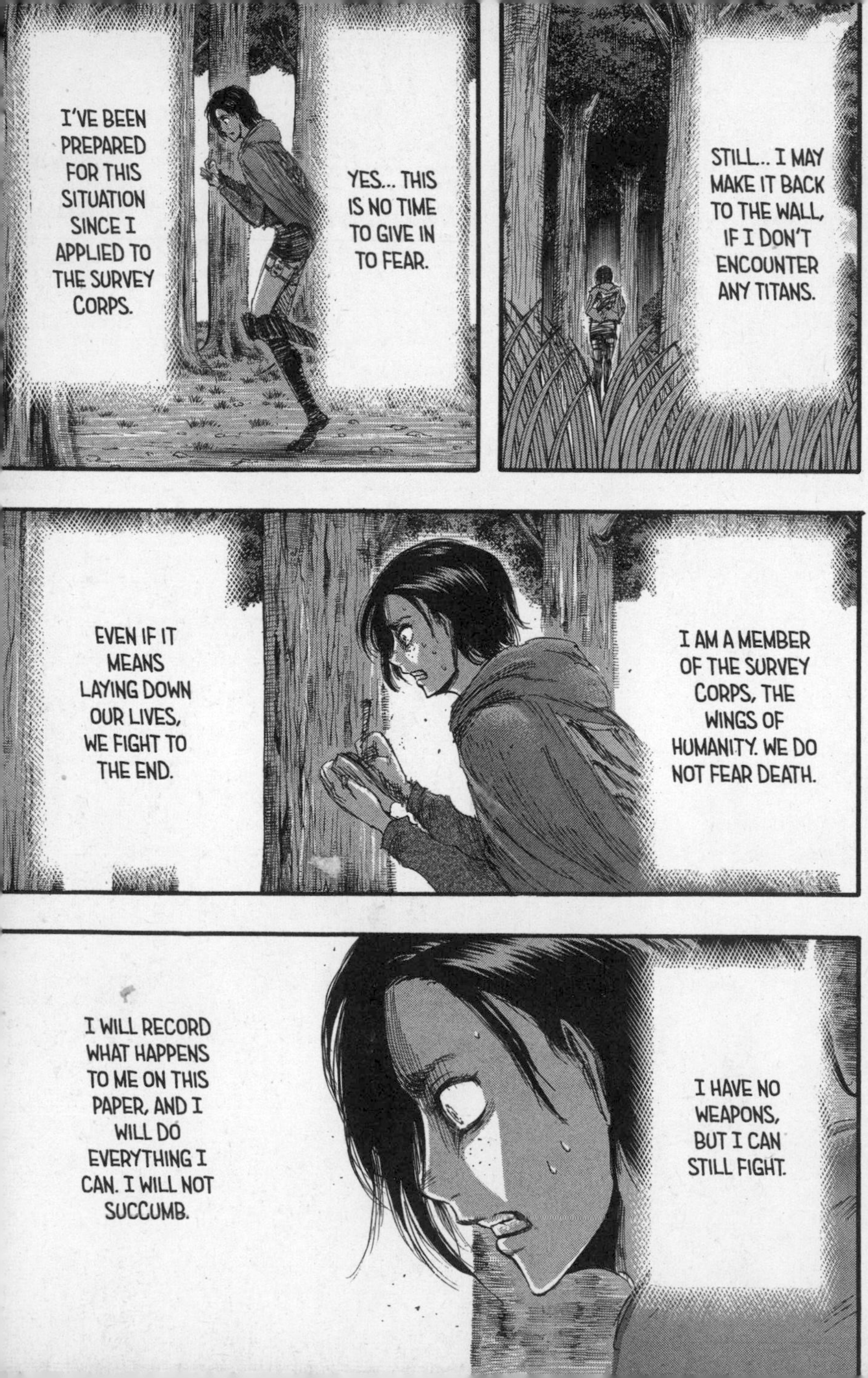
STILL... I MAY MAKE IT BACK TO THE WALL, IF I DON'T ENCOUNTER ANY TITANS.
YES... THIS IS NO TIME TO GIVE IN TO FEAR.
I'VE BEEN PREPARED FOR THIS SITUATION SINCE I APPLIED TO THE SURVEY CORPS.
I AM A MEMBER OF THE SURVEY CORPS, THE WINGS OF HUMANITY. WE DO NOT FEAR DEATH.
EVEN IF IT MEANS LAYING DOWN OUR LIVES, WE FIGHT TO THE END.
I HAVE NO WEAPONS, BUT I CAN STILL FIGHT.
I WILL RECORD WHAT HAPPENS TO ME ON THIS PAPER, AND I WILL DO EVERYTHING I CAN. I WILL NOT SUCCUMB.

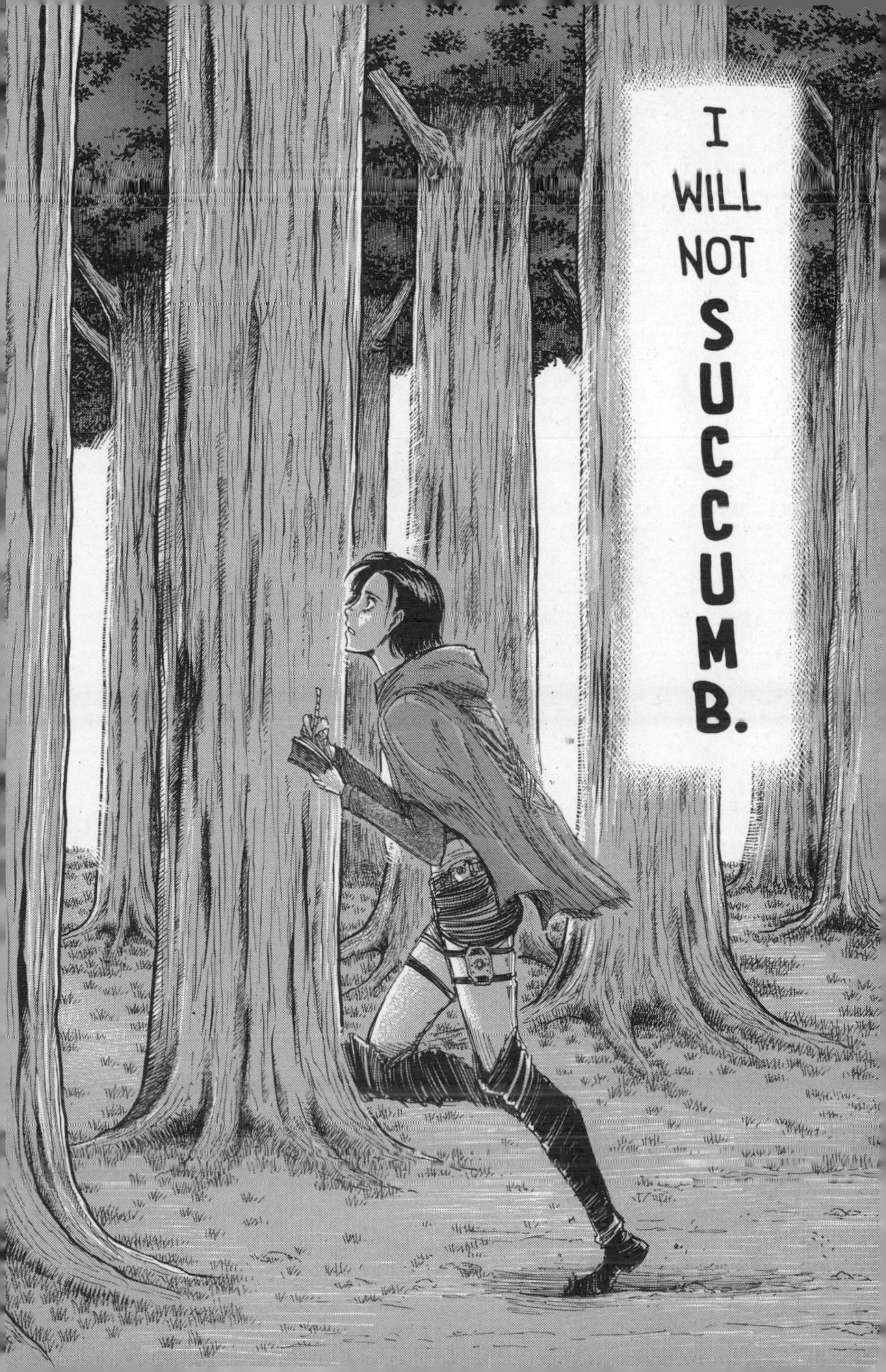
I WILL NOT SUCCUMB.

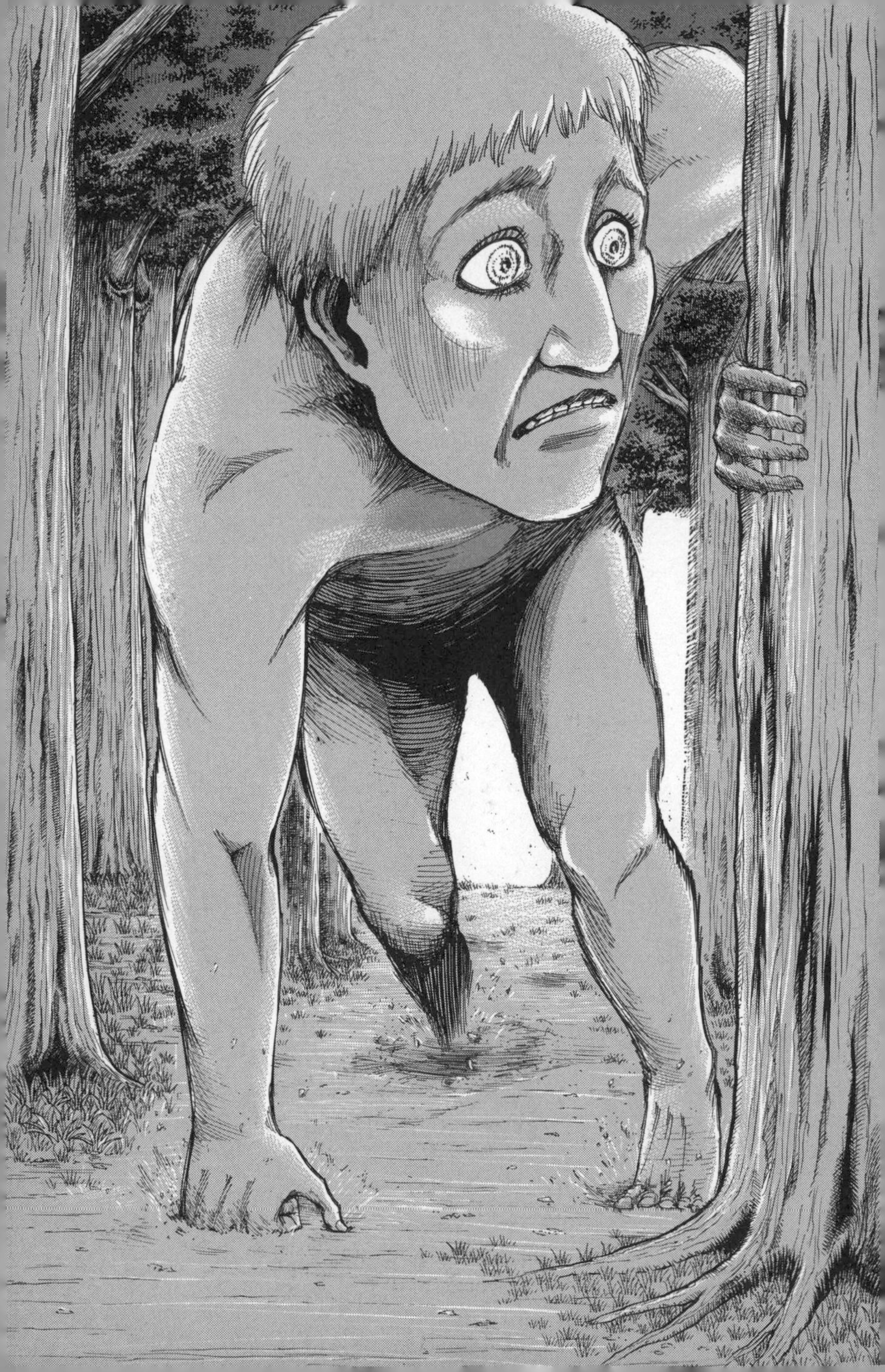

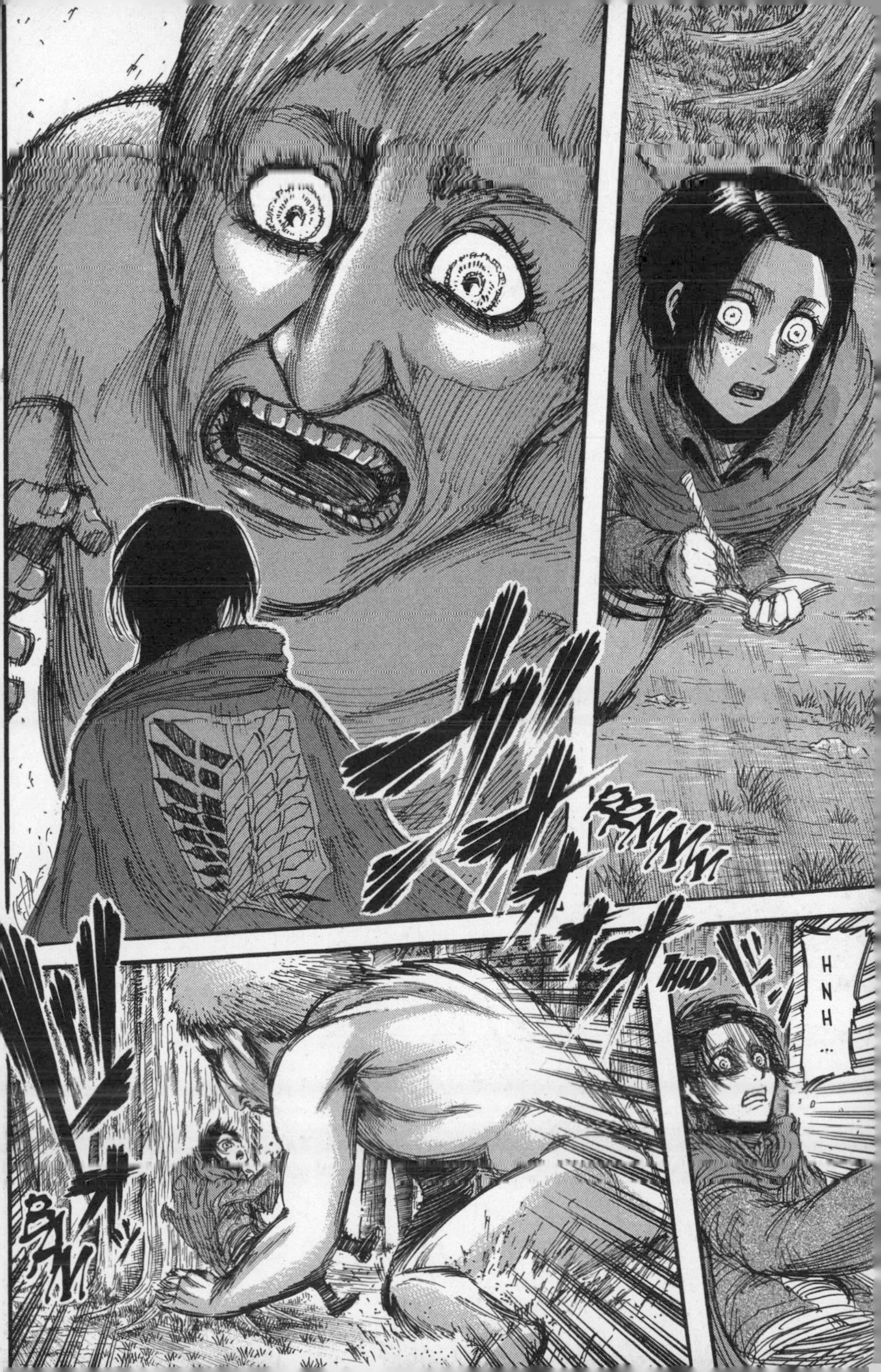
RRMMM
HNH ...
THUD
BAM

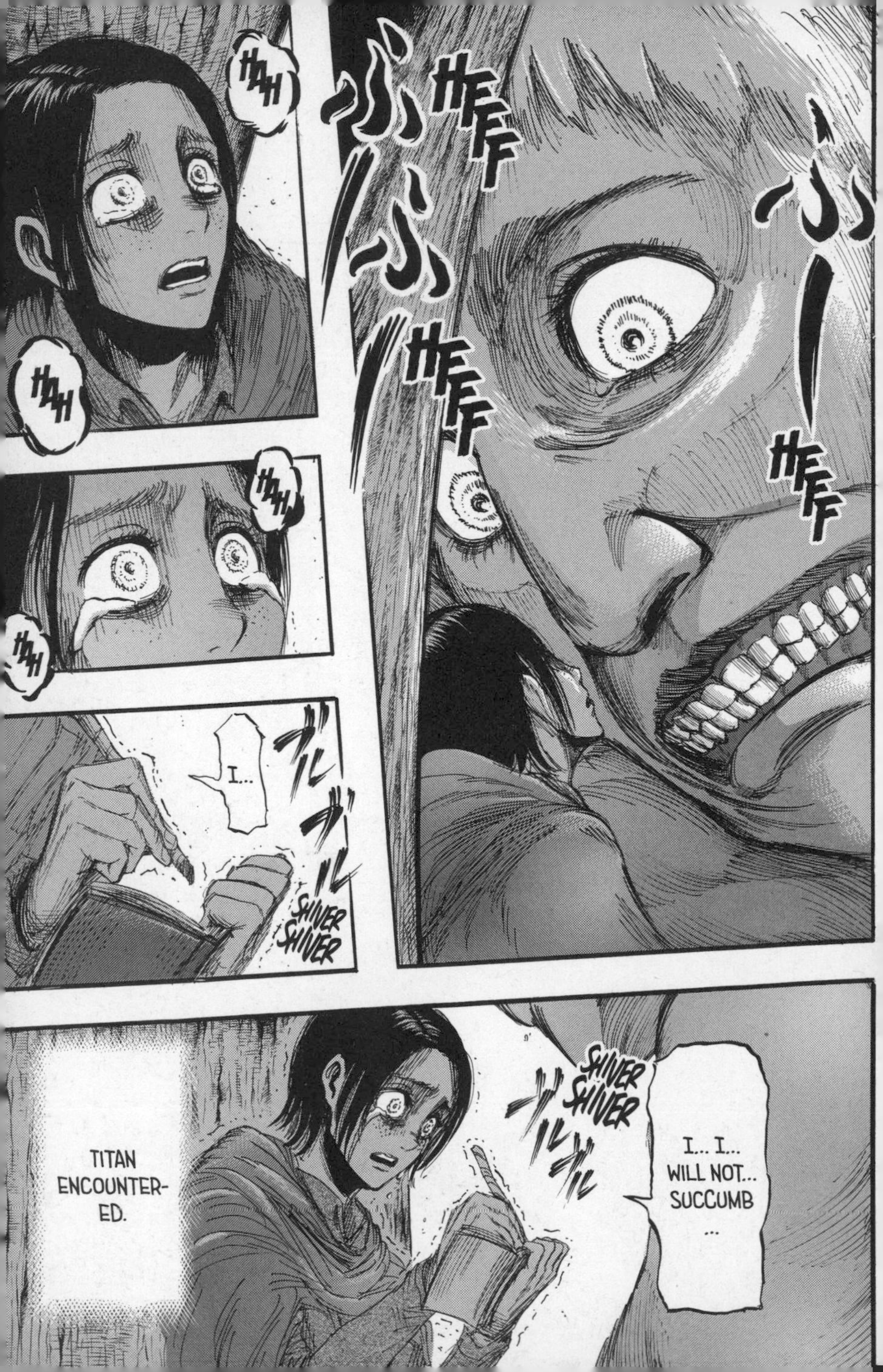
HEFF
HEFF
HEFF
HAH
HAH
HAH
HAH
I...
SHIVER SHIVER
I... I... WILL NOT... SUCCUMB ...
SHIVER SHIVER
TITAN ENCOUNTER-ED.

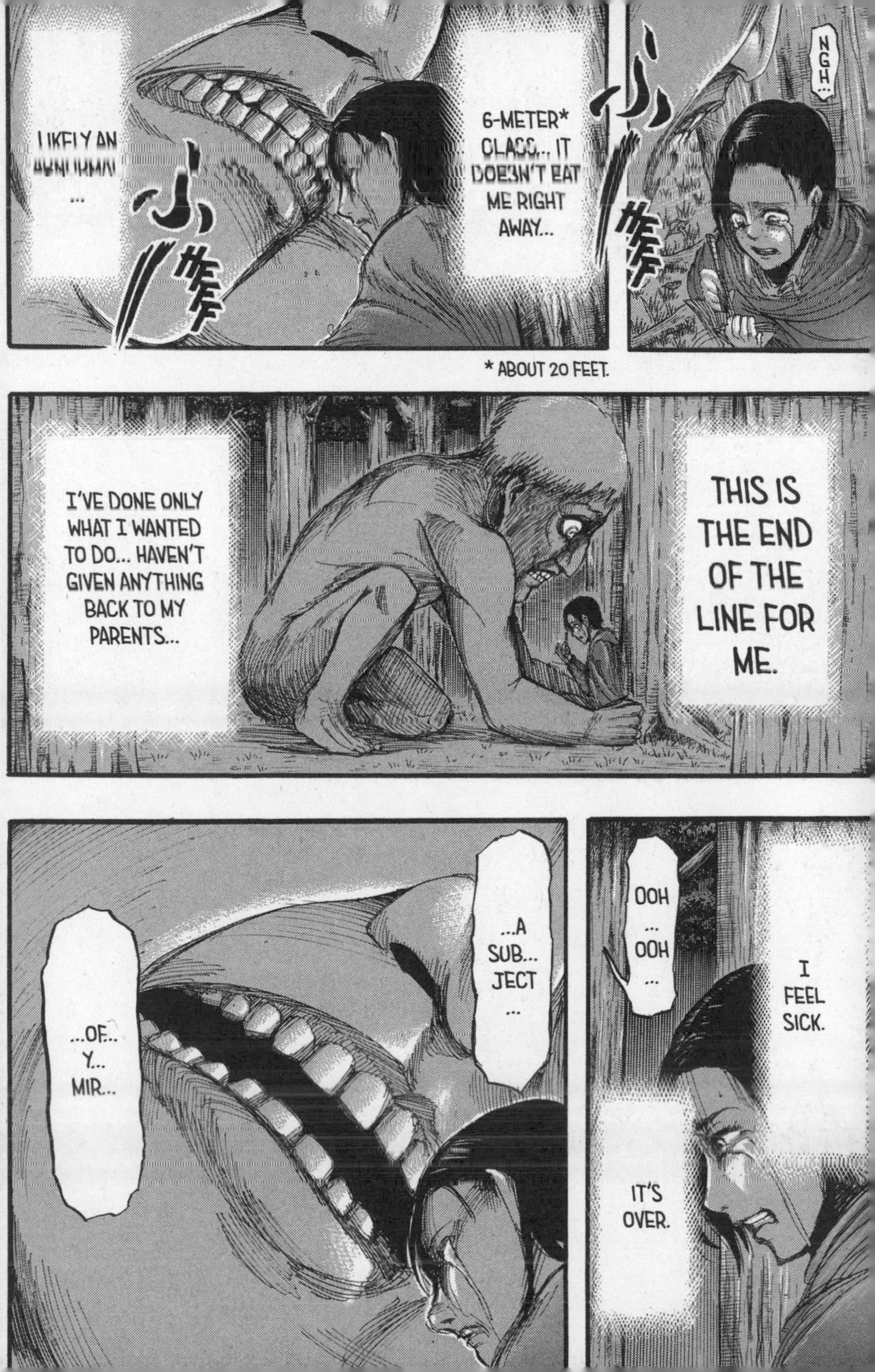
NGH...
HEFF
6-METER* CLASS... IT DOESN'T EAT ME RIGHT AWAY...
HEFF
LIKELY AN ABNORMAL ...
* ABOUT 20 FEET.
THIS IS THE END OF THE LINE FOR ME.
I'VE DONE ONLY WHAT I WANTED TO DO... HAVEN'T GIVEN ANYTHING BACK TO MY PARENTS...
OOH ... OOH ...
I FEEL SICK.
IT'S OVER.
...A SUB... JECT ...
...OF... Y... MIR...

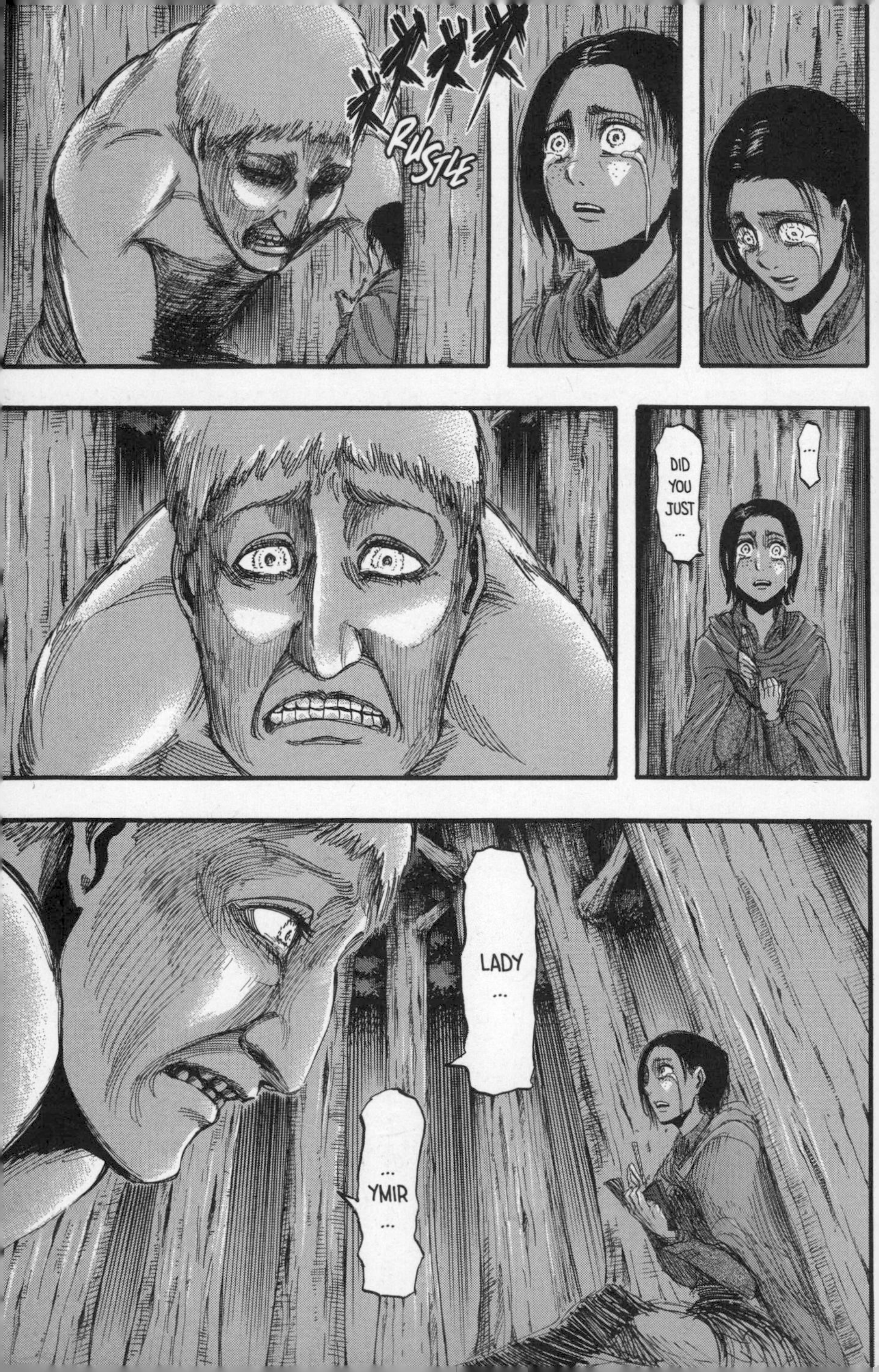
RUSTLE
...
DID YOU JUST ...
LADY ...
... YMIR ...

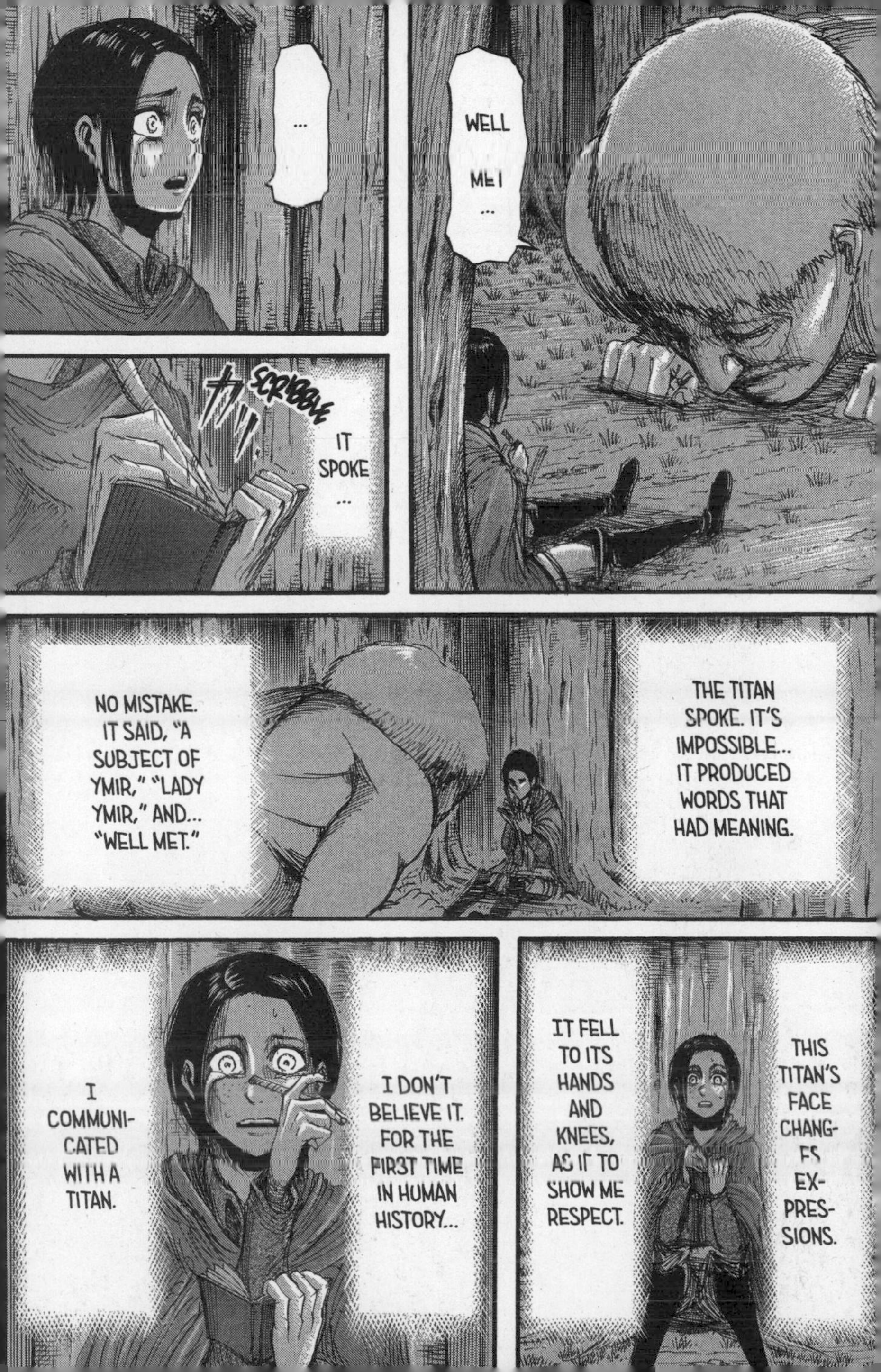
WELL MET ...
...
SCRIBBLE
IT SPOKE ...
THE TITAN SPOKE. IT'S IMPOSSIBLE... IT PRODUCED WORDS THAT HAD MEANING.
NO MISTAKE. IT SAID, "A SUBJECT OF YMIR," "LADY YMIR," AND... "WELL MET."
THIS TITAN'S FACE CHANGES EXPRESSIONS.
IT FELL TO ITS HANDS AND KNEES, AS IF TO SHOW ME RESPECT.
I DON'T BELIEVE IT. FOR THE FIRST TIME IN HUMAN HISTORY...
I COMMUNICATED WITH A TITAN.

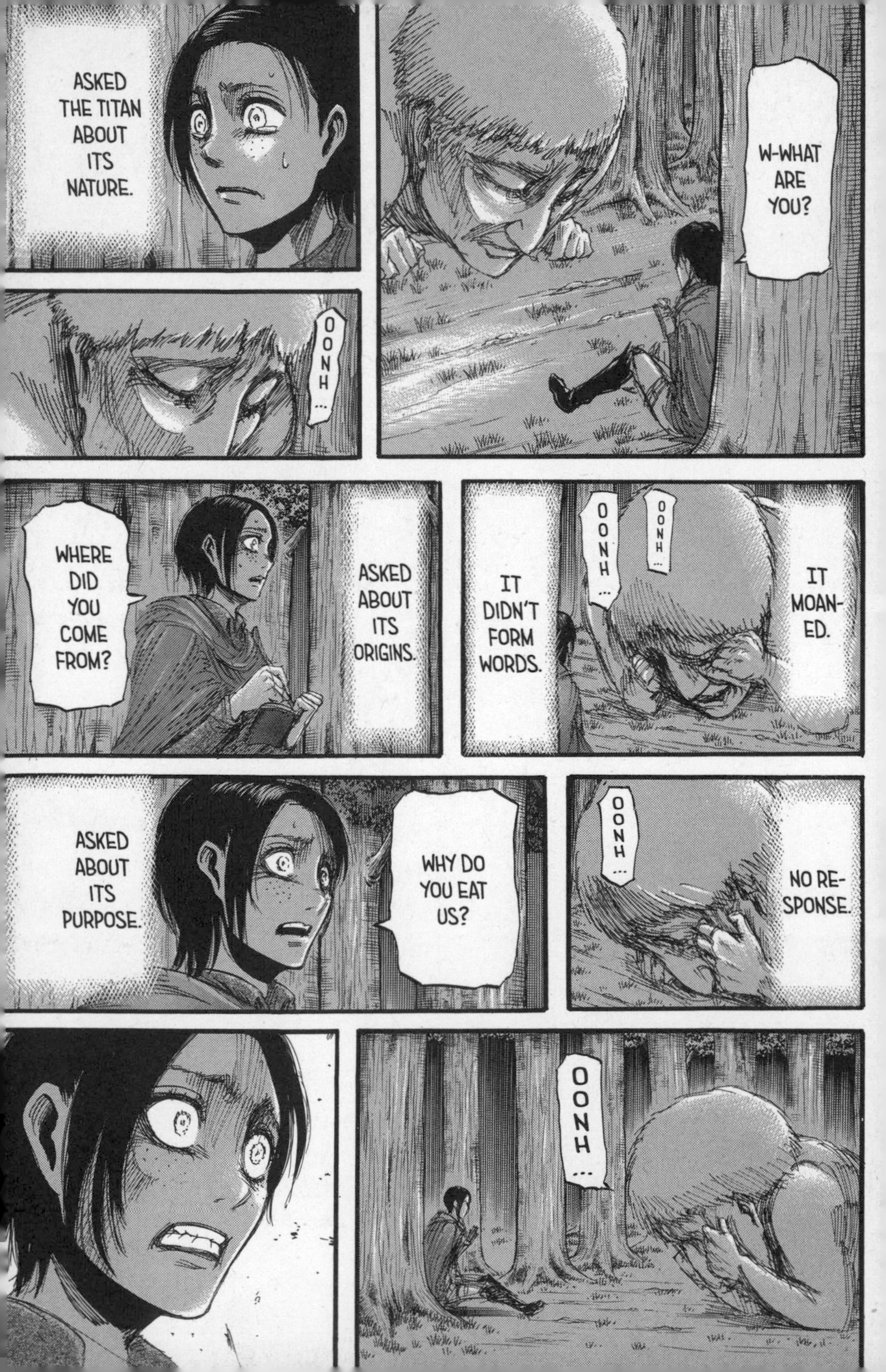
W-WHAT ARE YOU?
ASKED THE TITAN ABOUT ITS NATURE.
OONH...
IT MOAN-ED.
OONH...
OONH...
IT DIDN'T FORM WORDS.
ASKED ABOUT ITS ORIGINS.
WHERE DID YOU COME FROM?
NO RE-SPONSE.
OONH...
WHY DO YOU EAT US?
ASKED ABOUT ITS PURPOSE.
OONH...

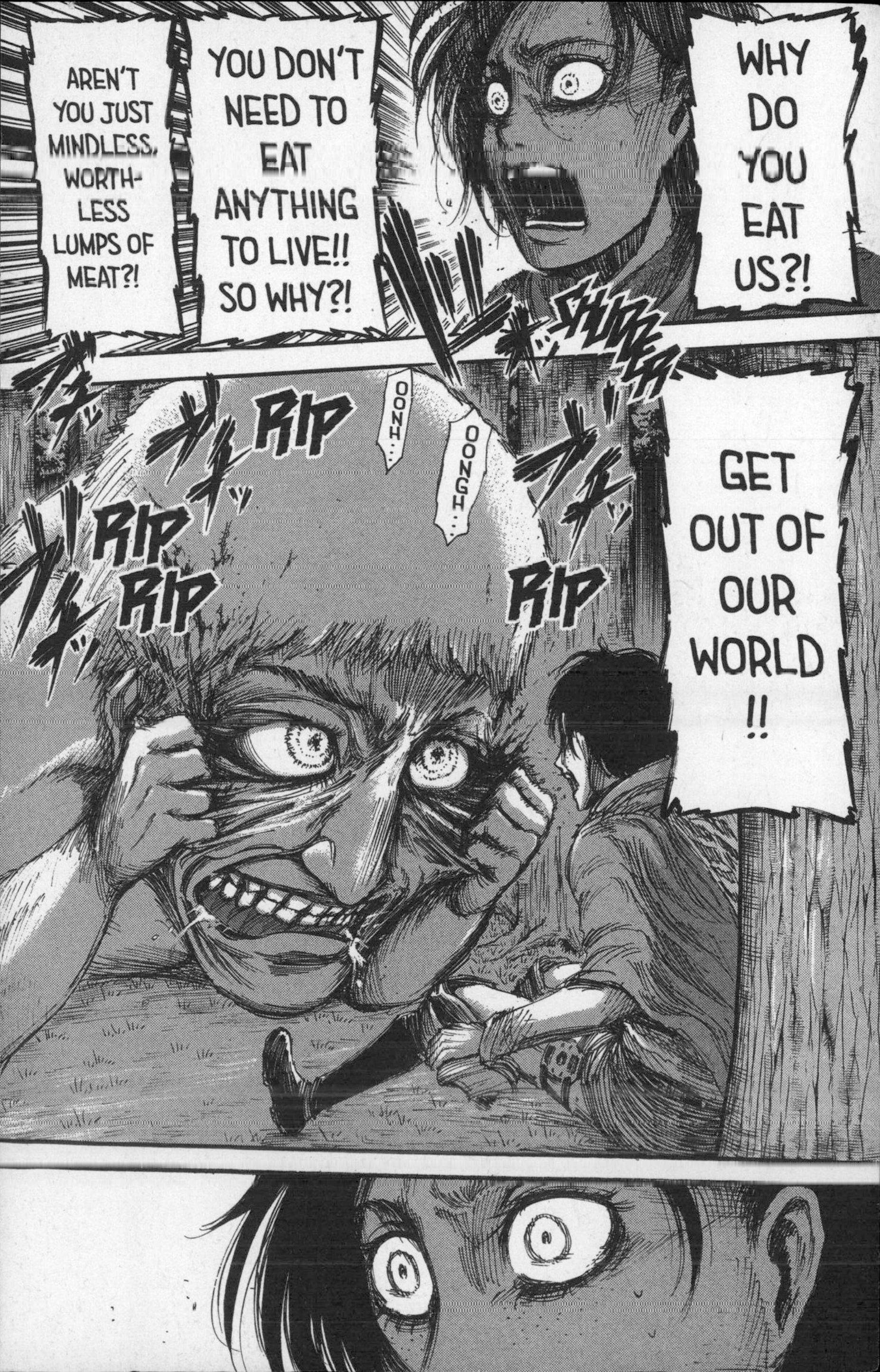

WHY DO YOU EAT US?!
YOU DON'T NEED TO EAT ANYTHING TO LIVE!! SO WHY?!
AREN'T YOU JUST MINDLESS, WORTHLESS LUMPS OF MEAT?!
GET OUT OF OUR WORLD!!
RIP
OONGH...
OONH...
RIP
RIP
RIP

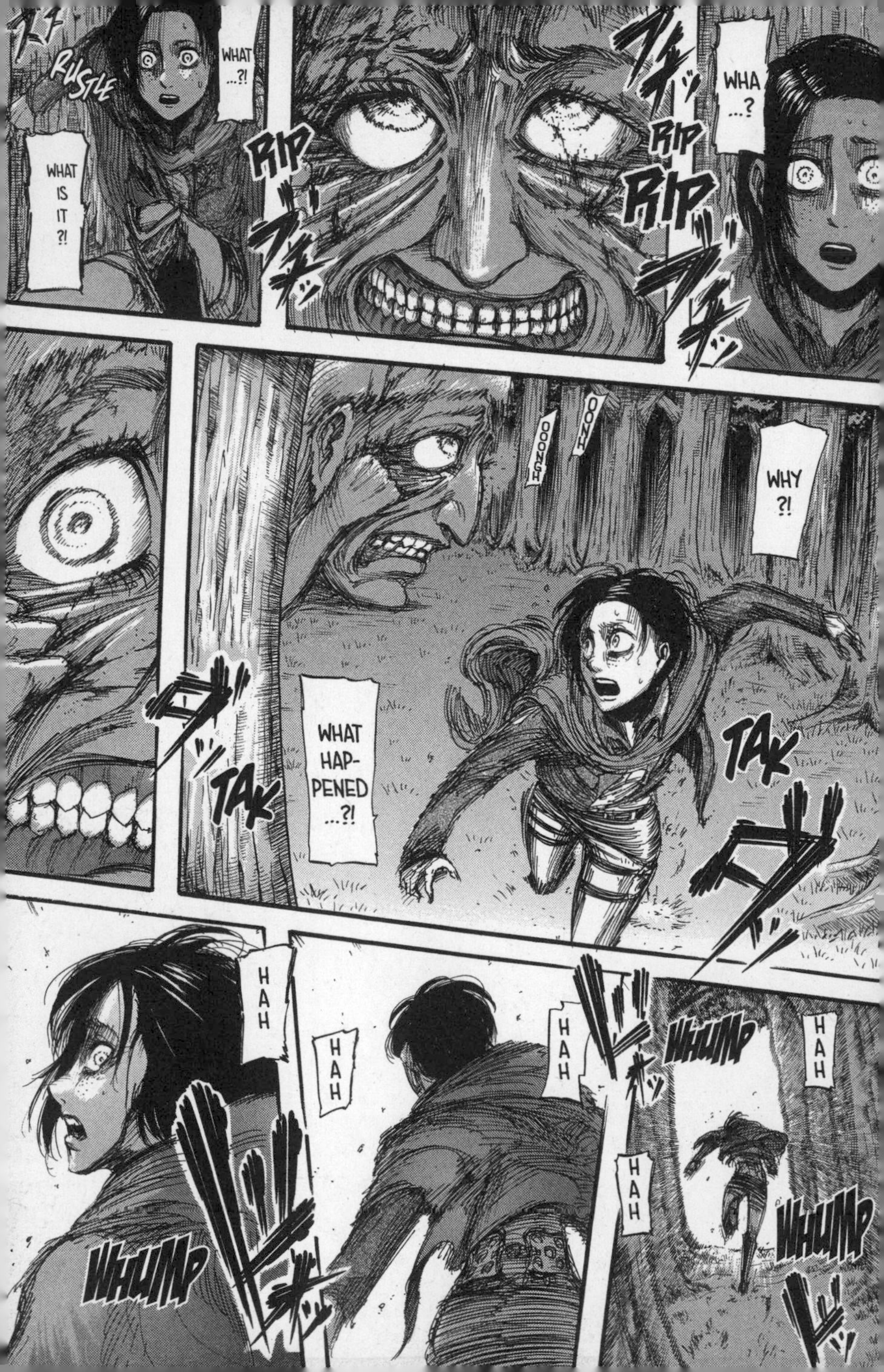
WHA ...?
RIP
RIP
RIP
RUSTLE
WHAT ...?!
WHAT IS IT ?!
OOONH
OOONGH
WHY ?!
TAK
WHAT HAP-PENED ...?!
TAK
HAH HAH
WHUMP
WHUMP
HAH HAH
HAH HAH
HAH HAH
HAH HAH
WHUMP

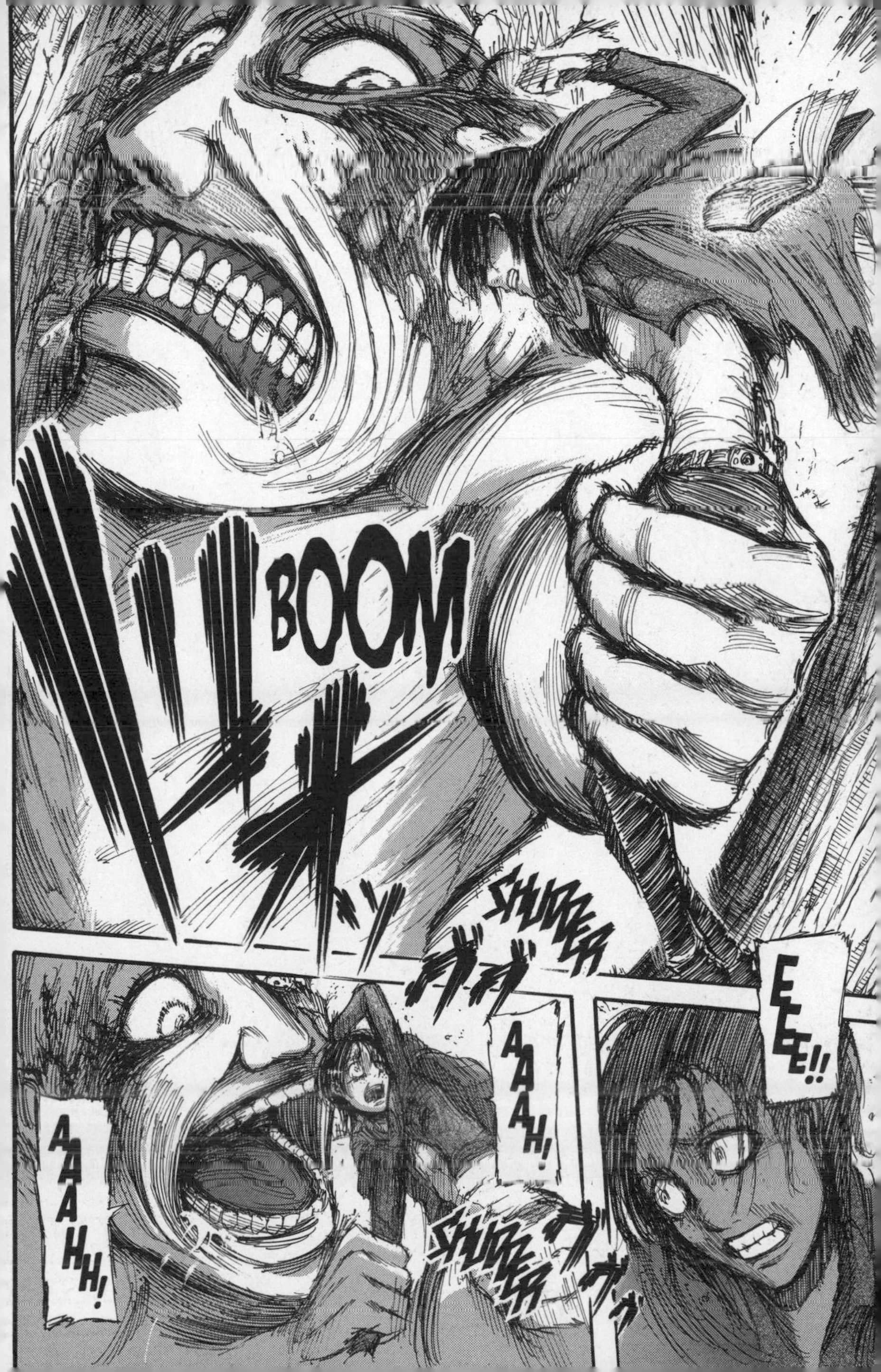
BOOM
SHUDDER
EEEE!!
AAAH!
AAAAHH!
SHUDDER

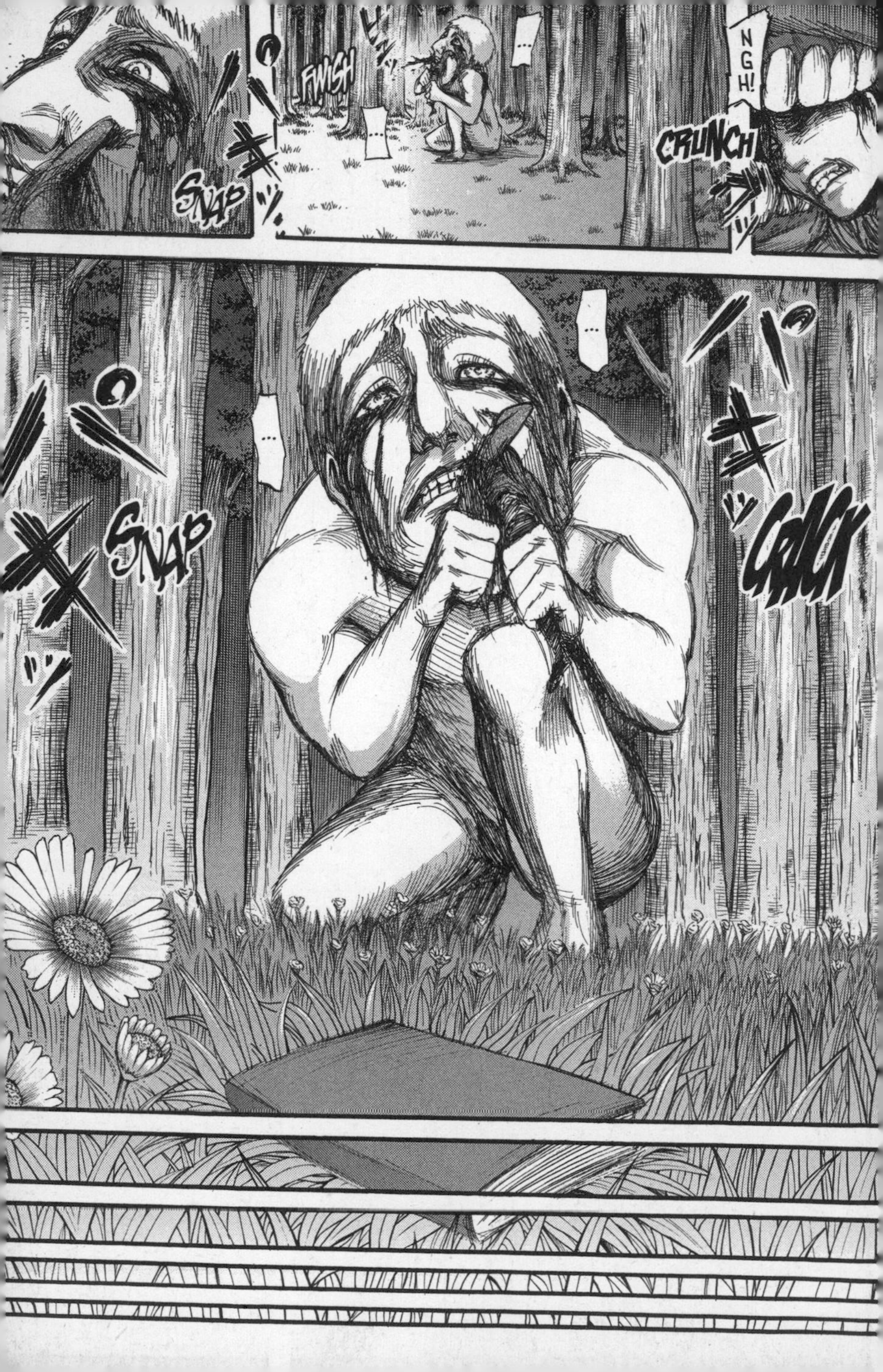
NGH!
CRUNCH
...
FWISH
...
SNAP
...
...
CRACK
SNAP

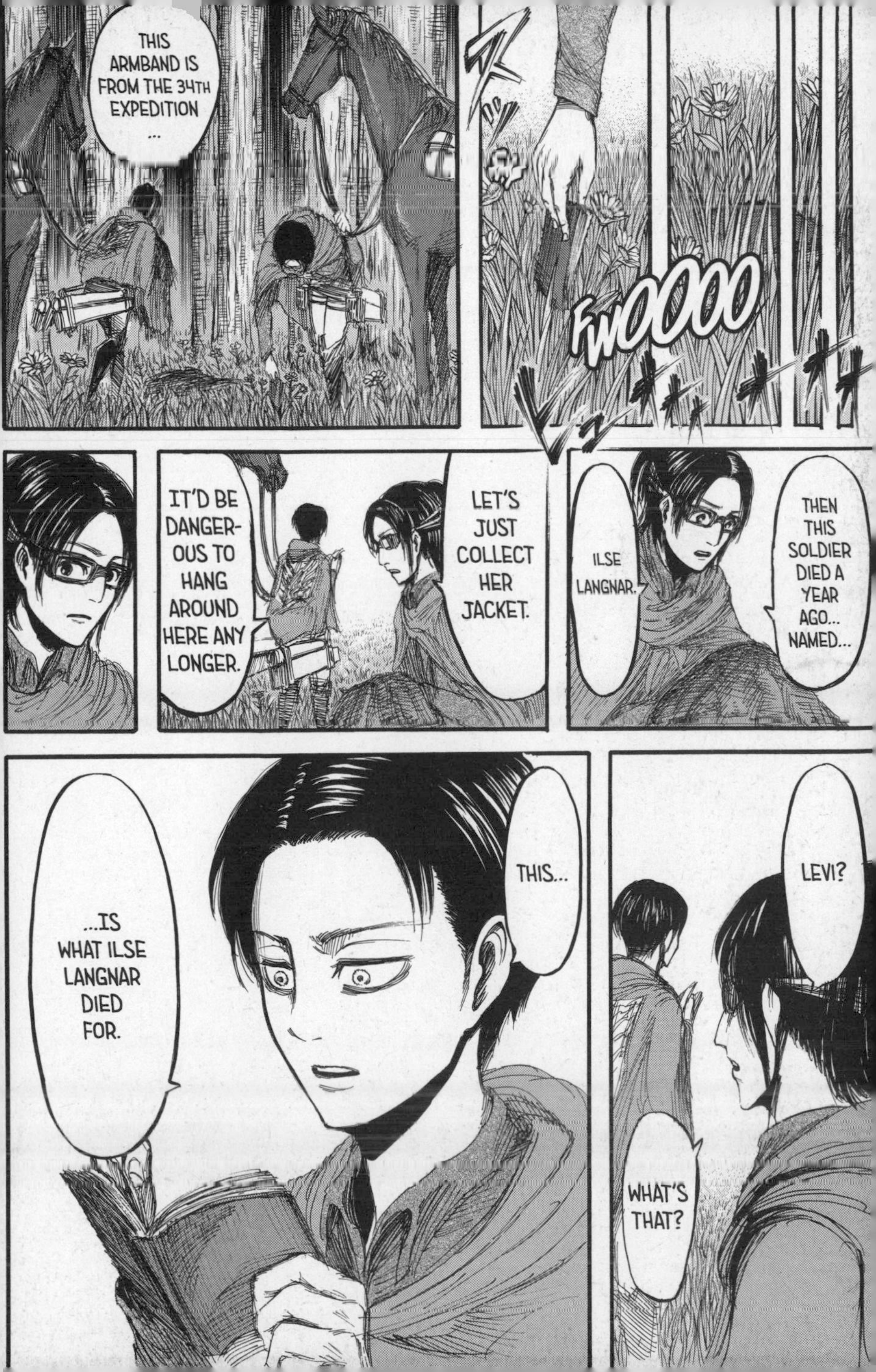
FWOOOO
THIS ARMBAND IS FROM THE 34TH EXPEDITION ...
THEN THIS SOLDIER DIED A YEAR AGO... NAMED...
ILSE LANGNAR.
LET'S JUST COLLECT HER JACKET.
IT'D BE DANGER-OUS TO HANG AROUND HERE ANY LONGER.
LEVI?
WHAT'S THAT?
THIS...
...IS WHAT ILSE LANGNAR DIED FOR.

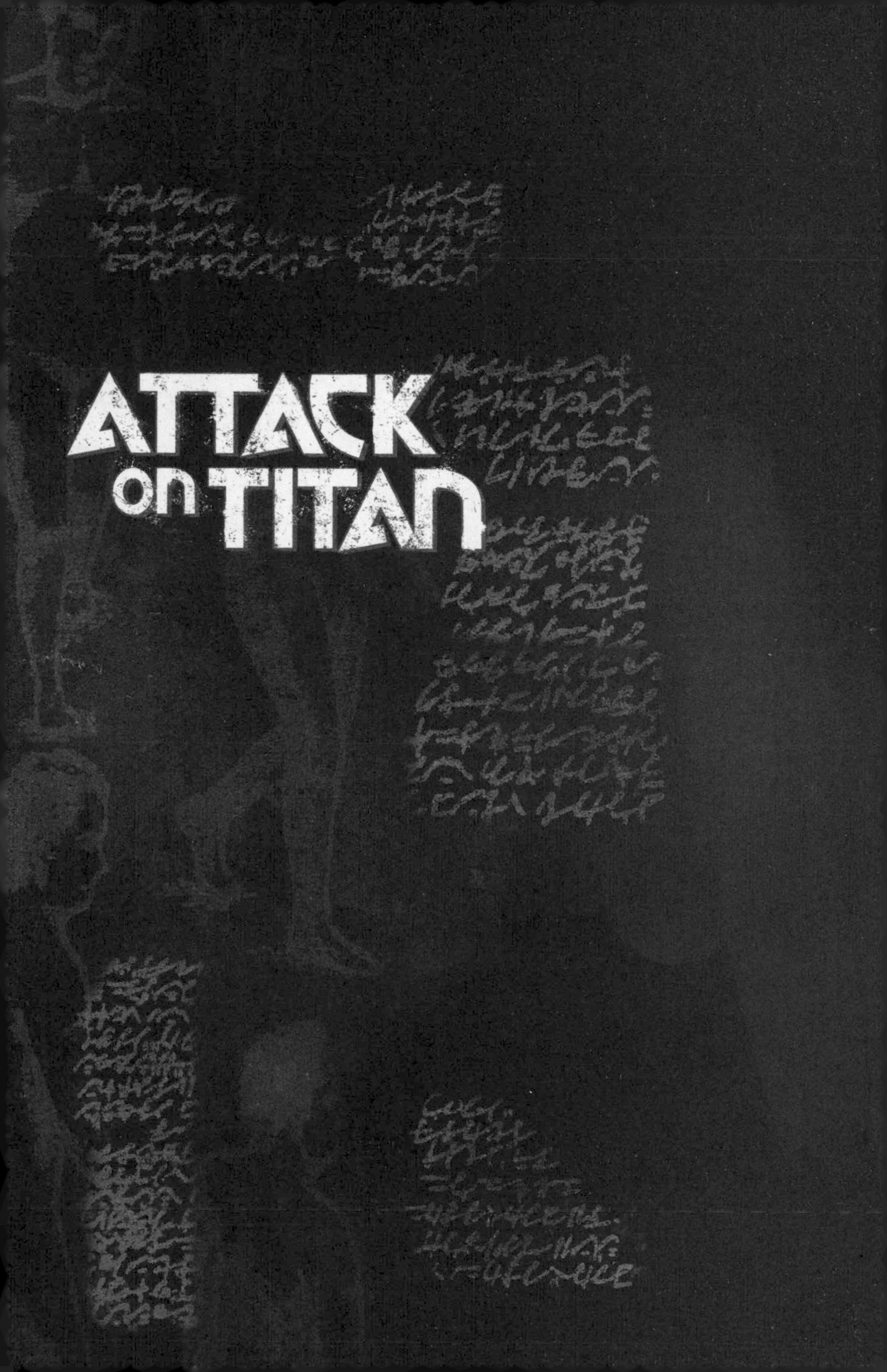
ATTACK on TITAN

ATTACK ON TITAN

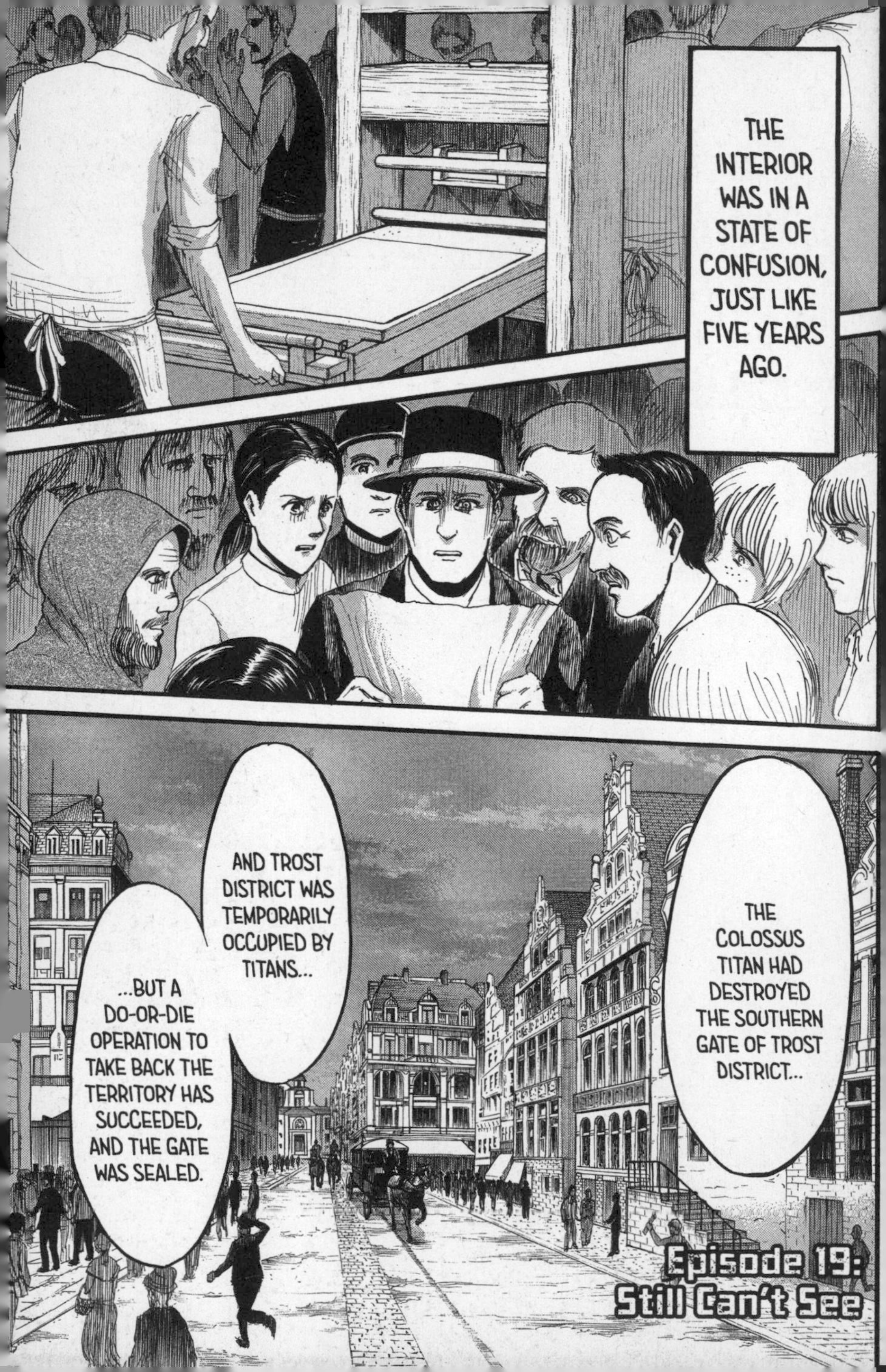
THE INTERIOR WAS IN A STATE OF CONFUSION, JUST LIKE FIVE YEARS AGO.
THE COLOSSUS TITAN HAD DESTROYED THE SOUTHERN GATE OF TROST DISTRICT...
AND TROST DISTRICT WAS TEMPORARILY OCCUPIED BY TITANS...
...BUT A DO-OR-DIE OPERATION TO TAKE BACK THE TERRITORY HAS SUCCEEDED, AND THE GATE WAS SEALED.
Episode 19: Still Can't See

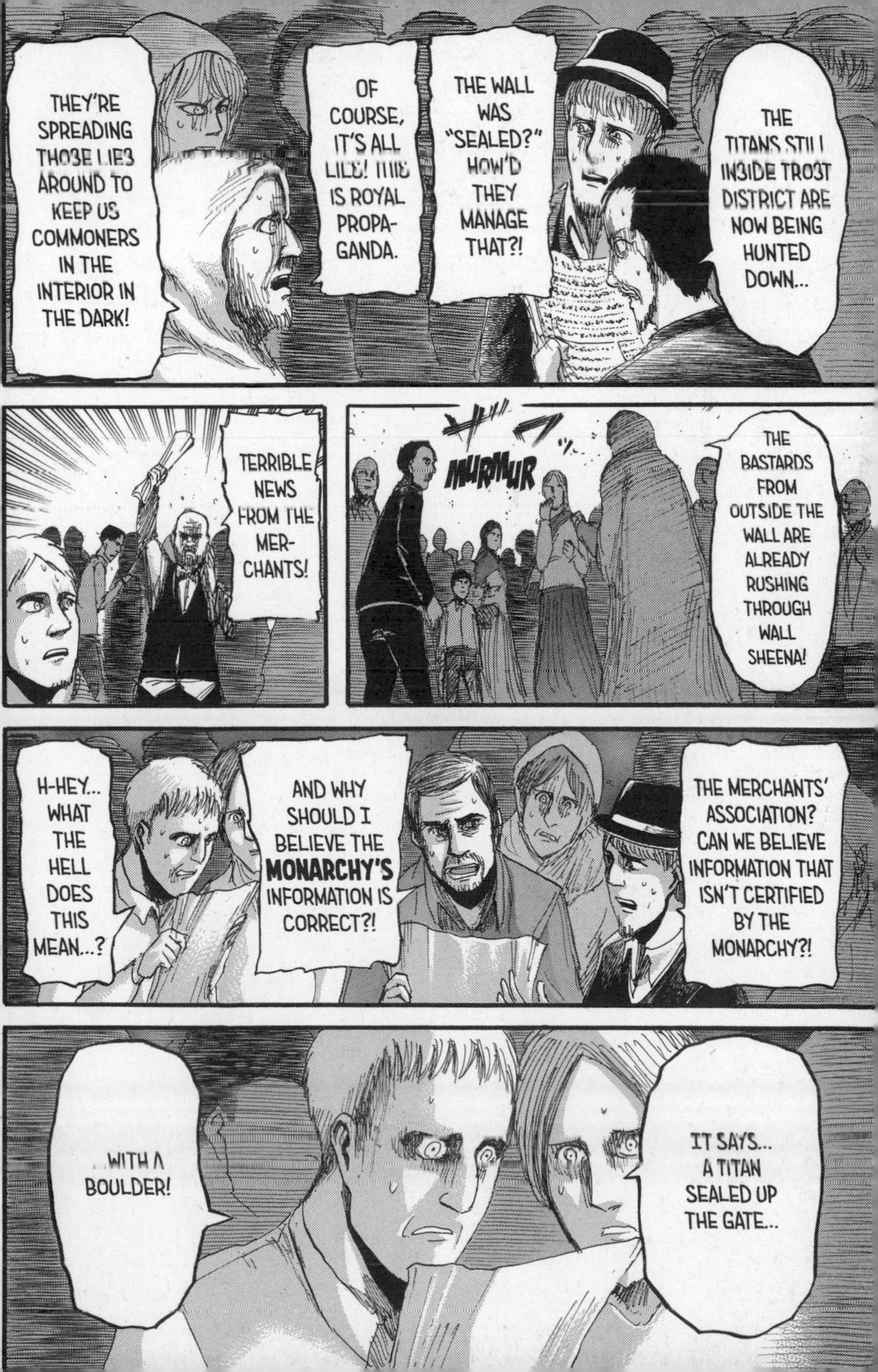
THE TITANS STILL INSIDE TROST DISTRICT ARE NOW BEING HUNTED DOWN...
THE WALL WAS "SEALED?" HOW'D THEY MANAGE THAT?!
OF COURSE, IT'S ALL LIES! THIS IS ROYAL PROPAGANDA.
THEY'RE SPREADING THOSE LIES AROUND TO KEEP US COMMONERS IN THE INTERIOR IN THE DARK!
MURMUR
THE BASTARDS FROM OUTSIDE THE WALL ARE ALREADY RUSHING THROUGH WALL SHEENA!
TERRIBLE NEWS FROM THE MERCHANTS!
THE MERCHANTS' ASSOCIATION? CAN WE BELIEVE INFORMATION THAT ISN'T CERTIFIED BY THE MONARCHY?!
AND WHY SHOULD I BELIEVE THE **MONARCHY'S** INFORMATION IS CORRECT?!
H-HEY... WHAT THE HELL DOES THIS MEAN...?
IT SAYS... A TITAN SEALED UP THE GATE...
...WITH A BOULDER!

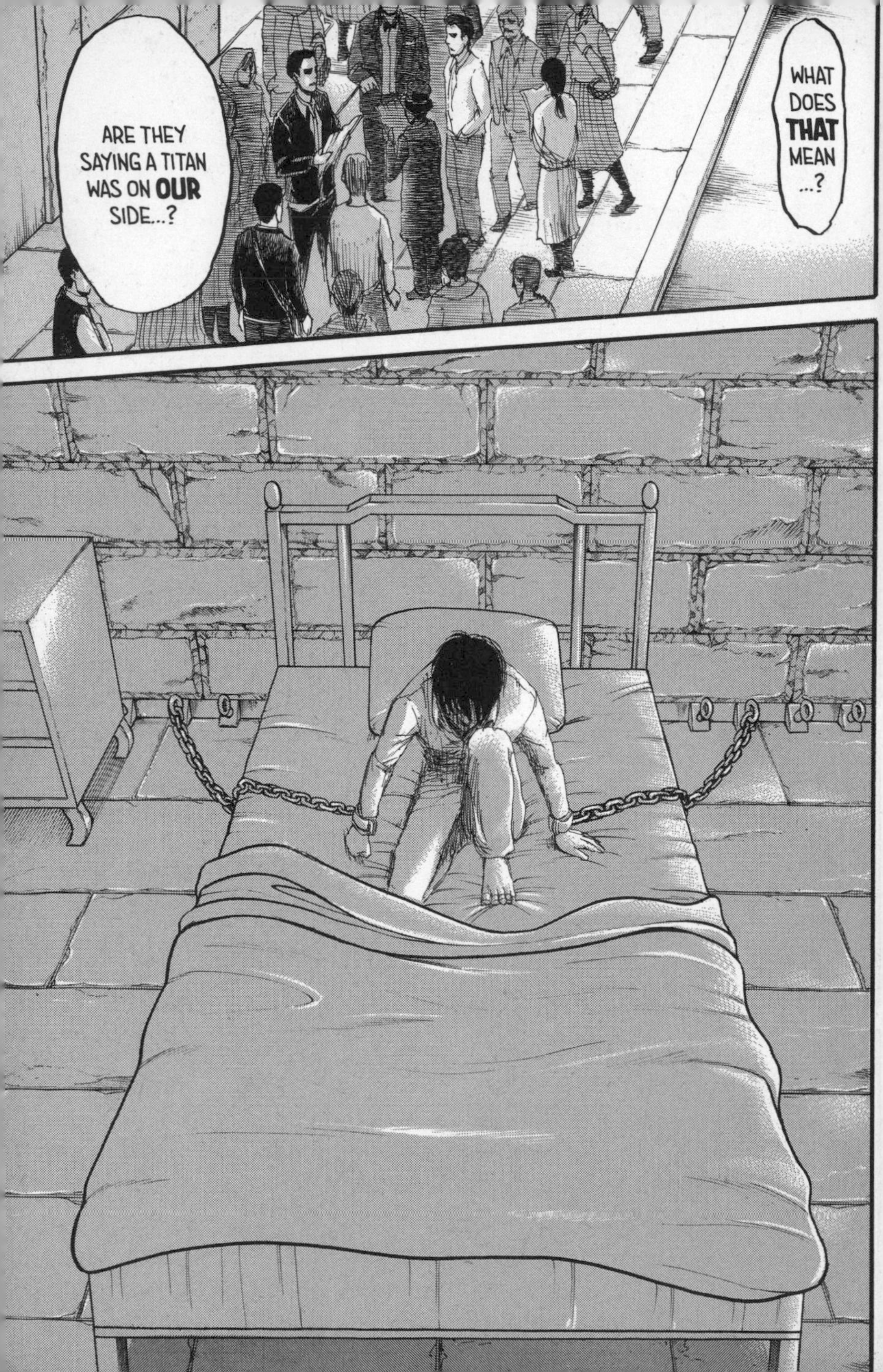
WHAT DOES **THAT** MEAN ...?
ARE THEY SAYING A TITAN WAS ON **OUR** SIDE...?

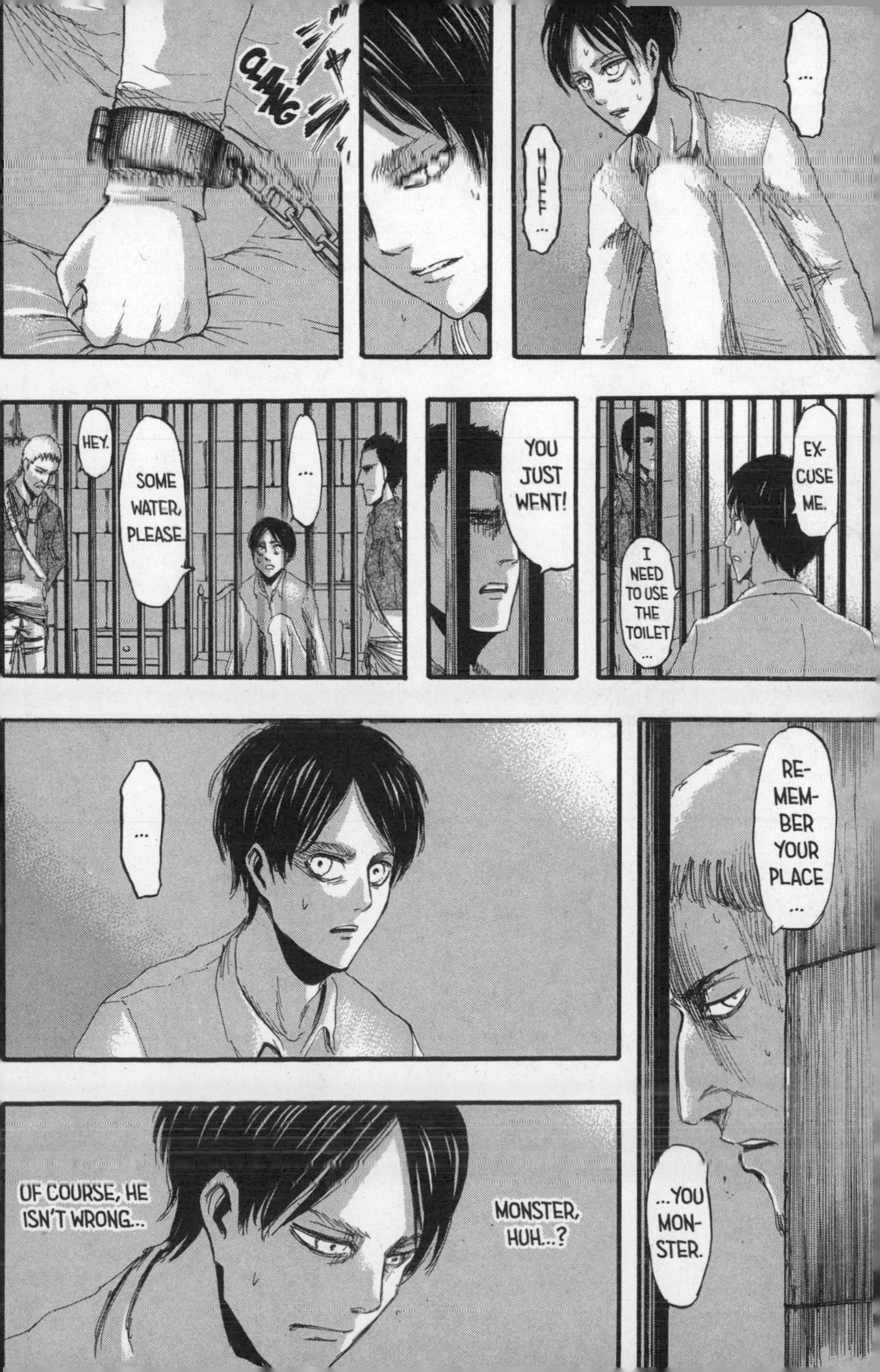
...
HUFF ...
CLANG
EX-CUSE ME.
I NEED TO USE THE TOILET ...
YOU JUST WENT!
...
HEY.
SOME WATER, PLEASE.
RE-MEM-BER YOUR PLACE ...
...YOU MON-STER.
...
MONSTER, HUH...?
OF COURSE, HE ISN'T WRONG...

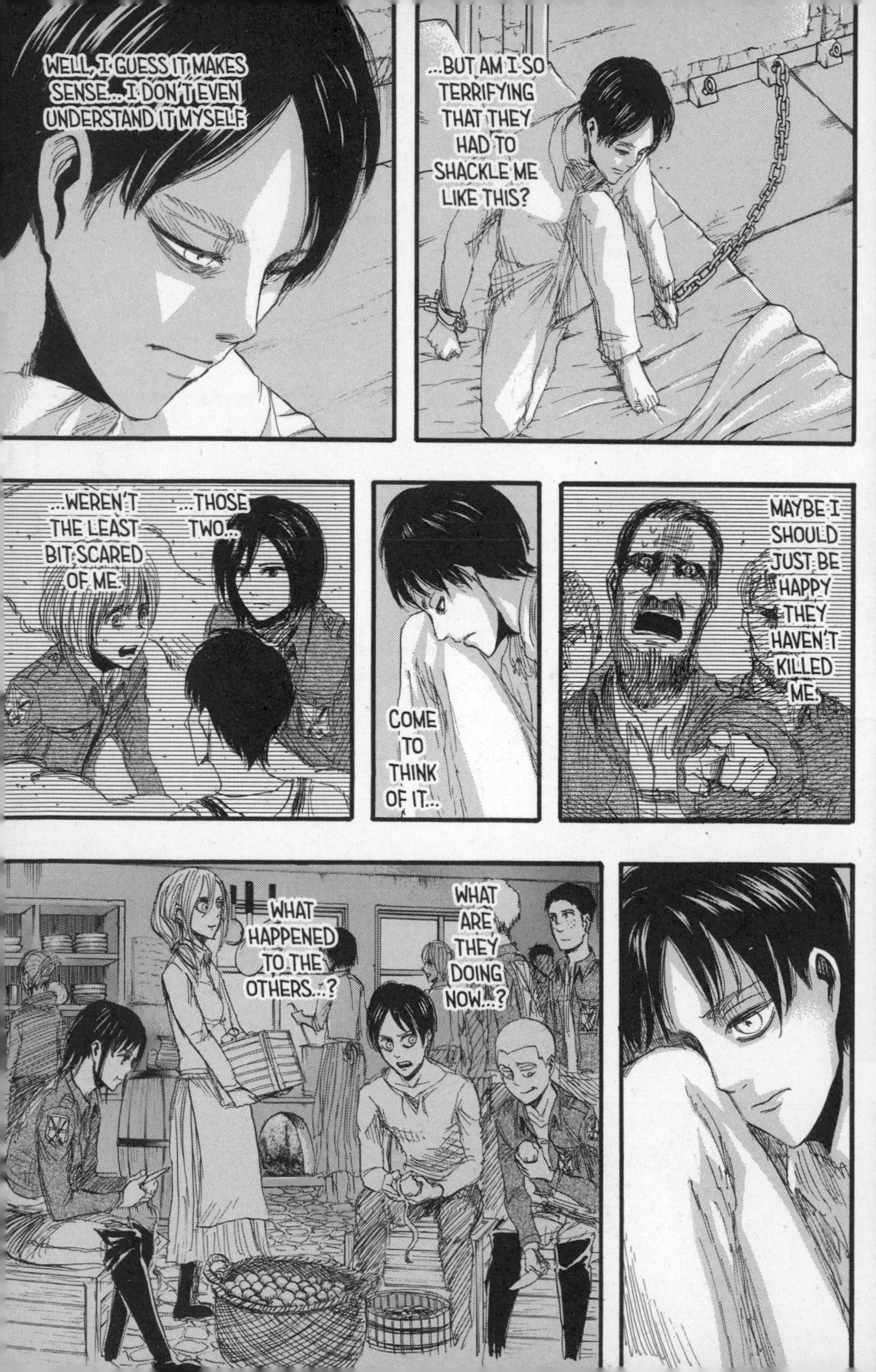
...BUT AM I SO TERRIFYING THAT THEY HAD TO SHACKLE ME LIKE THIS?
WELL, I GUESS IT MAKES SENSE... I DON'T EVEN UNDERSTAND IT MYSELF.
MAYBE I SHOULD JUST BE HAPPY THEY HAVEN'T KILLED ME.
COME TO THINK OF IT...
...THOSE TWO...
...WEREN'T THE LEAST BIT SCARED OF ME.
WHAT ARE THEY DOING NOW...?
WHAT HAPPENED TO THE OTHERS...?

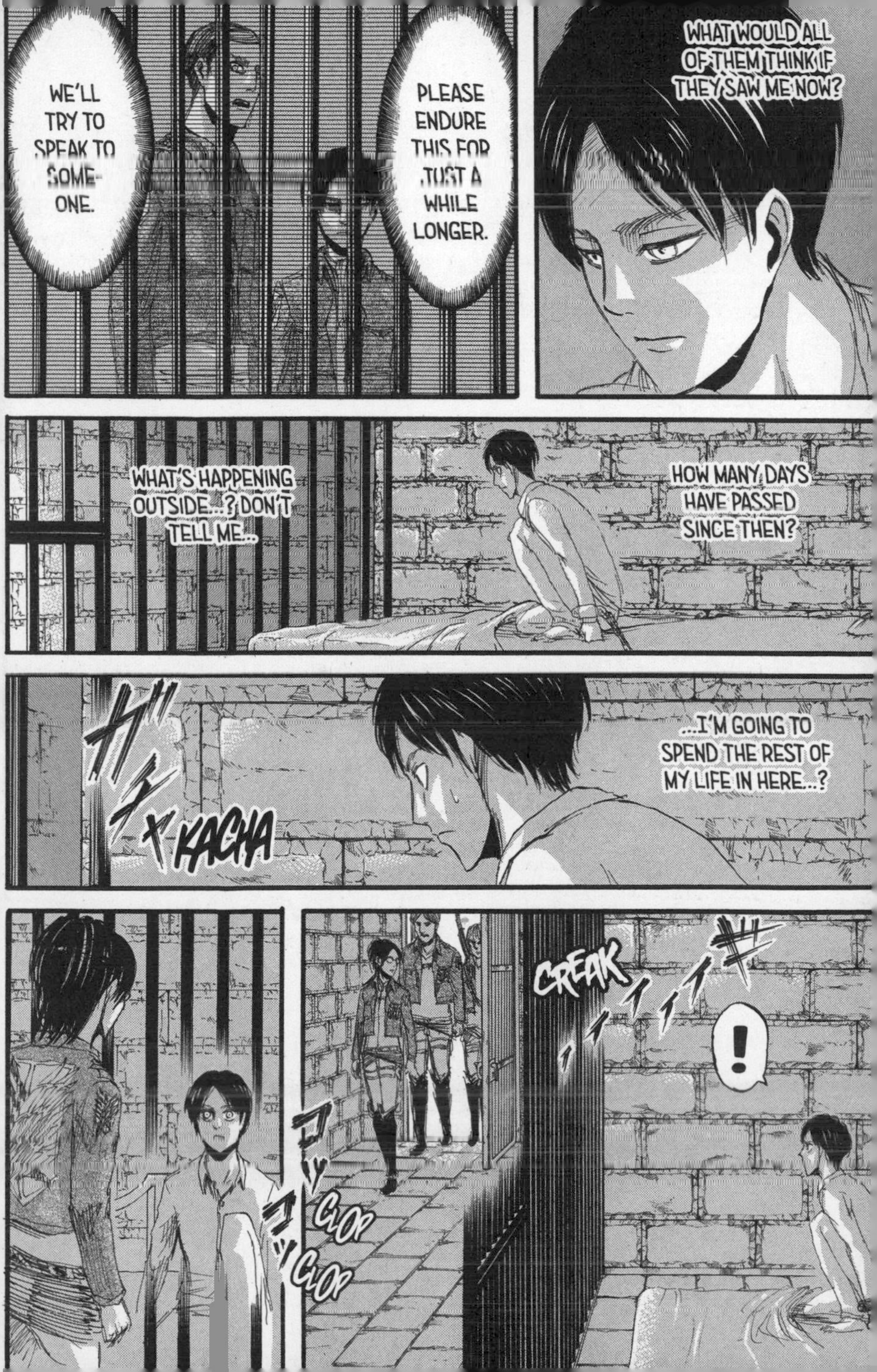
WHAT WOULD ALL OF THEM THINK IF THEY SAW ME NOW?
PLEASE ENDURE THIS FOR JUST A WHILE LONGER.
WE'LL TRY TO SPEAK TO SOME-ONE.
HOW MANY DAYS HAVE PASSED SINCE THEN?
WHAT'S HAPPENING OUTSIDE...? DON'T TELL ME...
...I'M GOING TO SPEND THE REST OF MY LIFE IN HERE...?
KACHA
CREAK
!
CLOP
CLOP

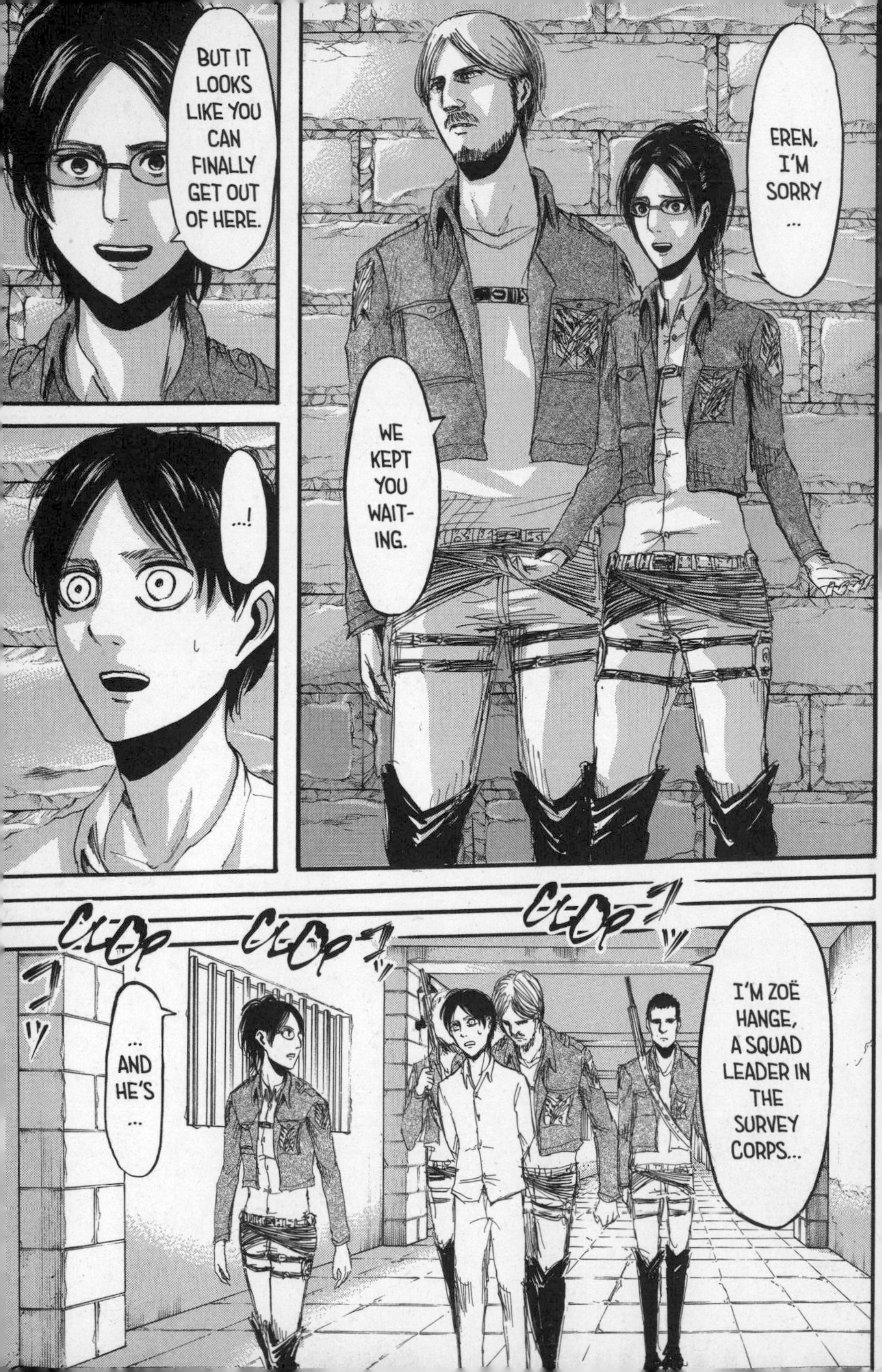
EREN, I'M SORRY ...
WE KEPT YOU WAIT-ING.
BUT IT LOOKS LIKE YOU CAN FINALLY GET OUT OF HERE.
...!
CLOP
CLOP
CLOP
I'M ZOË HANGE, A SQUAD LEADER IN THE SURVEY CORPS...
... AND HE'S ...

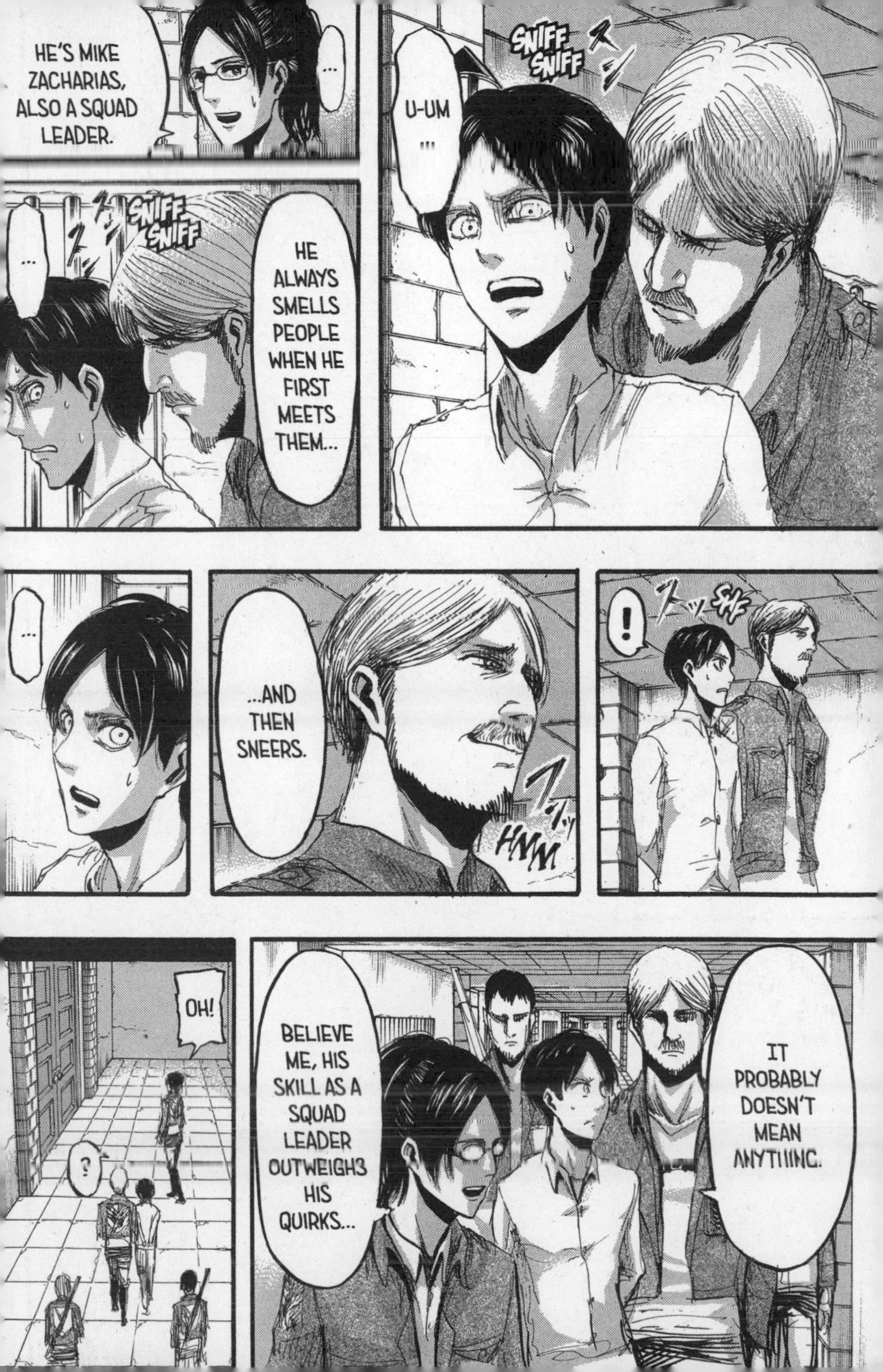
SNIFF SNIFF
U-UM ...
...
HE'S MIKE ZACHARIAS, ALSO A SQUAD LEADER.
HE ALWAYS SMELLS PEOPLE WHEN HE FIRST MEETS THEM...
SNIFF SNIFF
...
!
SHF
...AND THEN SNEERS.
HMM
...
IT PROBABLY DOESN'T MEAN ANYTHING.
BELIEVE ME, HIS SKILL AS A SQUAD LEADER OUTWEIGHS HIS QUIRKS...
OH!
?

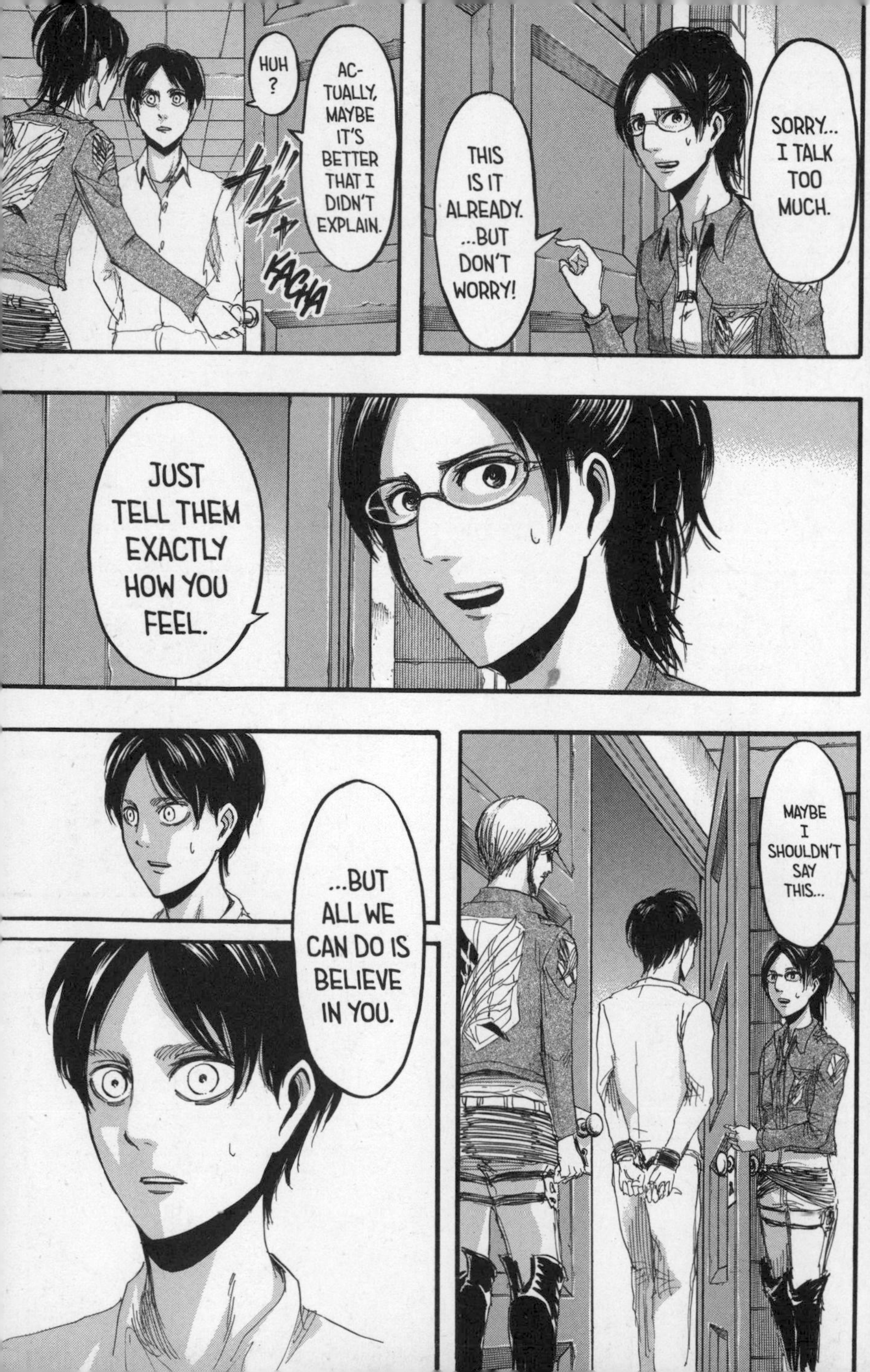
SORRY... I TALK TOO MUCH.
THIS IS IT ALREADY. ...BUT DON'T WORRY!
AC-TUALLY, MAYBE IT'S BETTER THAT I DIDN'T EXPLAIN.
HUH?
KACHA
JUST TELL THEM EXACTLY HOW YOU FEEL.
MAYBE I SHOULDN'T SAY THIS...
...BUT ALL WE CAN DO IS BELIEVE IN YOU.

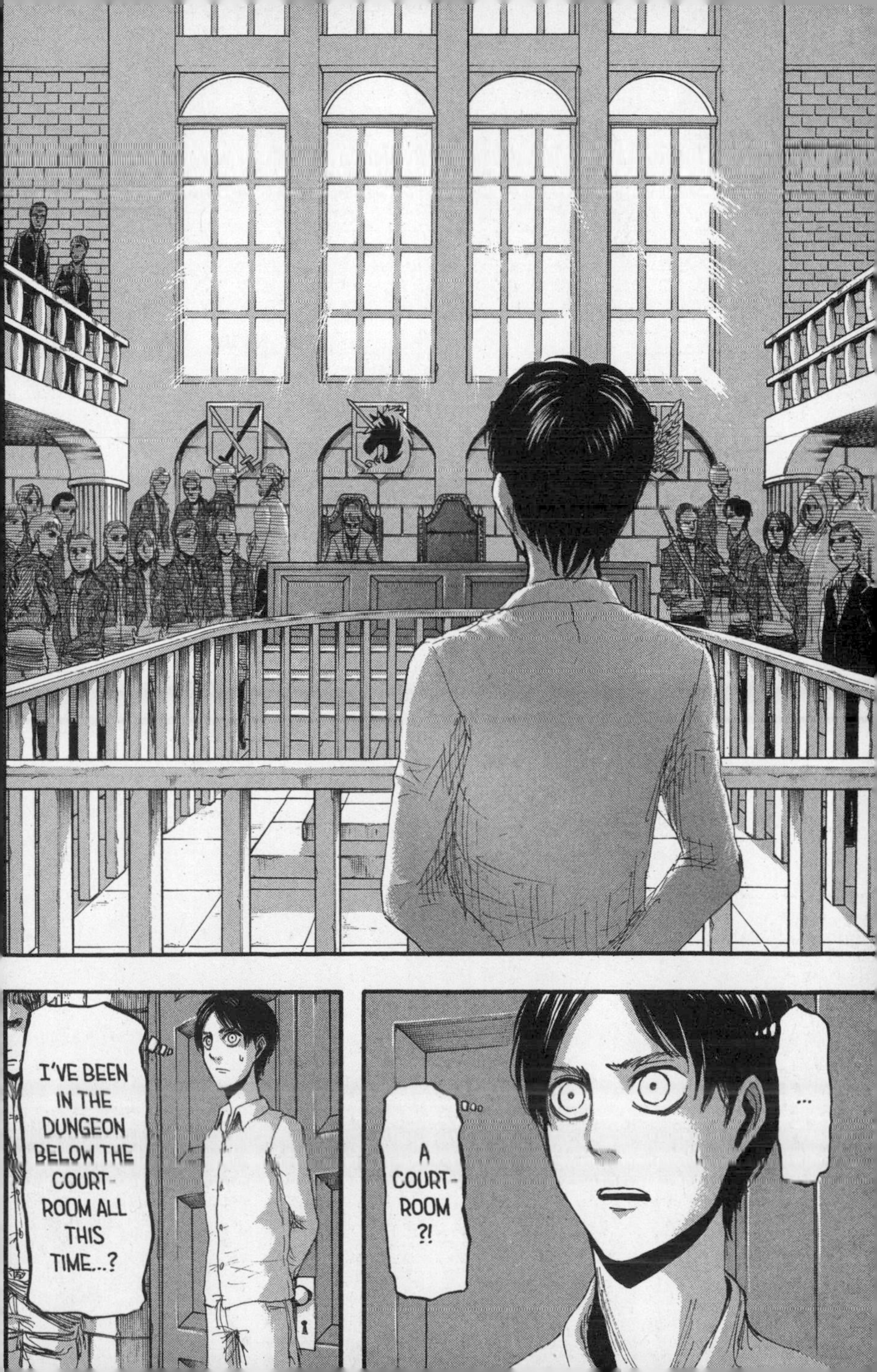
...
A COURT-ROOM?!
I'VE BEEN IN THE DUNGEON BELOW THE COURT-ROOM ALL THIS TIME...?

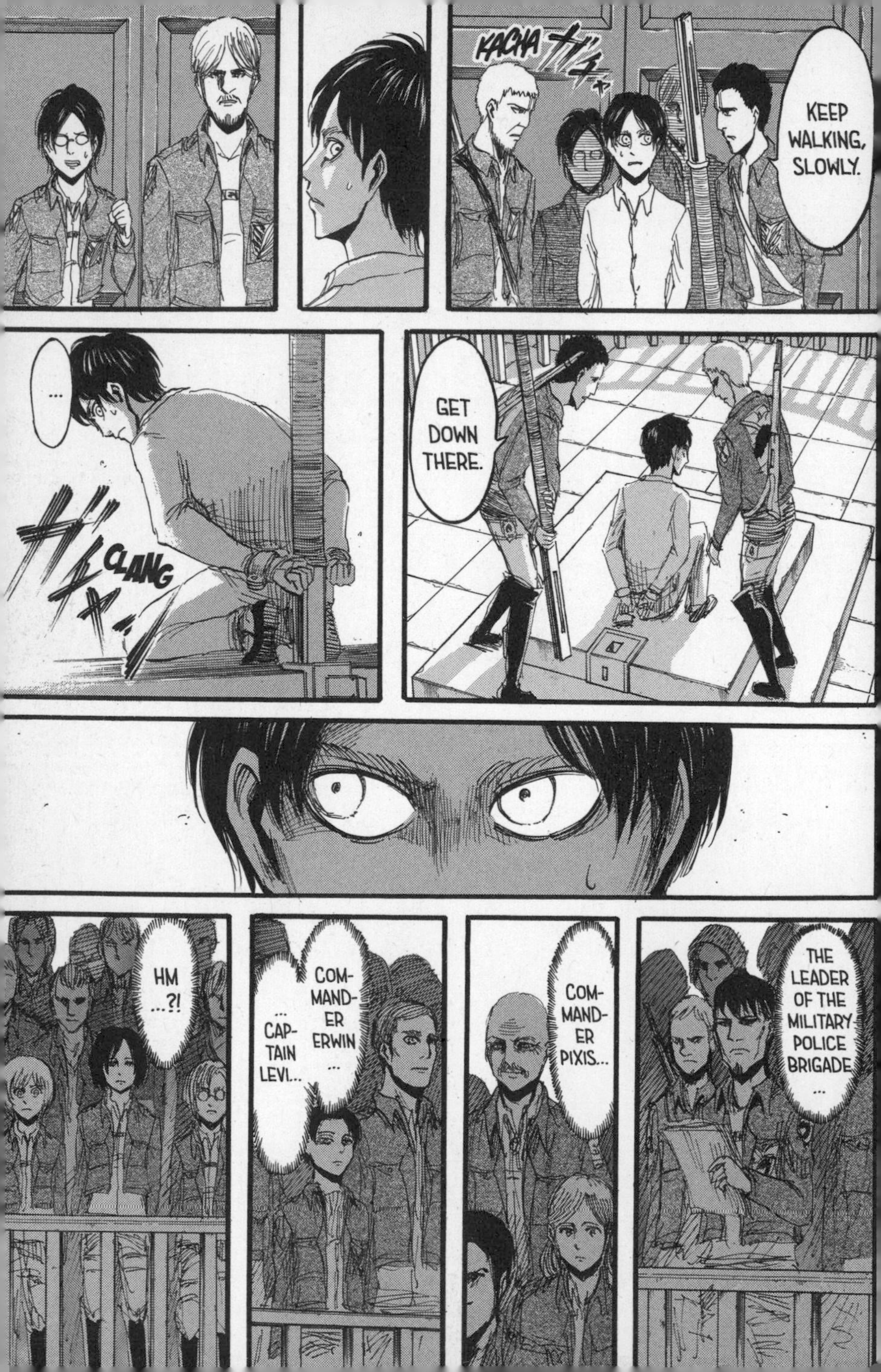
KEEP WALKING, SLOWLY.
KACHA
GET DOWN THERE.
...
CLANG
THE LEADER OF THE MILITARY POLICE BRIGADE...
COM-MAND-ER PIXIS...
COM-MAND-ER ERWIN...
...CAP-TAIN LEVI...
HM...?!

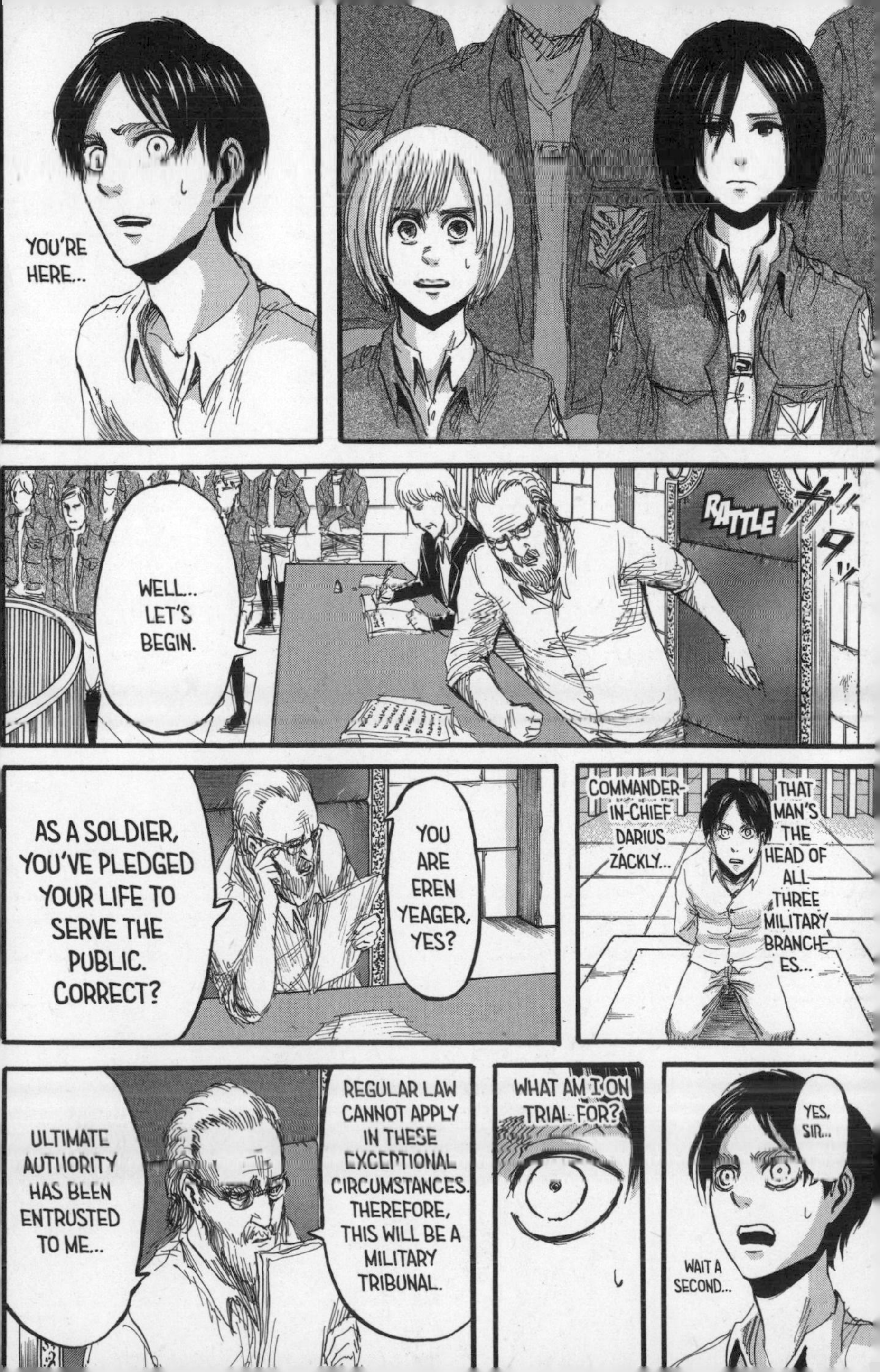
YOU'RE HERE...
RATTLE
WELL... LET'S BEGIN.
THAT MAN'S THE HEAD OF ALL THREE MILITARY BRANCHES...
COMMANDER-IN-CHIEF DARIUS ZACKLY...
YOU ARE EREN YEAGER, YES?
AS A SOLDIER, YOU'VE PLEDGED YOUR LIFE TO SERVE THE PUBLIC. CORRECT?
YES, SIR...
WAIT A SECOND...
WHAT AM I ON TRIAL FOR?
REGULAR LAW CANNOT APPLY IN THESE EXCEPTIONAL CIRCUMSTANCES. THEREFORE, THIS WILL BE A MILITARY TRIBUNAL.
ULTIMATE AUTHORITY HAS BEEN ENTRUSTED TO ME...

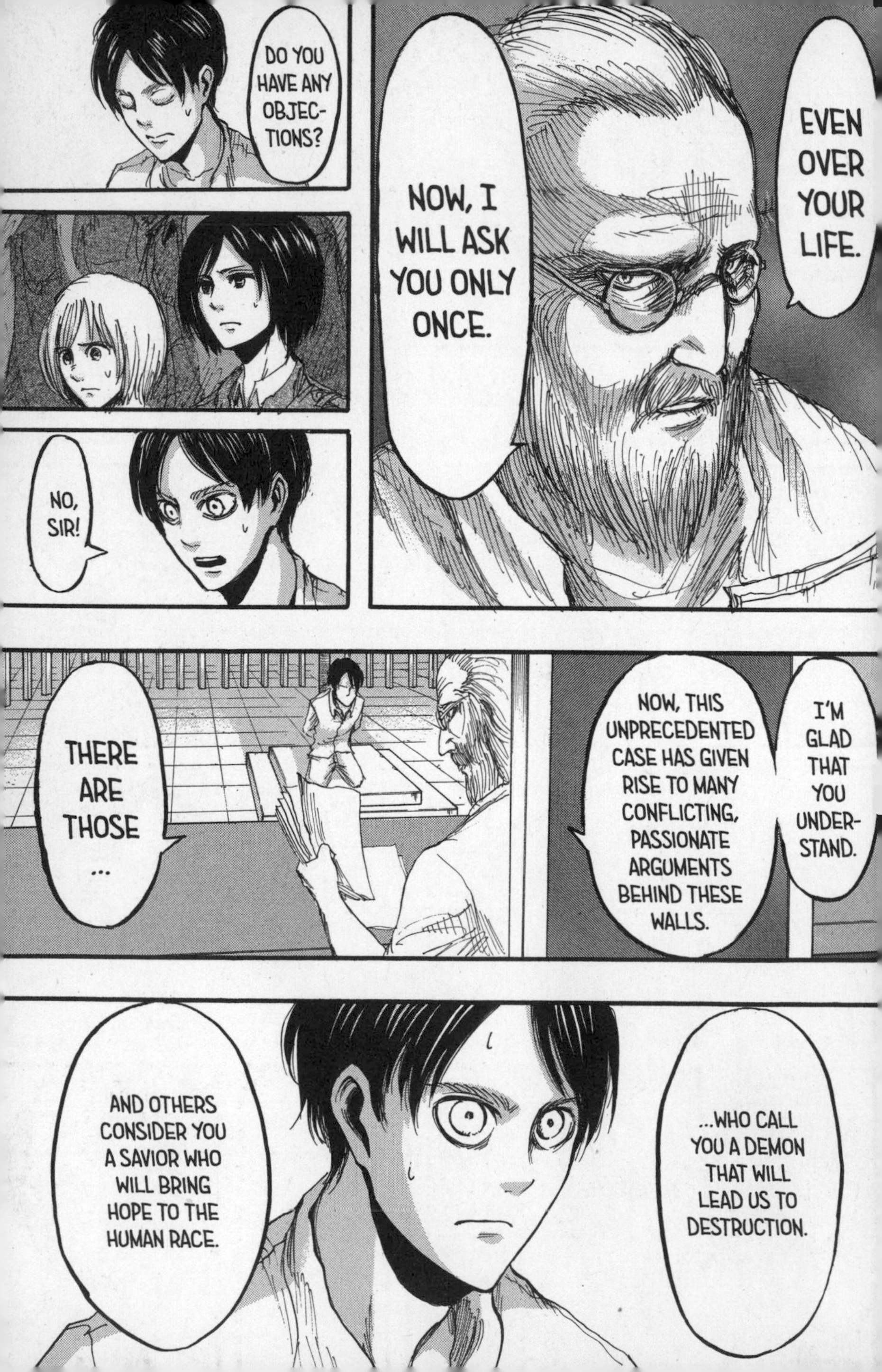
EVEN OVER YOUR LIFE.
NOW, I WILL ASK YOU ONLY ONCE.
DO YOU HAVE ANY OBJEC-TIONS?
NO, SIR!
I'M GLAD THAT YOU UNDER-STAND.
NOW, THIS UNPRECEDENTED CASE HAS GIVEN RISE TO MANY CONFLICTING, PASSIONATE ARGUMENTS BEHIND THESE WALLS.
THERE ARE THOSE ...
...WHO CALL YOU A DEMON THAT WILL LEAD US TO DESTRUCTION.
AND OTHERS CONSIDER YOU A SAVIOR WHO WILL BRING HOPE TO THE HUMAN RACE.

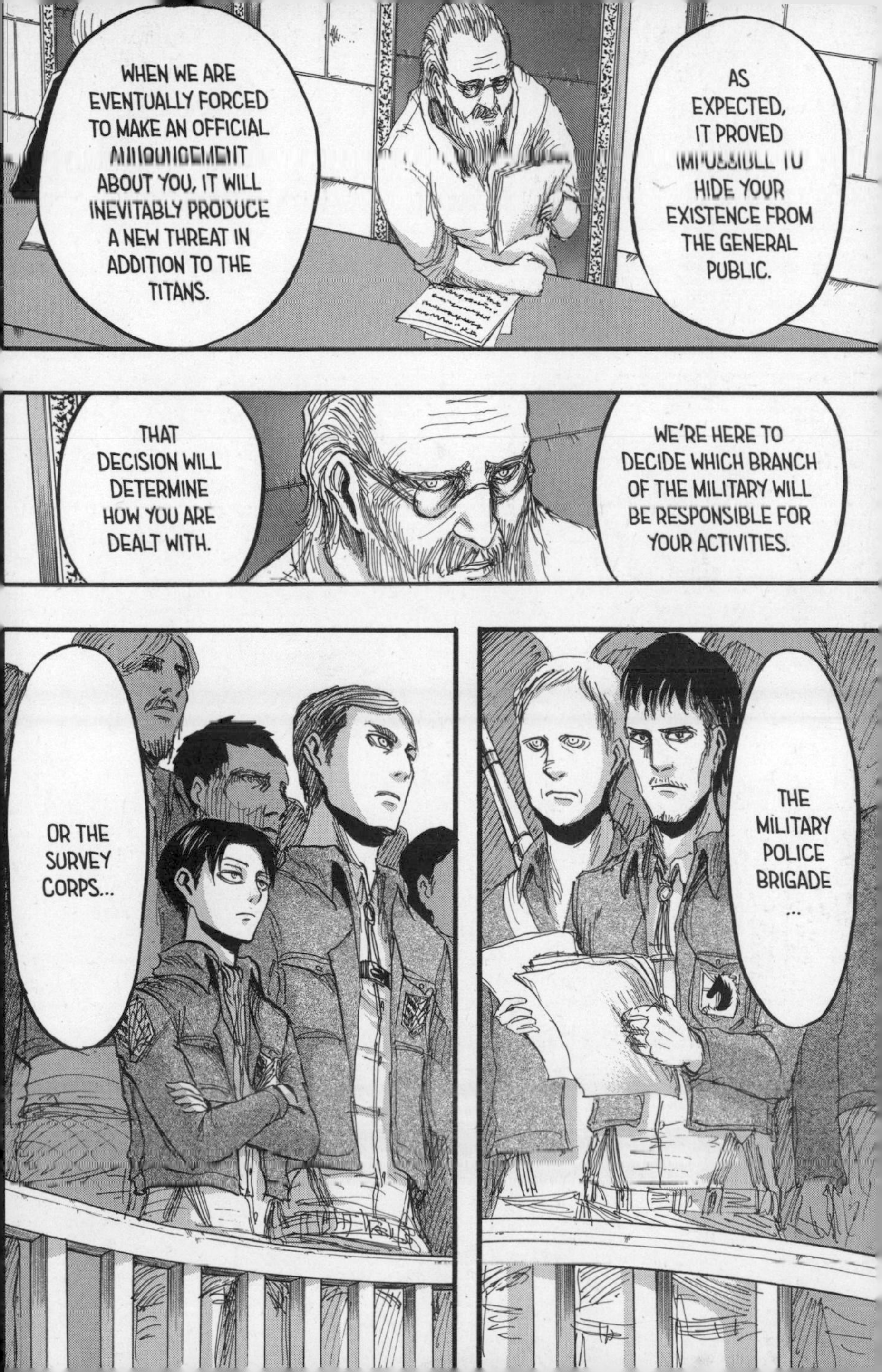
AS EXPECTED, IT PROVED IMPOSSIBLE TO HIDE YOUR EXISTENCE FROM THE GENERAL PUBLIC.
WHEN WE ARE EVENTUALLY FORCED TO MAKE AN OFFICIAL ANNOUNCEMENT ABOUT YOU, IT WILL INEVITABLY PRODUCE A NEW THREAT IN ADDITION TO THE TITANS.
WE'RE HERE TO DECIDE WHICH BRANCH OF THE MILITARY WILL BE RESPONSIBLE FOR YOUR ACTIVITIES.
THAT DECISION WILL DETERMINE HOW YOU ARE DEALT WITH.
THE MILITARY POLICE BRIGADE ...
OR THE SURVEY CORPS...

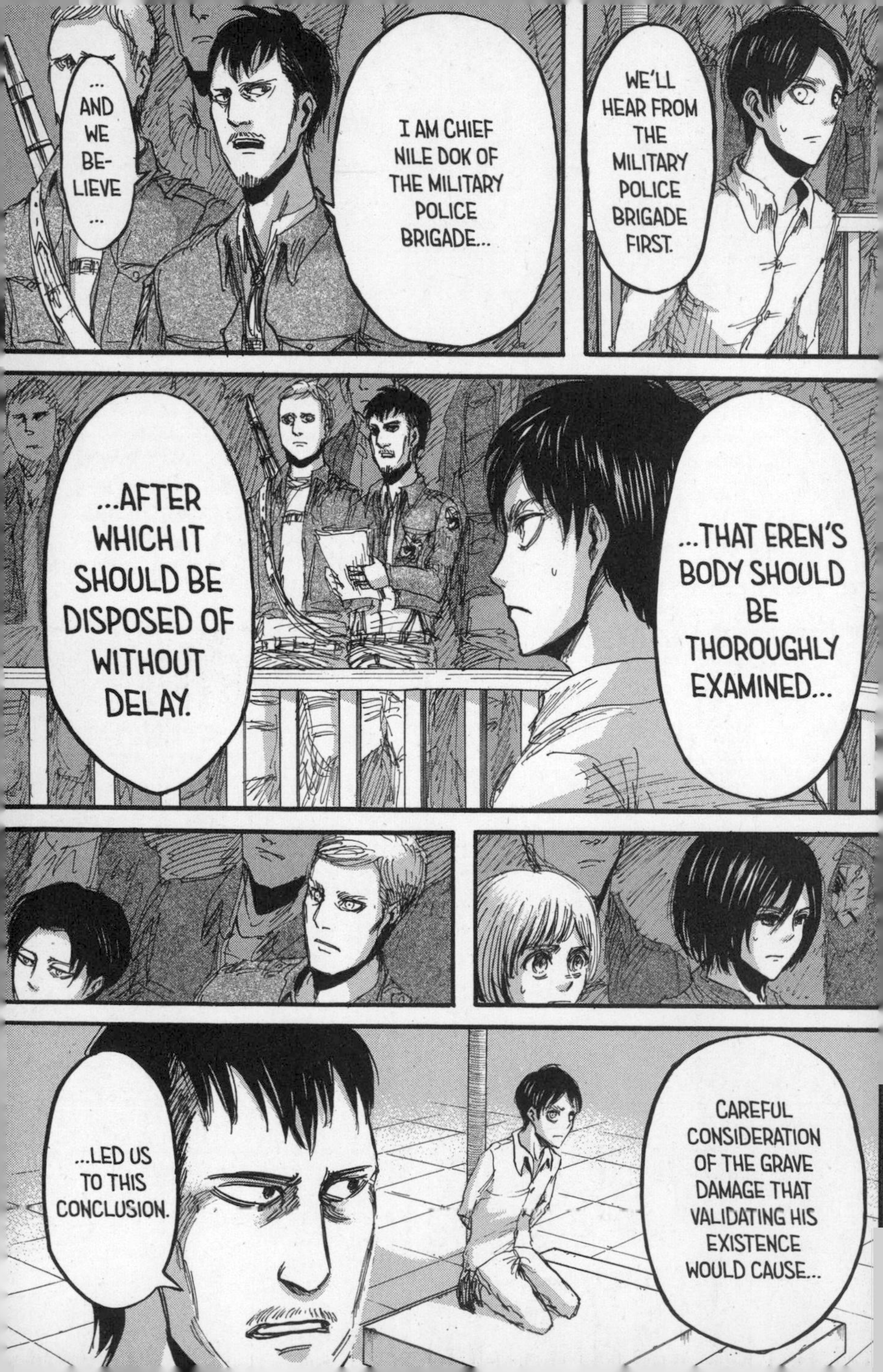
WE'LL HEAR FROM THE MILITARY POLICE BRIGADE FIRST.
I AM CHIEF NILE DOK OF THE MILITARY POLICE BRIGADE...
... AND WE BE- LIEVE ...
...THAT EREN'S BODY SHOULD BE THOROUGHLY EXAMINED...
...AFTER WHICH IT SHOULD BE DISPOSED OF WITHOUT DELAY.
CAREFUL CONSIDERATION OF THE GRAVE DAMAGE THAT VALIDATING HIS EXISTENCE WOULD CAUSE...
...LED US TO THIS CONCLUSION.

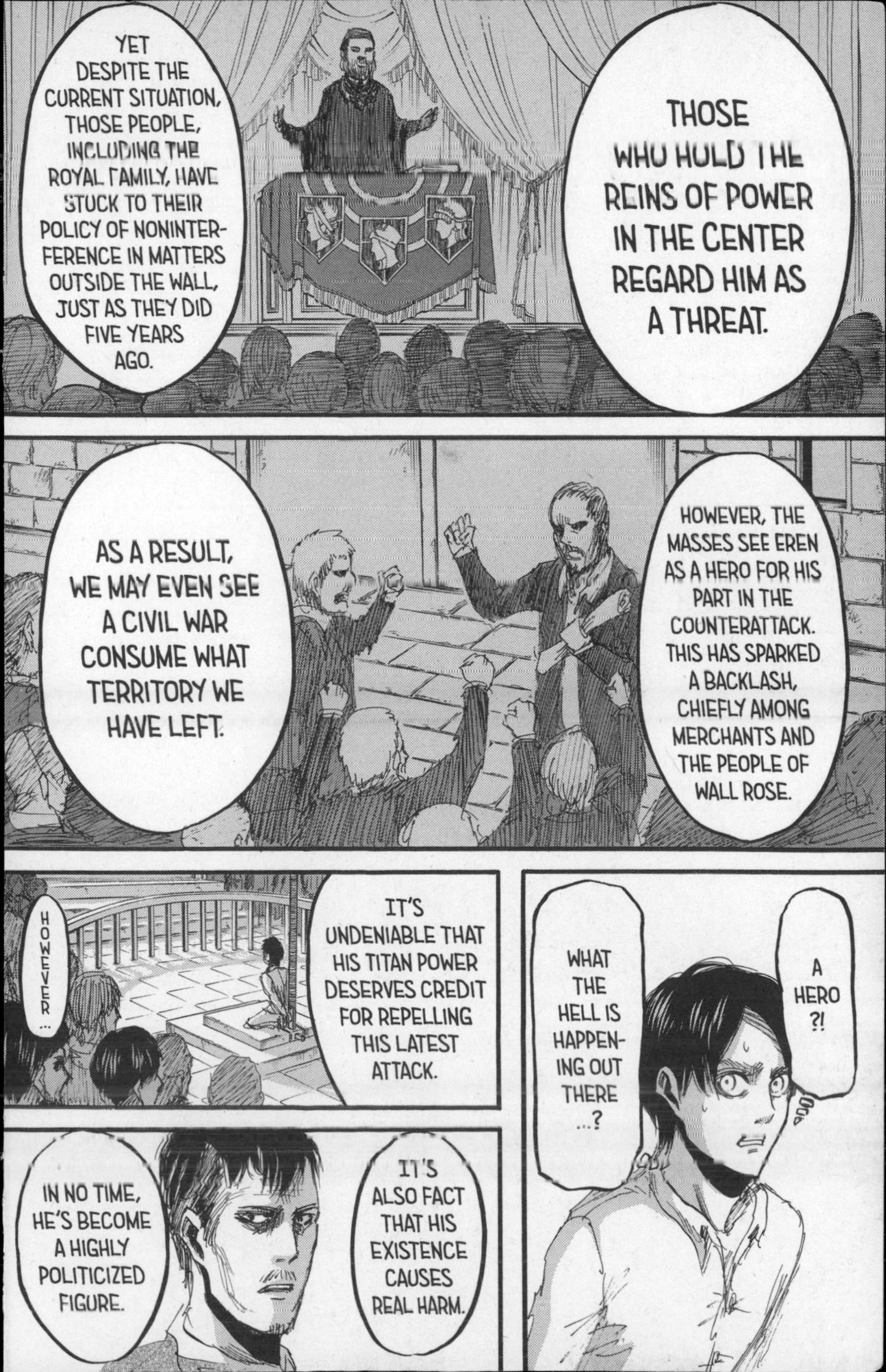
THOSE WHO HOLD THE REINS OF POWER IN THE CENTER REGARD HIM AS A THREAT.
YET DESPITE THE CURRENT SITUATION, THOSE PEOPLE, INCLUDING THE ROYAL FAMILY, HAVE STUCK TO THEIR POLICY OF NONINTERFERENCE IN MATTERS OUTSIDE THE WALL, JUST AS THEY DID FIVE YEARS AGO.
HOWEVER, THE MASSES SEE EREN AS A HERO FOR HIS PART IN THE COUNTERATTACK. THIS HAS SPARKED A BACKLASH, CHIEFLY AMONG MERCHANTS AND THE PEOPLE OF WALL ROSE.
AS A RESULT, WE MAY EVEN SEE A CIVIL WAR CONSUME WHAT TERRITORY WE HAVE LEFT.
A HERO ?!
WHAT THE HELL IS HAPPENING OUT THERE ...?
IT'S UNDENIABLE THAT HIS TITAN POWER DESERVES CREDIT FOR REPELLING THIS LATEST ATTACK.
HOWEVER ...
IT'S ALSO FACT THAT HIS EXISTENCE CAUSES REAL HARM.
IN NO TIME, HE'S BECOME A HIGHLY POLITICIZED FIGURE.

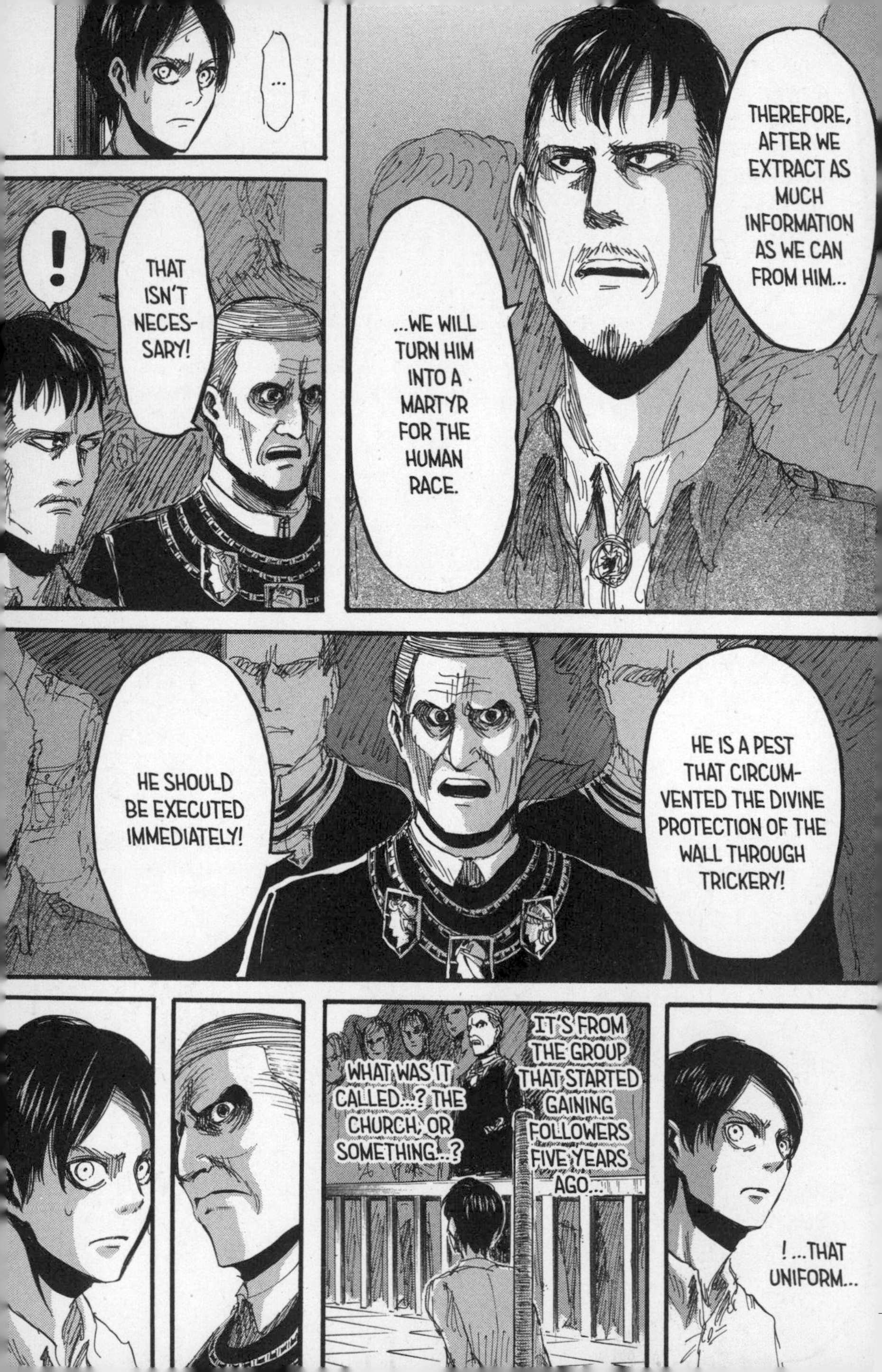
THEREFORE, AFTER WE EXTRACT AS MUCH INFORMATION AS WE CAN FROM HIM...
...WE WILL TURN HIM INTO A MARTYR FOR THE HUMAN RACE.
...
THAT ISN'T NECES-SARY!
!
HE IS A PEST THAT CIRCUM-VENTED THE DIVINE PROTECTION OF THE WALL THROUGH TRICKERY!
HE SHOULD BE EXECUTED IMMEDIATELY!
! ...THAT UNIFORM...
IT'S FROM THE GROUP THAT STARTED GAINING FOLLOWERS FIVE YEARS AGO...
WHAT WAS IT CALLED...? THE CHURCH, OR SOMETHING...?

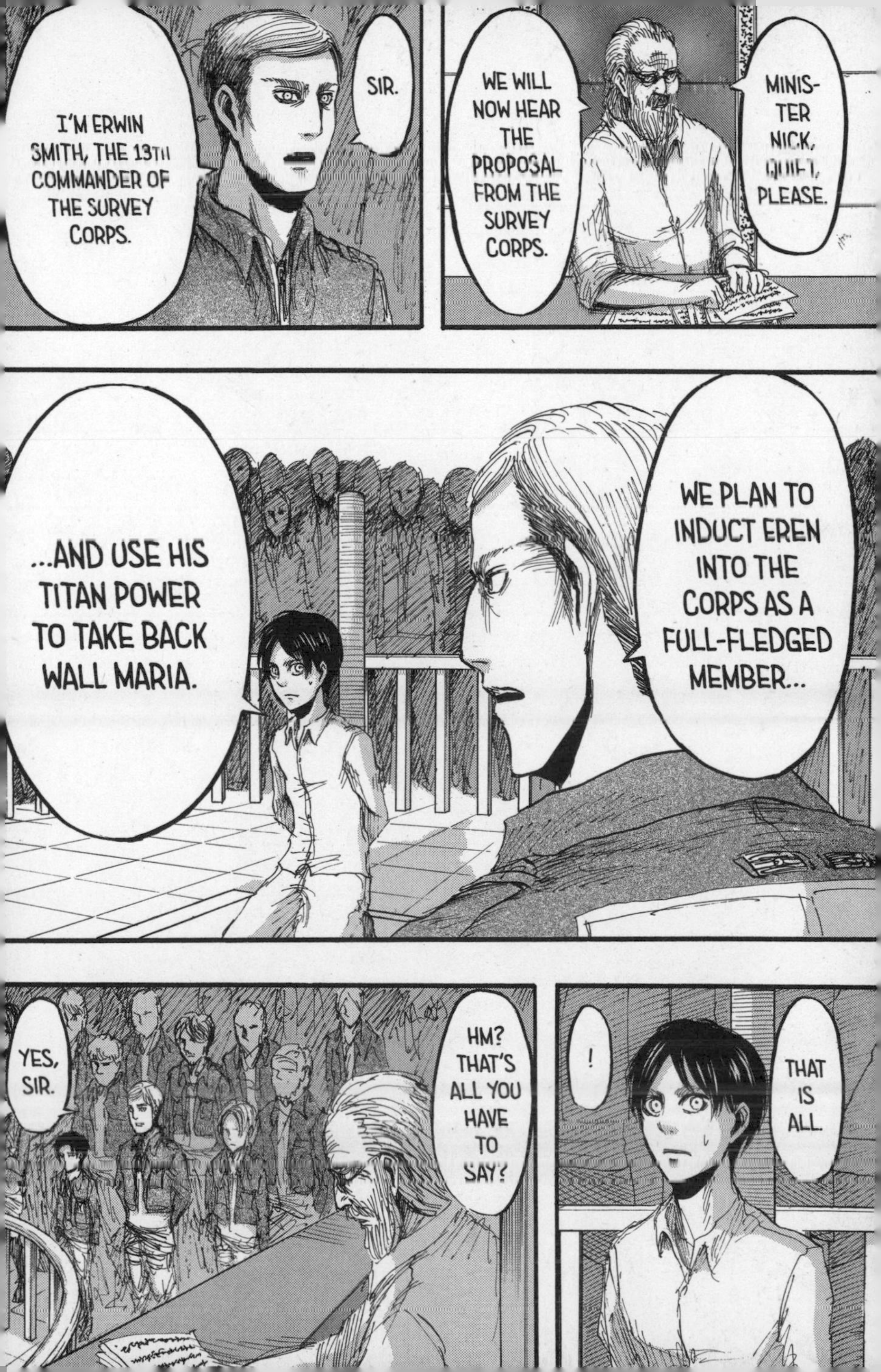
MINISTER NICK, QUIET, PLEASE.
WE WILL NOW HEAR THE PROPOSAL FROM THE SURVEY CORPS.
SIR.
I'M ERWIN SMITH, THE 13TH COMMANDER OF THE SURVEY CORPS.
WE PLAN TO INDUCT EREN INTO THE CORPS AS A FULL-FLEDGED MEMBER...
...AND USE HIS TITAN POWER TO TAKE BACK WALL MARIA.
THAT IS ALL.
!
HM? THAT'S ALL YOU HAVE TO SAY?
YES, SIR.

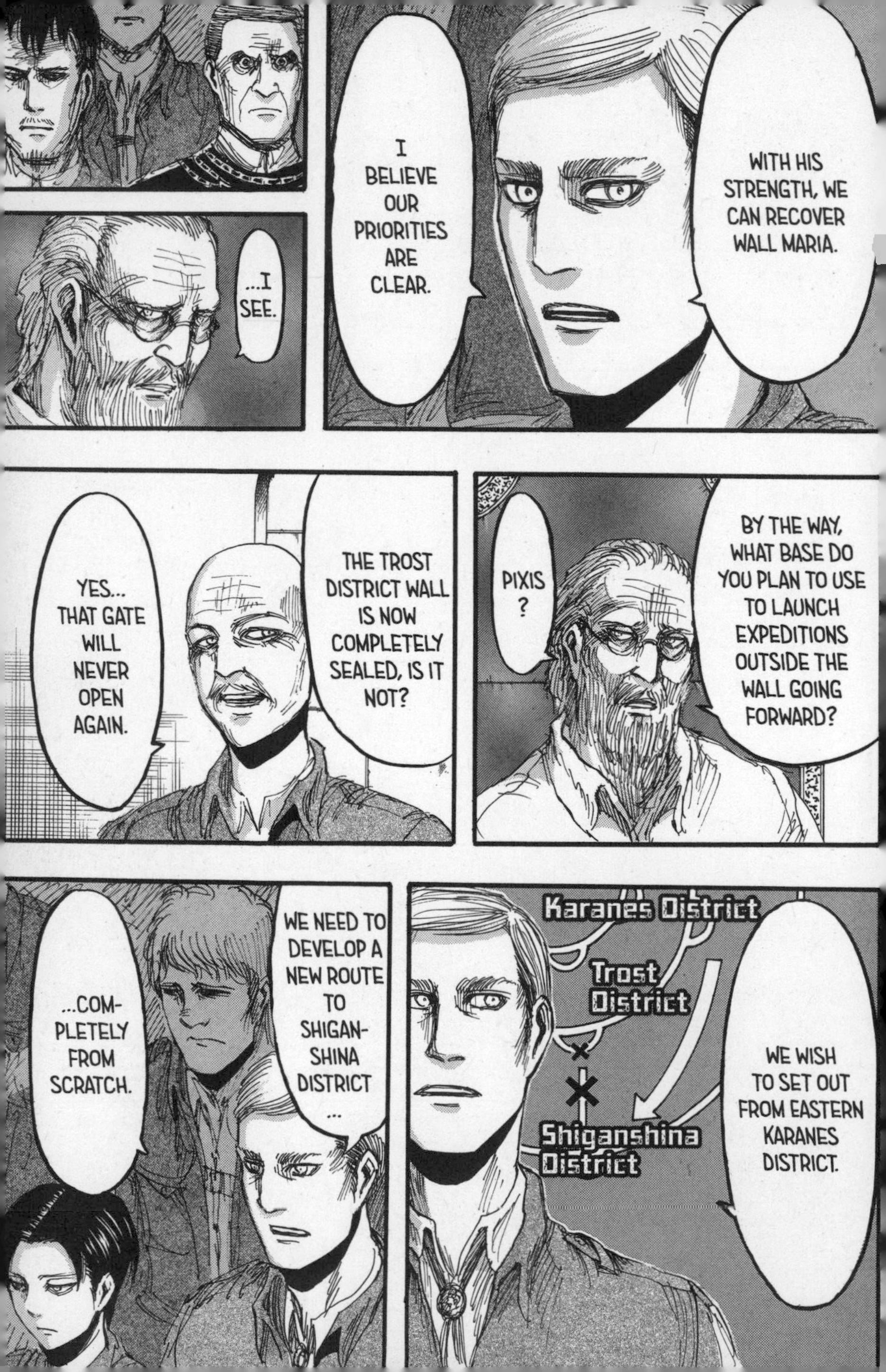
WITH HIS STRENGTH, WE CAN RECOVER WALL MARIA.
I BELIEVE OUR PRIORITIES ARE CLEAR.
...I SEE.
BY THE WAY, WHAT BASE DO YOU PLAN TO USE TO LAUNCH EXPEDITIONS OUTSIDE THE WALL GOING FORWARD?
PIXIS ?
THE TROST DISTRICT WALL IS NOW COMPLETELY SEALED, IS IT NOT?
YES... THAT GATE WILL NEVER OPEN AGAIN.
Karanes District
Trost District
Shiganshina District
WE WISH TO SET OUT FROM EASTERN KARANES DISTRICT.
WE NEED TO DEVELOP A NEW ROUTE TO SHIGANSHINA DISTRICT ...
...COMPLETELY FROM SCRATCH.

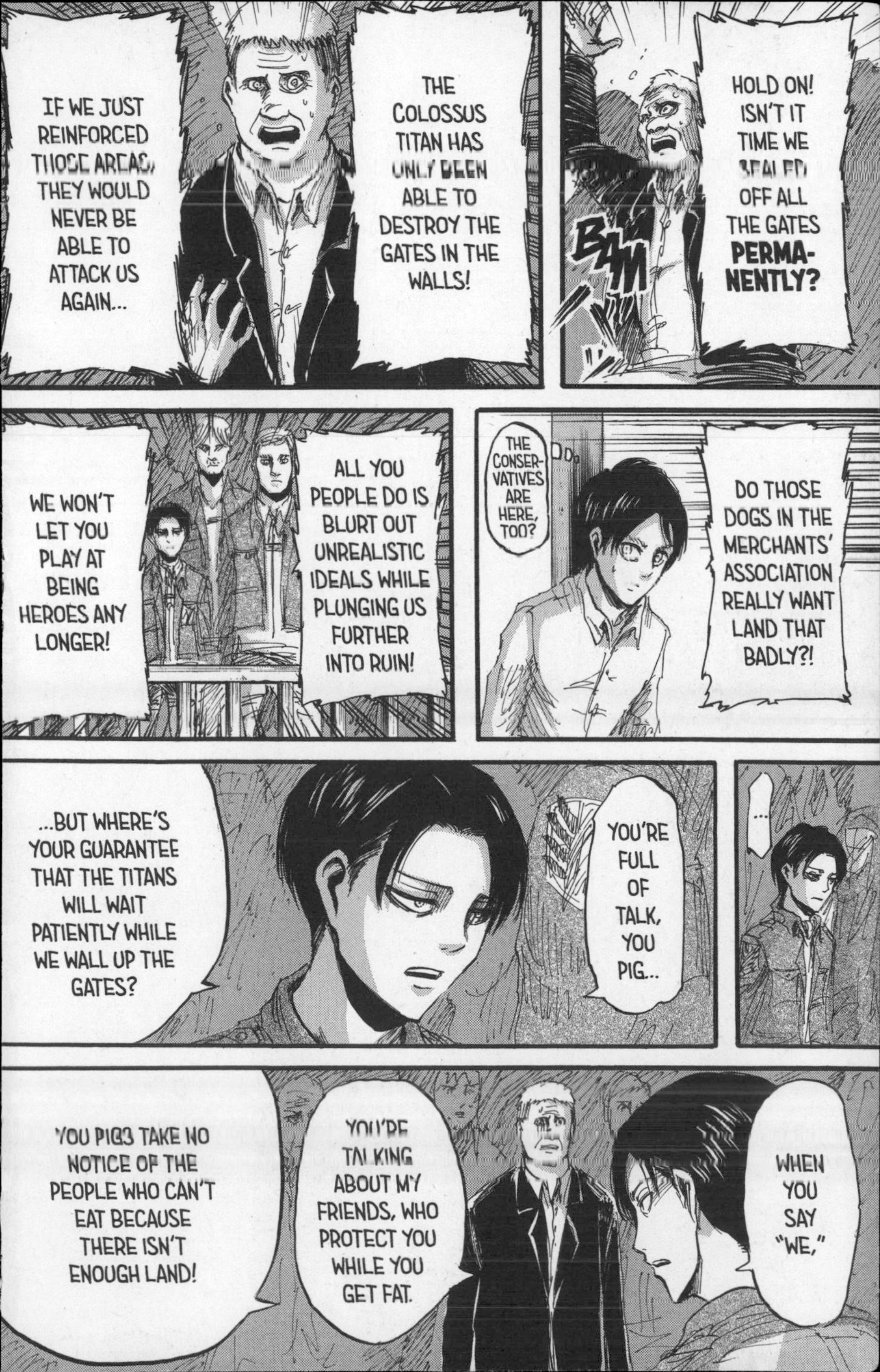
HOLD ON! ISN'T IT TIME WE SEALED OFF ALL THE GATES **PERMA-NENTLY?**
BAM
THE COLOSSUS TITAN HAS ONLY BEEN ABLE TO DESTROY THE GATES IN THE WALLS!
IF WE JUST REINFORCED THOSE AREAS, THEY WOULD NEVER BE ABLE TO ATTACK US AGAIN...
DO THOSE DOGS IN THE MERCHANTS' ASSOCIATION REALLY WANT LAND THAT BADLY?!
THE CONSER-VATIVES ARE HERE, TOO?
ALL YOU PEOPLE DO IS BLURT OUT UNREALISTIC IDEALS WHILE PLUNGING US FURTHER INTO RUIN!
WE WON'T LET YOU PLAY AT BEING HEROES ANY LONGER!
...
YOU'RE FULL OF TALK, YOU PIG...
...BUT WHERE'S YOUR GUARANTEE THAT THE TITANS WILL WAIT PATIENTLY WHILE WE WALL UP THE GATES?
WHEN YOU SAY "WE,"
YOU'RE TALKING ABOUT MY FRIENDS, WHO PROTECT YOU WHILE YOU GET FAT.
YOU PIGS TAKE NO NOTICE OF THE PEOPLE WHO CAN'T EAT BECAUSE THERE ISN'T ENOUGH LAND!

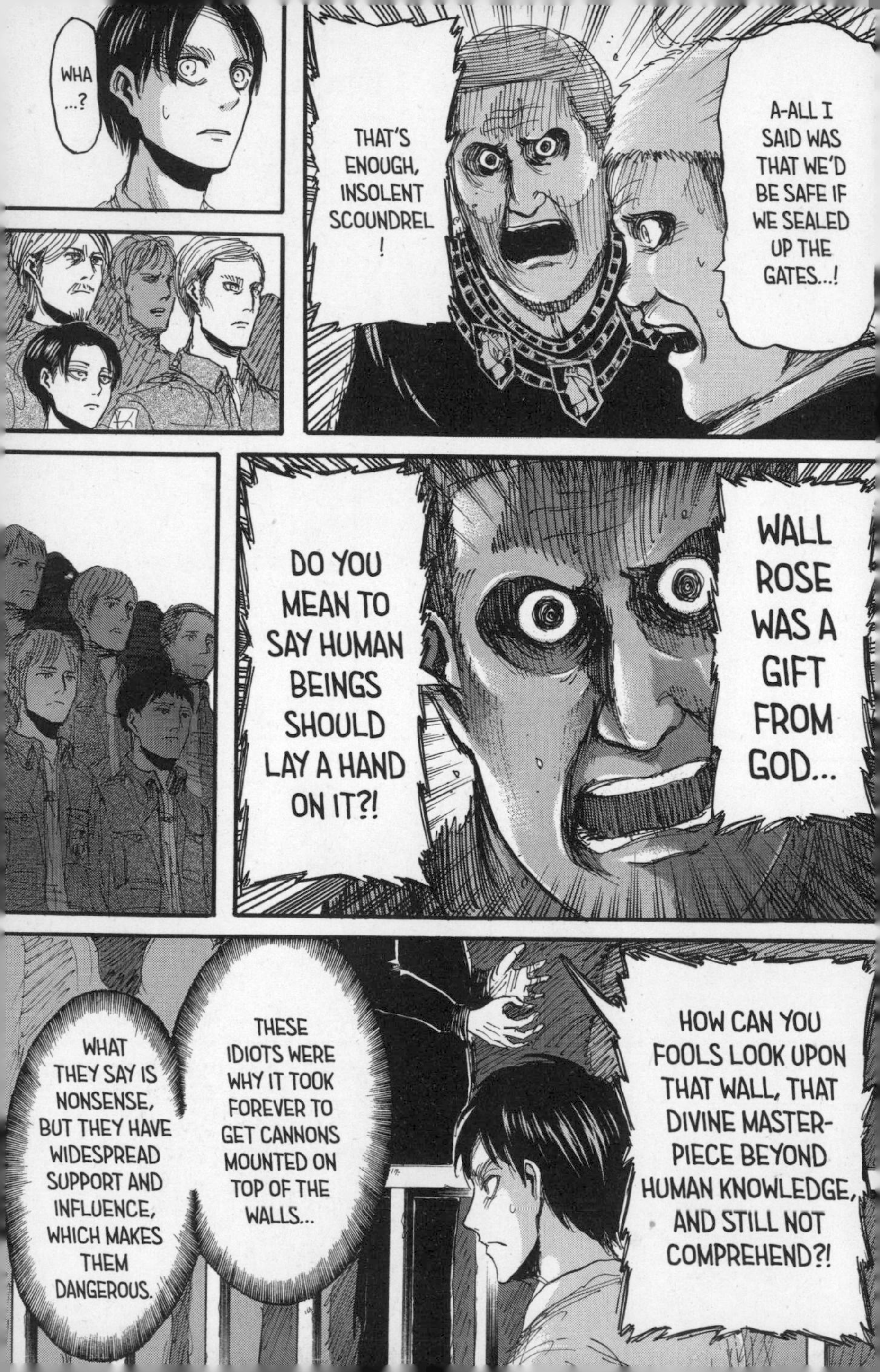
A-ALL I SAID WAS THAT WE'D BE SAFE IF WE SEALED UP THE GATES...!
THAT'S ENOUGH, INSOLENT SCOUNDREL!
WHA...?
WALL ROSE WAS A GIFT FROM GOD...
DO YOU MEAN TO SAY HUMAN BEINGS SHOULD LAY A HAND ON IT?!
HOW CAN YOU FOOLS LOOK UPON THAT WALL, THAT DIVINE MASTER-PIECE BEYOND HUMAN KNOWLEDGE, AND STILL NOT COMPREHEND?!
THESE IDIOTS WERE WHY IT TOOK FOREVER TO GET CANNONS MOUNTED ON TOP OF THE WALLS...
WHAT THEY SAY IS NONSENSE, BUT THEY HAVE WIDESPREAD SUPPORT AND INFLUENCE, WHICH MAKES THEM DANGEROUS.

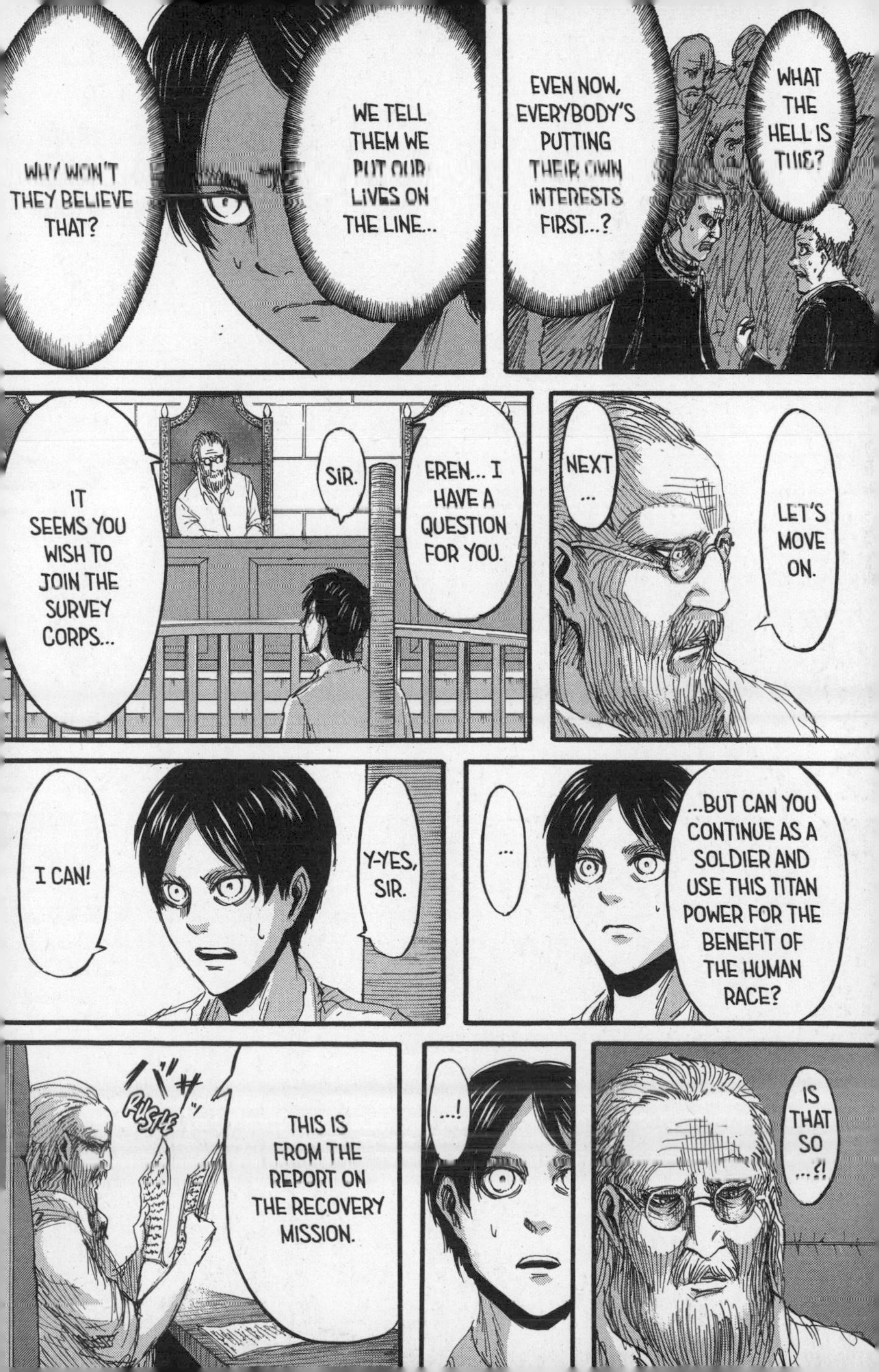
WHAT THE HELL IS THIS?
EVEN NOW, EVERYBODY'S PUTTING THEIR OWN INTERESTS FIRST...?
WE TELL THEM WE PUT OUR LIVES ON THE LINE...
WHY WON'T THEY BELIEVE THAT?
NEXT...
LET'S MOVE ON.
EREN... I HAVE A QUESTION FOR YOU.
SIR.
IT SEEMS YOU WISH TO JOIN THE SURVEY CORPS...
...BUT CAN YOU CONTINUE AS A SOLDIER AND USE THIS TITAN POWER FOR THE BENEFIT OF THE HUMAN RACE?
...
Y-YES, SIR.
I CAN!
IS THAT SO...?!
...!
バサッ
RUSTLE
THIS IS FROM THE REPORT ON THE RECOVERY MISSION.

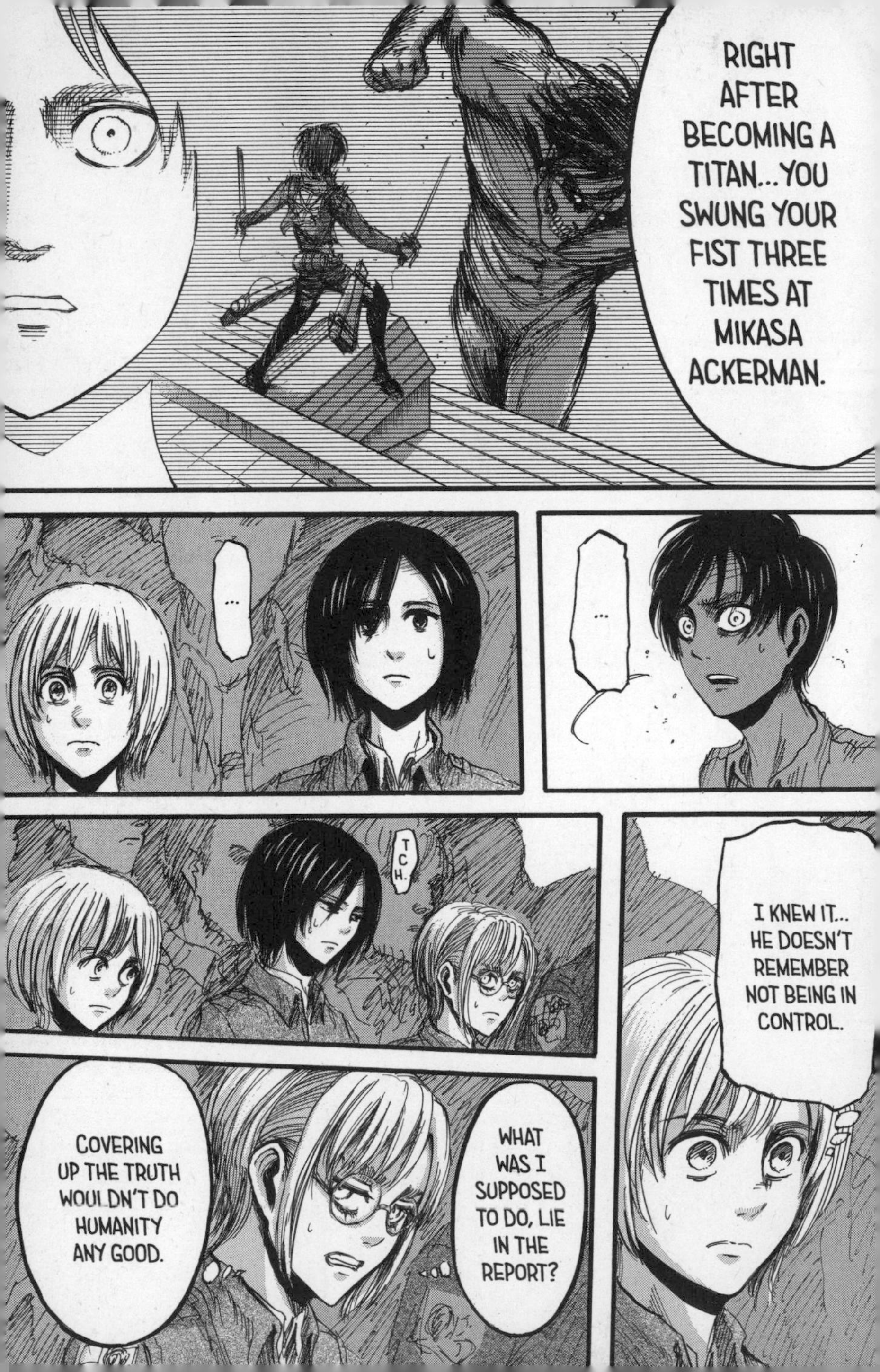
RIGHT AFTER BECOMING A TITAN... YOU SWUNG YOUR FIST THREE TIMES AT MIKASA ACKERMAN.
...
...
I KNEW IT... HE DOESN'T REMEMBER NOT BEING IN CONTROL.
TCH.
WHAT WAS I SUPPOSED TO DO, LIE IN THE REPORT?
COVERING UP THE TRUTH WOULDN'T DO HUMANITY ANY GOOD.

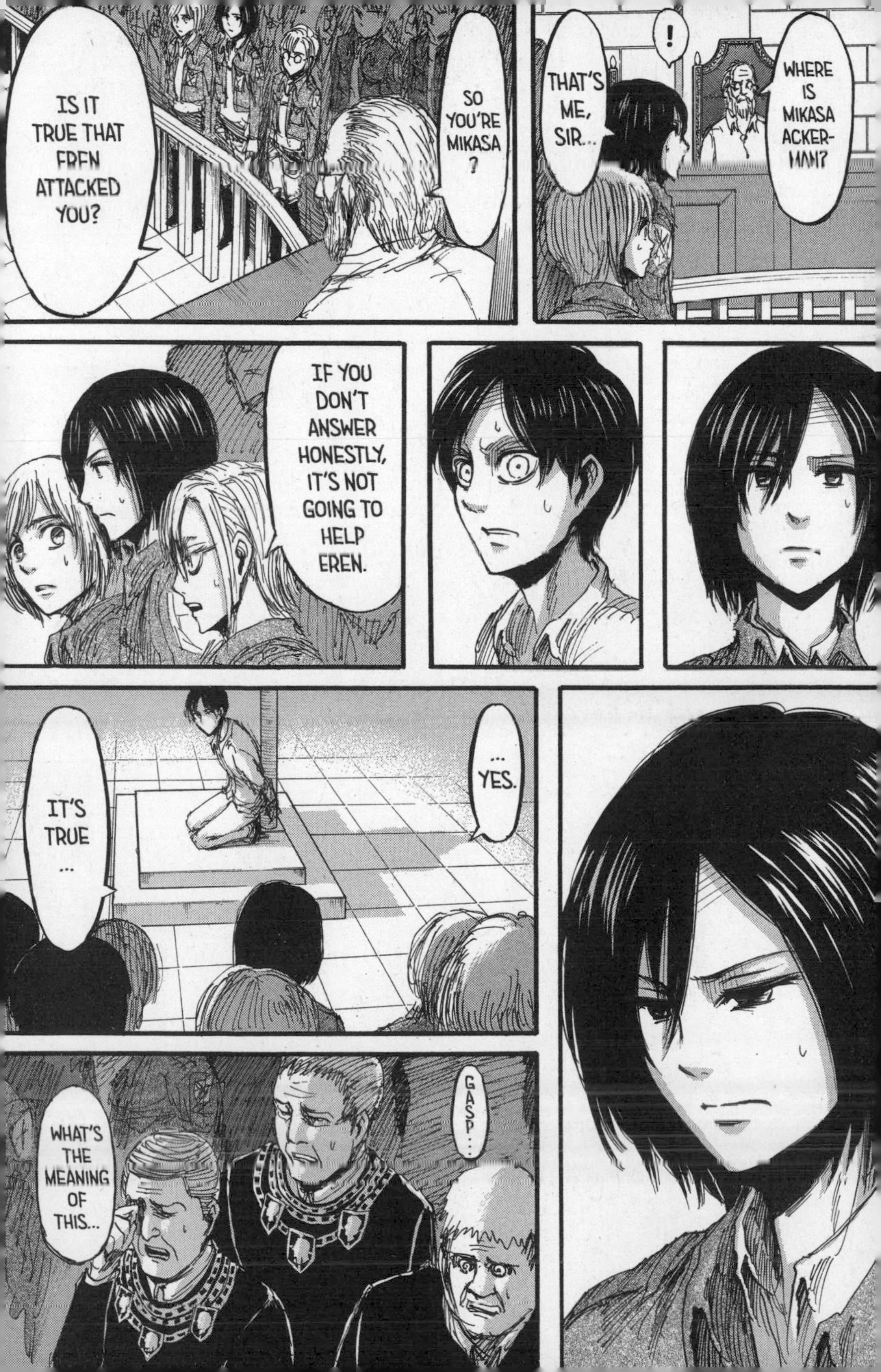
WHERE IS MIKASA ACKERMAN?
!
THAT'S ME, SIR...
SO YOU'RE MIKASA?
IS IT TRUE THAT EREN ATTACKED YOU?
IF YOU DON'T ANSWER HONESTLY, IT'S NOT GOING TO HELP EREN.
...YES.
IT'S TRUE...
GASP...
WHAT'S THE MEANING OF THIS...

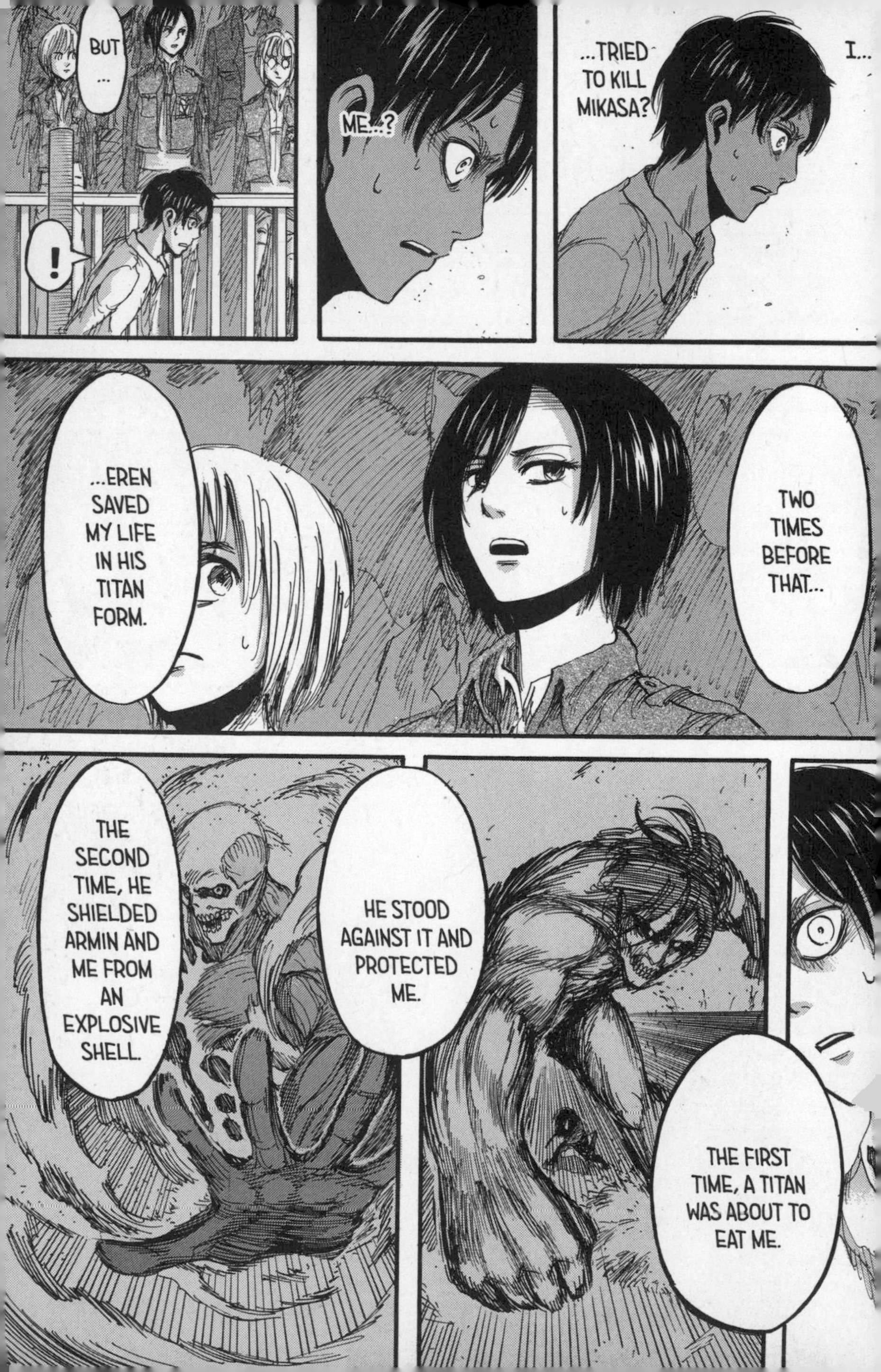
I...
...TRIED TO KILL MIKASA?
ME...?
BUT ...
!
TWO TIMES BEFORE THAT...
...EREN SAVED MY LIFE IN HIS TITAN FORM.
THE FIRST TIME, A TITAN WAS ABOUT TO EAT ME.
HE STOOD AGAINST IT AND PROTECTED ME.
THE SECOND TIME, HE SHIELDED ARMIN AND ME FROM AN EXPLOSIVE SHELL.

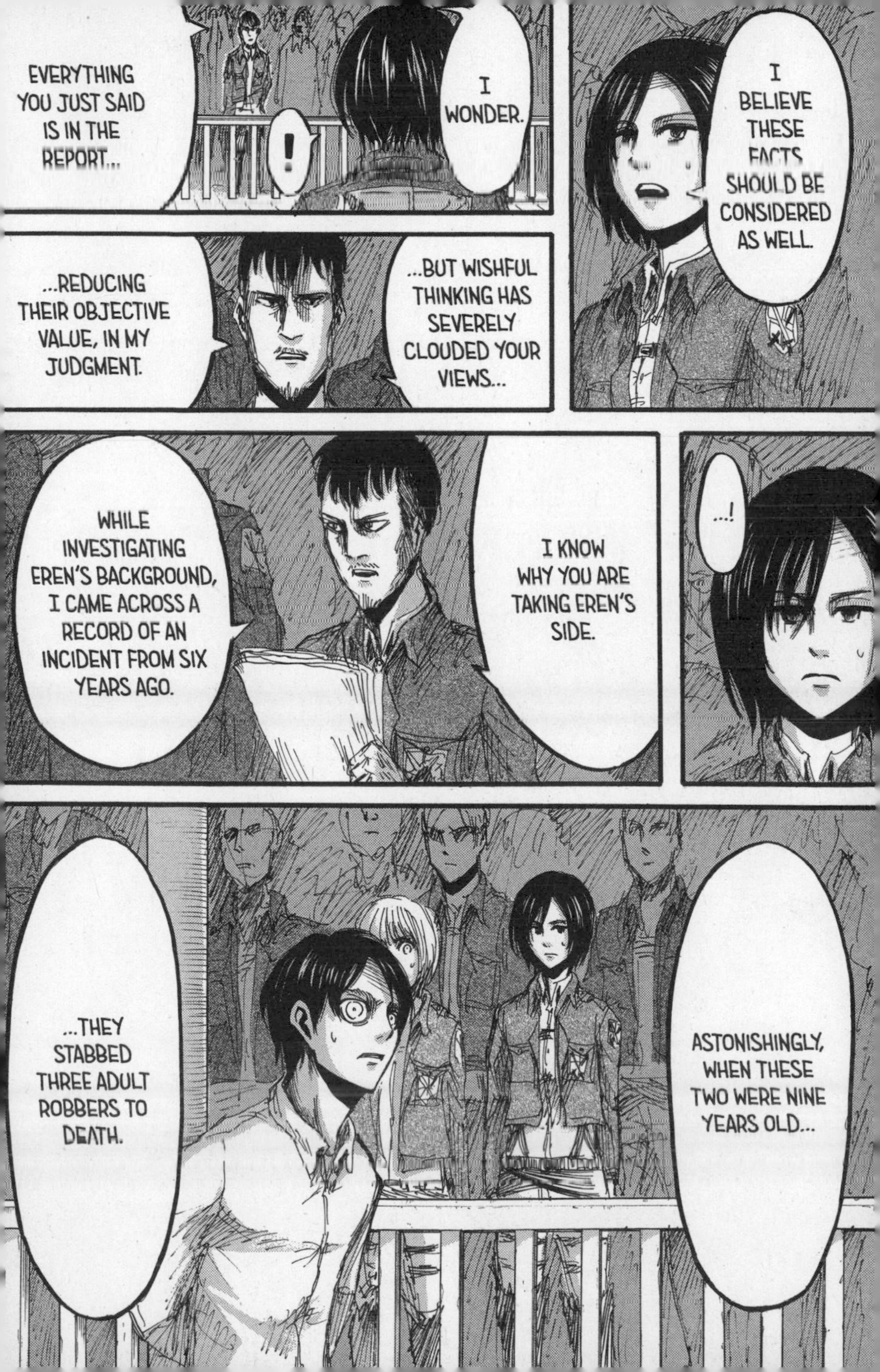
I BELIEVE THESE FACTS SHOULD BE CONSIDERED AS WELL.
I WONDER.
!
EVERYTHING YOU JUST SAID IS IN THE REPORT...
...BUT WISHFUL THINKING HAS SEVERELY CLOUDED YOUR VIEWS...
...REDUCING THEIR OBJECTIVE VALUE, IN MY JUDGMENT.
...!
I KNOW WHY YOU ARE TAKING EREN'S SIDE.
WHILE INVESTIGATING EREN'S BACKGROUND, I CAME ACROSS A RECORD OF AN INCIDENT FROM SIX YEARS AGO.
ASTONISHINGLY, WHEN THESE TWO WERE NINE YEARS OLD...
...THEY STABBED THREE ADULT ROBBERS TO DEATH.

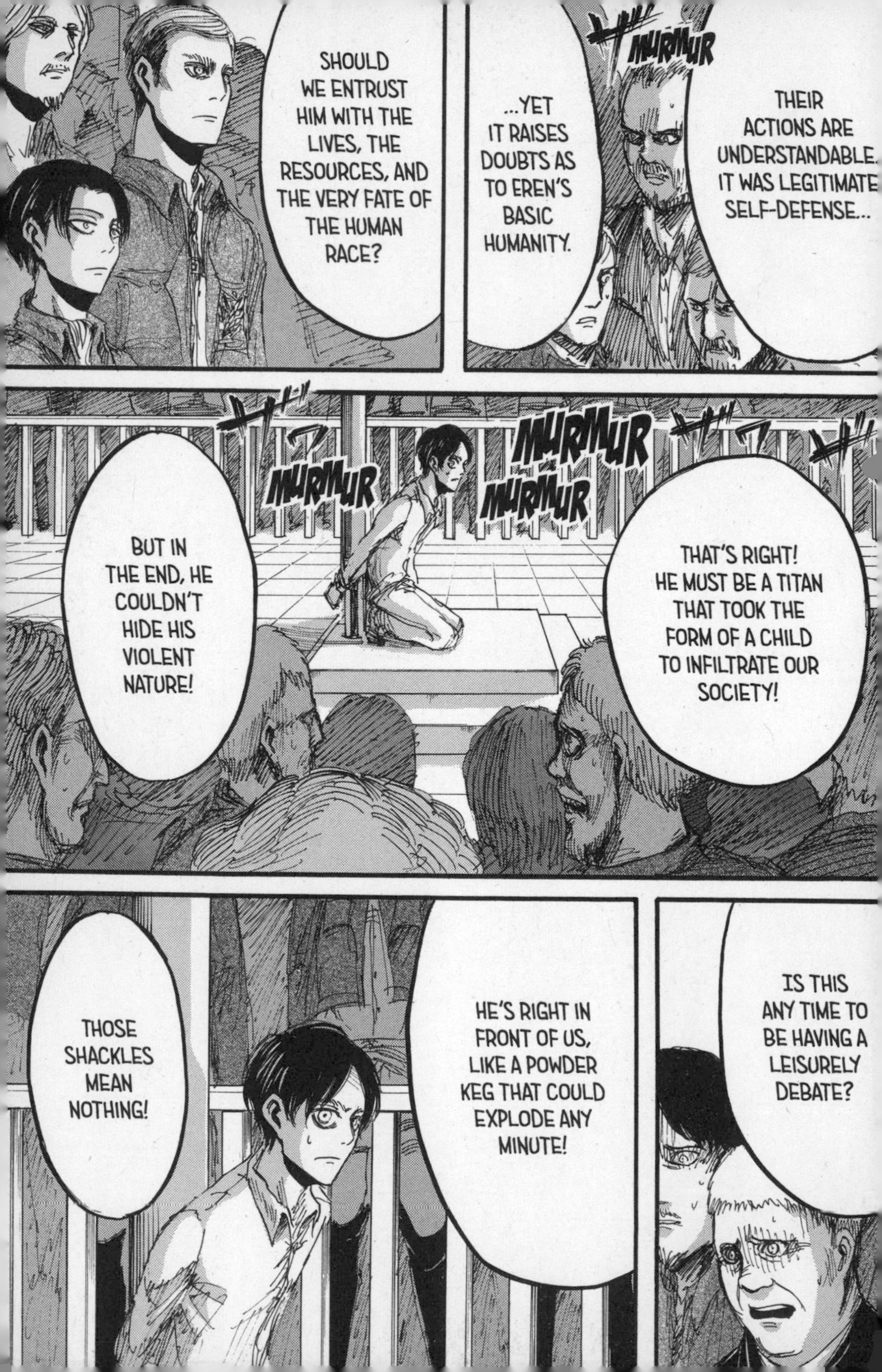
MURMUR
THEIR ACTIONS ARE UNDERSTANDABLE. IT WAS LEGITIMATE SELF-DEFENSE...
...YET IT RAISES DOUBTS AS TO EREN'S BASIC HUMANITY.
SHOULD WE ENTRUST HIM WITH THE LIVES, THE RESOURCES, AND THE VERY FATE OF THE HUMAN RACE?
MURMUR
MURMUR
MURMUR
THAT'S RIGHT! HE MUST BE A TITAN THAT TOOK THE FORM OF A CHILD TO INFILTRATE OUR SOCIETY!
BUT IN THE END, HE COULDN'T HIDE HIS VIOLENT NATURE!
IS THIS ANY TIME TO BE HAVING A LEISURELY DEBATE?
HE'S RIGHT IN FRONT OF US, LIKE A POWDER KEG THAT COULD EXPLODE ANY MINUTE!
THOSE SHACKLES MEAN NOTHING!

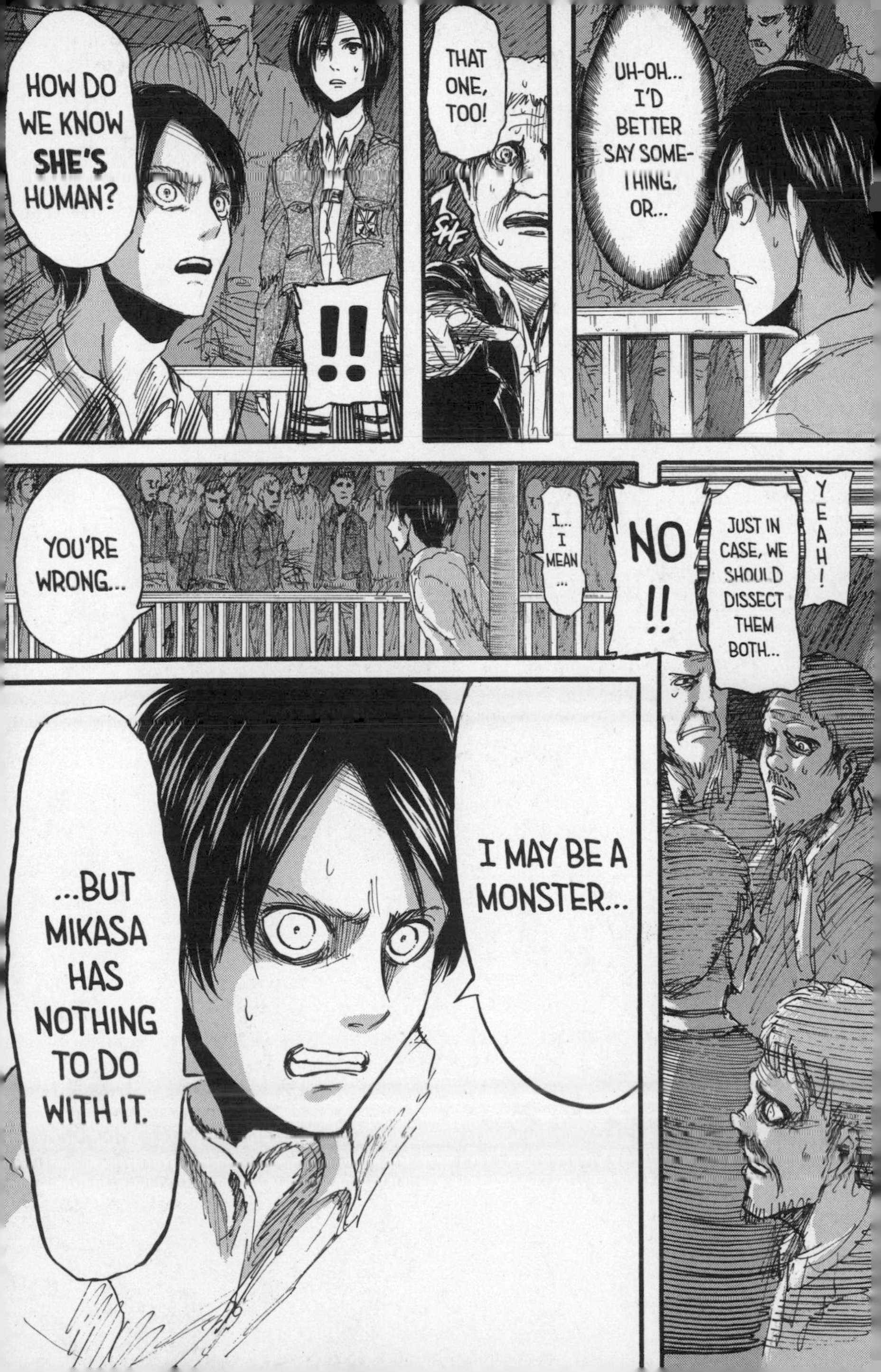
UH-OH... I'D BETTER SAY SOME-THING, OR...
THAT ONE, TOO!
HOW DO WE KNOW **SHE'S** HUMAN?
!!
YEAH!
JUST IN CASE, WE SHOULD DISSECT THEM BOTH...
NO!!
I... I MEAN...
YOU'RE WRONG...
I MAY BE A MONSTER...
...BUT MIKASA HAS NOTHING TO DO WITH IT.

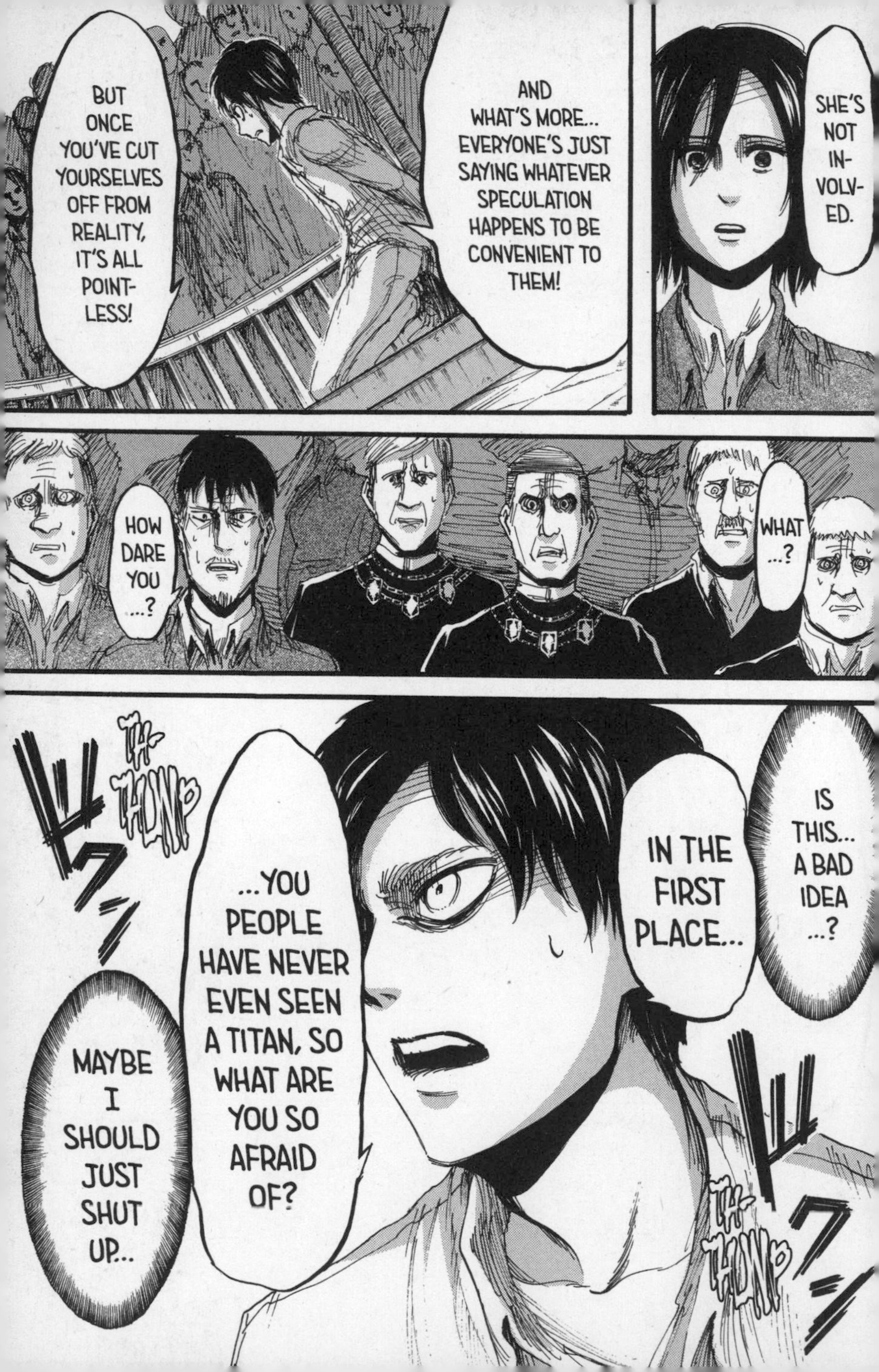
SHE'S NOT INVOLVED.
AND WHAT'S MORE... EVERYONE'S JUST SAYING WHATEVER SPECULATION HAPPENS TO BE CONVENIENT TO THEM!
BUT ONCE YOU'VE CUT YOURSELVES OFF FROM REALITY, IT'S ALL POINTLESS!
WHAT ...?
HOW DARE YOU ...?
IS THIS... A BAD IDEA ...?
IN THE FIRST PLACE...
TH THUMP
...YOU PEOPLE HAVE NEVER EVEN SEEN A TITAN, SO WHAT ARE YOU SO AFRAID OF?
TH THUMP
MAYBE I SHOULD JUST SHUT UP...

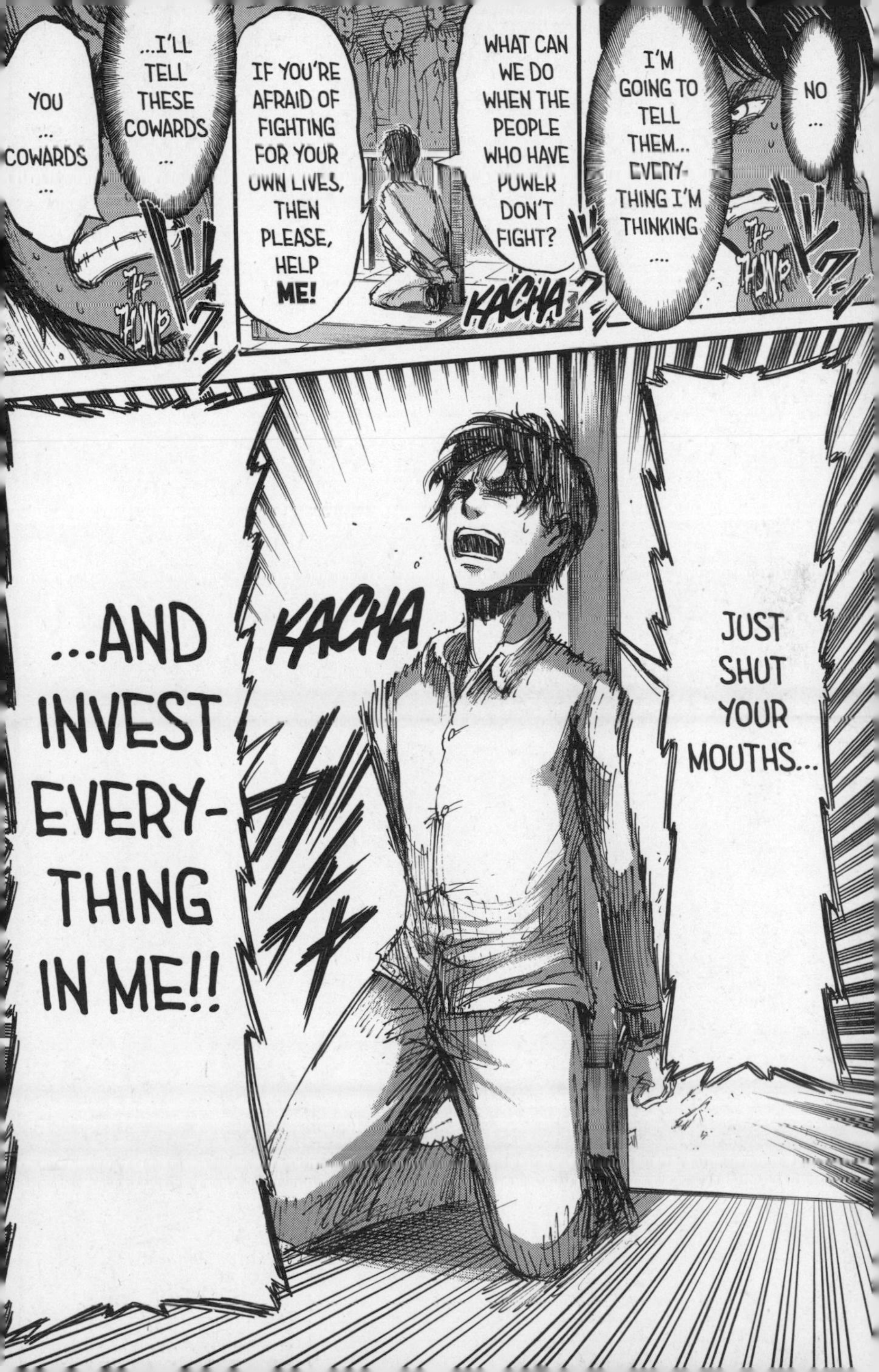
NO ...
I'M GOING TO TELL THEM... EVERY-THING I'M THINKING ....
TH-THUMP
WHAT CAN WE DO WHEN THE PEOPLE WHO HAVE POWER DON'T FIGHT?
IF YOU'RE AFRAID OF FIGHTING FOR YOUR OWN LIVES, THEN PLEASE, HELP **ME!**
KACHA
...I'LL TELL THESE COWARDS ...
YOU ... COWARDS ...
TH-THUMP
JUST SHUT YOUR MOUTHS...
KACHA
...AND INVEST EVERY-THING IN ME!!

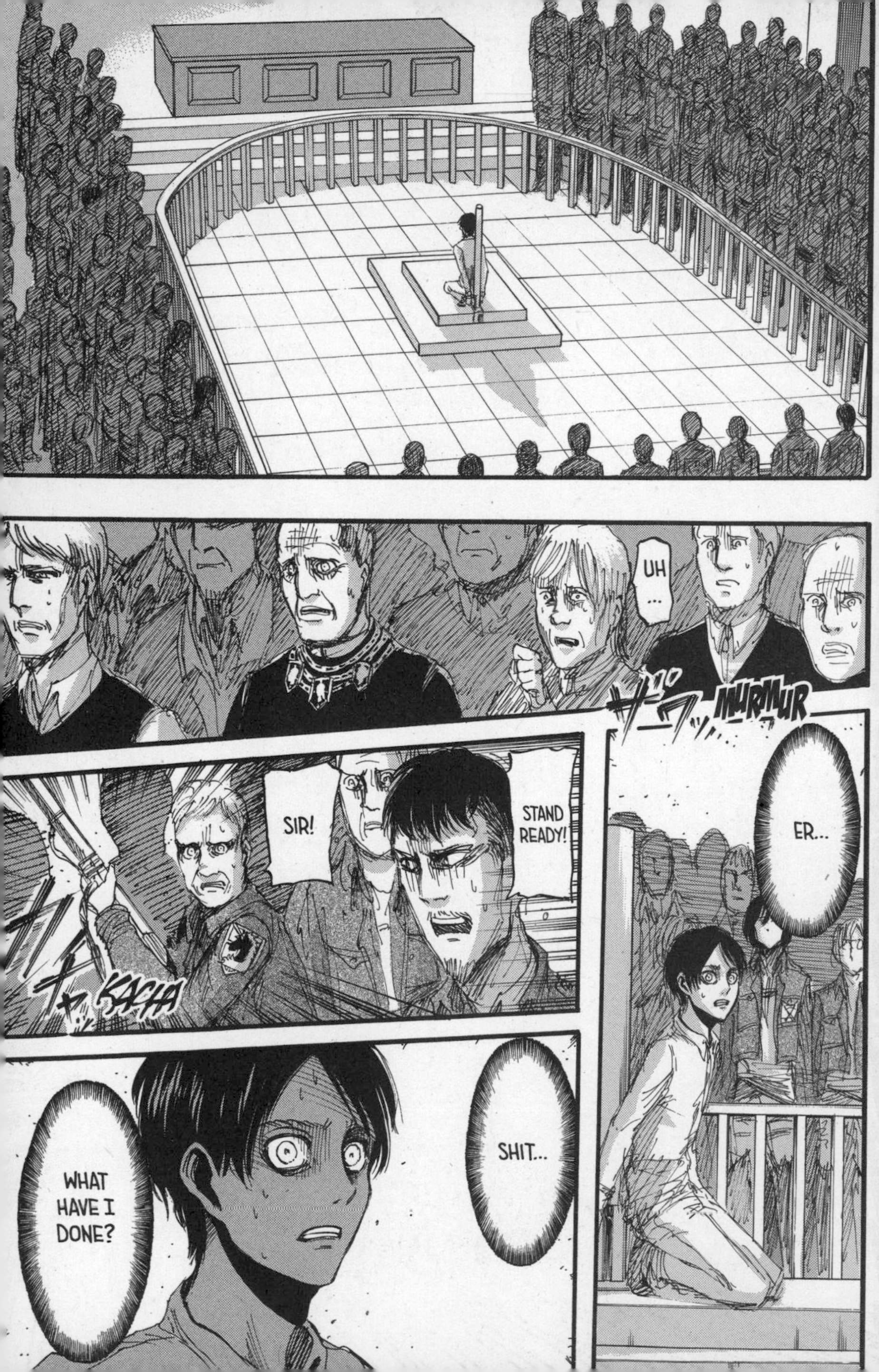
UH ...
MURMUR
ER...
STAND READY!
SIR!
KACHA
SHIT...
WHAT HAVE I DONE?

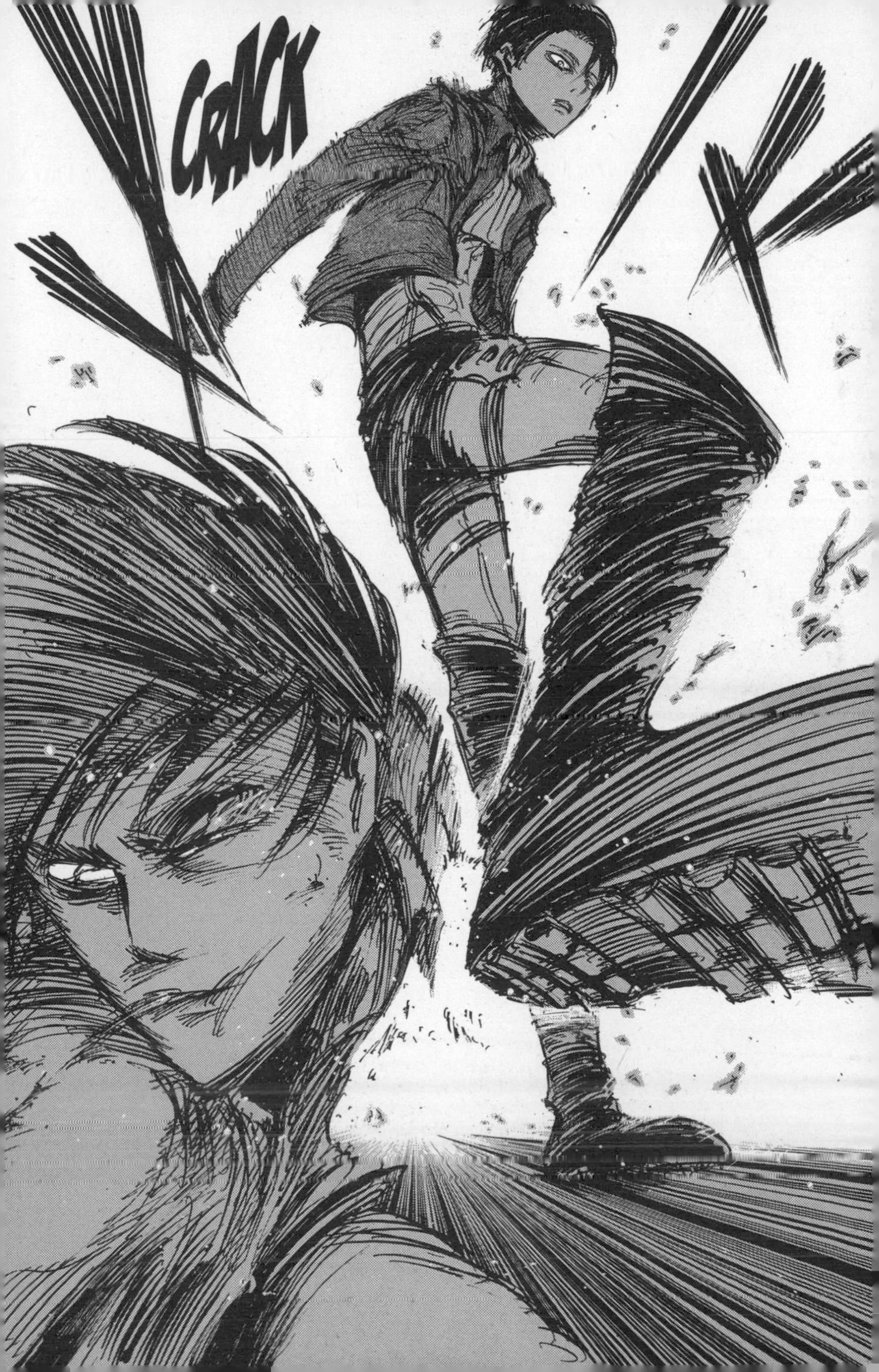
CRACK

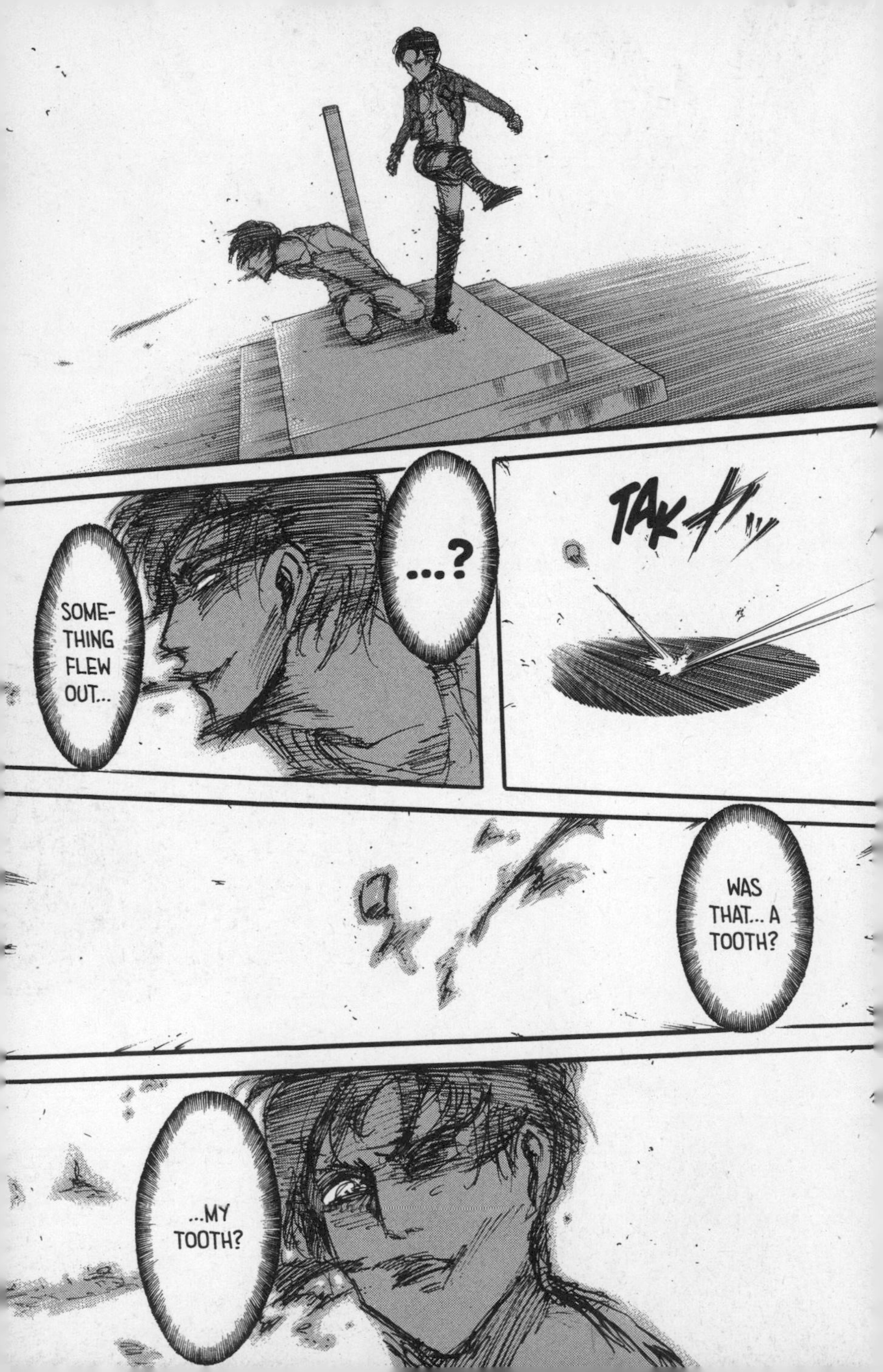
TAK
...?
SOME-THING FLEW OUT...
WAS THAT... A TOOTH?
...MY TOOTH?

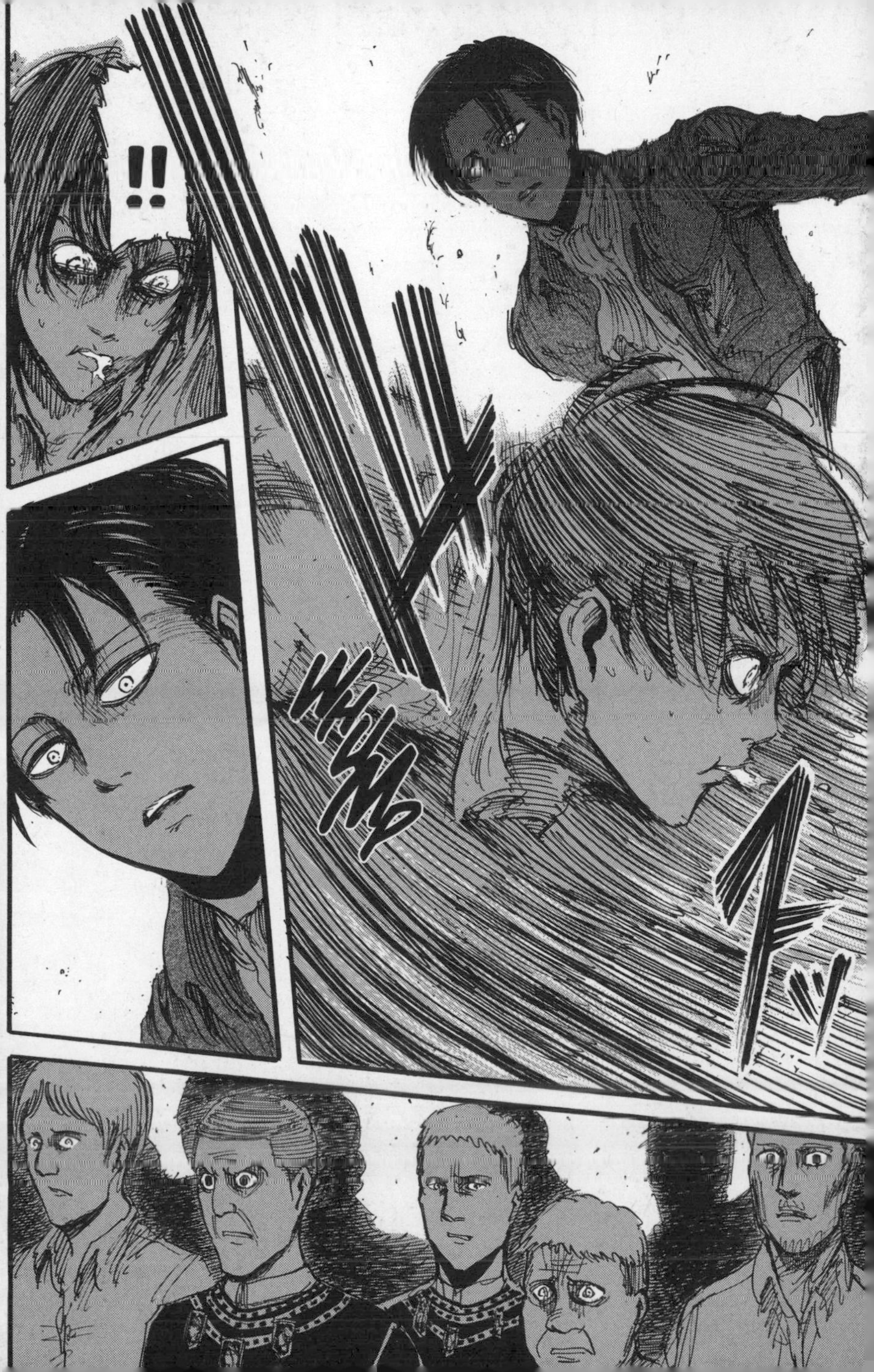
!!
WHUMP

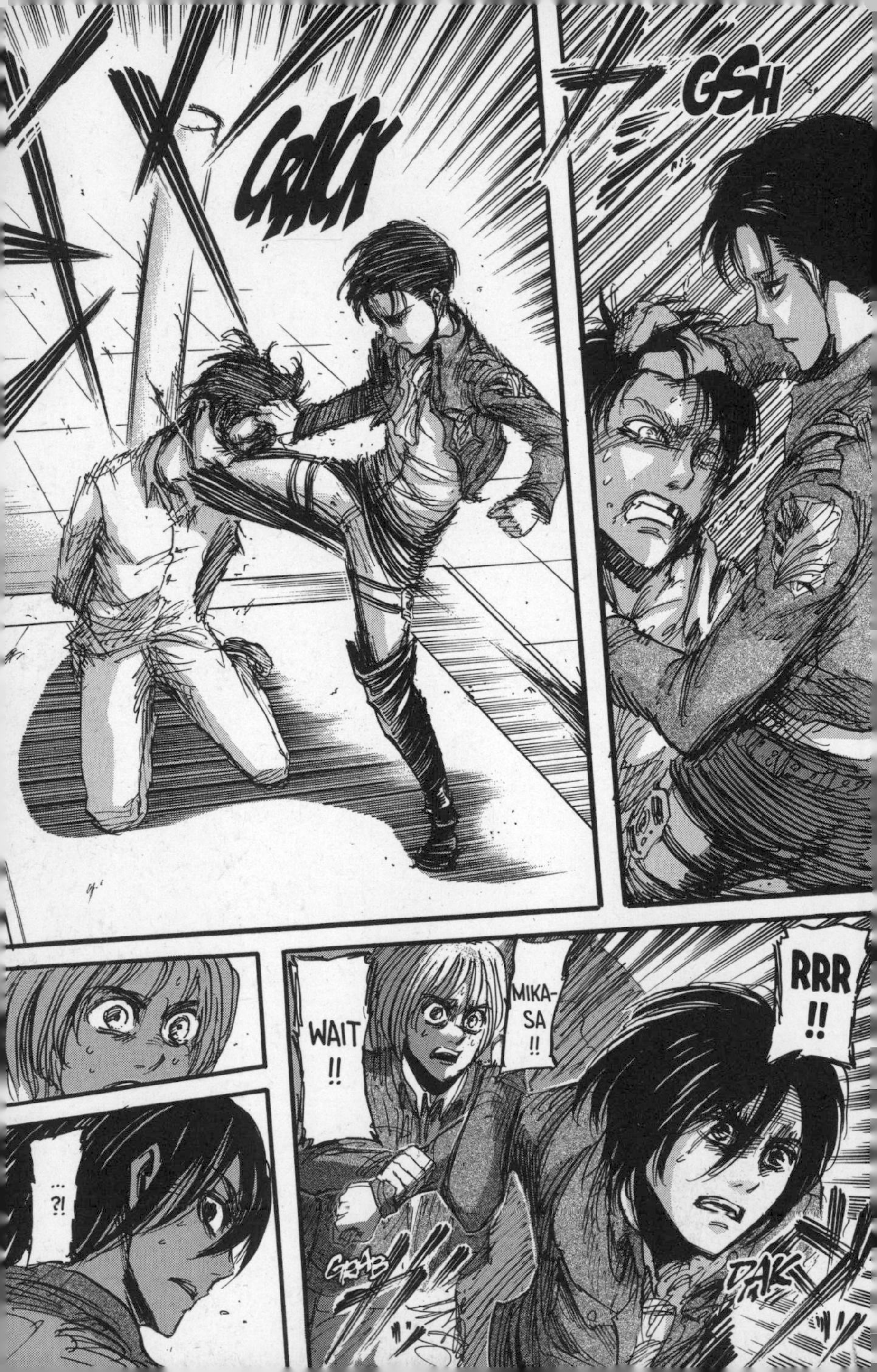
GSH
CRACK
RRR !!
MIKA-SA !!
WAIT !!
DAK
GRAB
...?!

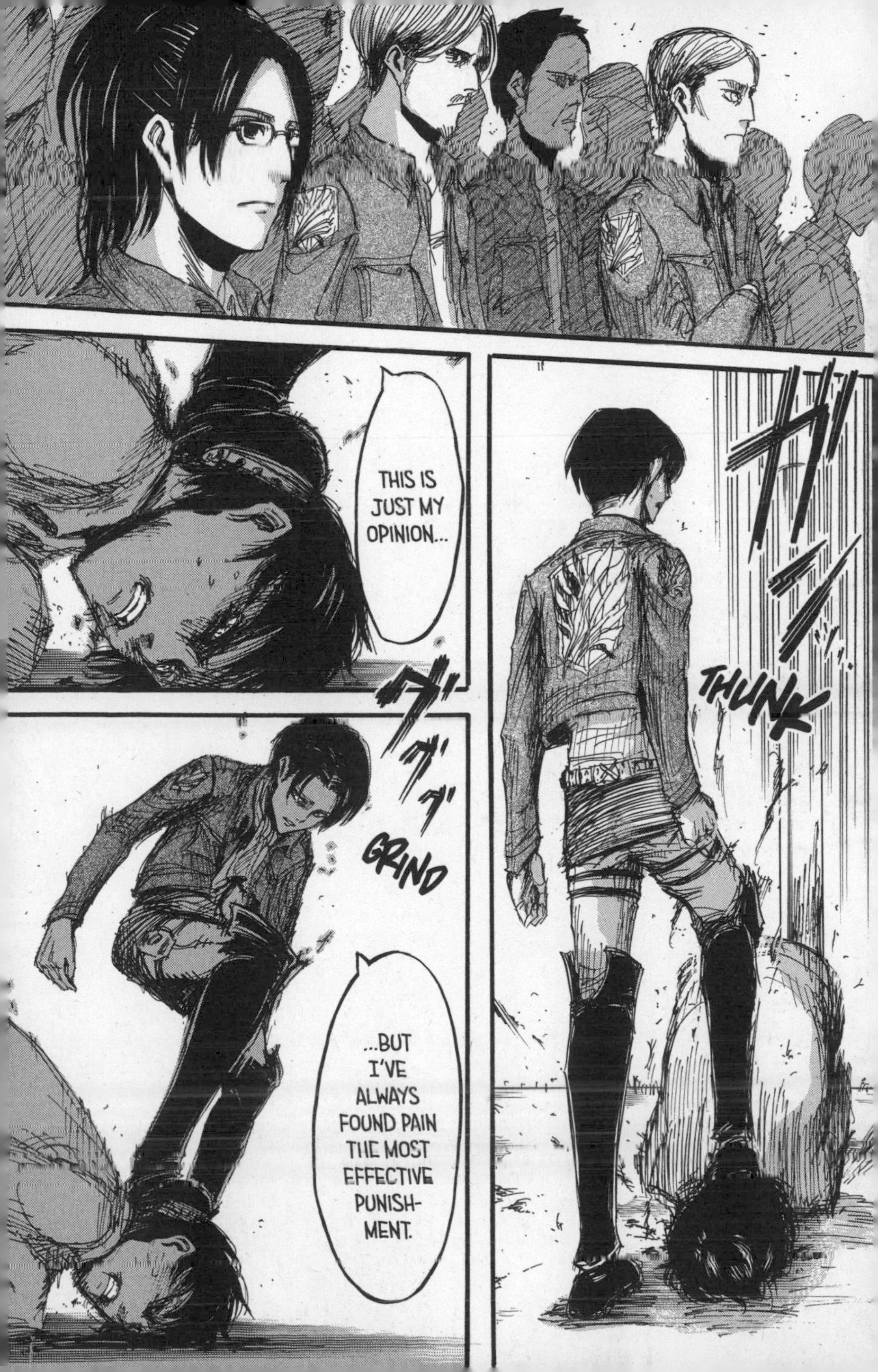
THUNK
THIS IS JUST MY OPINION...
GRIND
...BUT I'VE ALWAYS FOUND PAIN THE MOST EFFECTIVE PUNISH-MENT.

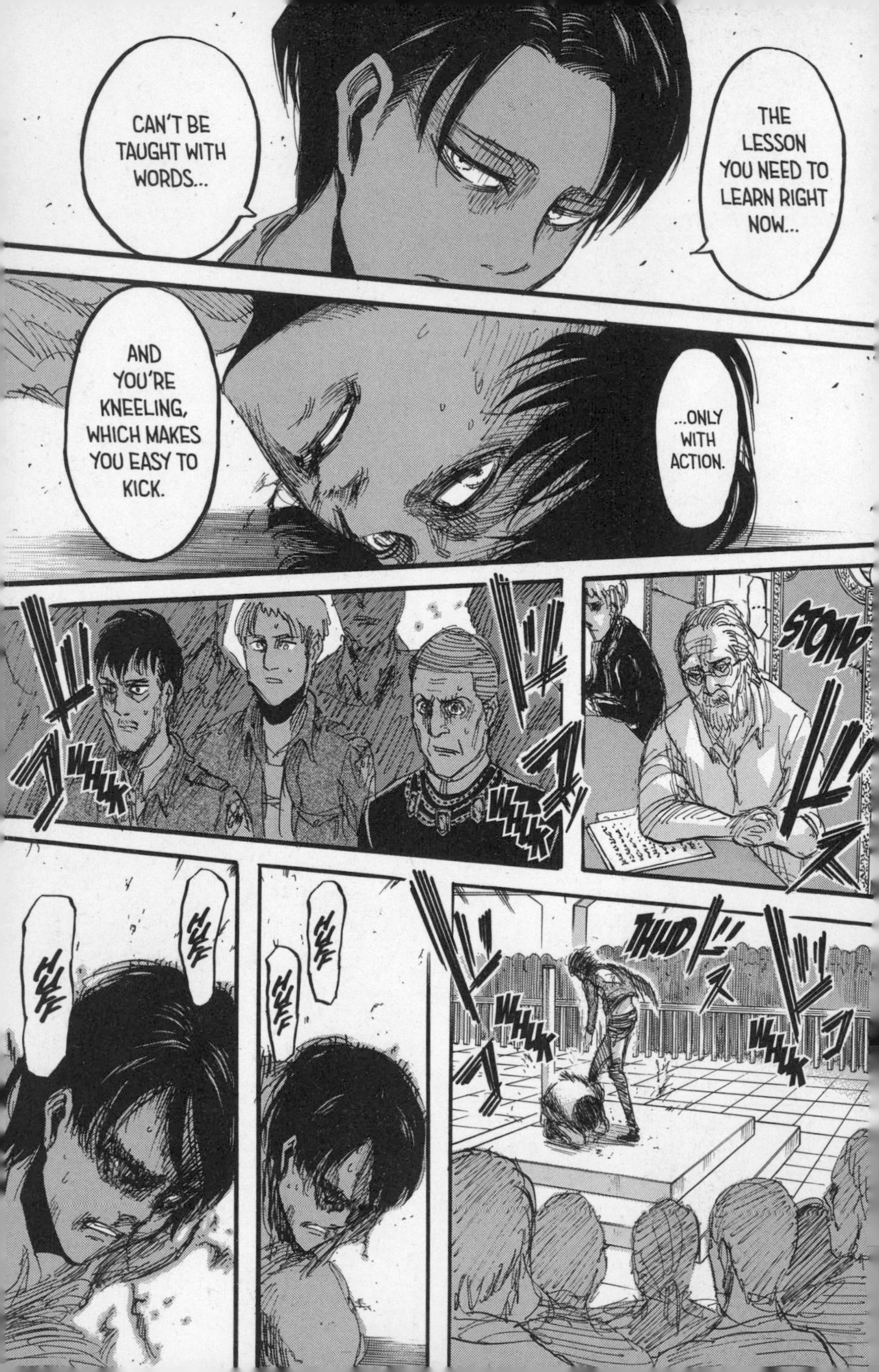
THE LESSON YOU NEED TO LEARN RIGHT NOW...
CAN'T BE TAUGHT WITH WORDS...
...ONLY WITH ACTION.
AND YOU'RE KNEELING, WHICH MAKES YOU EASY TO KICK.
STOMP
WHUK
WHUK
THUD
WHUK
WHUK

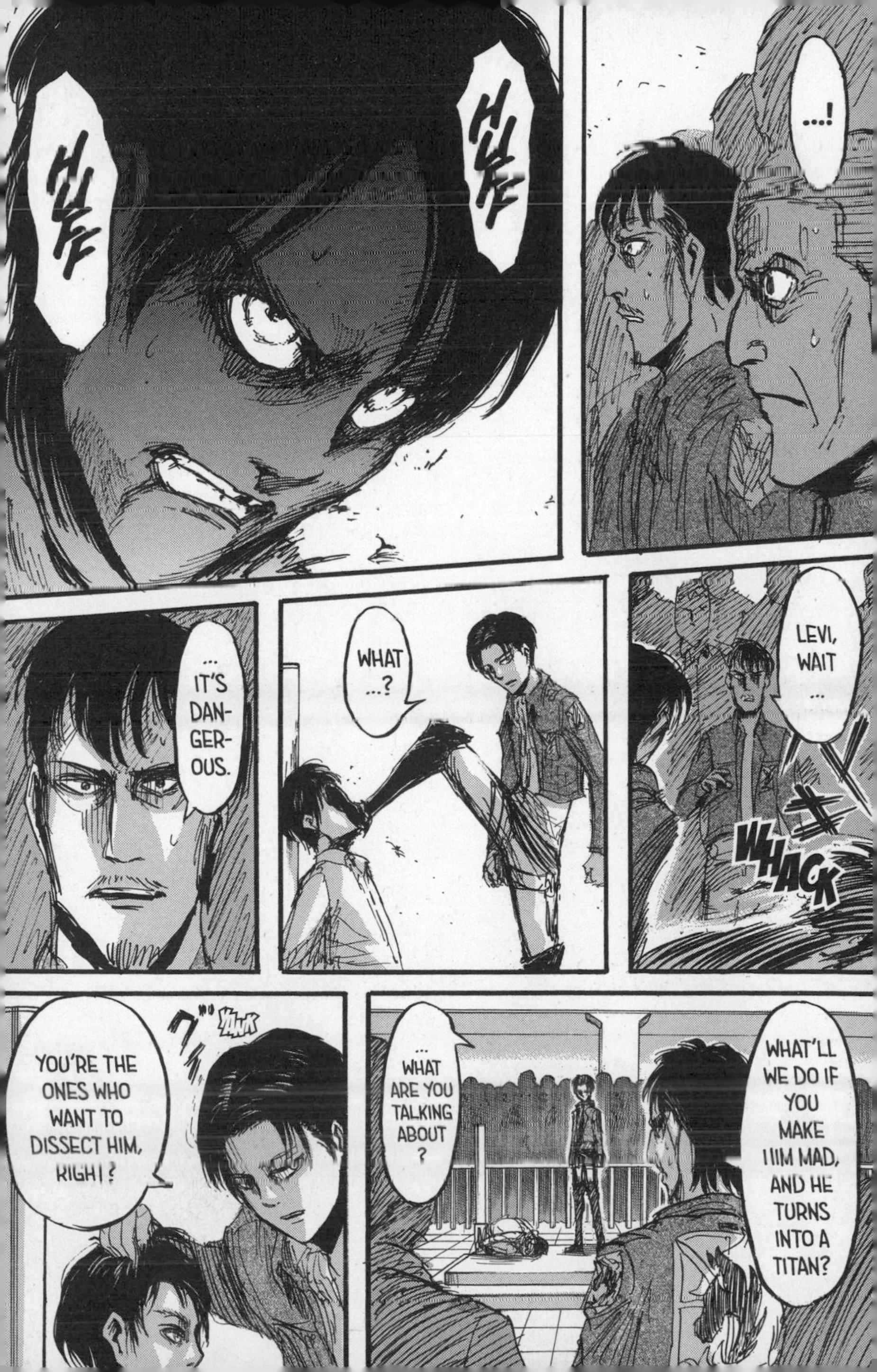
...!
HUFF
HUFF
LEVI, WAIT ...
WHACK
WHAT ...?
... IT'S DANGEROUS.
WHAT'LL WE DO IF YOU MAKE HIM MAD, AND HE TURNS INTO A TITAN?
... WHAT ARE YOU TALKING ABOUT ?
YANK
YOU'RE THE ONES WHO WANT TO DISSECT HIM, RIGHT?

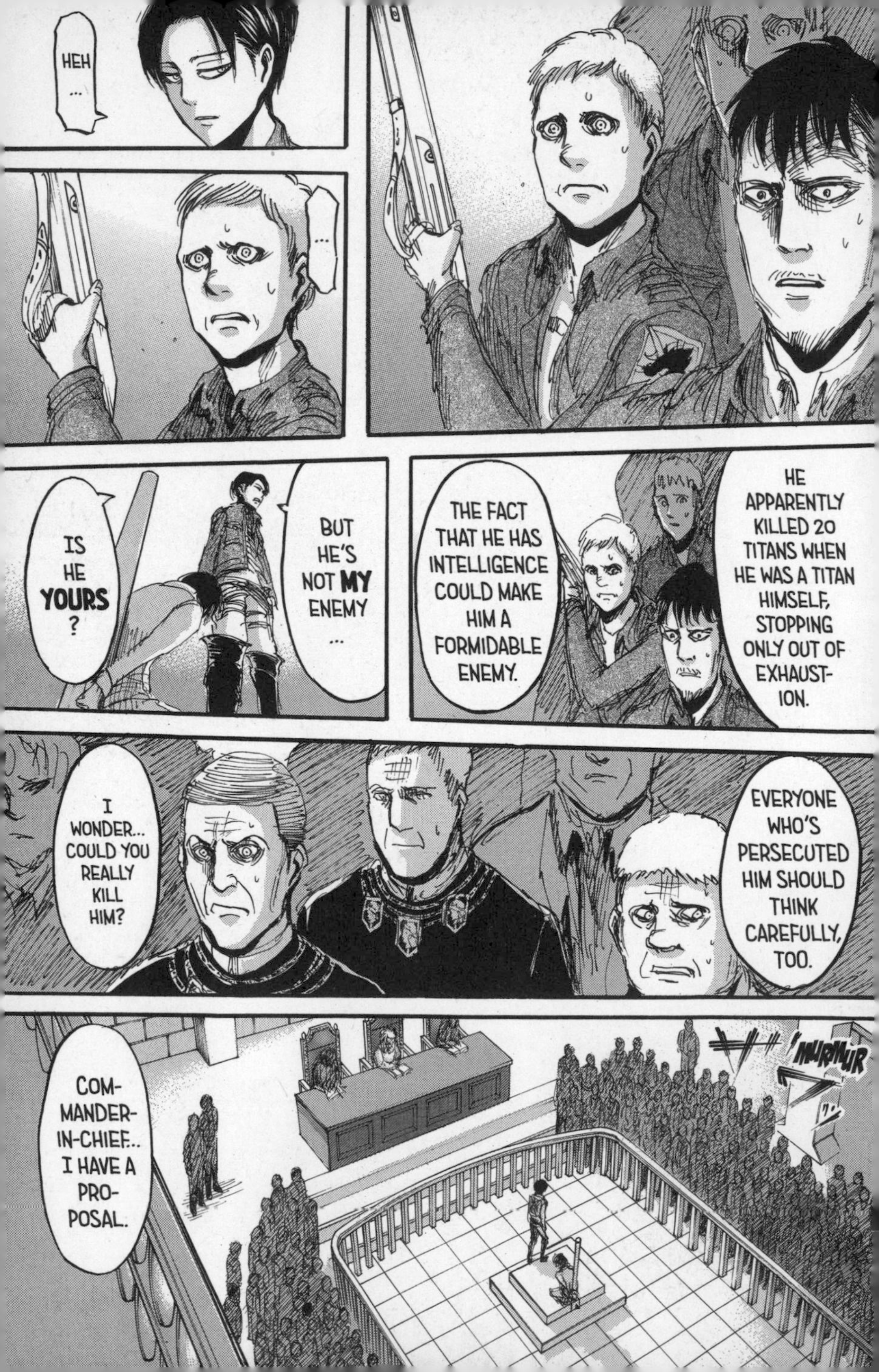
HEH ...
...
HE APPARENTLY KILLED 20 TITANS WHEN HE WAS A TITAN HIMSELF, STOPPING ONLY OUT OF EXHAUST-ION.
THE FACT THAT HE HAS INTELLIGENCE COULD MAKE HIM A FORMIDABLE ENEMY.
BUT HE'S NOT MY ENEMY ...
IS HE YOURS ?
EVERYONE WHO'S PERSECUTED HIM SHOULD THINK CAREFULLY, TOO.
I WONDER... COULD YOU REALLY KILL HIM?
MURMUR
COM-MANDER-IN-CHIEF... I HAVE A PRO-POSAL.

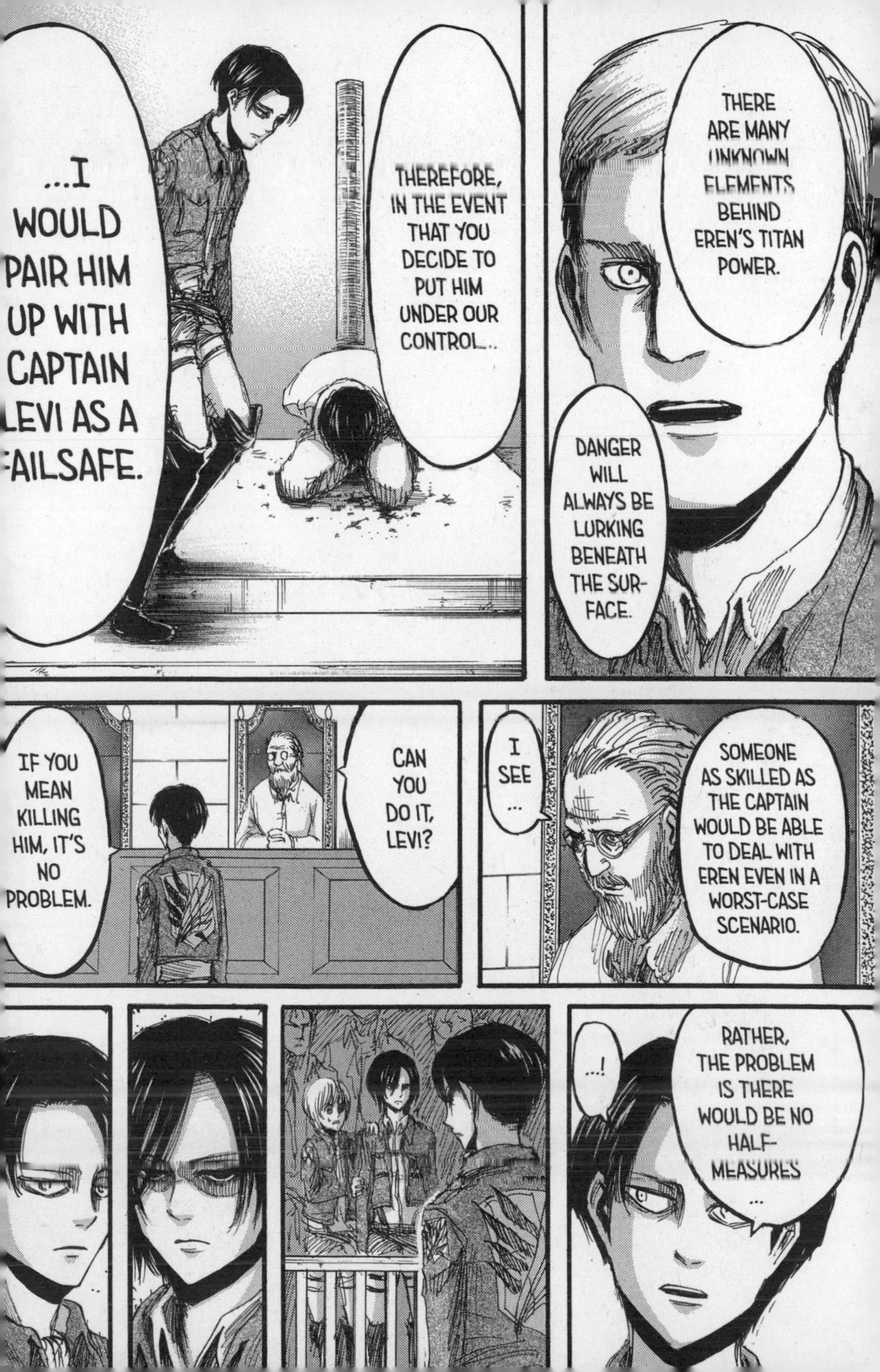
THERE ARE MANY UNKNOWN ELEMENTS BEHIND EREN'S TITAN POWER.
DANGER WILL ALWAYS BE LURKING BENEATH THE SUR-FACE.
THEREFORE, IN THE EVENT THAT YOU DECIDE TO PUT HIM UNDER OUR CONTROL...
...I WOULD PAIR HIM UP WITH CAPTAIN LEVI AS A FAILSAFE.
SOMEONE AS SKILLED AS THE CAPTAIN WOULD BE ABLE TO DEAL WITH EREN EVEN IN A WORST-CASE SCENARIO.
I SEE...
CAN YOU DO IT, LEVI?
IF YOU MEAN KILLING HIM, IT'S NO PROBLEM.
RATHER, THE PROBLEM IS THERE WOULD BE NO HALF-MEASURES...
...!

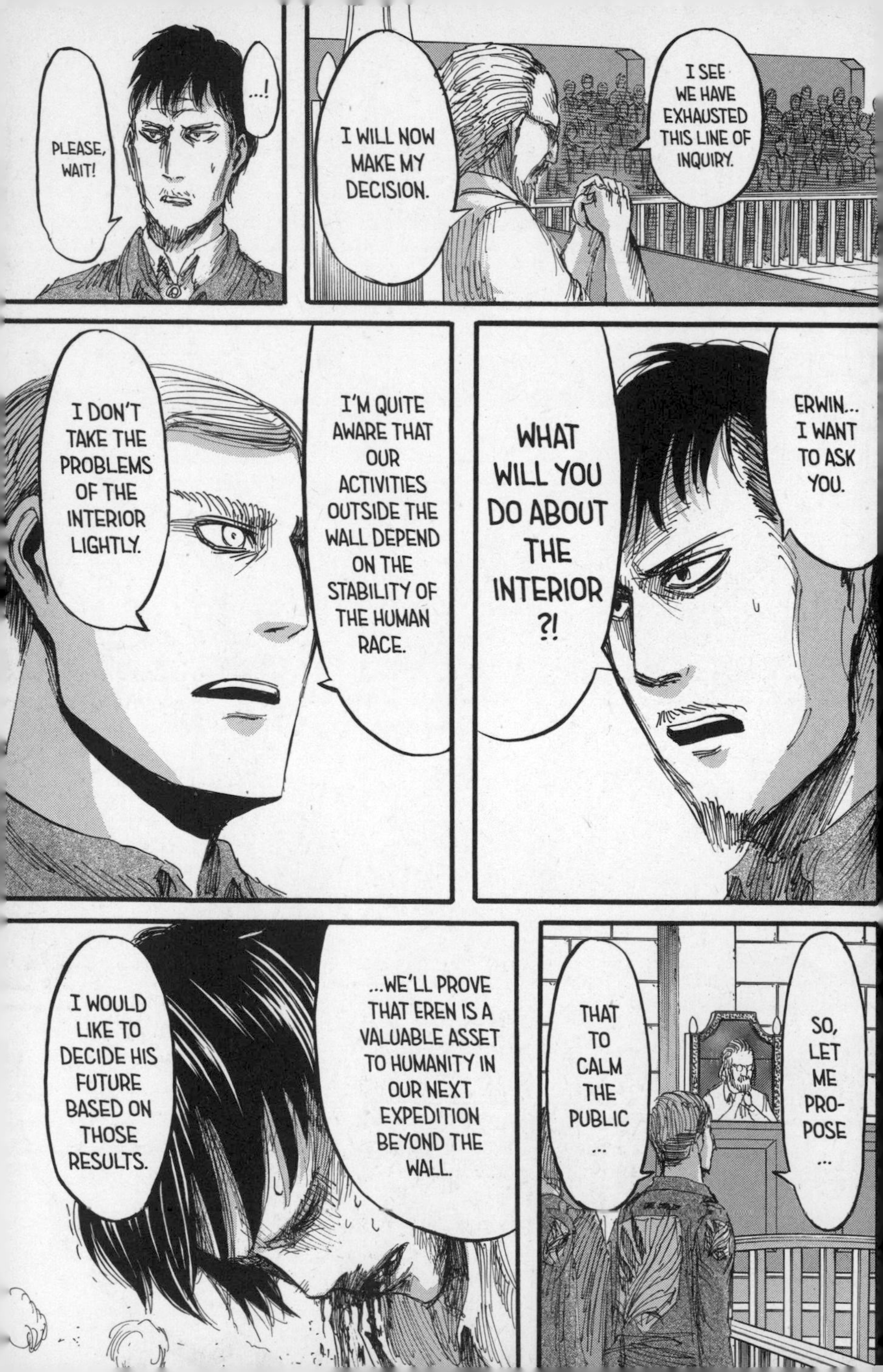
I SEE WE HAVE EXHAUSTED THIS LINE OF INQUIRY.
I WILL NOW MAKE MY DECISION.
...!
PLEASE, WAIT!
ERWIN... I WANT TO ASK YOU.
WHAT WILL YOU DO ABOUT THE INTERIOR ?!
I'M QUITE AWARE THAT OUR ACTIVITIES OUTSIDE THE WALL DEPEND ON THE STABILITY OF THE HUMAN RACE.
I DON'T TAKE THE PROBLEMS OF THE INTERIOR LIGHTLY.
SO, LET ME PRO-POSE ...
THAT TO CALM THE PUBLIC ...
...WE'LL PROVE THAT EREN IS A VALUABLE ASSET TO HUMANITY IN OUR NEXT EXPEDITION BEYOND THE WALL.
I WOULD LIKE TO DECIDE HIS FUTURE BASED ON THOSE RESULTS.

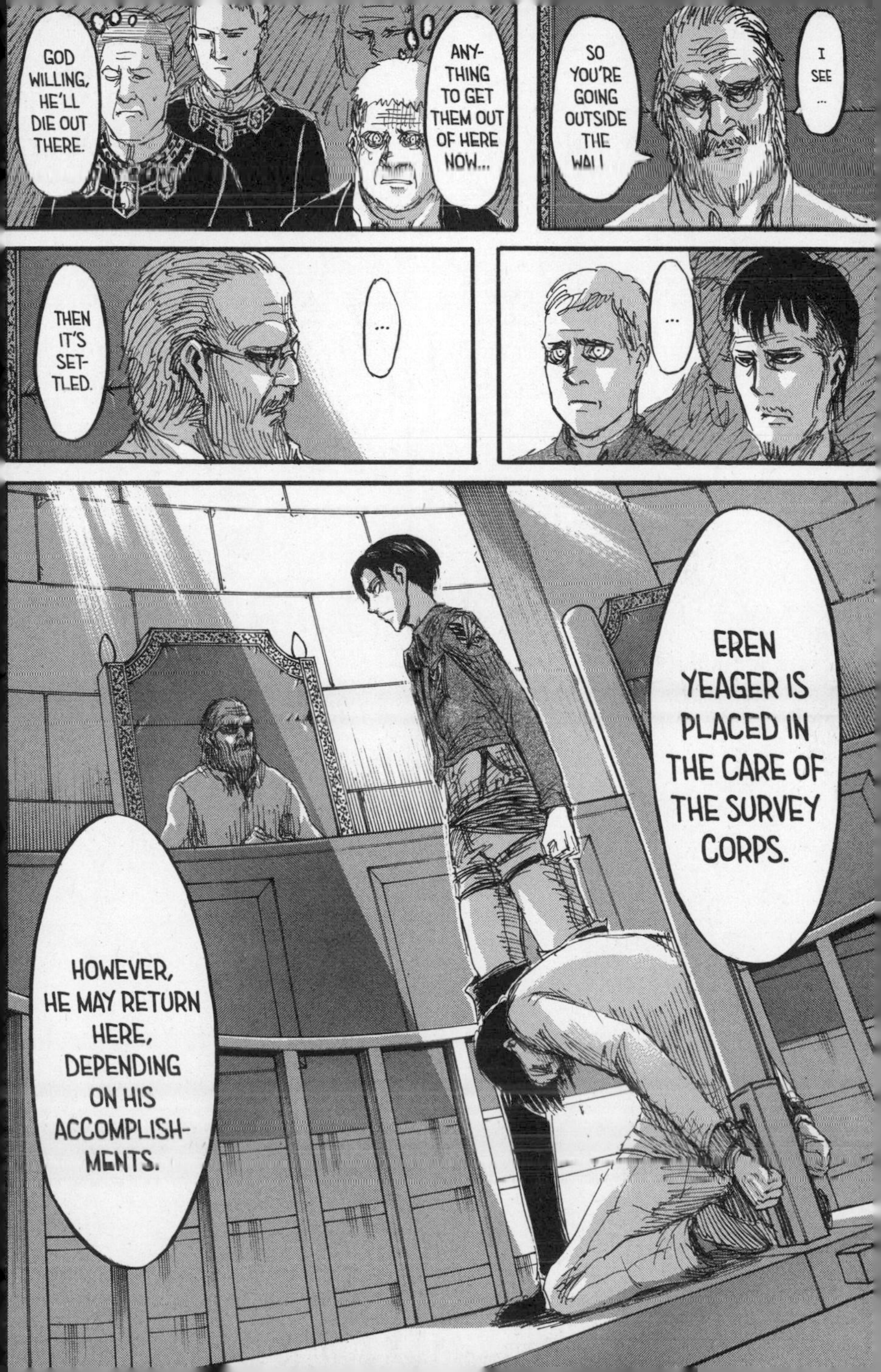
I SEE ...
SO YOU'RE GOING OUTSIDE THE WALL
ANY-THING TO GET THEM OUT OF HERE NOW...
GOD WILLING, HE'LL DIE OUT THERE.
...
...
THEN IT'S SET-TLED.
EREN YEAGER IS PLACED IN THE CARE OF THE SURVEY CORPS.
HOWEVER, HE MAY RETURN HERE, DEPENDING ON HIS ACCOMPLISH-MENTS.

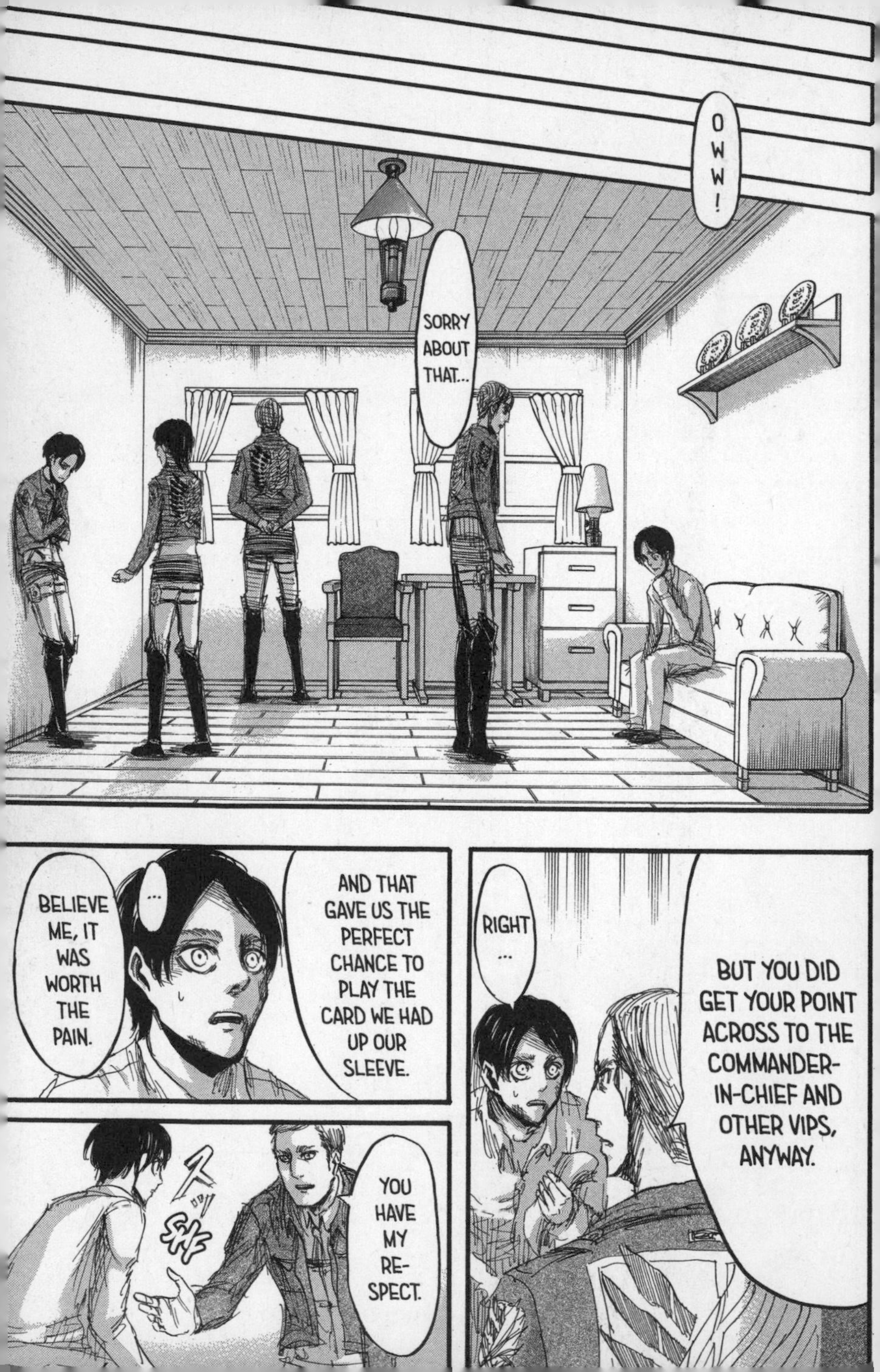
OWW!
SORRY ABOUT THAT...
BUT YOU DID GET YOUR POINT ACROSS TO THE COMMANDER-IN-CHIEF AND OTHER VIPS, ANYWAY.
RIGHT...
AND THAT GAVE US THE PERFECT CHANCE TO PLAY THE CARD WE HAD UP OUR SLEEVE.
...
BELIEVE ME, IT WAS WORTH THE PAIN.
YOU HAVE MY RE-SPECT.
SK

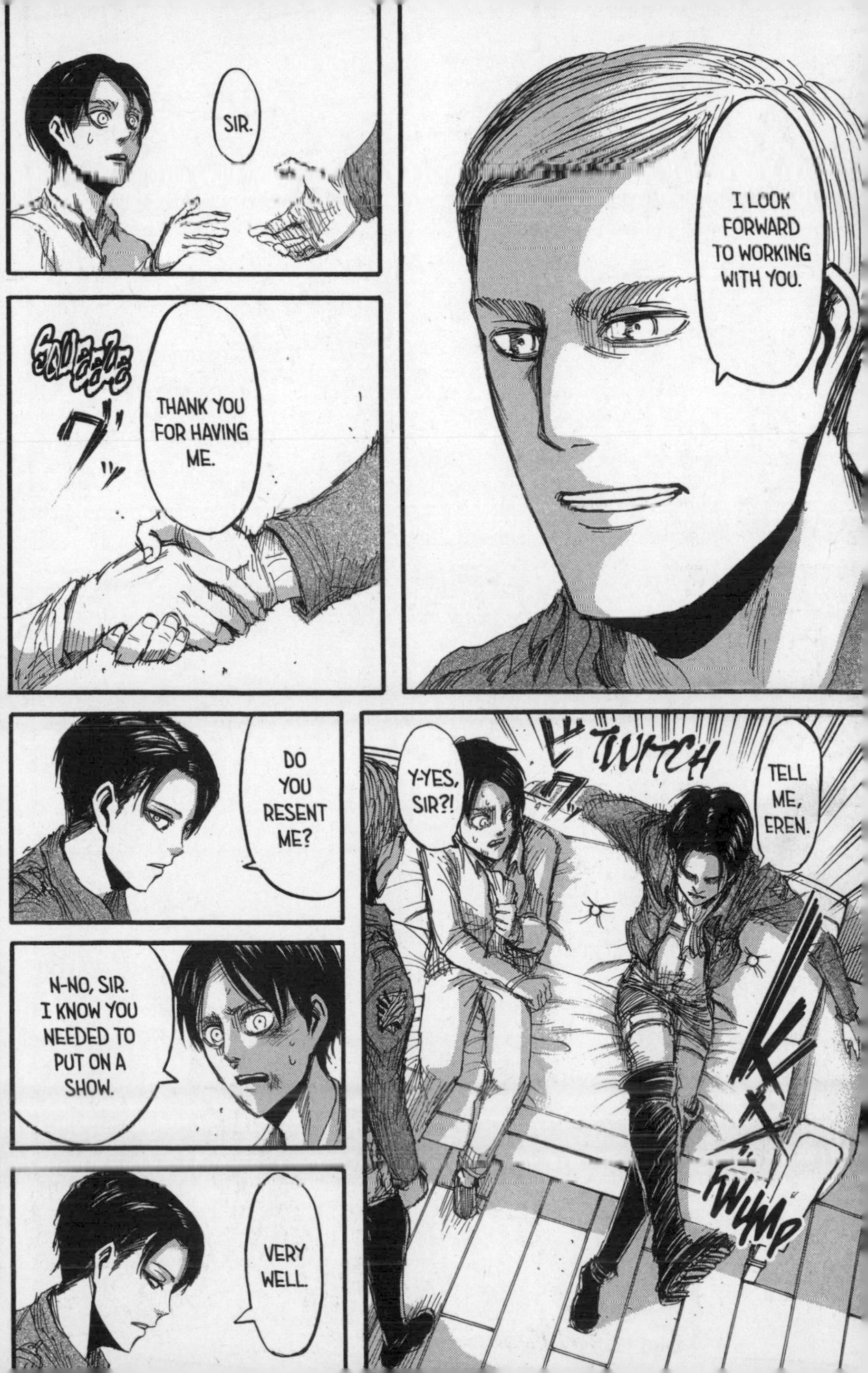
I LOOK FORWARD TO WORKING WITH YOU.
SIR.
THANK YOU FOR HAVING ME.
TELL ME, EREN.
TWITCH
Y-YES, SIR?!
KWUMP
DO YOU RESENT ME?
N-NO, SIR. I KNOW YOU NEEDED TO PUT ON A SHOW.
VERY WELL.

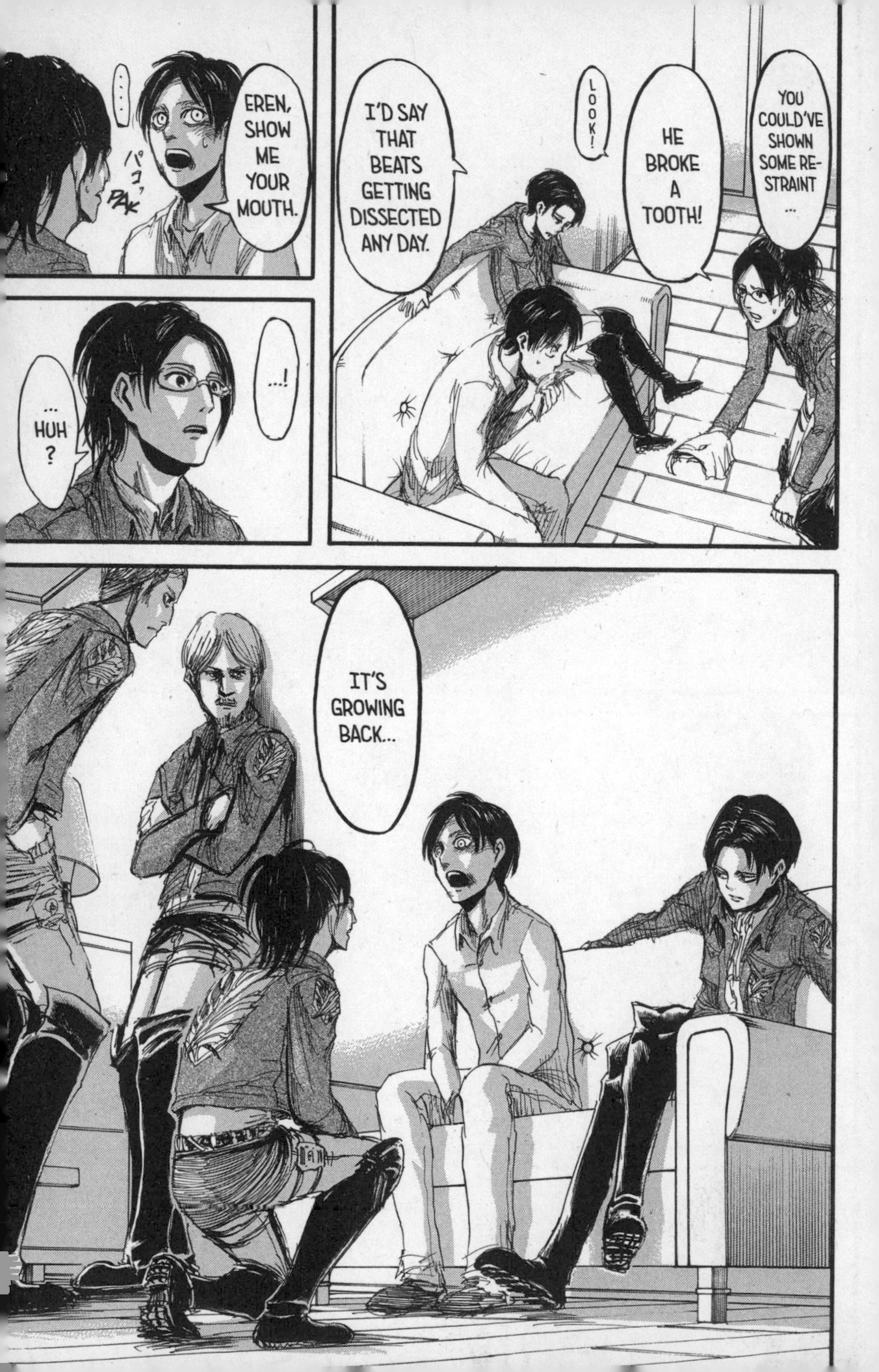
YOU COULD'VE SHOWN SOME RE-STRAINT...
HE BROKE A TOOTH!
LOOK!
I'D SAY THAT BEATS GETTING DISSECTED ANY DAY.
EREN, SHOW ME YOUR MOUTH.
. . .
パコッ
PAK
...!
...HUH?
IT'S GROWING BACK...

ATTACK on TITAN

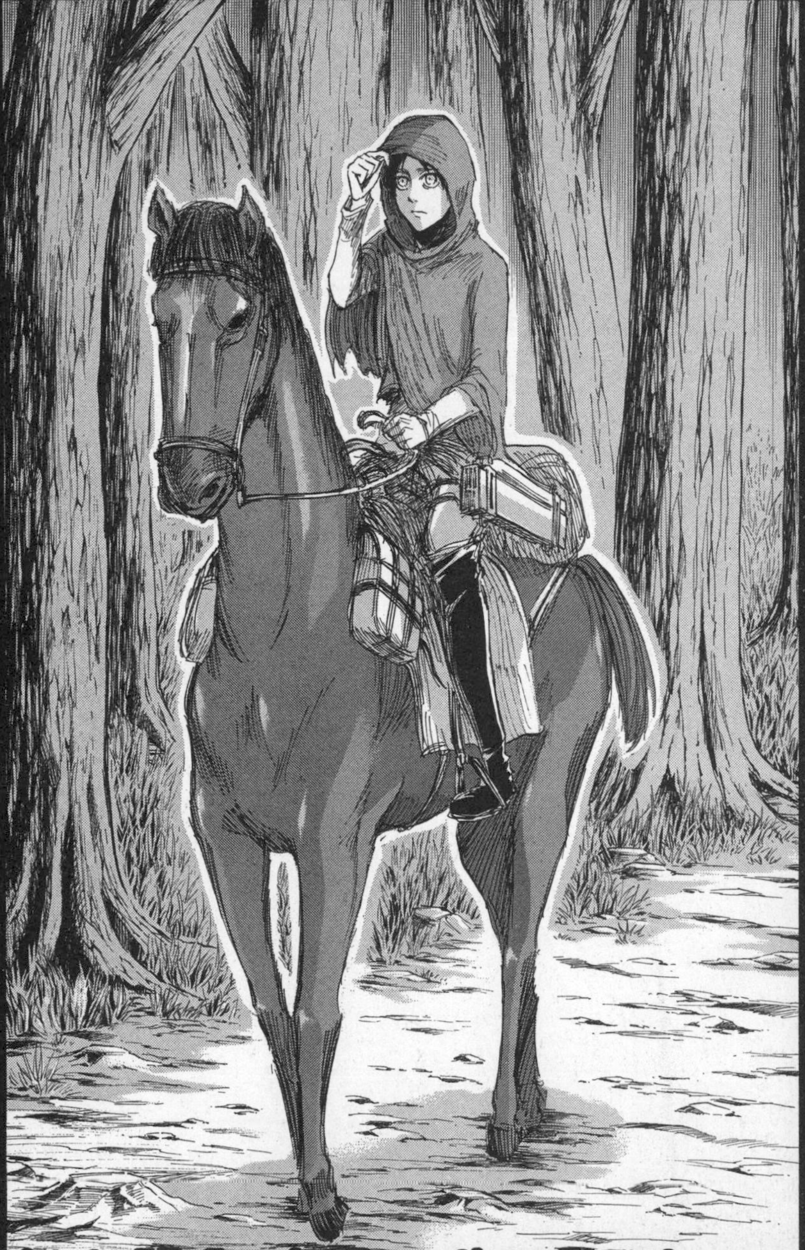

Episode 20: Special Operations Squad

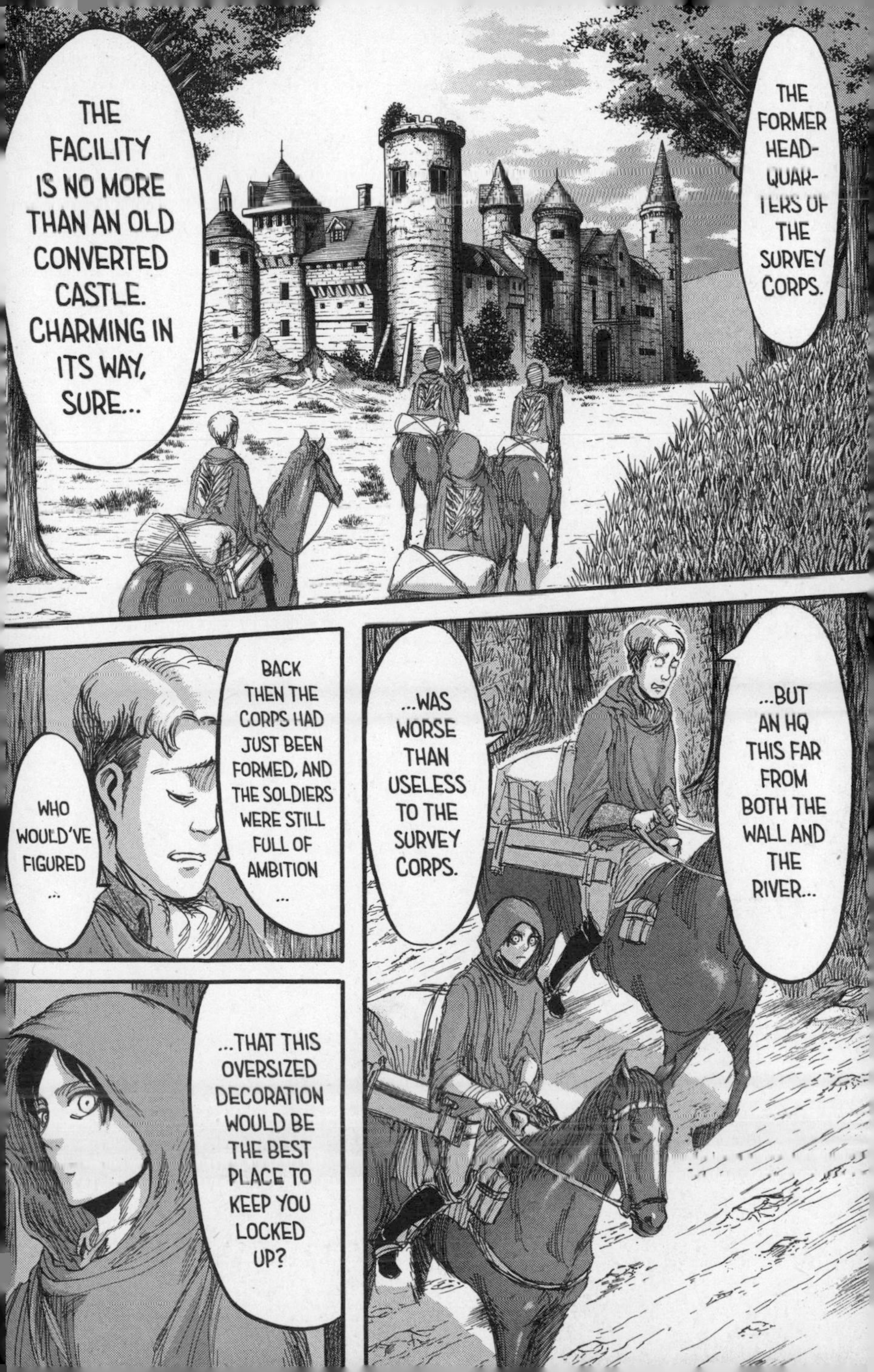
THE FORMER HEADQUARTERS OF THE SURVEY CORPS.
THE FACILITY IS NO MORE THAN AN OLD CONVERTED CASTLE. CHARMING IN ITS WAY, SURE...
...BUT AN HQ THIS FAR FROM BOTH THE WALL AND THE RIVER...
...WAS WORSE THAN USELESS TO THE SURVEY CORPS.
BACK THEN THE CORPS HAD JUST BEEN FORMED, AND THE SOLDIERS WERE STILL FULL OF AMBITION...
WHO WOULD'VE FIGURED...
...THAT THIS OVERSIZED DECORATION WOULD BE THE BEST PLACE TO KEEP YOU LOCKED UP?

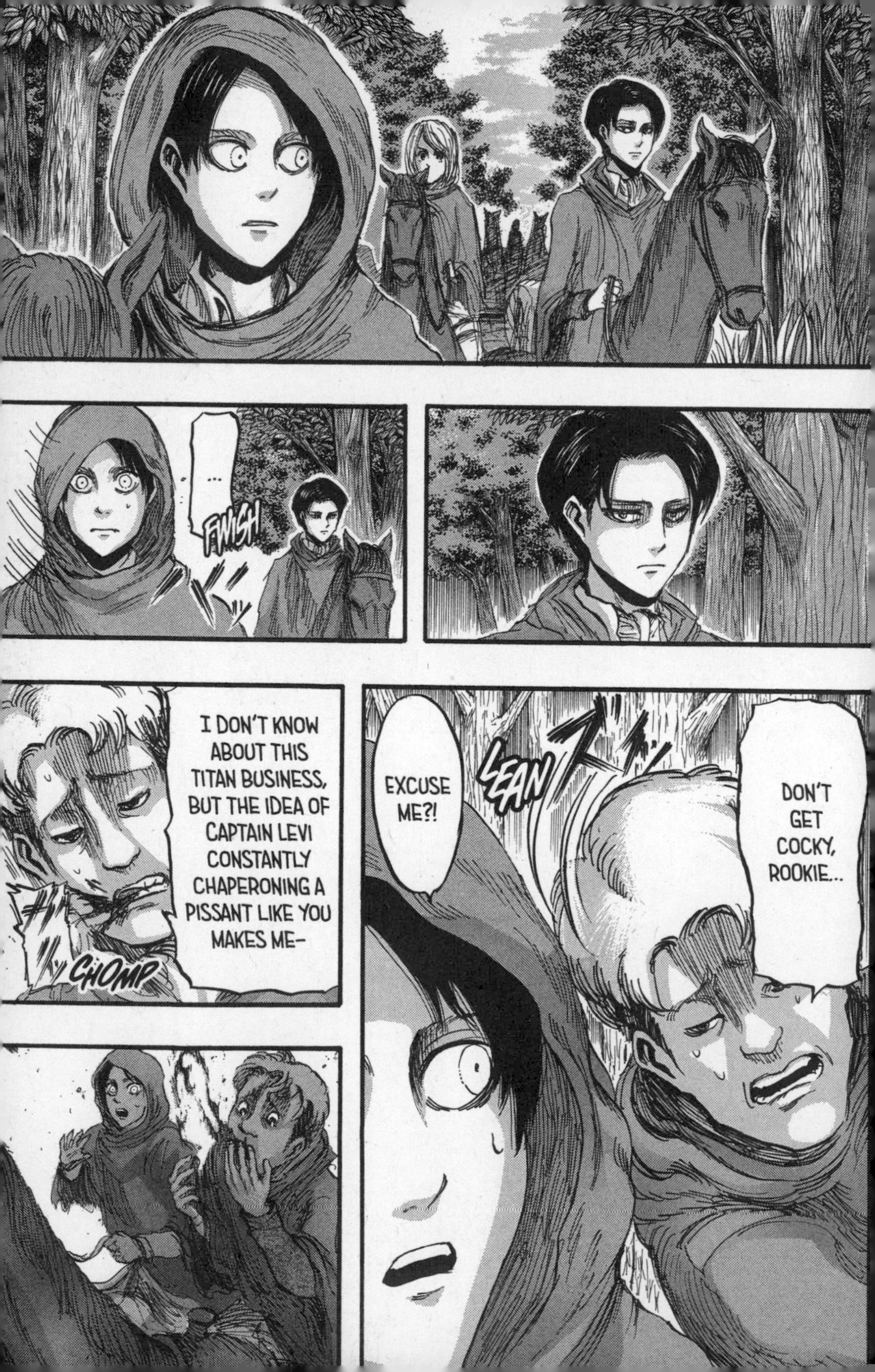
...
FWISH
DON'T GET COCKY, ROOKIE...
LEAN
EXCUSE ME?!
I DON'T KNOW ABOUT THIS TITAN BUSINESS, BUT THE IDEA OF CAPTAIN LEVI CONSTANTLY CHAPERONING A PISSANT LIKE YOU MAKES ME–
CHOMP

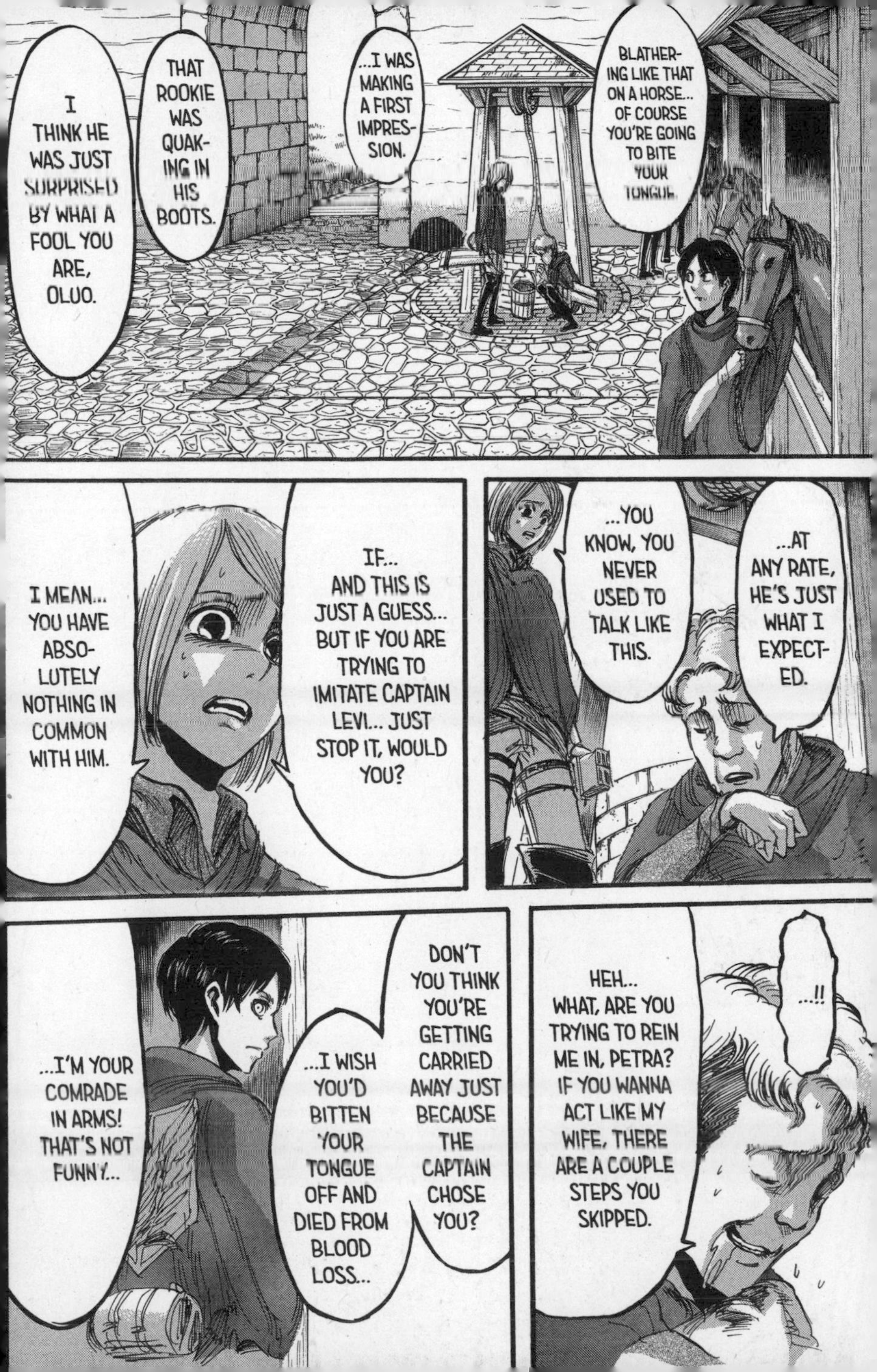
BLATHERING LIKE THAT ON A HORSE... OF COURSE YOU'RE GOING TO BITE YOUR TONGUE.
...I WAS MAKING A FIRST IMPRESSION.
THAT ROOKIE WAS QUAKING IN HIS BOOTS.
I THINK HE WAS JUST SURPRISED BY WHAT A FOOL YOU ARE, OLUO.
...AT ANY RATE, HE'S JUST WHAT I EXPECTED.
...YOU KNOW, YOU NEVER USED TO TALK LIKE THIS.
IF... AND THIS IS JUST A GUESS... BUT IF YOU ARE TRYING TO IMITATE CAPTAIN LEVI... JUST STOP IT, WOULD YOU?
I MEAN... YOU HAVE ABSOLUTELY NOTHING IN COMMON WITH HIM.
...!!
HEH... WHAT, ARE YOU TRYING TO REIN ME IN, PETRA? IF YOU WANNA ACT LIKE MY WIFE, THERE ARE A COUPLE STEPS YOU SKIPPED.
DON'T YOU THINK YOU'RE GETTING CARRIED AWAY JUST BECAUSE THE CAPTAIN CHOSE YOU?
...I WISH YOU'D BITTEN YOUR TONGUE OFF AND DIED FROM BLOOD LOSS...
...I'M YOUR COMRADE IN ARMS! THAT'S NOT FUNNY...

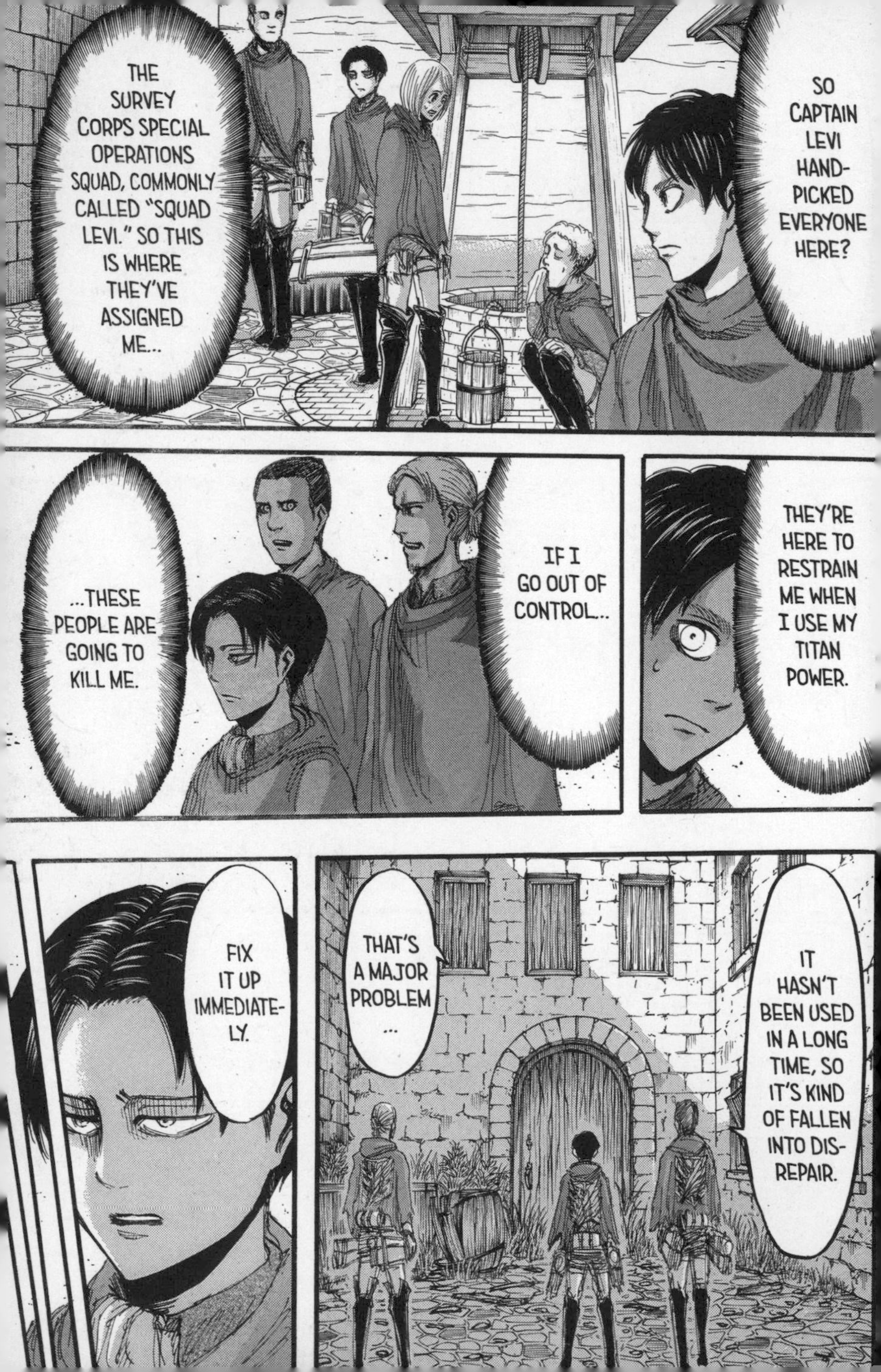
SO CAPTAIN LEVI HAND-PICKED EVERYONE HERE?
THE SURVEY CORPS SPECIAL OPERATIONS SQUAD, COMMONLY CALLED "SQUAD LEVI." SO THIS IS WHERE THEY'VE ASSIGNED ME...
THEY'RE HERE TO RESTRAIN ME WHEN I USE MY TITAN POWER.
IF I GO OUT OF CONTROL...
...THESE PEOPLE ARE GOING TO KILL ME.
IT HASN'T BEEN USED IN A LONG TIME, SO IT'S KIND OF FALLEN INTO DIS-REPAIR.
THAT'S A MAJOR PROBLEM ...
FIX IT UP IMMEDIATE-LY.

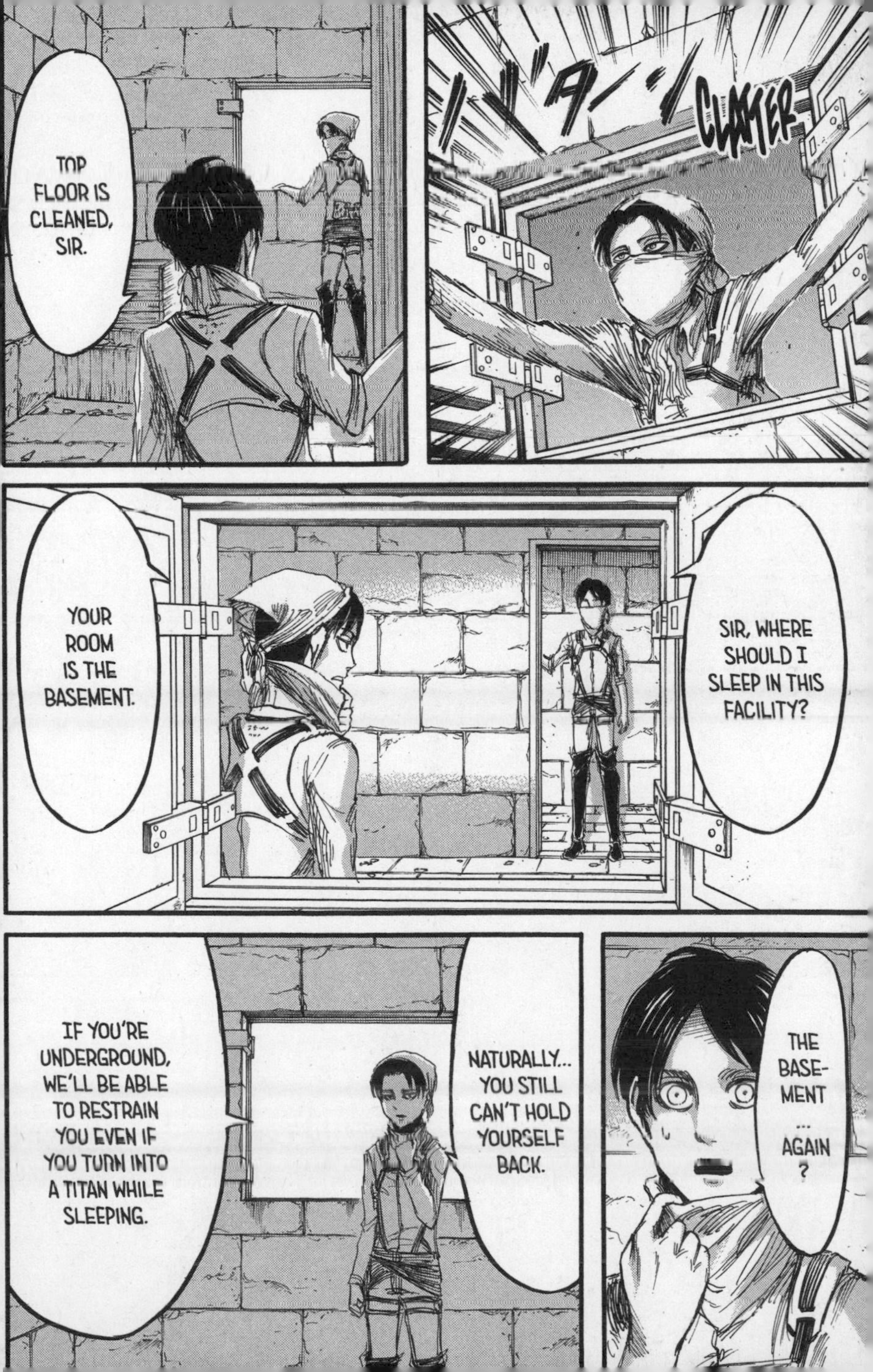
CLATTER
TOP FLOOR IS CLEANED, SIR.
SIR, WHERE SHOULD I SLEEP IN THIS FACILITY?
YOUR ROOM IS THE BASEMENT.
THE BASEMENT ... AGAIN?
NATURALLY... YOU STILL CAN'T HOLD YOURSELF BACK.
IF YOU'RE UNDERGROUND, WE'LL BE ABLE TO RESTRAIN YOU EVEN IF YOU TURN INTO A TITAN WHILE SLEEPING.

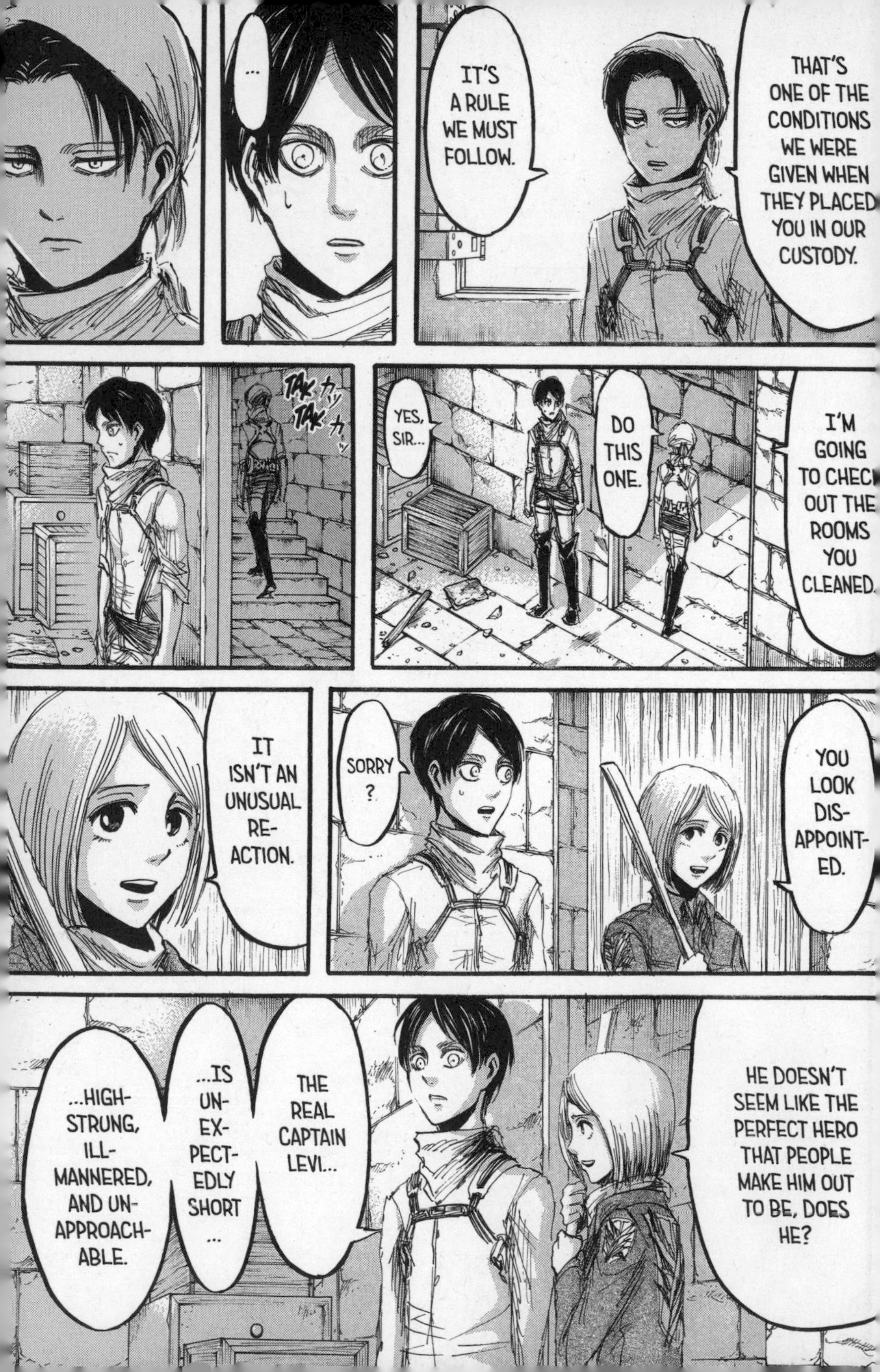
THAT'S ONE OF THE CONDITIONS WE WERE GIVEN WHEN THEY PLACED YOU IN OUR CUSTODY.
IT'S A RULE WE MUST FOLLOW.
...
I'M GOING TO CHEC OUT THE ROOMS YOU CLEANED.
DO THIS ONE.
YES, SIR...
TAK カッ
TAK カッ
YOU LOOK DIS-APPOINT-ED.
SORRY ?
IT ISN'T AN UNUSUAL RE-ACTION.
HE DOESN'T SEEM LIKE THE PERFECT HERO THAT PEOPLE MAKE HIM OUT TO BE, DOES HE?
THE REAL CAPTAIN LEVI...
...IS UN-EX-PECT-EDLY SHORT...
...HIGH-STRUNG, ILL-MANNERED, AND UN-APPROACH-ABLE.

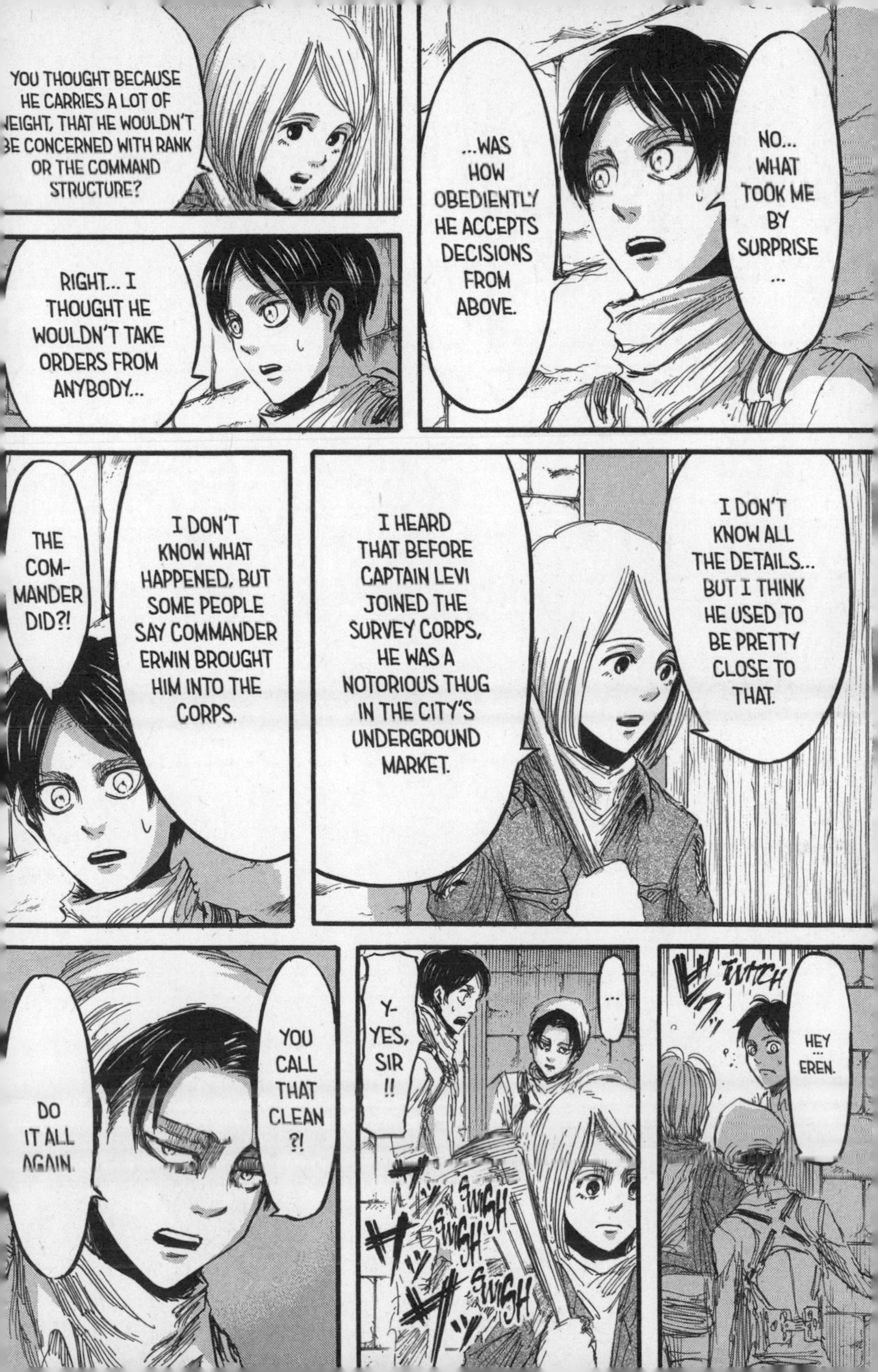

NO... WHAT TOOK ME BY SURPRISE ...
...WAS HOW OBEDIENTLY HE ACCEPTS DECISIONS FROM ABOVE.
YOU THOUGHT BECAUSE HE CARRIES A LOT OF WEIGHT, THAT HE WOULDN'T BE CONCERNED WITH RANK OR THE COMMAND STRUCTURE?
RIGHT... I THOUGHT HE WOULDN'T TAKE ORDERS FROM ANYBODY...
I DON'T KNOW ALL THE DETAILS... BUT I THINK HE USED TO BE PRETTY CLOSE TO THAT.
I HEARD THAT BEFORE CAPTAIN LEVI JOINED THE SURVEY CORPS, HE WAS A NOTORIOUS THUG IN THE CITY'S UNDERGROUND MARKET.
I DON'T KNOW WHAT HAPPENED, BUT SOME PEOPLE SAY COMMANDER ERWIN BROUGHT HIM INTO THE CORPS.
THE COM-MANDER DID?!
TWITCH
HEY EREN.
...
Y-YES, SIR!!
SWISH
SWISH
SWISH
YOU CALL THAT CLEAN?!
DO IT ALL AGAIN.

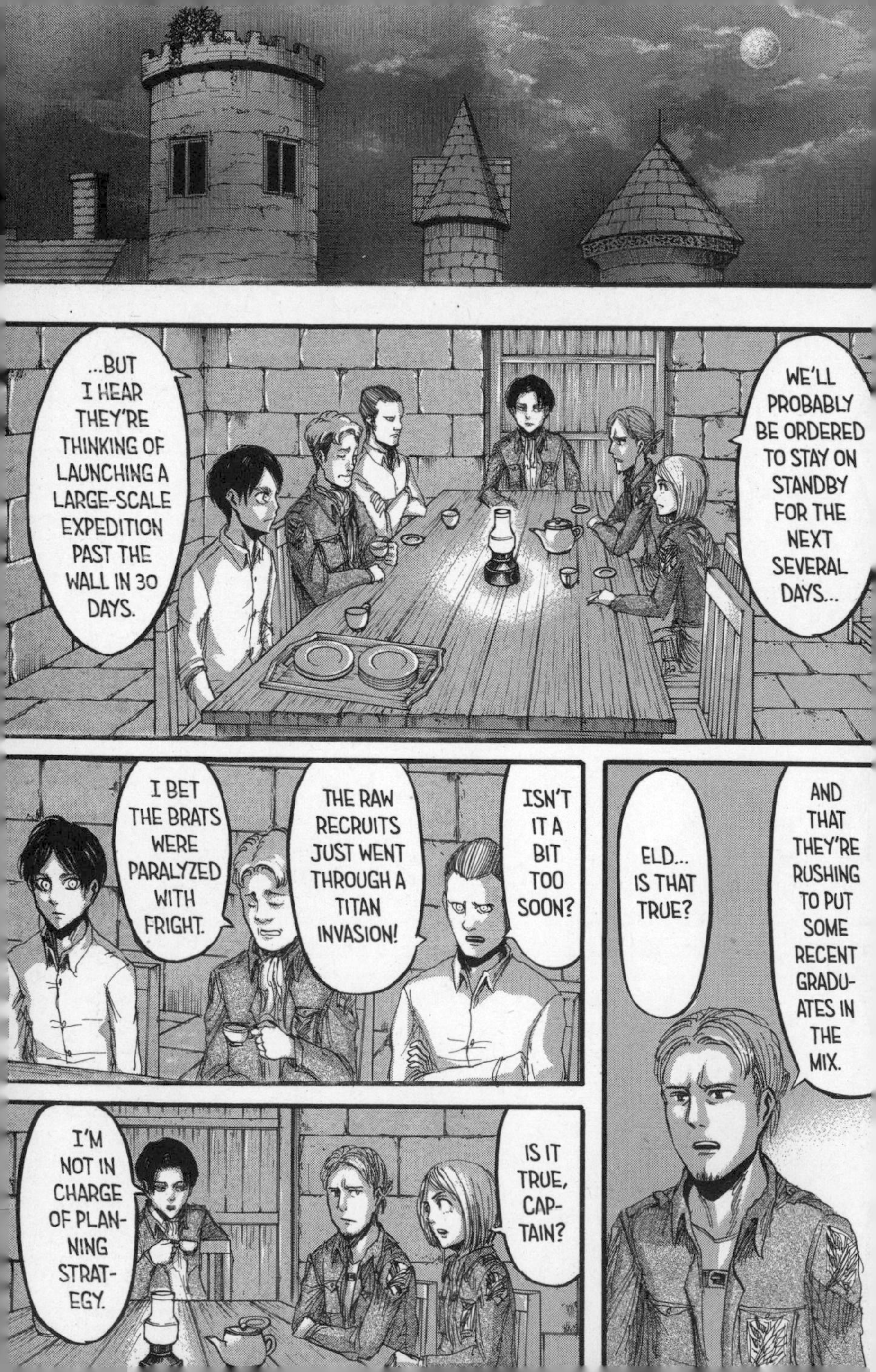
WE'LL PROBABLY BE ORDERED TO STAY ON STANDBY FOR THE NEXT SEVERAL DAYS...
...BUT I HEAR THEY'RE THINKING OF LAUNCHING A LARGE-SCALE EXPEDITION PAST THE WALL IN 30 DAYS.
AND THAT THEY'RE RUSHING TO PUT SOME RECENT GRADU-ATES IN THE MIX.
ELD... IS THAT TRUE?
ISN'T IT A BIT TOO SOON?
THE RAW RECRUITS JUST WENT THROUGH A TITAN INVASION!
I BET THE BRATS WERE PARALYZED WITH FRIGHT.
IS IT TRUE, CAP-TAIN?
I'M NOT IN CHARGE OF PLAN-NING STRAT-EGY.

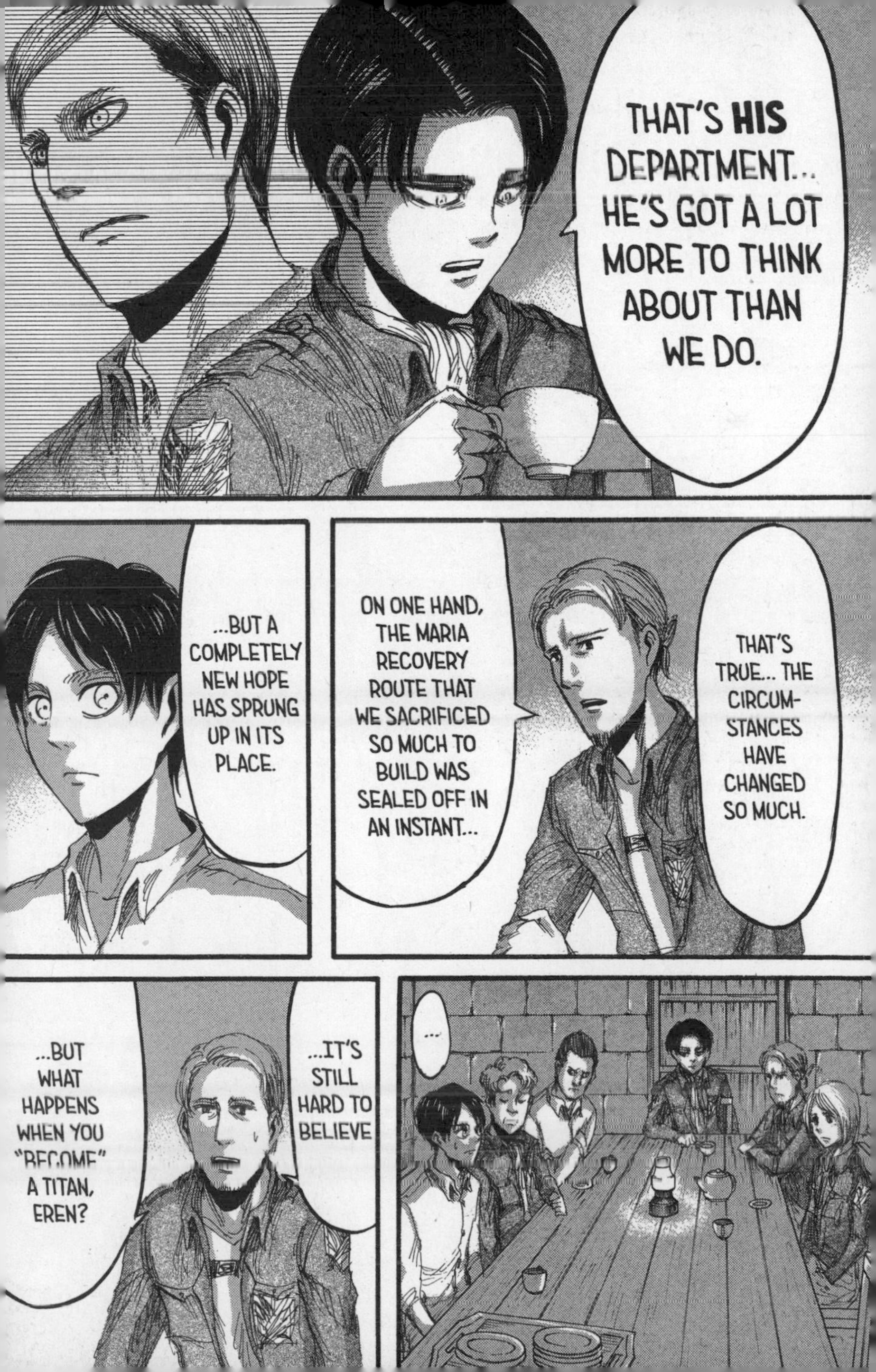
THAT'S **HIS** DEPARTMENT... HE'S GOT A LOT MORE TO THINK ABOUT THAN WE DO.
THAT'S TRUE... THE CIRCUM-STANCES HAVE CHANGED SO MUCH.
ON ONE HAND, THE MARIA RECOVERY ROUTE THAT WE SACRIFICED SO MUCH TO BUILD WAS SEALED OFF IN AN INSTANT...
...BUT A COMPLETELY NEW HOPE HAS SPRUNG UP IN ITS PLACE.
...
...IT'S STILL HARD TO BELIEVE
...BUT WHAT HAPPENS WHEN YOU "BECOME" A TITAN, EREN?

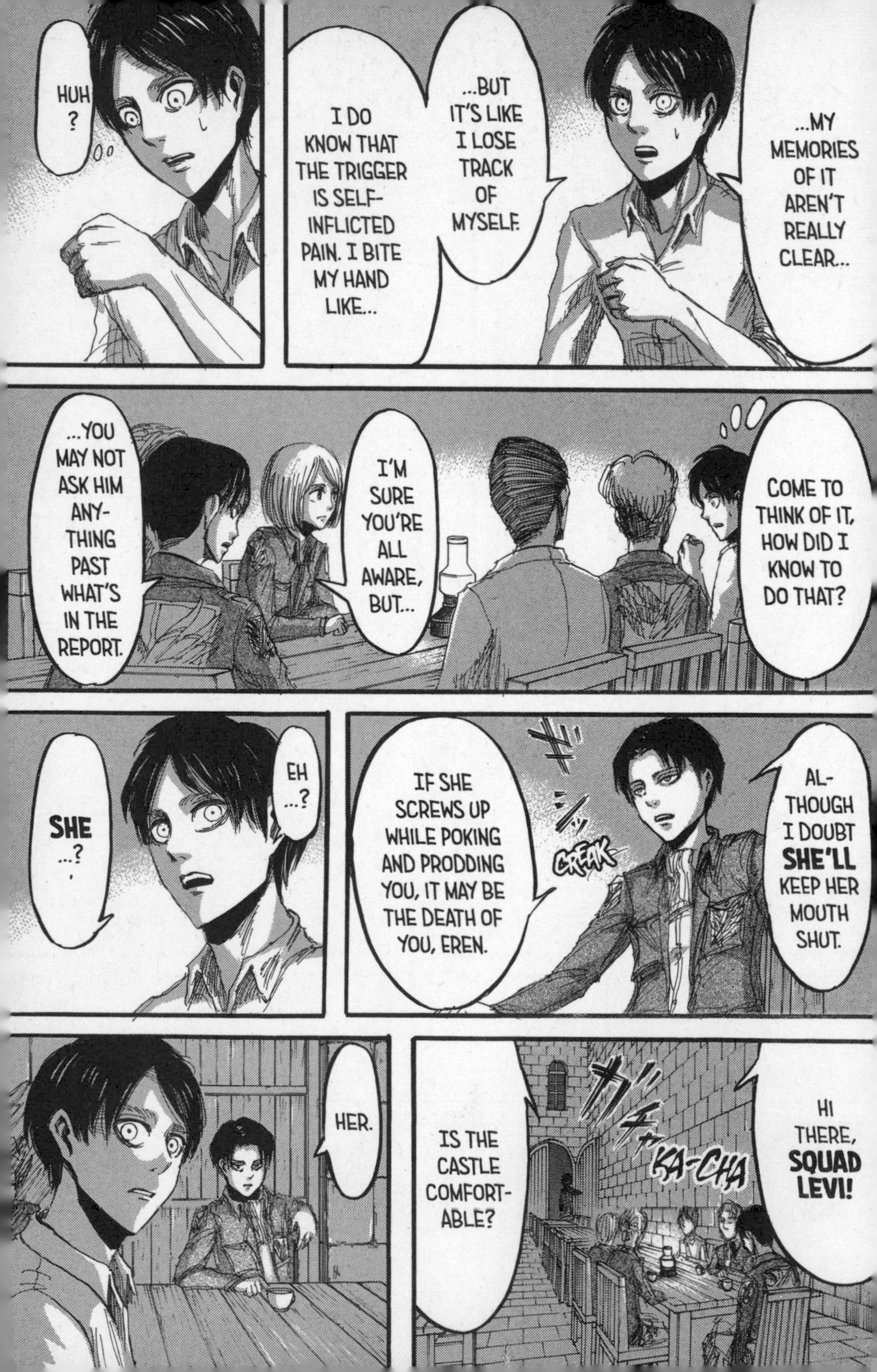
...MY MEMORIES OF IT AREN'T REALLY CLEAR...
...BUT IT'S LIKE I LOSE TRACK OF MYSELF.
I DO KNOW THAT THE TRIGGER IS SELF-INFLICTED PAIN. I BITE MY HAND LIKE...
HUH?
COME TO THINK OF IT, HOW DID I KNOW TO DO THAT?
I'M SURE YOU'RE ALL AWARE, BUT...
...YOU MAY NOT ASK HIM ANYTHING PAST WHAT'S IN THE REPORT.
ALTHOUGH I DOUBT **SHE'LL** KEEP HER MOUTH SHUT.
CREAK
IF SHE SCREWS UP WHILE POKING AND PRODDING YOU, IT MAY BE THE DEATH OF YOU, EREN.
EH...?
SHE...?
HI THERE, **SQUAD LEVI!**
KA-CHA
IS THE CASTLE COMFORTABLE?
HER.

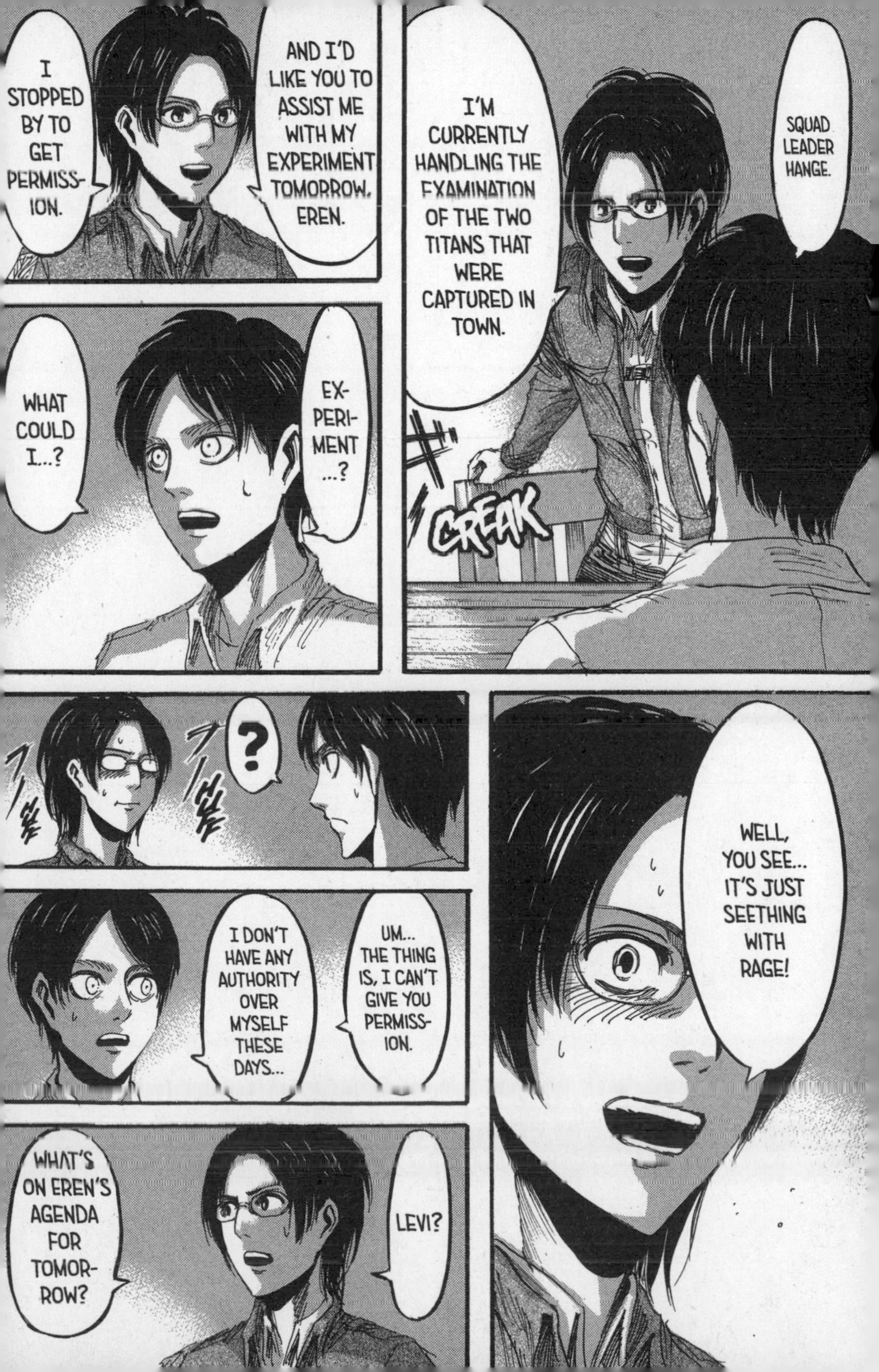
SQUAD LEADER HANGE.
I'M CURRENTLY HANDLING THE EXAMINATION OF THE TWO TITANS THAT WERE CAPTURED IN TOWN.
CREAK
AND I'D LIKE YOU TO ASSIST ME WITH MY EXPERIMENT TOMORROW, EREN.
I STOPPED BY TO GET PERMISSION.
EXPERIMENT...?
WHAT COULD I...?
WELL, YOU SEE... IT'S JUST SEETHING WITH RAGE!
?
UM... THE THING IS, I CAN'T GIVE YOU PERMISSION.
I DON'T HAVE ANY AUTHORITY OVER MYSELF THESE DAYS...
LEVI?
WHAT'S ON EREN'S AGENDA FOR TOMORROW?

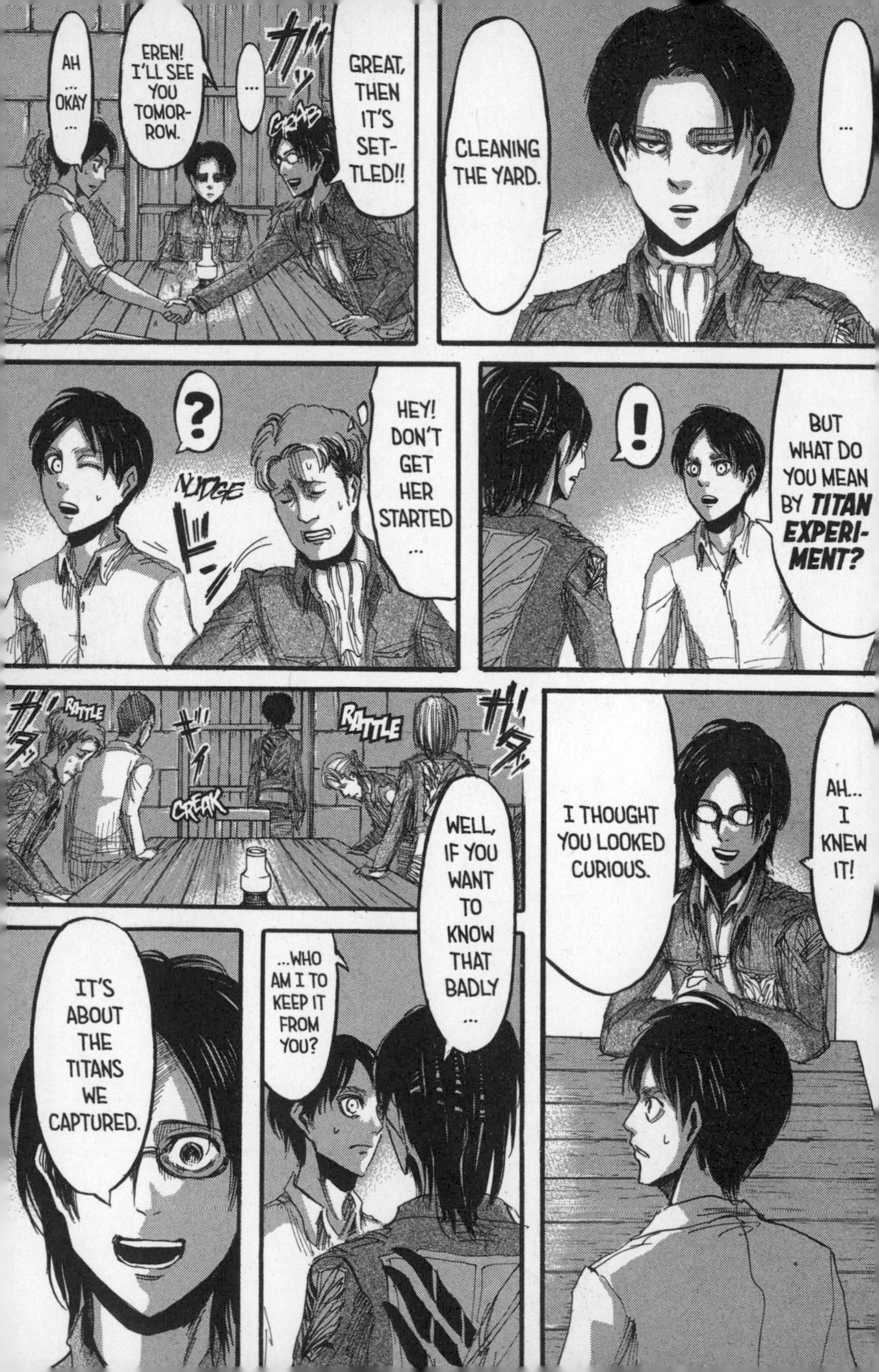
...
CLEANING THE YARD.
GREAT, THEN IT'S SETTLED!!
GRAB
...
EREN! I'LL SEE YOU TOMORROW.
AH ... OKAY ...
BUT WHAT DO YOU MEAN BY TITAN EXPERIMENT?
!
HEY! DON'T GET HER STARTED ...
?
NUDGE
AH... I KNEW IT!
I THOUGHT YOU LOOKED CURIOUS.
RATTLE
CREAK
RATTLE
WELL, IF YOU WANT TO KNOW THAT BADLY ...
...WHO AM I TO KEEP IT FROM YOU?
IT'S ABOUT THE TITANS WE CAPTURED.

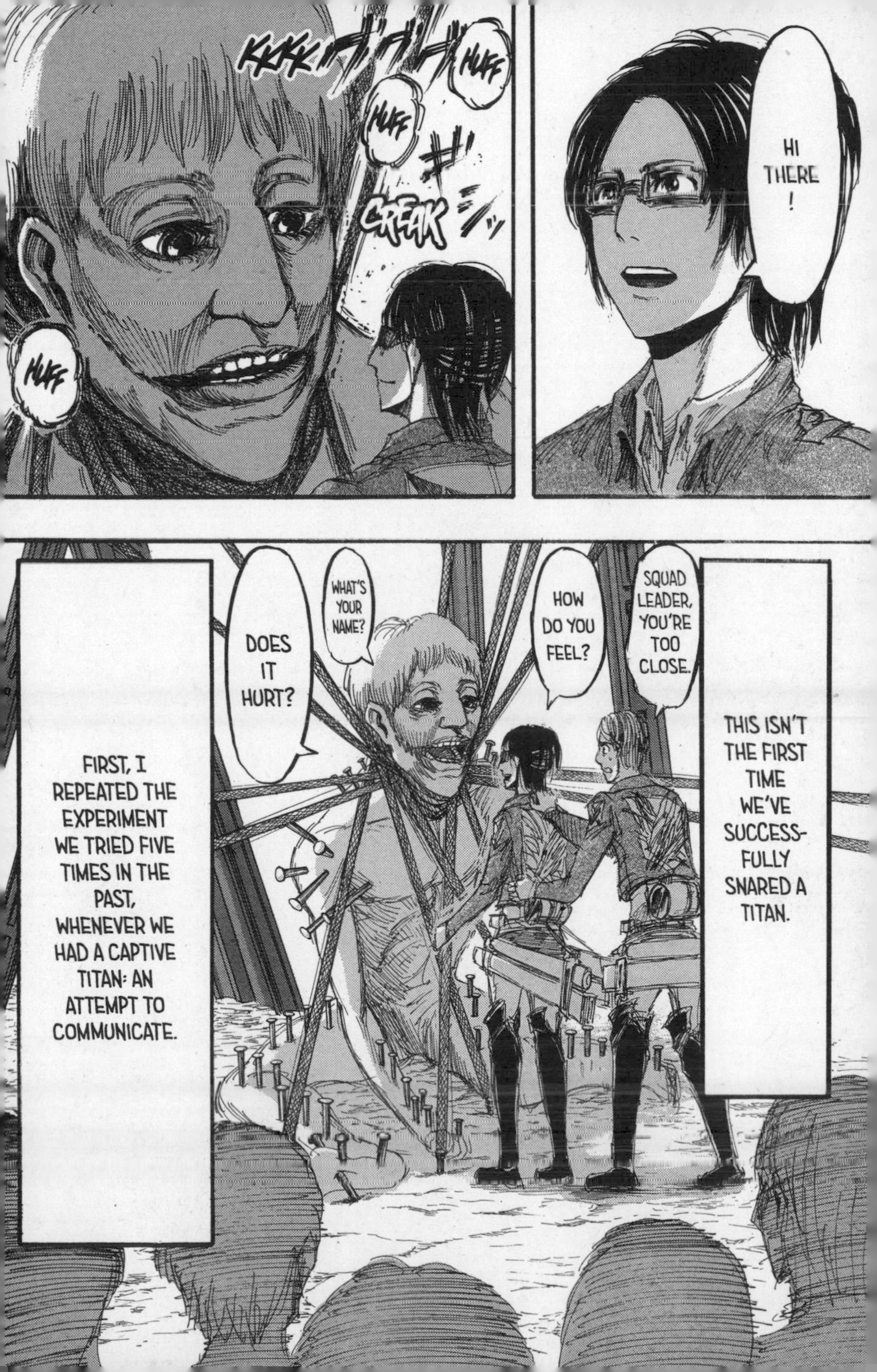
HI THERE!
KKKK
HUFF
HUFF
CREAK
HUFF
THIS ISN'T THE FIRST TIME WE'VE SUCCESSFULLY SNARED A TITAN.
SQUAD LEADER, YOU'RE TOO CLOSE.
HOW DO YOU FEEL?
WHAT'S YOUR NAME?
DOES IT HURT?
FIRST, I REPEATED THE EXPERIMENT WE TRIED FIVE TIMES IN THE PAST, WHENEVER WE HAD A CAPTIVE TITAN: AN ATTEMPT TO COMMUNICATE.

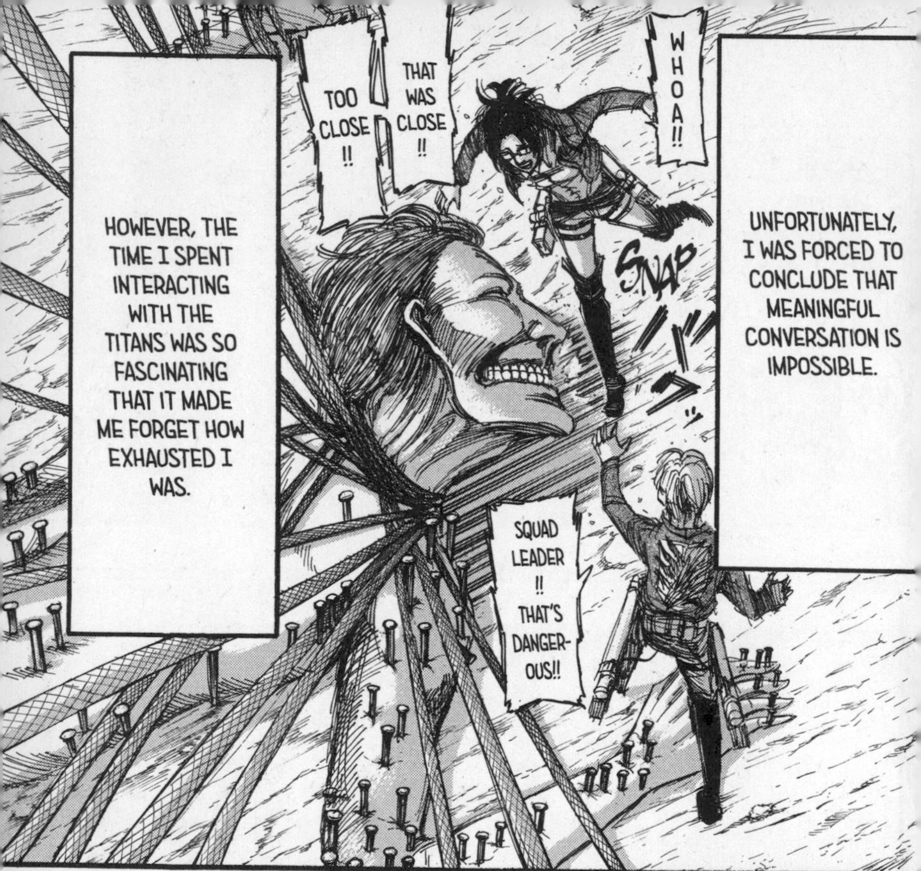
UNFORTUNATELY, I WAS FORCED TO CONCLUDE THAT MEANINGFUL CONVERSATION IS IMPOSSIBLE.
WHOA!!
THAT WAS CLOSE!!
TOO CLOSE!!
HOWEVER, THE TIME I SPENT INTERACTING WITH THE TITANS WAS SO FASCINATING THAT IT MADE ME FORGET HOW EXHAUSTED I WAS.
SNAP
SQUAD LEADER!! THAT'S DANGER-OUS!!

* ABOUT 13 FEET AND 23 FEET, RESPECTIVE

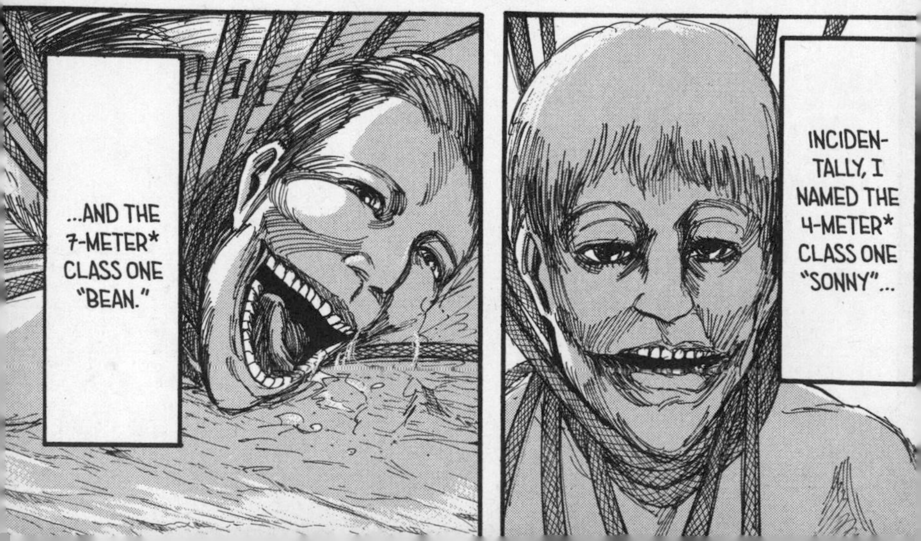
INCIDEN-TALLY, I NAMED THE 4-METER* CLASS ONE "SONNY"...
...AND THE 7-METER* CLASS ONE "BEAN."

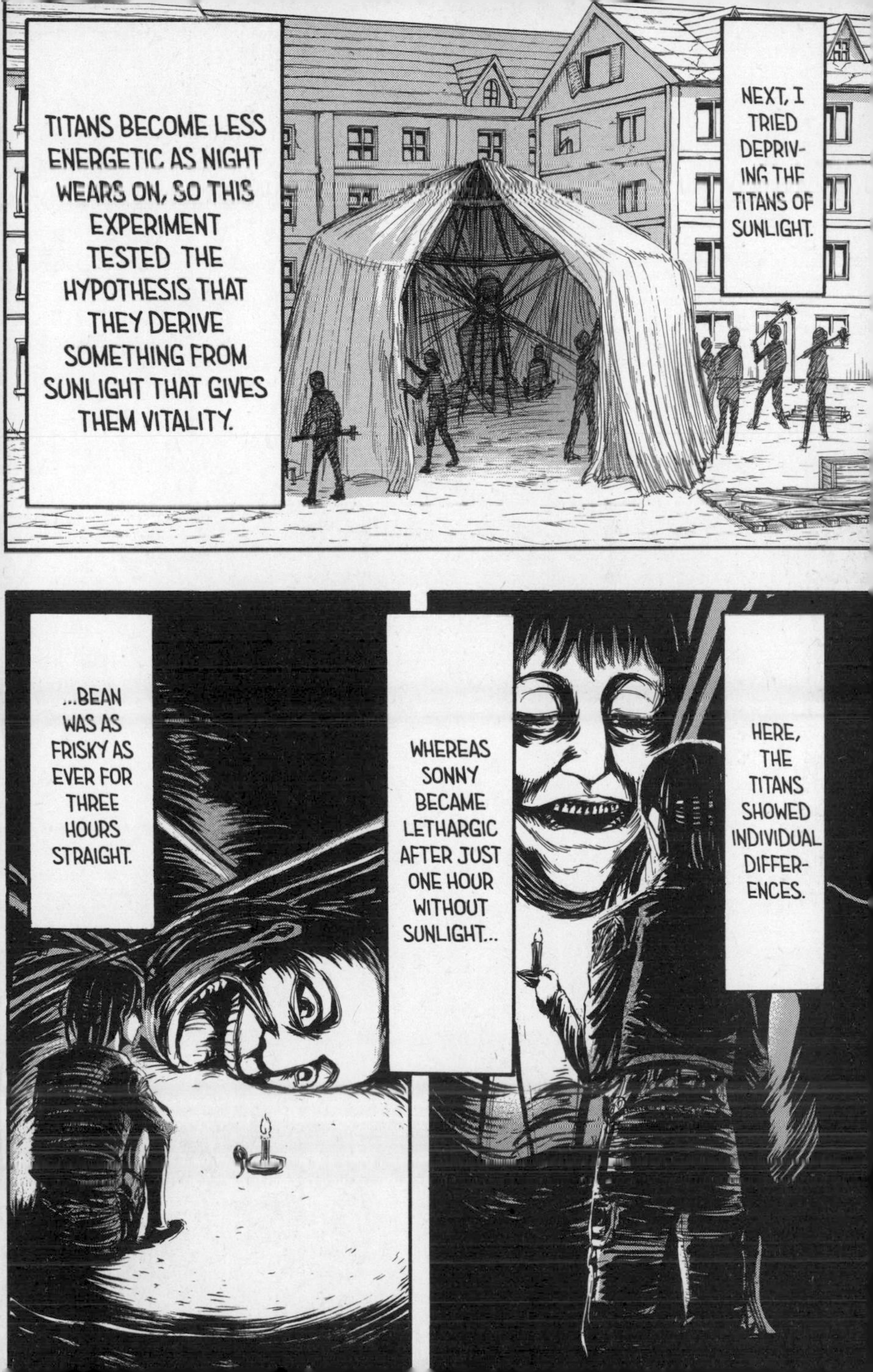
NEXT, I TRIED DEPRIVING THE TITANS OF SUNLIGHT.
TITANS BECOME LESS ENERGETIC AS NIGHT WEARS ON, SO THIS EXPERIMENT TESTED THE HYPOTHESIS THAT THEY DERIVE SOMETHING FROM SUNLIGHT THAT GIVES THEM VITALITY.
HERE, THE TITANS SHOWED INDIVIDUAL DIFFERENCES.
WHEREAS SONNY BECAME LETHARGIC AFTER JUST ONE HOUR WITHOUT SUNLIGHT...
...BEAN WAS AS FRISKY AS EVER FOR THREE HOURS STRAIGHT.

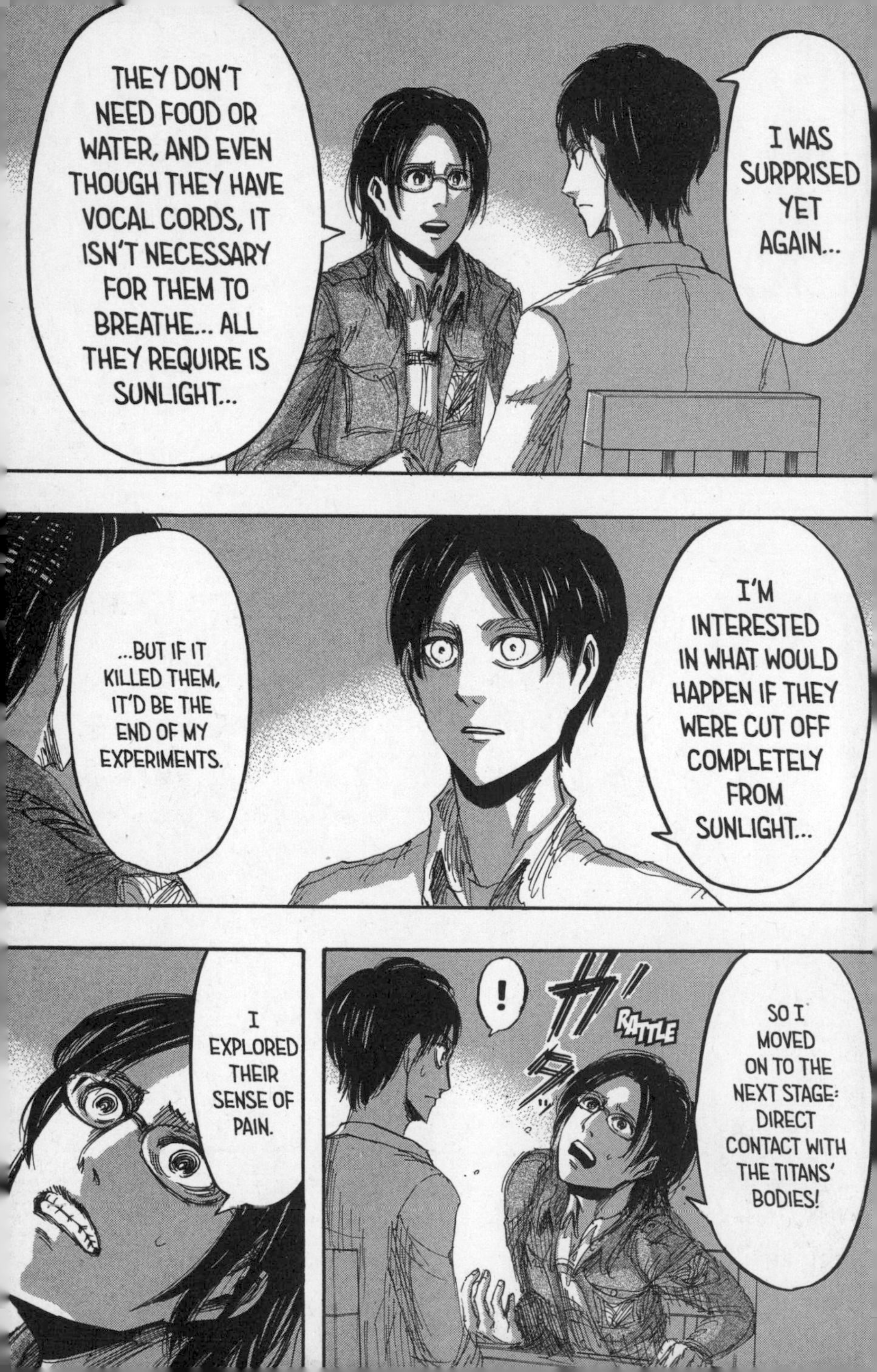
I WAS SURPRISED YET AGAIN...
THEY DON'T NEED FOOD OR WATER, AND EVEN THOUGH THEY HAVE VOCAL CORDS, IT ISN'T NECESSARY FOR THEM TO BREATHE... ALL THEY REQUIRE IS SUNLIGHT...
I'M INTERESTED IN WHAT WOULD HAPPEN IF THEY WERE CUT OFF COMPLETELY FROM SUNLIGHT...
...BUT IF IT KILLED THEM, IT'D BE THE END OF MY EXPERIMENTS.
SO I MOVED ON TO THE NEXT STAGE: DIRECT CONTACT WITH THE TITANS' BODIES!
RATTLE
!
I EXPLORED THEIR SENSE OF PAIN.

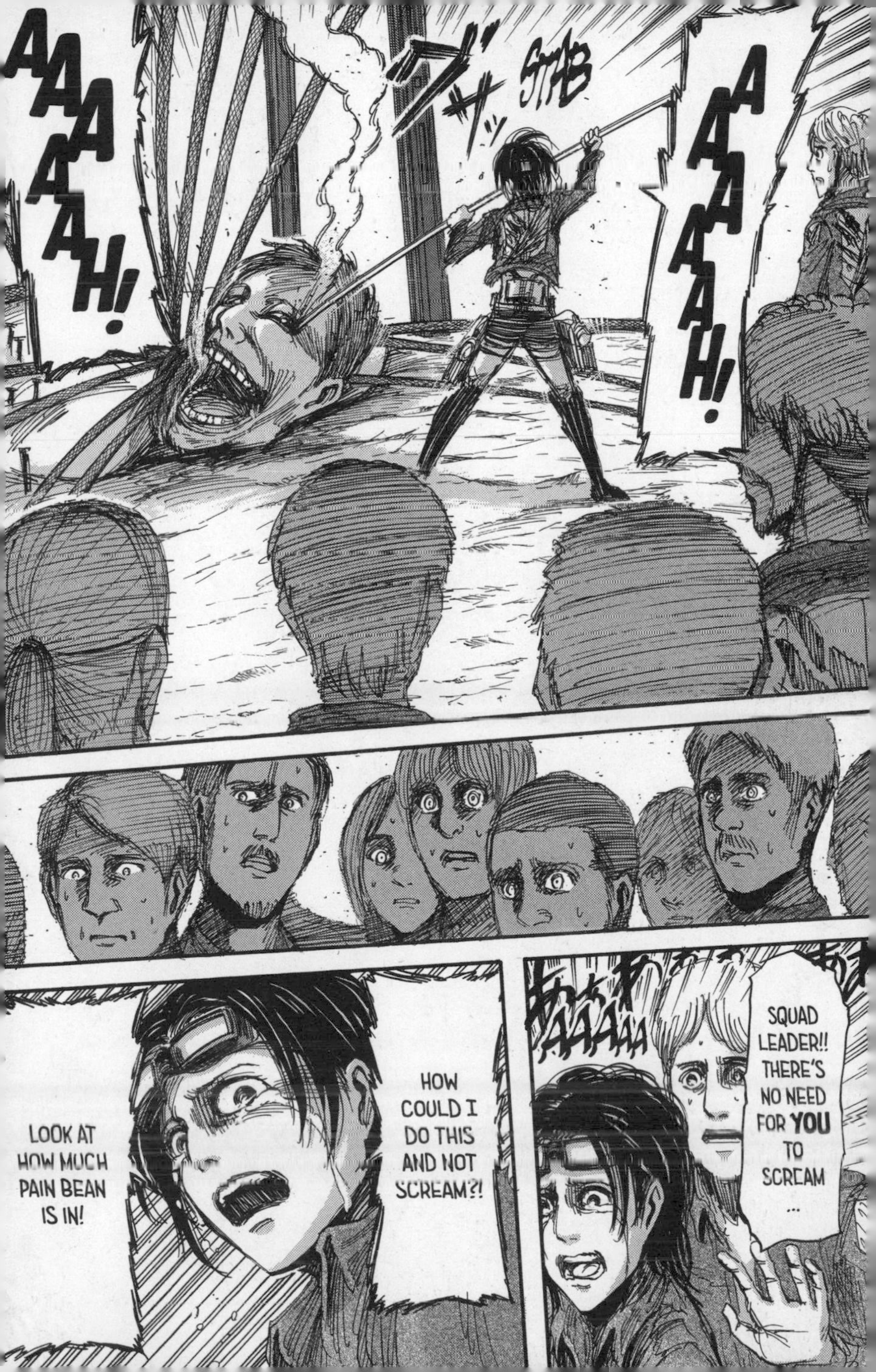
AAAAAH!
STAB
AAAAAH!
AAAAA
SQUAD LEADER!! THERE'S NO NEED FOR **YOU** TO SCREAM ...
HOW COULD I DO THIS AND NOT SCREAM?!
LOOK AT HOW MUCH PAIN BEAN IS IN!

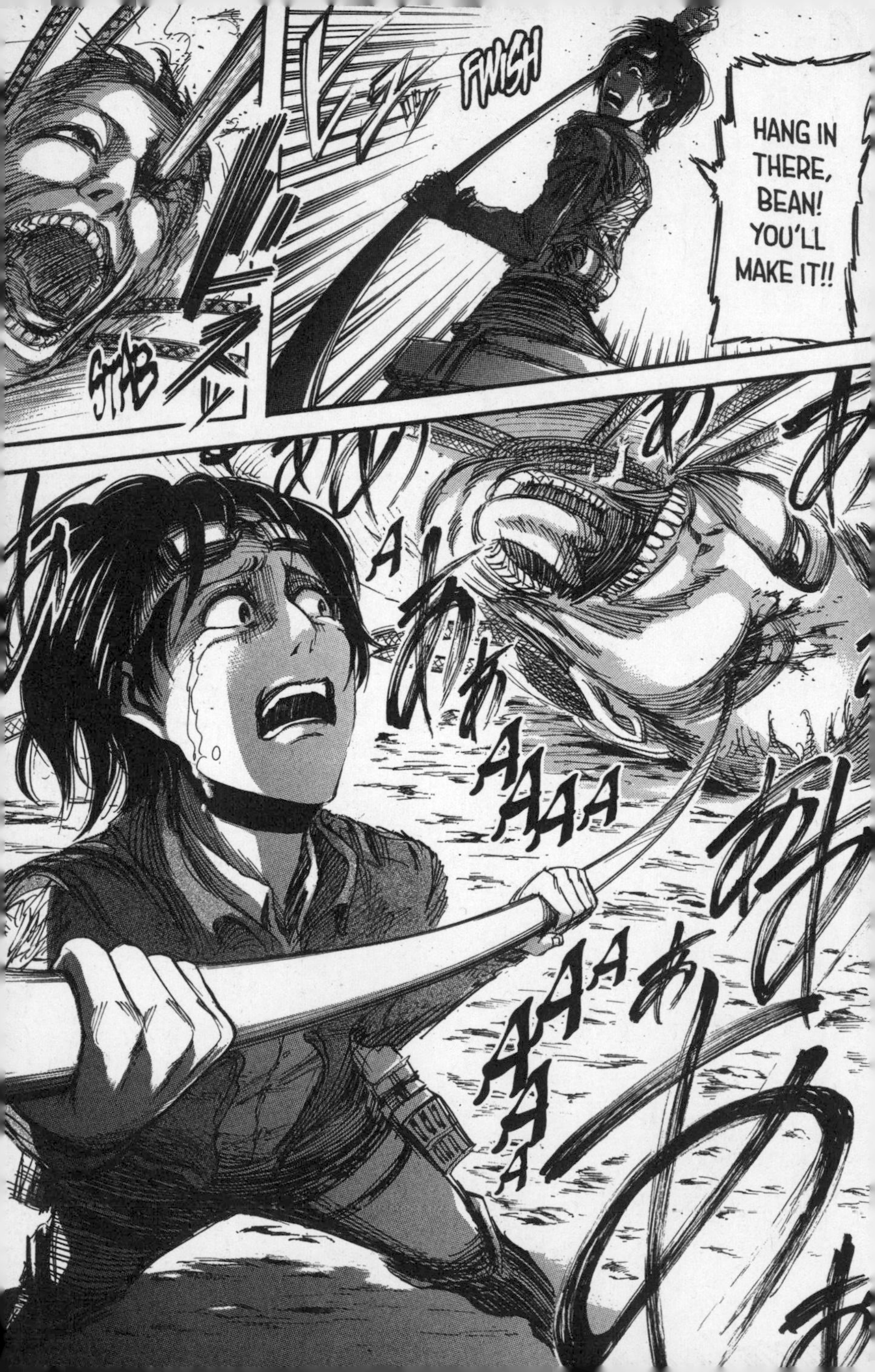
HANG IN THERE, BEAN! YOU'LL MAKE IT!!
FWISH
STAB
A
AAAA
AAAAAAA

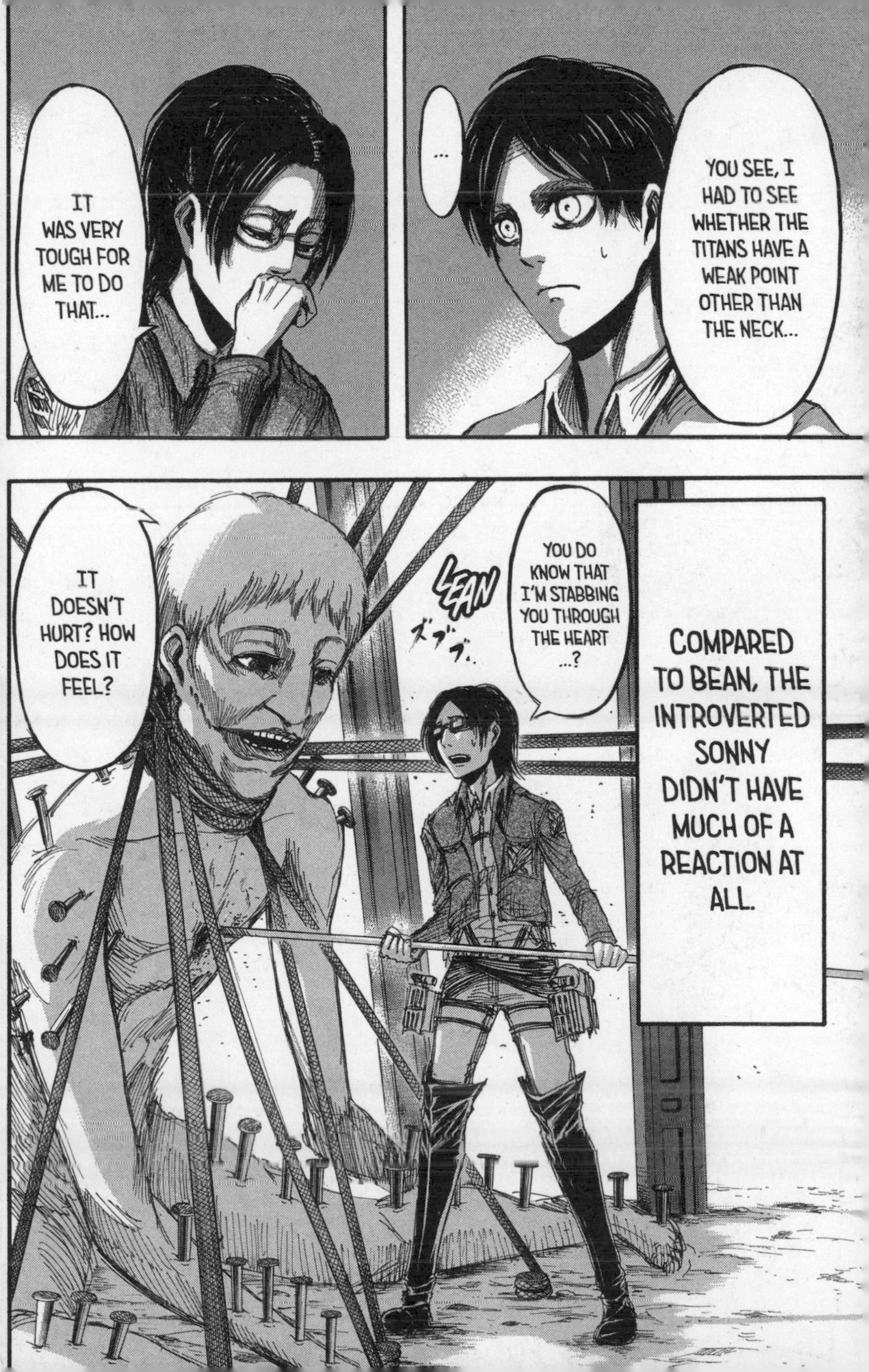
YOU SEE, I HAD TO SEE WHETHER THE TITANS HAVE A WEAK POINT OTHER THAN THE NECK...
...
IT WAS VERY TOUGH FOR ME TO DO THAT...
COMPARED TO BEAN, THE INTROVERTED SONNY DIDN'T HAVE MUCH OF A REACTION AT ALL.
YOU DO KNOW THAT I'M STABBING YOU THROUGH THE HEART ...?
LEAN
ズブブ
IT DOESN'T HURT? HOW DOES IT FEEL?

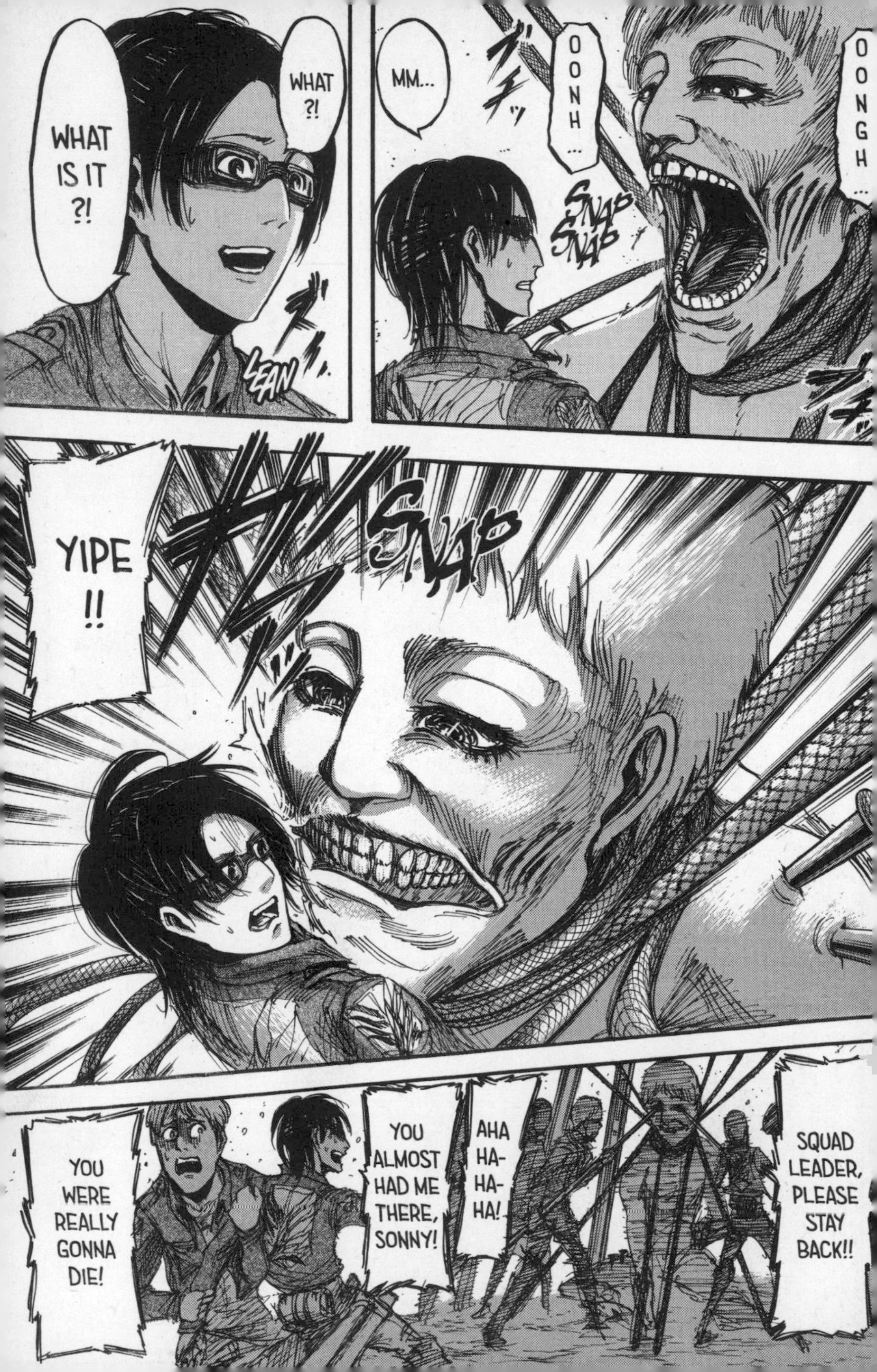
OONGH...
OONH...
SNAP SNAP
MM...
WHAT ?!
WHAT IS IT ?!
LEAN
SNAP
YIPE !!
SQUAD LEADER, PLEASE STAY BACK!!
AHA HA-HA-HA!
YOU ALMOST HAD ME THERE, SONNY!
YOU WERE REALLY GONNA DIE!

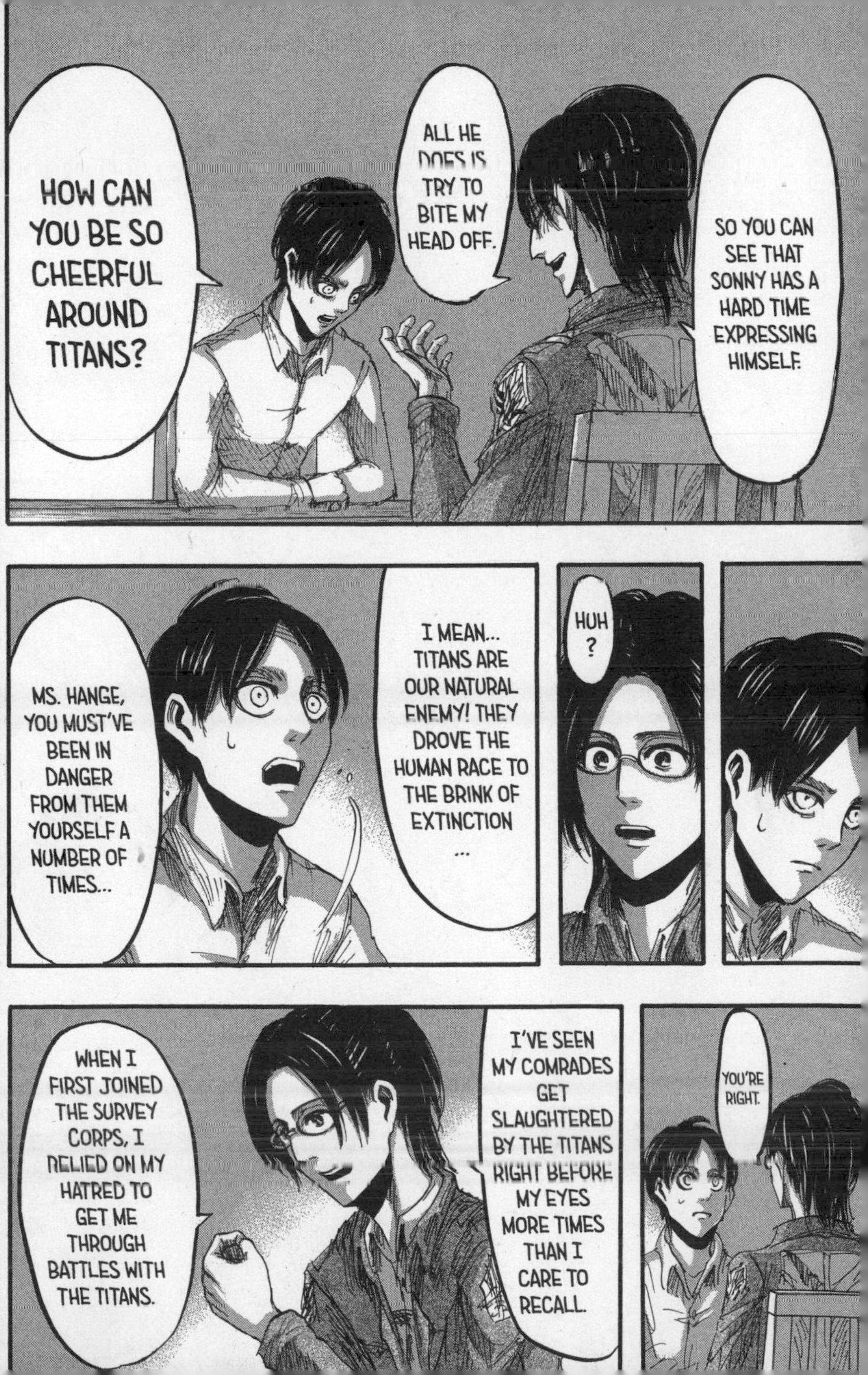
SO YOU CAN SEE THAT SONNY HAS A HARD TIME EXPRESSING HIMSELF.
ALL HE DOES IS TRY TO BITE MY HEAD OFF.
HOW CAN YOU BE SO CHEERFUL AROUND TITANS?
HUH ?
I MEAN... TITANS ARE OUR NATURAL ENEMY! THEY DROVE THE HUMAN RACE TO THE BRINK OF EXTINCTION ...
MS. HANGE, YOU MUST'VE BEEN IN DANGER FROM THEM YOURSELF A NUMBER OF TIMES...
YOU'RE RIGHT.
I'VE SEEN MY COMRADES GET SLAUGHTERED BY THE TITANS RIGHT BEFORE MY EYES MORE TIMES THAN I CARE TO RECALL.
WHEN I FIRST JOINED THE SURVEY CORPS, I RELIED ON MY HATRED TO GET ME THROUGH BATTLES WITH THE TITANS.

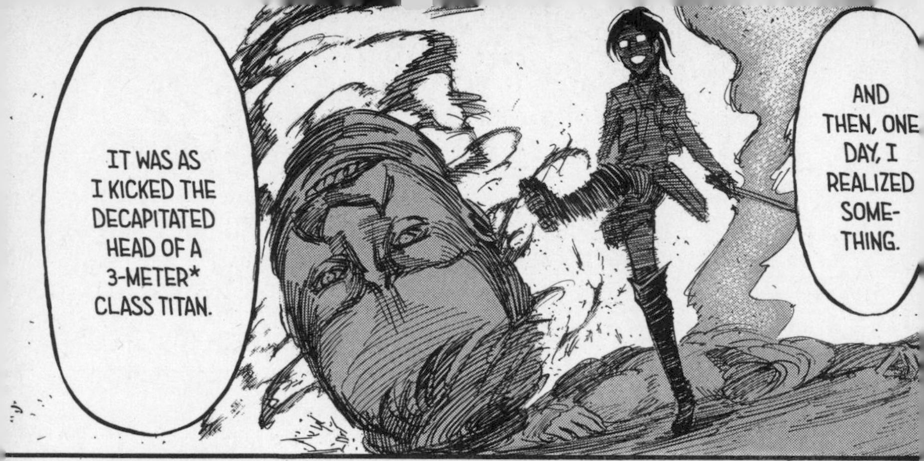
AND THEN, ONE DAY, I REALIZED SOME-THING.
IT WAS AS I KICKED THE DECAPITATED HEAD OF A 3-METER* CLASS TITAN.

* ABOUT 10 FEET.

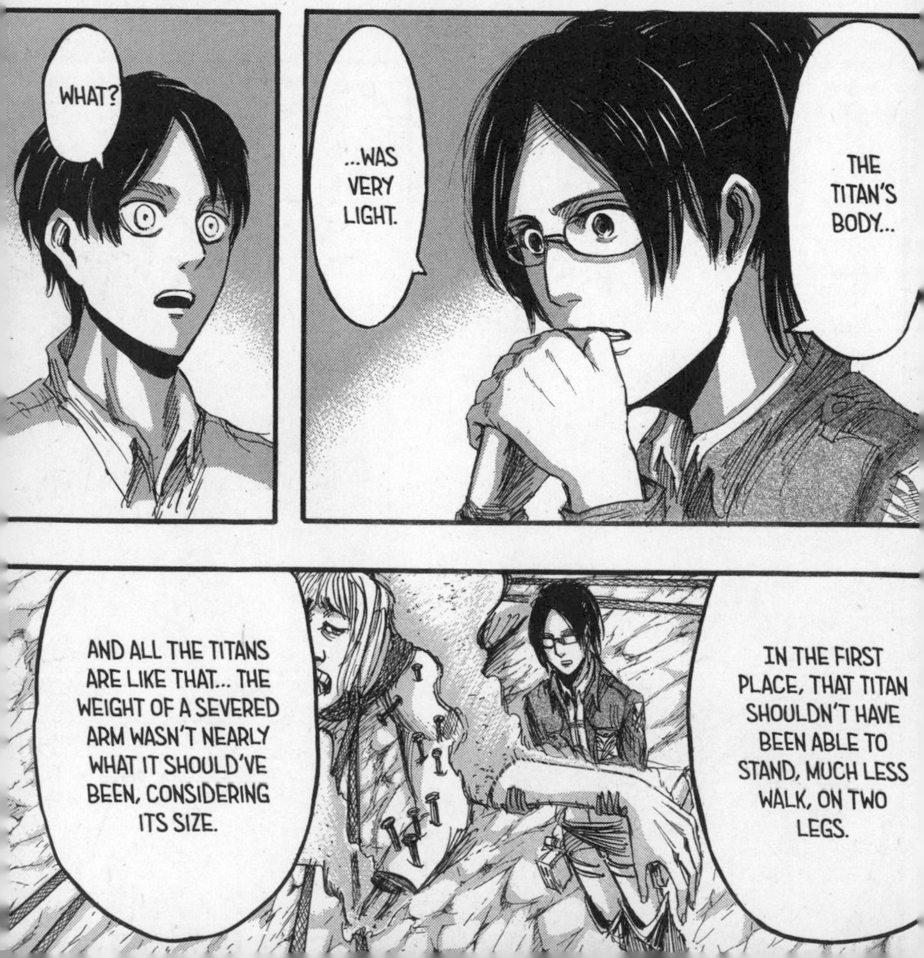
THE TITAN'S BODY...
...WAS VERY LIGHT.
WHAT?
IN THE FIRST PLACE, THAT TITAN SHOULDN'T HAVE BEEN ABLE TO STAND, MUCH LESS WALK, ON TWO LEGS.
AND ALL THE TITANS ARE LIKE THAT... THE WEIGHT OF A SEVERED ARM WASN'T NEARLY WHAT IT SHOULD'VE BEEN, CONSIDERING ITS SIZE.

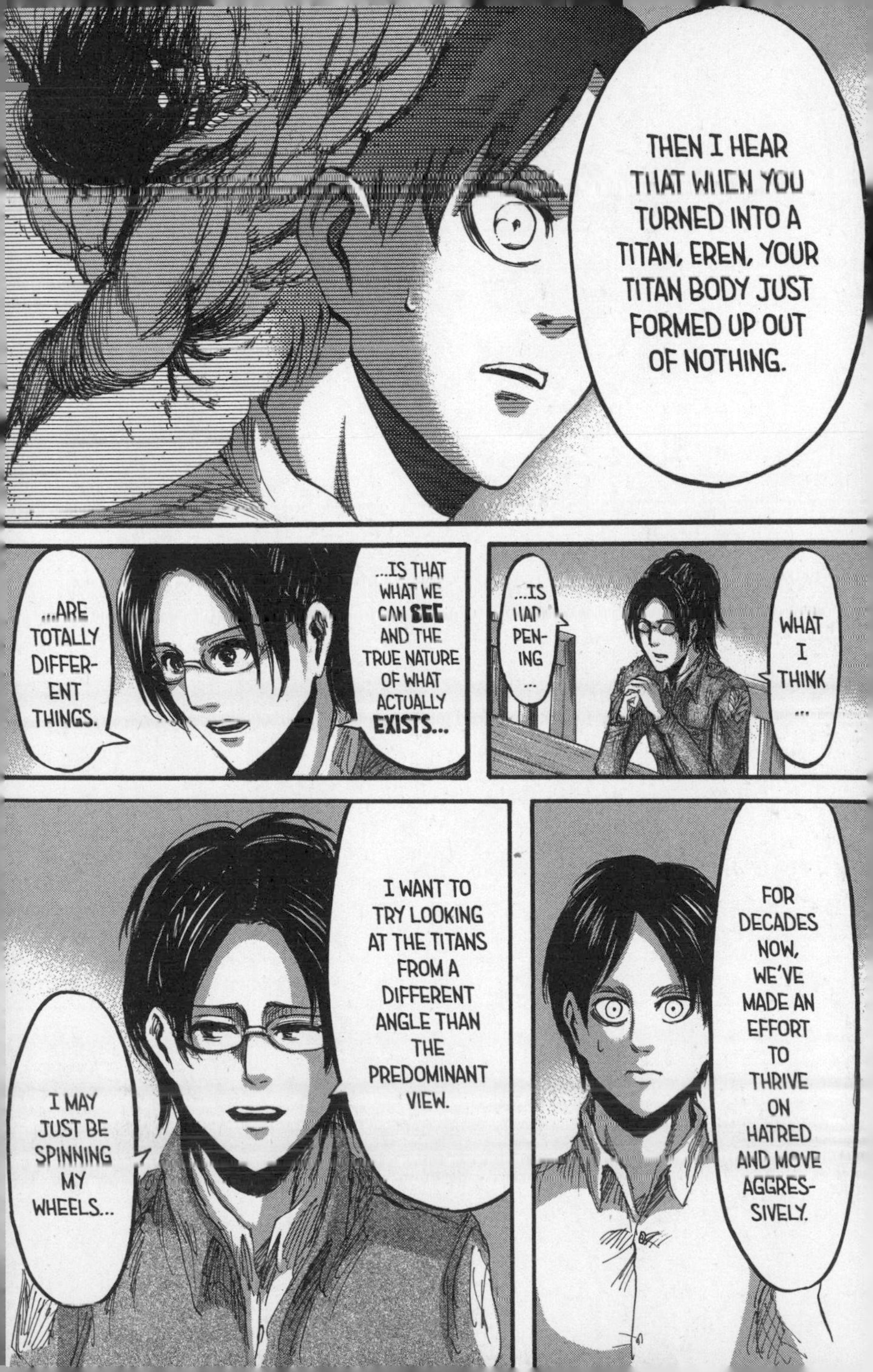
THEN I HEAR THAT WHEN YOU TURNED INTO A TITAN, EREN, YOUR TITAN BODY JUST FORMED UP OUT OF NOTHING.
WHAT I THINK...
...IS HAPPENING...
...IS THAT WHAT WE CAN SEE AND THE TRUE NATURE OF WHAT ACTUALLY EXISTS...
...ARE TOTALLY DIFFERENT THINGS.
FOR DECADES NOW, WE'VE MADE AN EFFORT TO THRIVE ON HATRED AND MOVE AGGRESSIVELY.
I WANT TO TRY LOOKING AT THE TITANS FROM A DIFFERENT ANGLE THAN THE PREDOMINANT VIEW.
I MAY JUST BE SPINNING MY WHEELS...

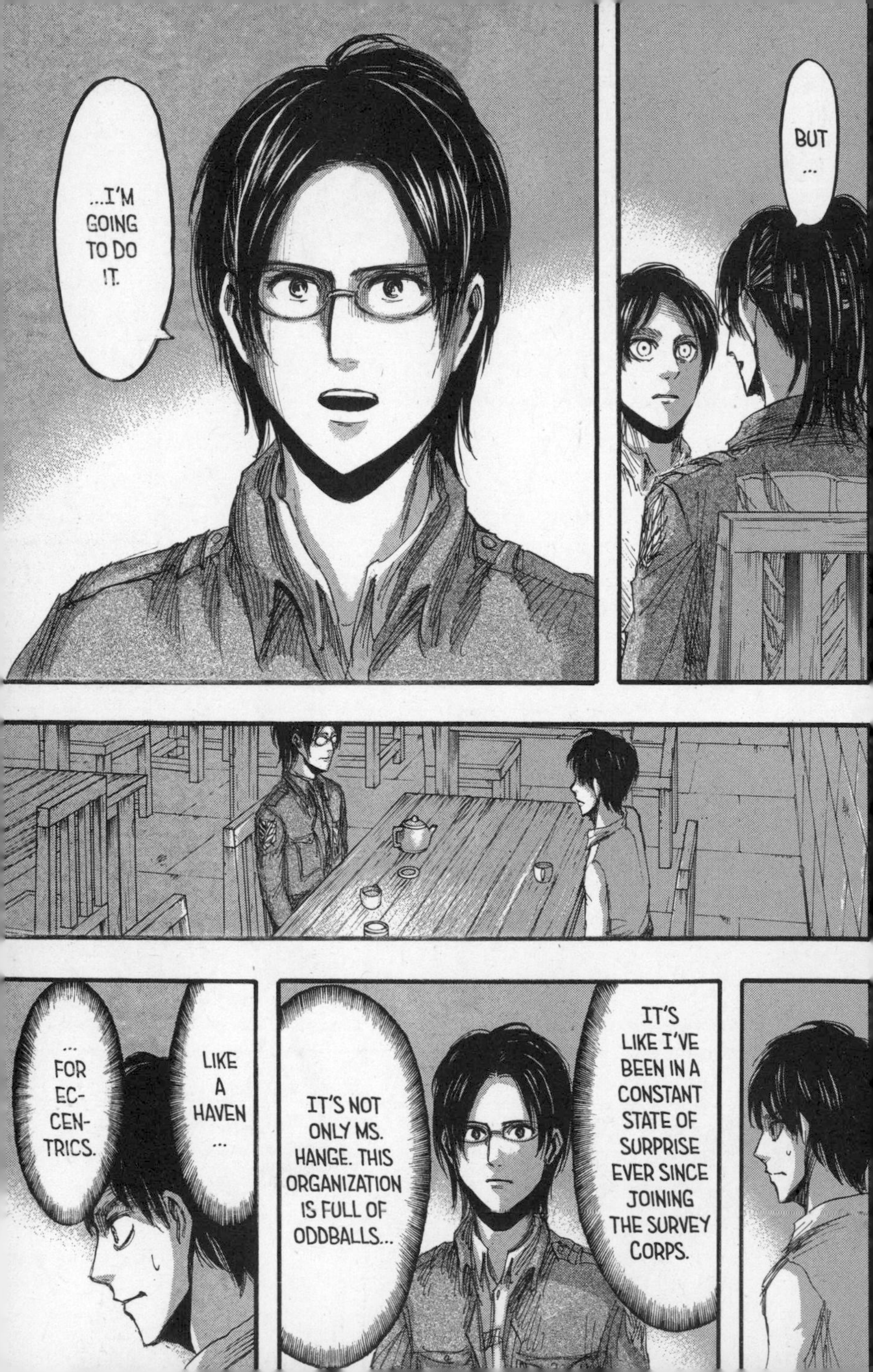
BUT ...
...I'M GOING TO DO IT.
IT'S LIKE I'VE BEEN IN A CONSTANT STATE OF SURPRISE EVER SINCE JOINING THE SURVEY CORPS.
IT'S NOT ONLY MS. HANGE. THIS ORGANIZATION IS FULL OF ODDBALLS...
LIKE A HAVEN ...
... FOR EC-CEN-TRICS.

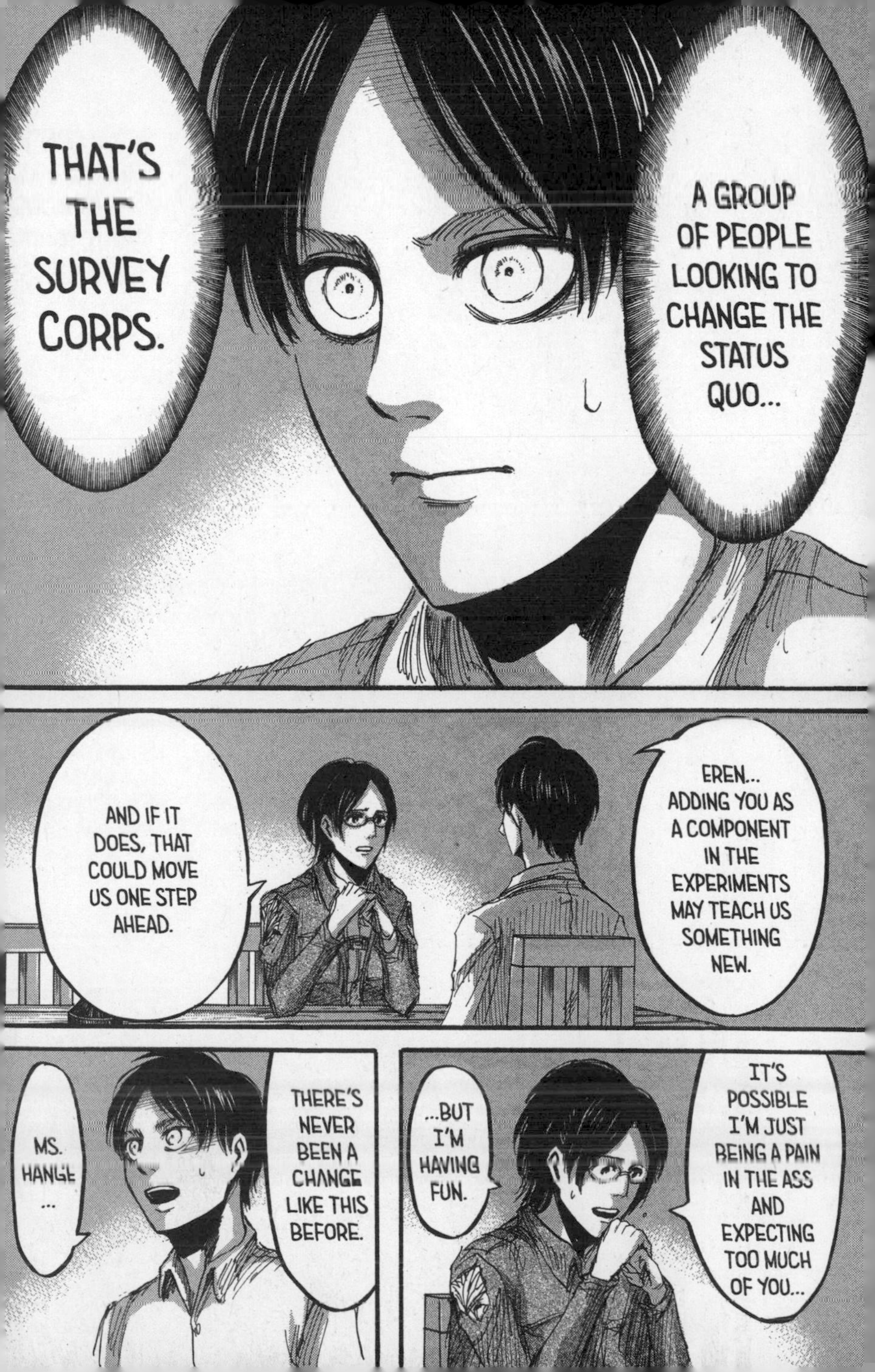
A GROUP OF PEOPLE LOOKING TO CHANGE THE STATUS QUO...
THAT'S THE SURVEY CORPS.
EREN... ADDING YOU AS A COMPONENT IN THE EXPERIMENTS MAY TEACH US SOMETHING NEW.
AND IF IT DOES, THAT COULD MOVE US ONE STEP AHEAD.
IT'S POSSIBLE I'M JUST BEING A PAIN IN THE ASS AND EXPECTING TOO MUCH OF YOU...
...BUT I'M HAVING FUN.
THERE'S NEVER BEEN A CHANGE LIKE THIS BEFORE.
MS. HANGE ...

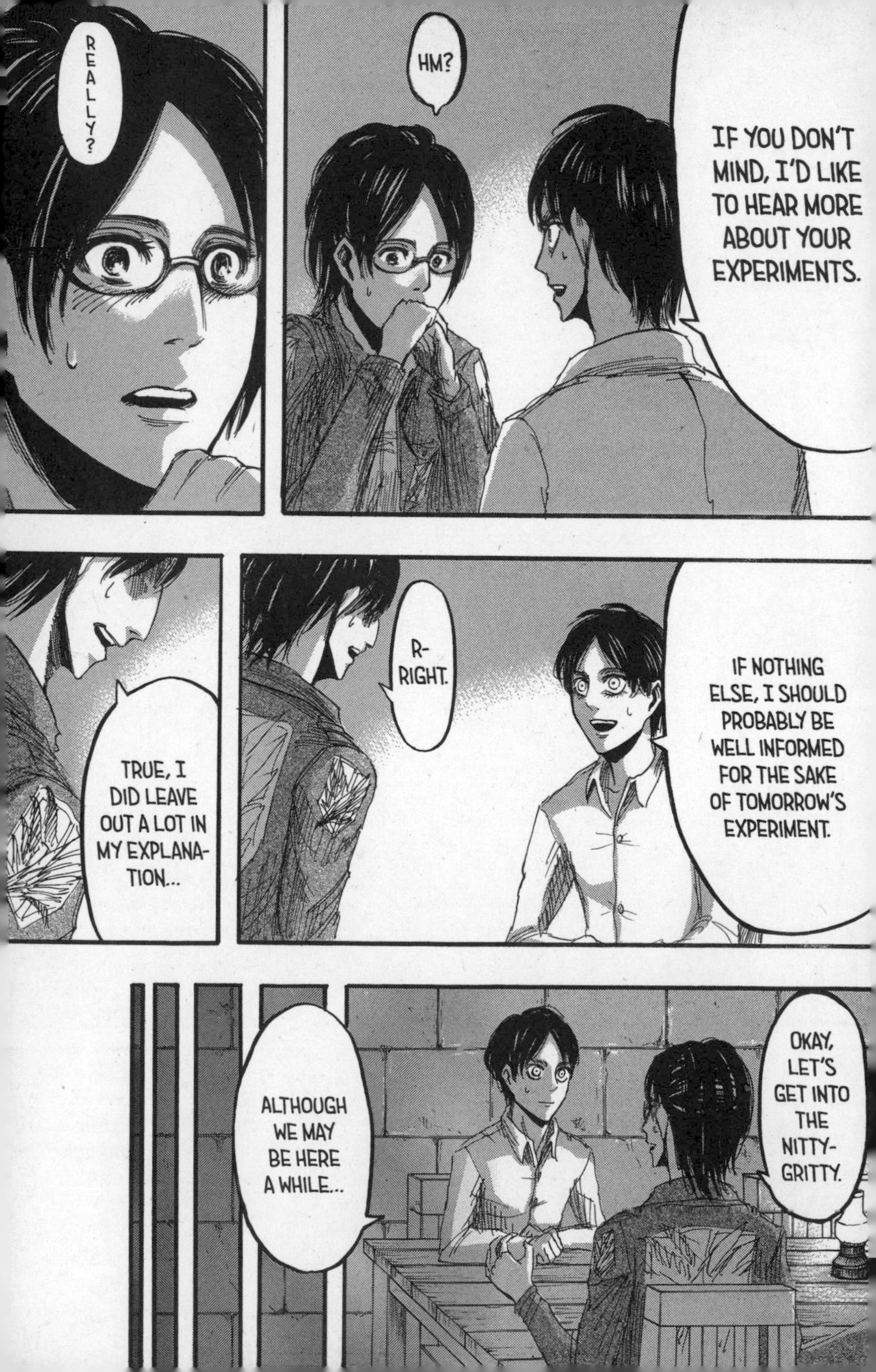
IF YOU DON'T MIND, I'D LIKE TO HEAR MORE ABOUT YOUR EXPERIMENTS.
HM?
REALLY?
IF NOTHING ELSE, I SHOULD PROBABLY BE WELL INFORMED FOR THE SAKE OF TOMORROW'S EXPERIMENT.
R-RIGHT.
TRUE, I DID LEAVE OUT A LOT IN MY EXPLANATION...
OKAY, LET'S GET INTO THE NITTY-GRITTY.
ALTHOUGH WE MAY BE HERE A WHILE...

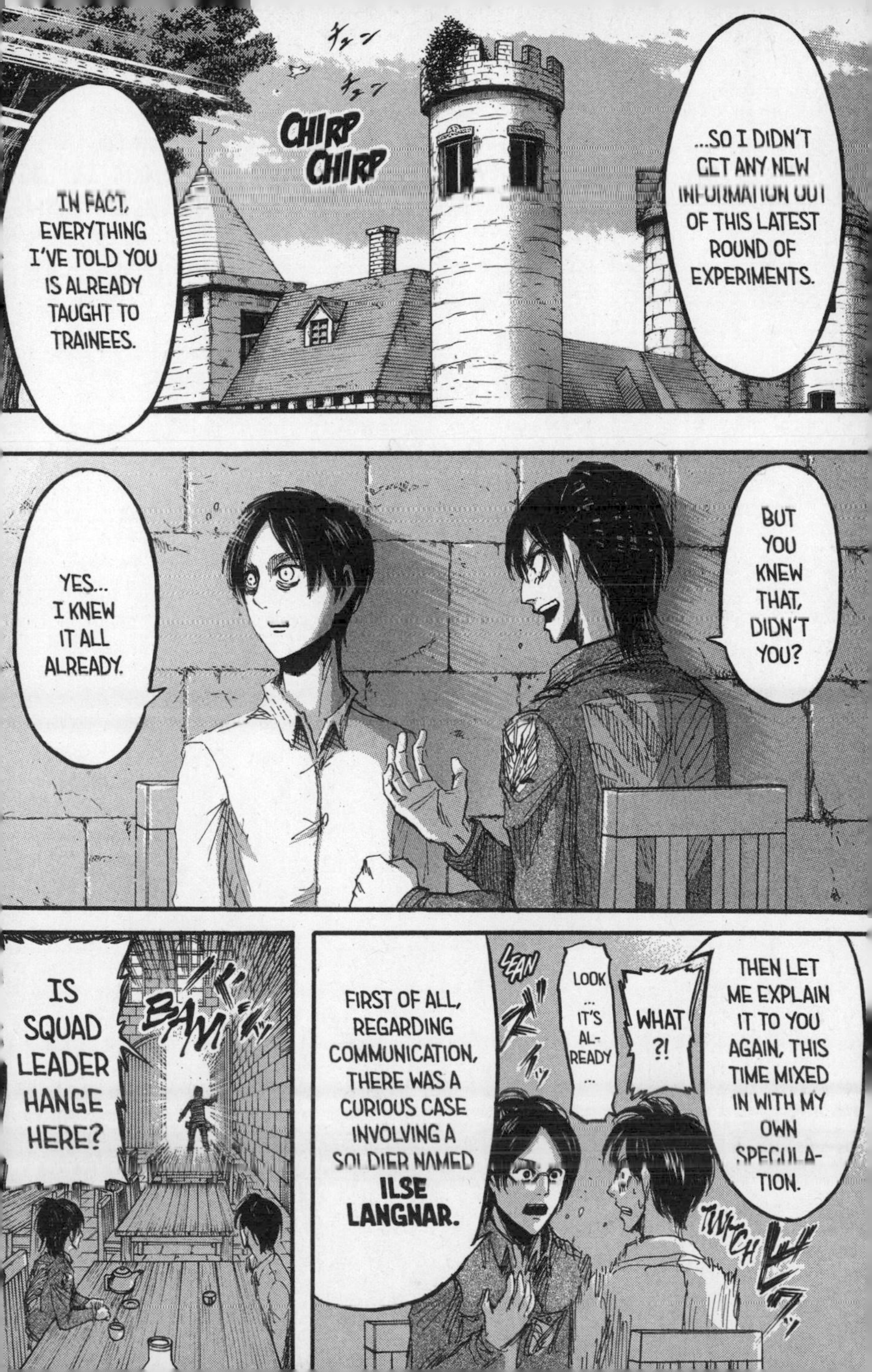
...SO I DIDN'T GET ANY NEW INFORMATION OUT OF THIS LATEST ROUND OF EXPERIMENTS.
CHIRP CHIRP
IN FACT, EVERYTHING I'VE TOLD YOU IS ALREADY TAUGHT TO TRAINEES.
BUT YOU KNEW THAT, DIDN'T YOU?
YES... I KNEW IT ALL ALREADY.
THEN LET ME EXPLAIN IT TO YOU AGAIN, THIS TIME MIXED IN WITH MY OWN SPECULATION.
TWITCH
WHAT?!
LOOK... IT'S ALREADY...
LEAN
FIRST OF ALL, REGARDING COMMUNICATION, THERE WAS A CURIOUS CASE INVOLVING A SOLDIER NAMED ILSE LANGNAR.
BAM
IS SQUAD LEADER HANGE HERE?

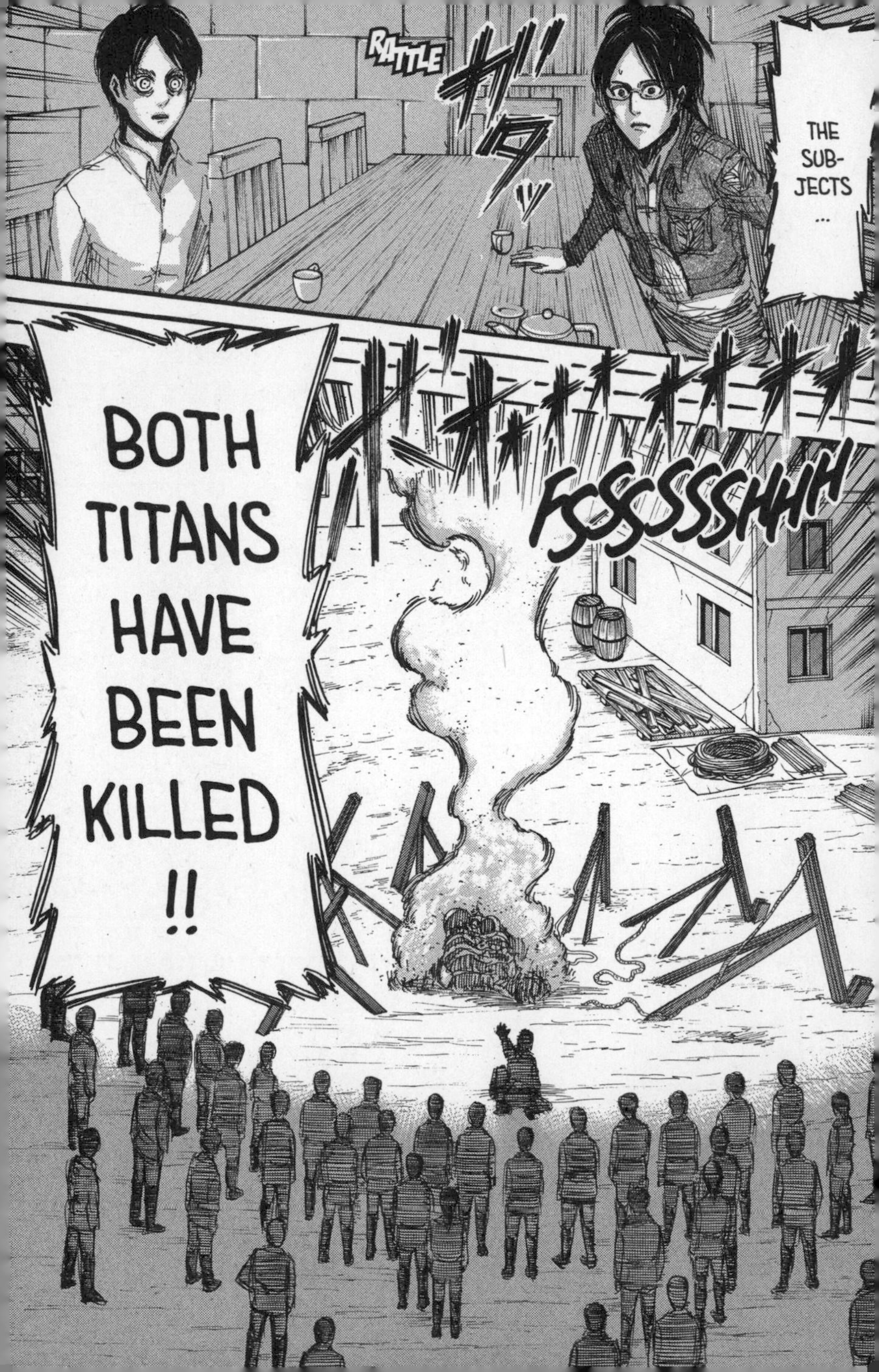
THE SUB-JECTS ...
RATTLE
FSSSSSSHHH
BOTH TITANS HAVE BEEN KILLED !!

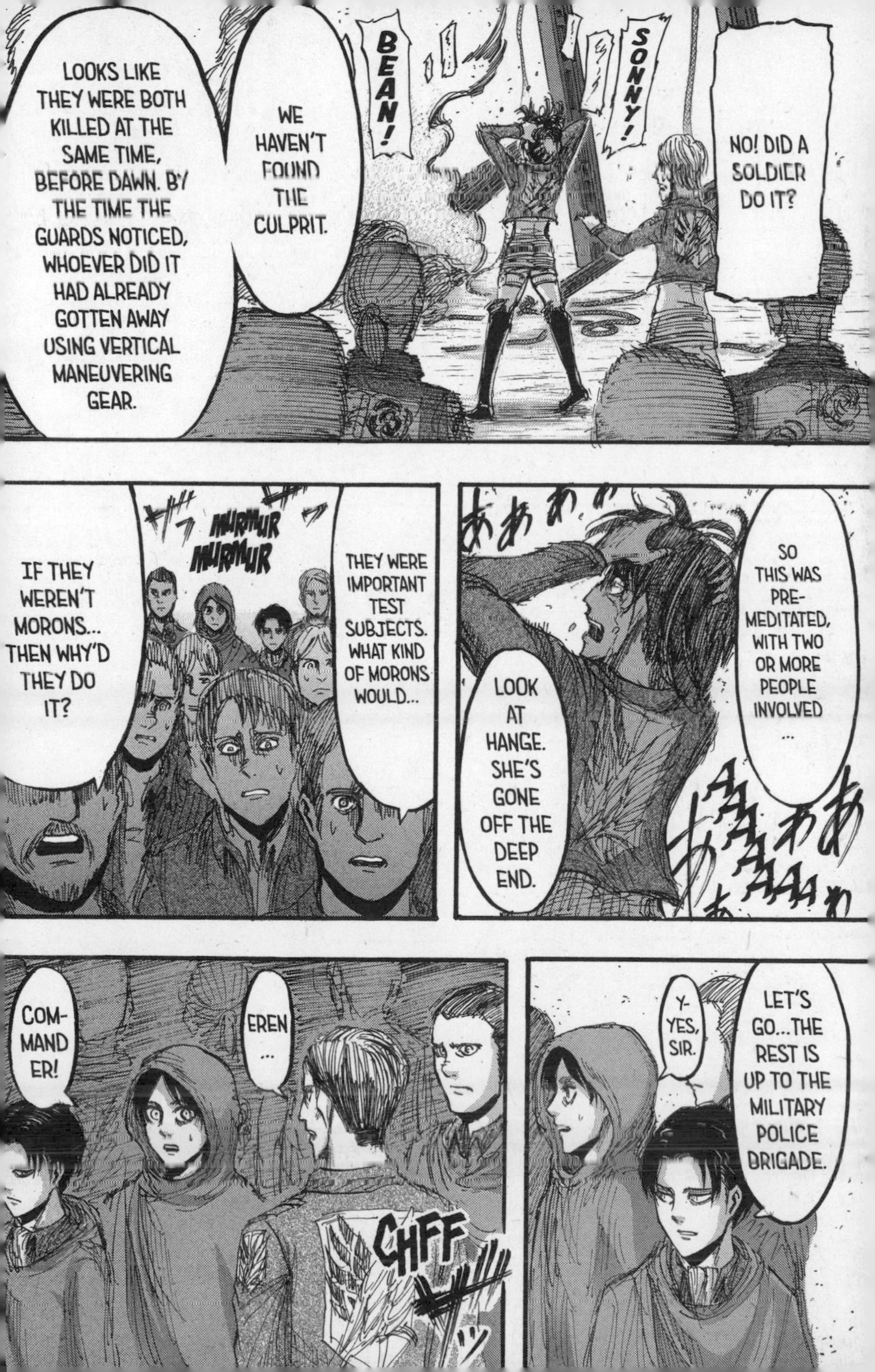
NO! DID A SOLDIER DO IT?
SONNY!
BEAN!
WE HAVEN'T FOUND THE CULPRIT.
LOOKS LIKE THEY WERE BOTH KILLED AT THE SAME TIME, BEFORE DAWN. BY THE TIME THE GUARDS NOTICED, WHOEVER DID IT HAD ALREADY GOTTEN AWAY USING VERTICAL MANEUVERING GEAR.
SO THIS WAS PRE-MEDITATED, WITH TWO OR MORE PEOPLE INVOLVED...
LOOK AT HANGE. SHE'S GONE OFF THE DEEP END.
THEY WERE IMPORTANT TEST SUBJECTS. WHAT KIND OF MORONS WOULD...
MURMUR MURMUR
IF THEY WEREN'T MORONS... THEN WHY'D THEY DO IT?
LET'S GO...THE REST IS UP TO THE MILITARY POLICE BRIGADE.
Y-YES, SIR.
EREN...
COM-MANDER!
CHFF

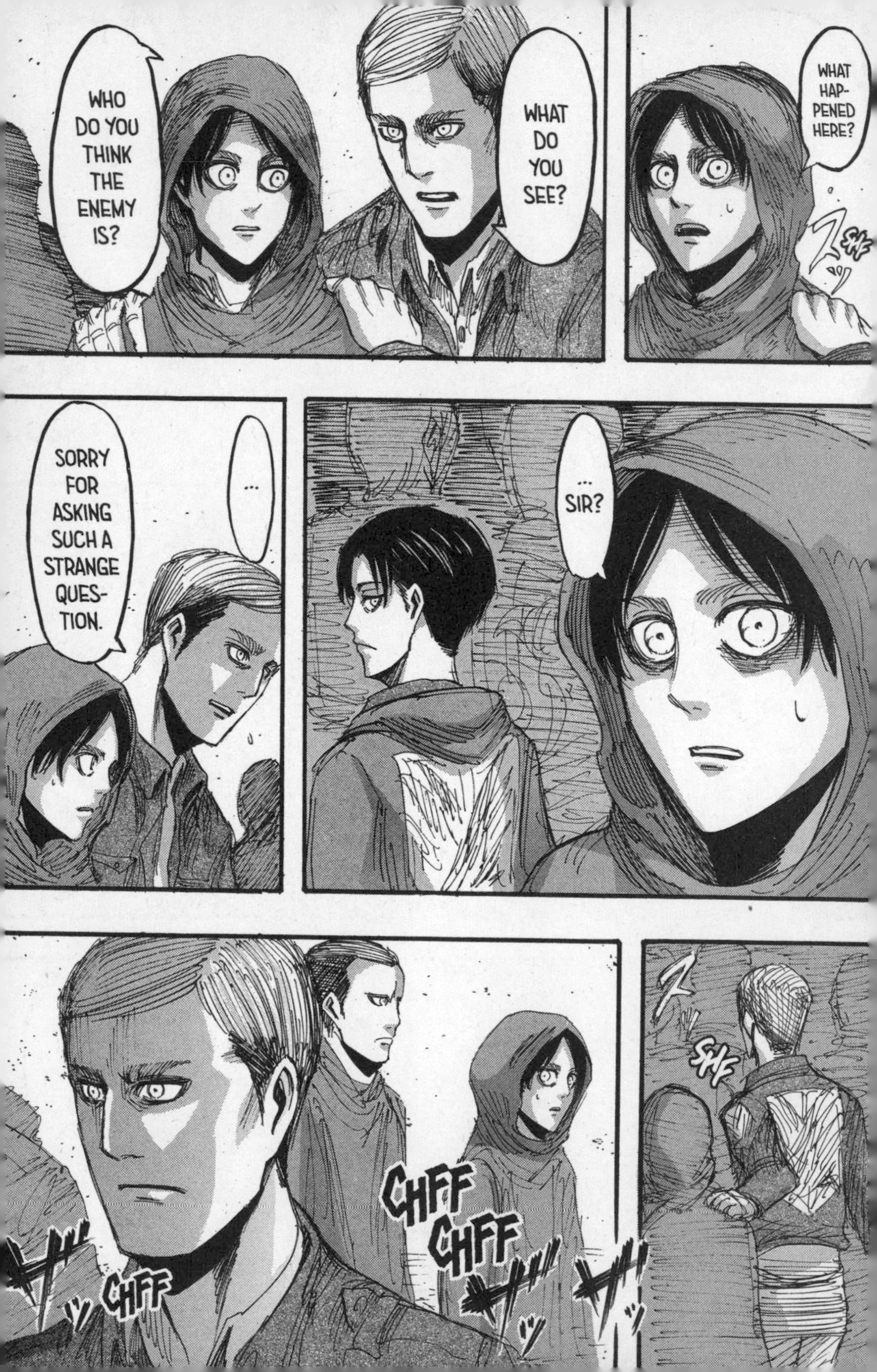
WHAT HAP-PENED HERE?
SHF
WHAT DO YOU SEE?
WHO DO YOU THINK THE ENEMY IS?
... SIR?
...
SORRY FOR ASKING SUCH A STRANGE QUES-TION.
SHF
CHFF CHFF
CHFF

ATTACK on TITAN

Episode 21: Opening the Gate

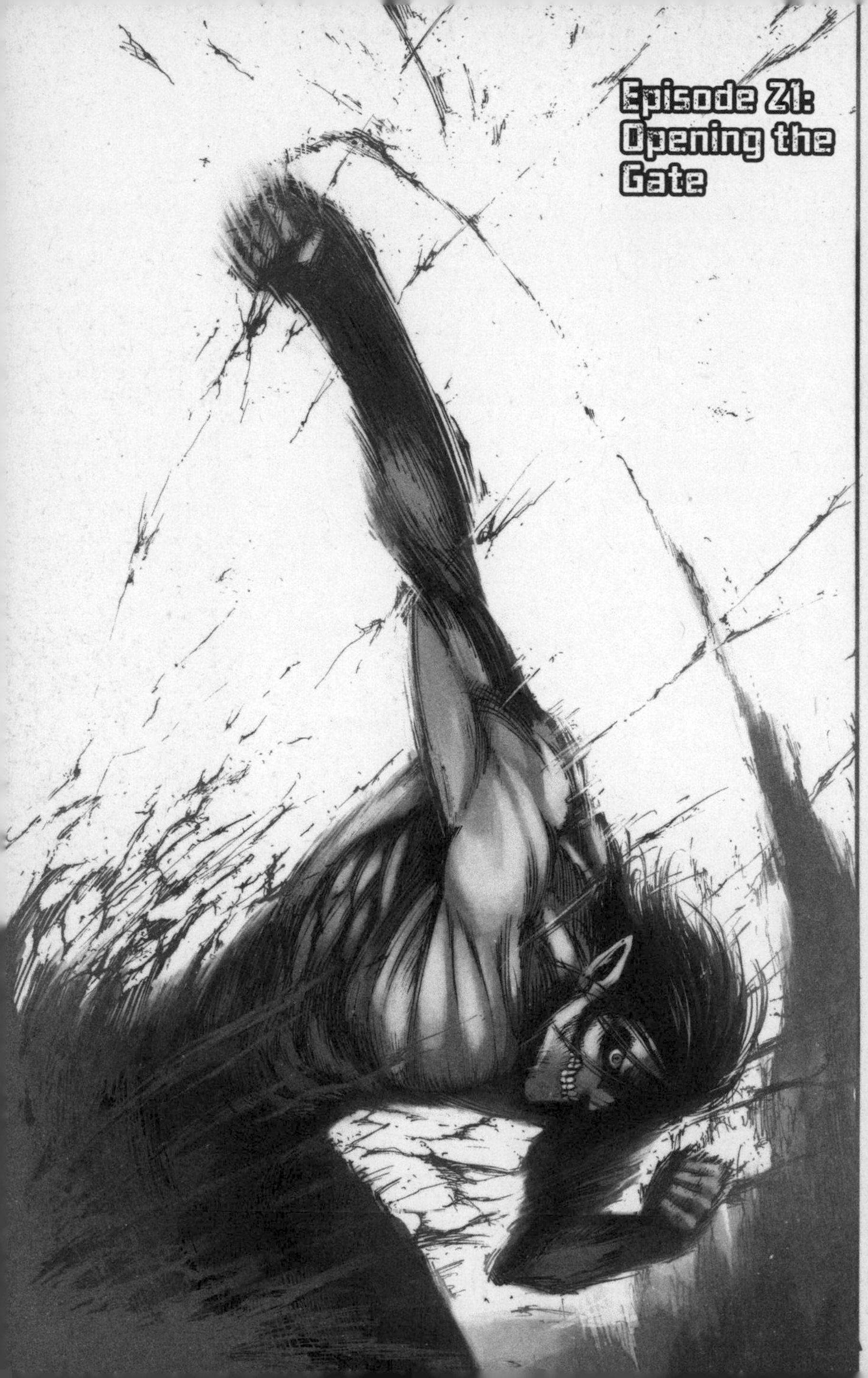

Rejected Cover Idea

THE MOOD DIDN'T FIT
WITH THE WORLD.

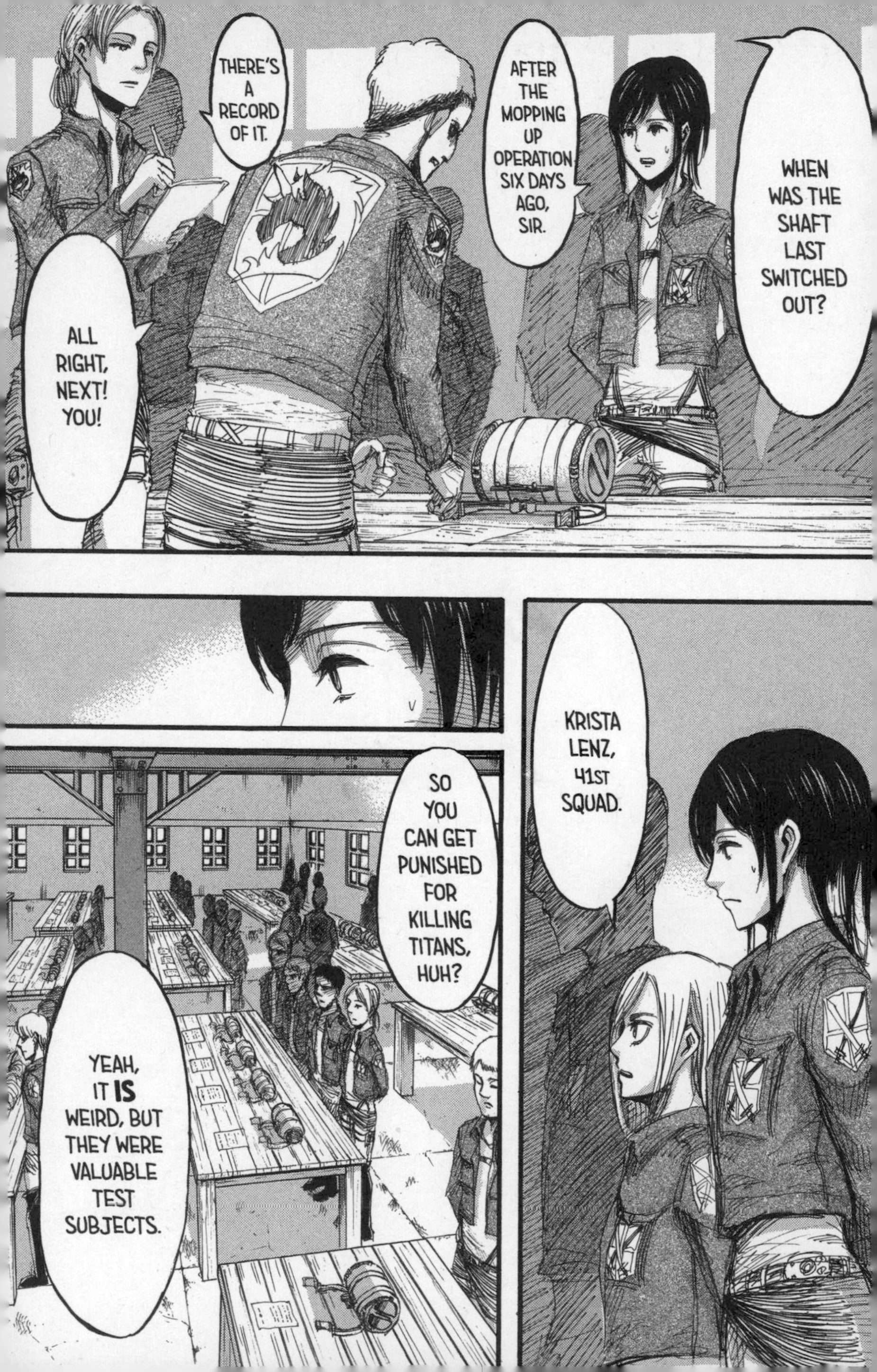
WHEN WAS THE SHAFT LAST SWITCHED OUT?
AFTER THE MOPPING UP OPERATION SIX DAYS AGO, SIR.
THERE'S A RECORD OF IT.
ALL RIGHT, NEXT! YOU!
KRISTA LENZ, 41ST SQUAD.
SO YOU CAN GET PUNISHED FOR KILLING TITANS, HUH?
YEAH, IT **IS** WEIRD, BUT THEY WERE VALUABLE TEST SUBJECTS.

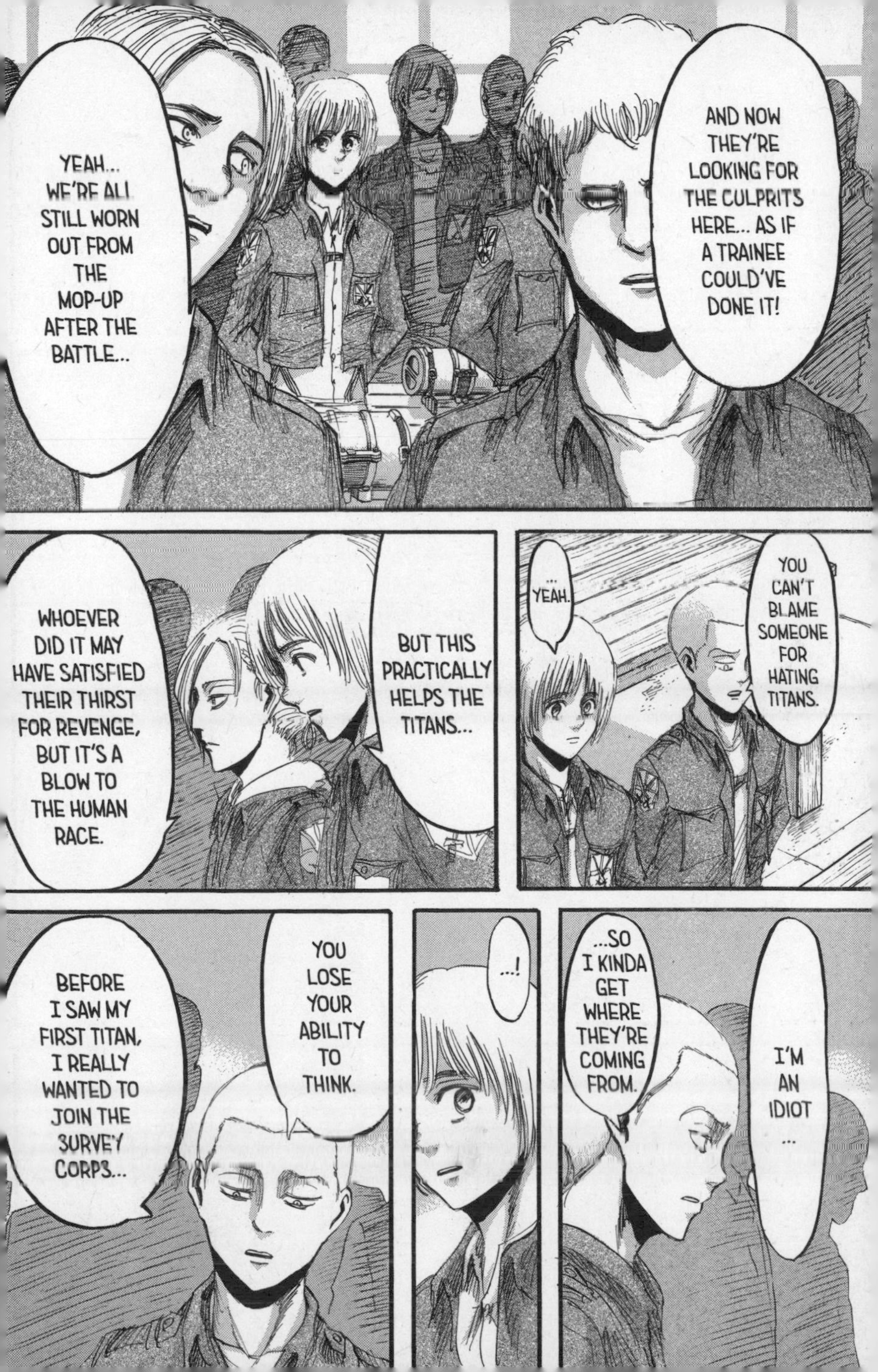
AND NOW THEY'RE LOOKING FOR THE CULPRITS HERE... AS IF A TRAINEE COULD'VE DONE IT!
YEAH... WE'RE ALL STILL WORN OUT FROM THE MOP-UP AFTER THE BATTLE...
YOU CAN'T BLAME SOMEONE FOR HATING TITANS.
...YEAH.
BUT THIS PRACTICALLY HELPS THE TITANS...
WHOEVER DID IT MAY HAVE SATISFIED THEIR THIRST FOR REVENGE, BUT IT'S A BLOW TO THE HUMAN RACE.
I'M AN IDIOT...
...SO I KINDA GET WHERE THEY'RE COMING FROM.
...!
YOU LOSE YOUR ABILITY TO THINK.
BEFORE I SAW MY FIRST TITAN, I REALLY WANTED TO JOIN THE SURVEY CORPS...

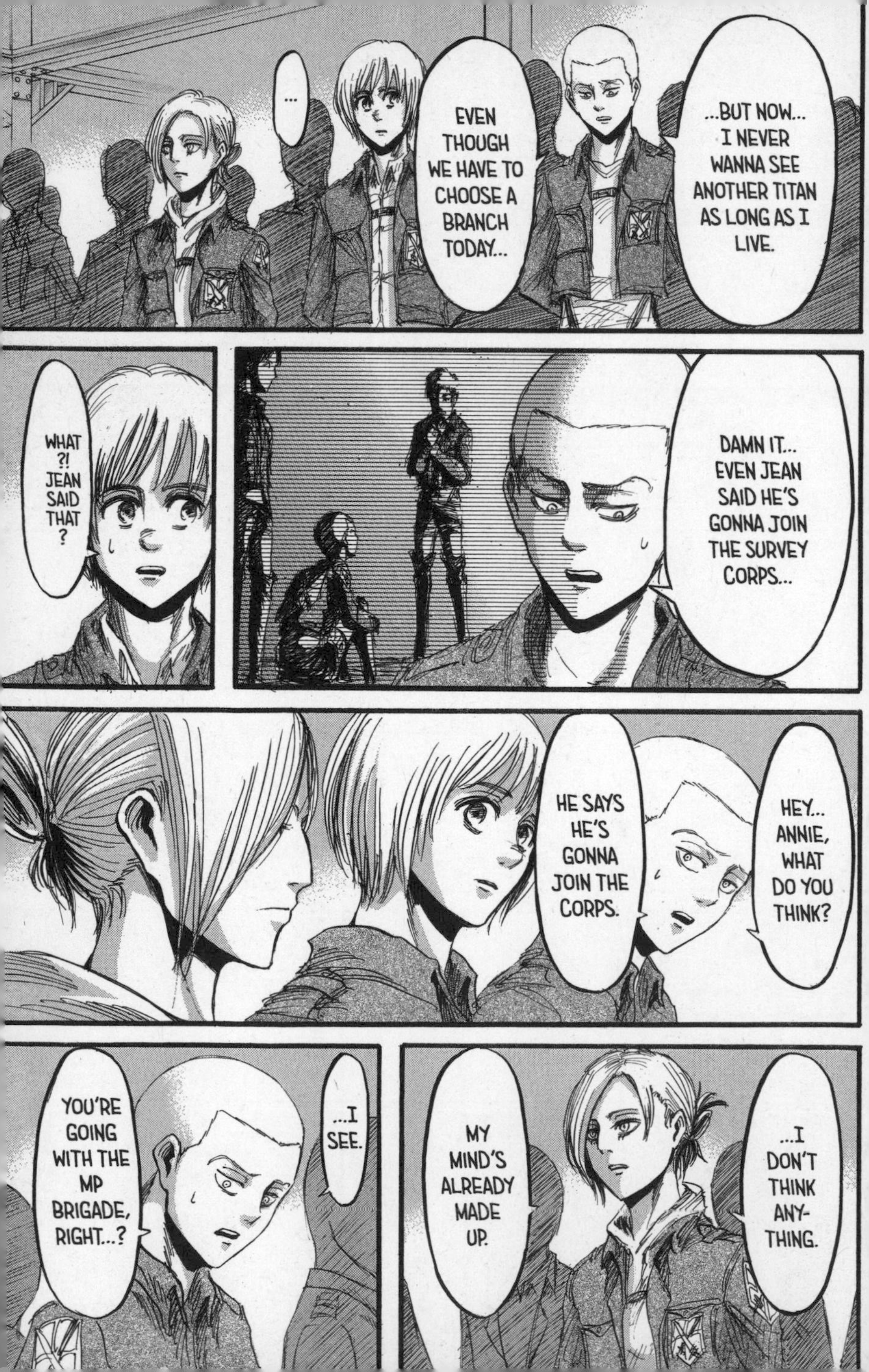
...BUT NOW... I NEVER WANNA SEE ANOTHER TITAN AS LONG AS I LIVE.
EVEN THOUGH WE HAVE TO CHOOSE A BRANCH TODAY...
...
DAMN IT... EVEN JEAN SAID HE'S GONNA JOIN THE SURVEY CORPS...
WHAT?! JEAN SAID THAT?
HEY... ANNIE, WHAT DO YOU THINK?
HE SAYS HE'S GONNA JOIN THE CORPS.
...I DON'T THINK ANY-THING.
MY MIND'S ALREADY MADE UP.
...I SEE.
YOU'RE GOING WITH THE MP BRIGADE, RIGHT...?

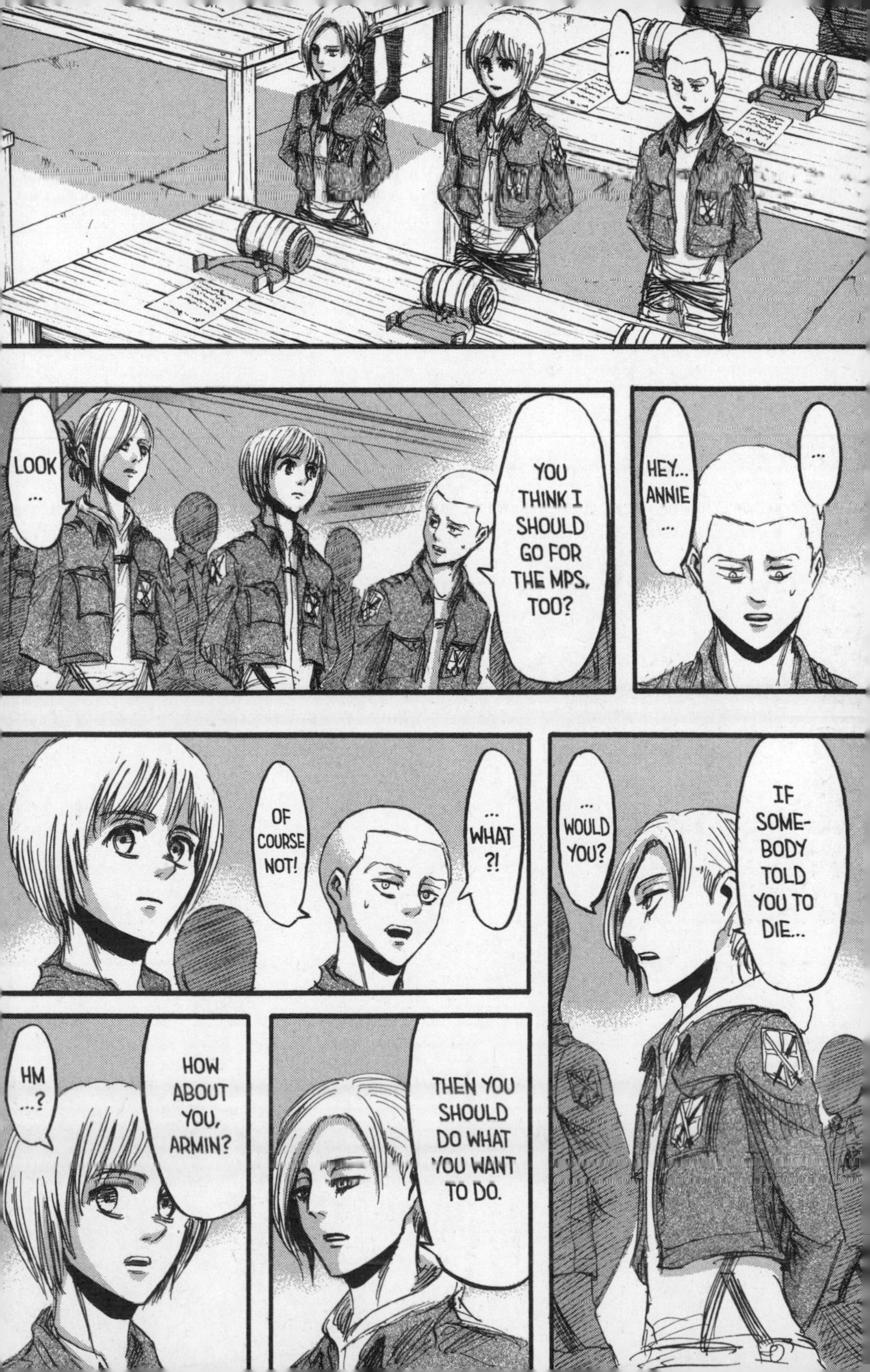
...
...
HEY... ANNIE ...
YOU THINK I SHOULD GO FOR THE MPS, TOO?
LOOK ...
IF SOME-BODY TOLD YOU TO DIE...
... WOULD YOU?
... WHAT ?!
OF COURSE NOT!
THEN YOU SHOULD DO WHAT YOU WANT TO DO.
HOW ABOUT YOU, ARMIN?
HM ...?

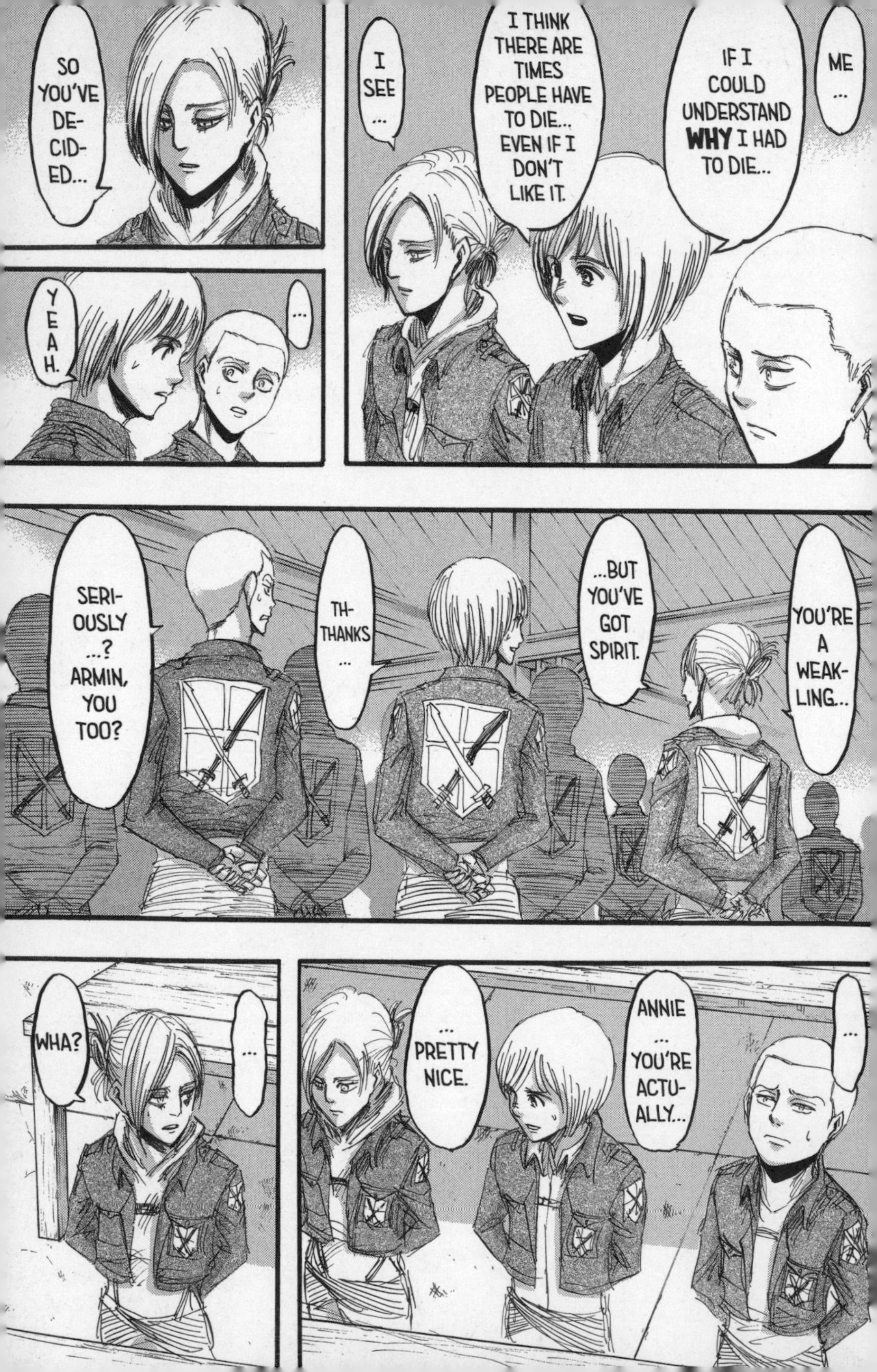
ME ...
IF I COULD UNDERSTAND WHY I HAD TO DIE...
I THINK THERE ARE TIMES PEOPLE HAVE TO DIE... EVEN IF I DON'T LIKE IT.
I SEE ...
SO YOU'VE DE-CID-ED...
...
YEAH.
YOU'RE A WEAK-LING...
...BUT YOU'VE GOT SPIRIT.
TH-THANKS ...
SERI-OUSLY ...? ARMIN, YOU TOO?
...
ANNIE ... YOU'RE ACTU-ALLY...
... PRETTY NICE.
...
WHA?

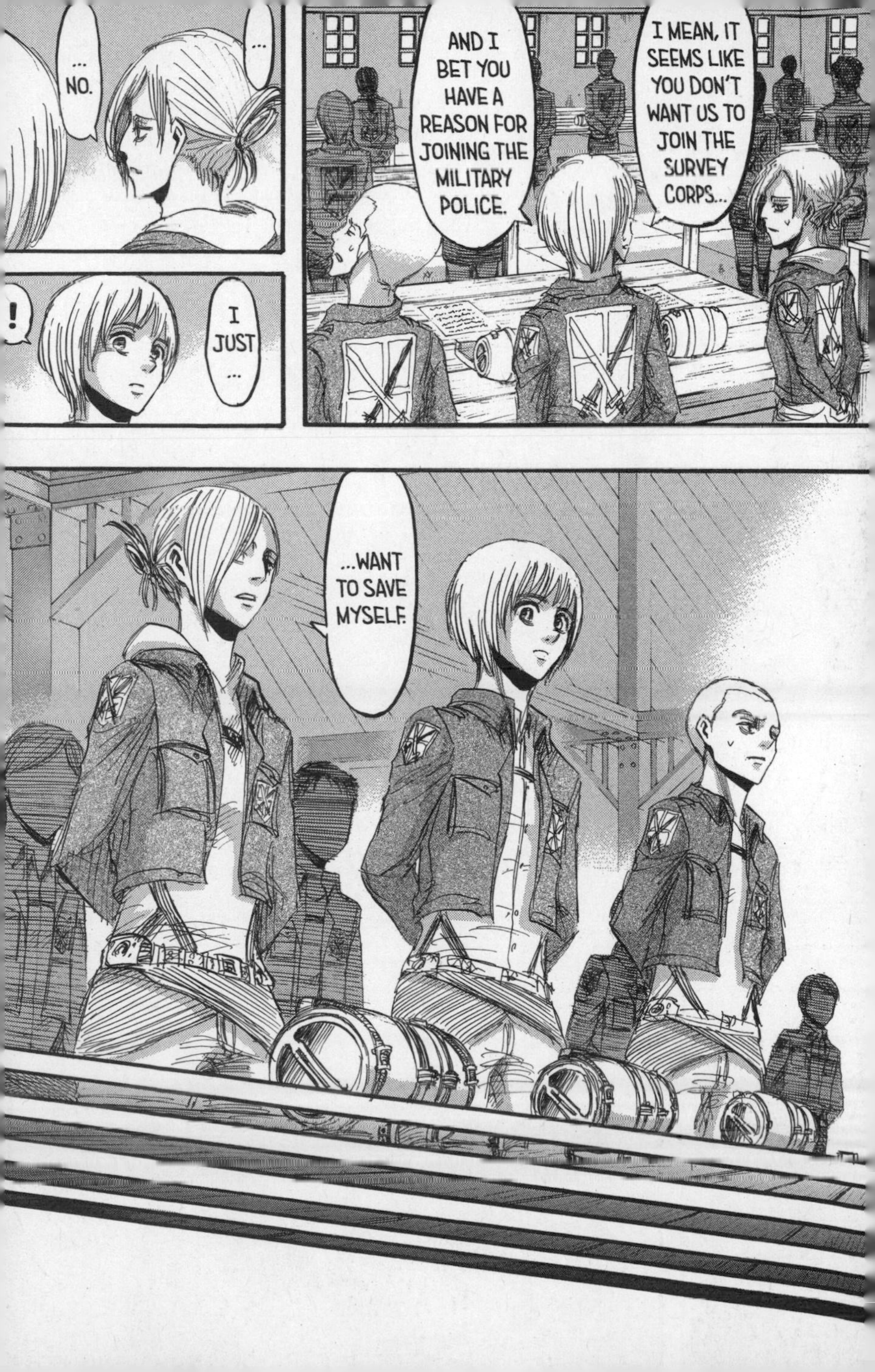
I MEAN, IT SEEMS LIKE YOU DON'T WANT US TO JOIN THE SURVEY CORPS...
AND I BET YOU HAVE A REASON FOR JOINING THE MILITARY POLICE.
...
... NO.
!
I JUST ...
...WANT TO SAVE MYSELF.

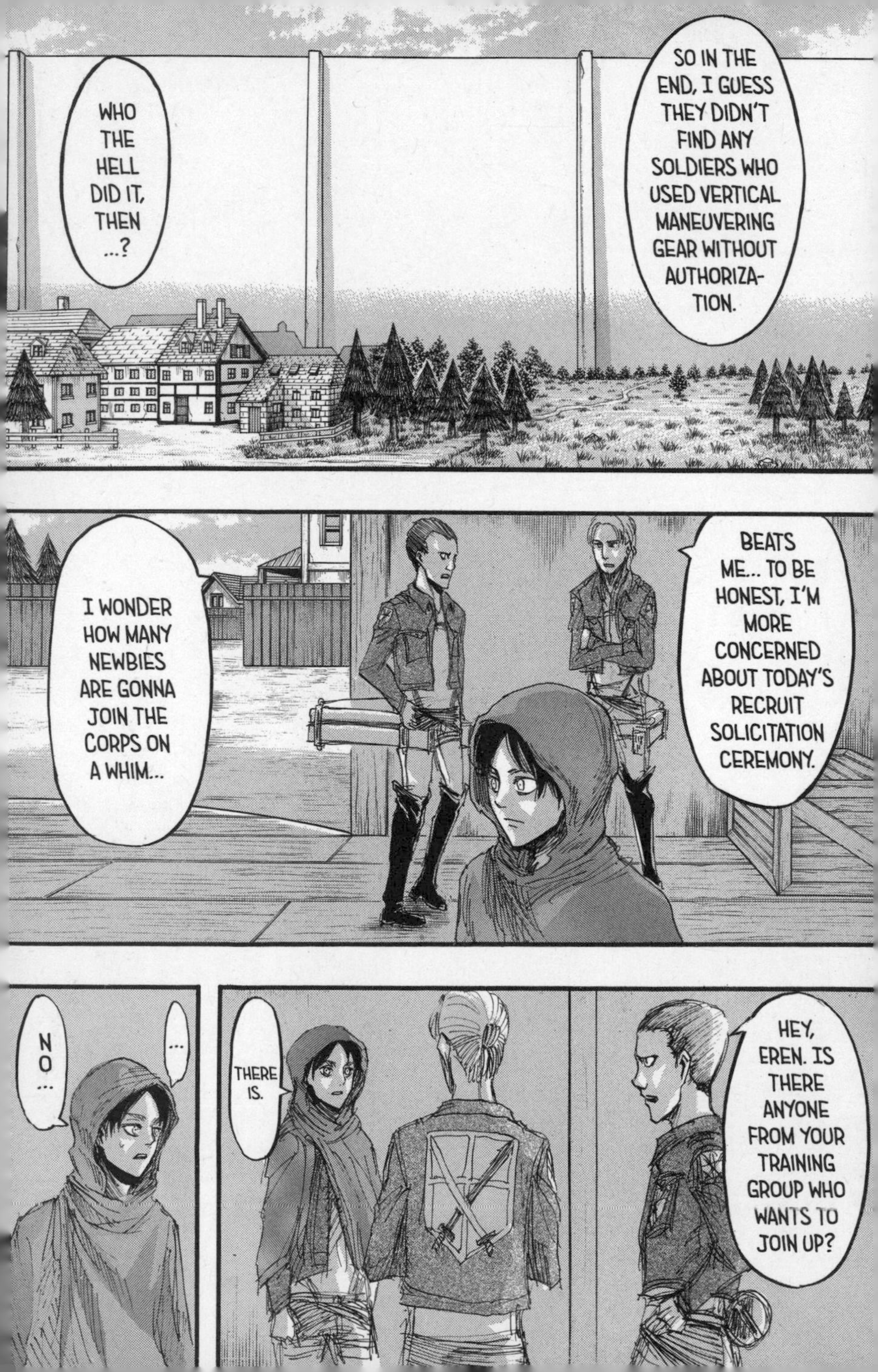
SO IN THE END, I GUESS THEY DIDN'T FIND ANY SOLDIERS WHO USED VERTICAL MANEUVERING GEAR WITHOUT AUTHORIZATION.
WHO THE HELL DID IT, THEN ...?
BEATS ME... TO BE HONEST, I'M MORE CONCERNED ABOUT TODAY'S RECRUIT SOLICITATION CEREMONY.
I WONDER HOW MANY NEWBIES ARE GONNA JOIN THE CORPS ON A WHIM...
HEY, EREN. IS THERE ANYONE FROM YOUR TRAINING GROUP WHO WANTS TO JOIN UP?
THERE IS.
...
NO...

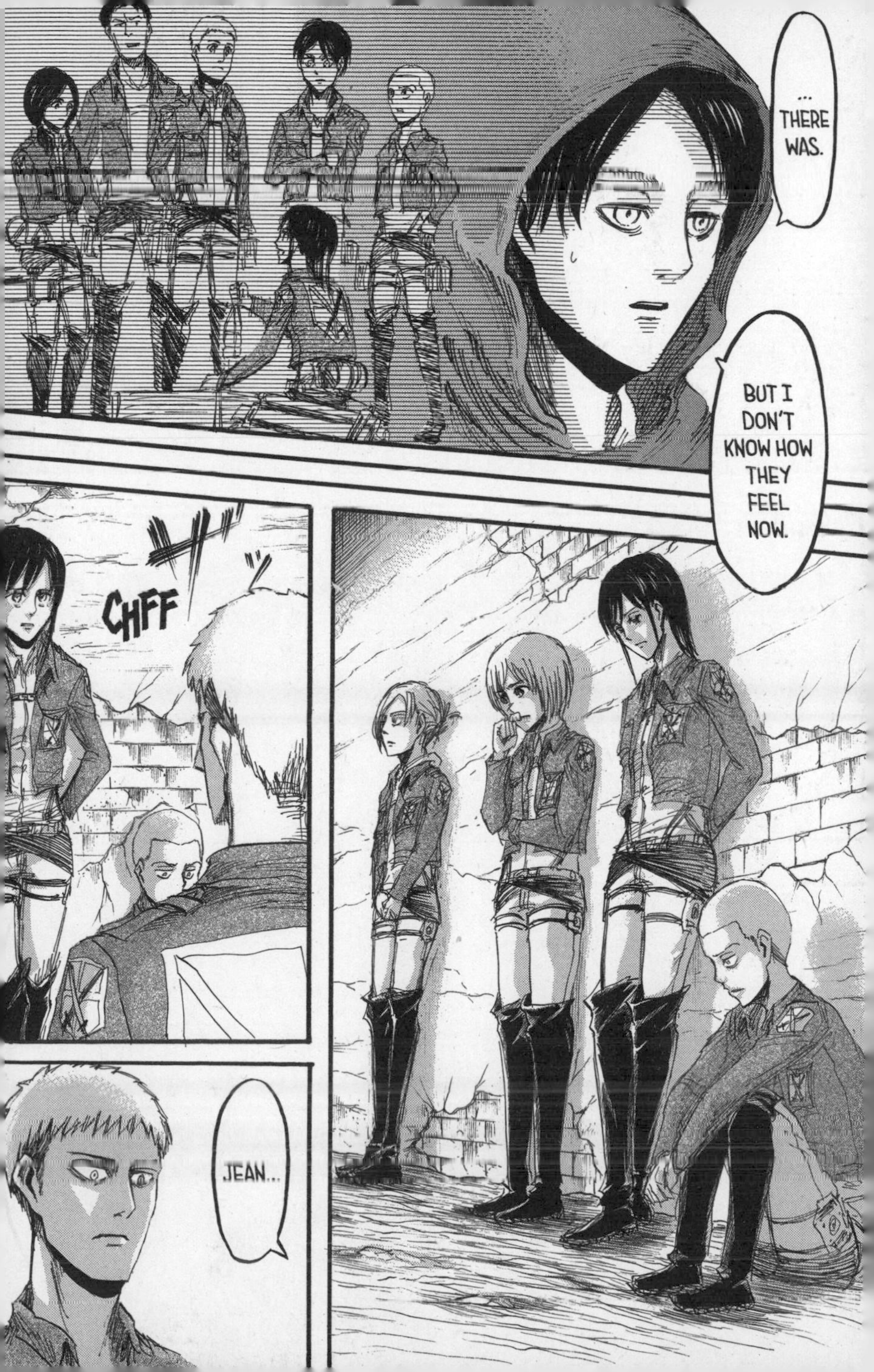
... THERE WAS.
BUT I DON'T KNOW HOW THEY FEEL NOW.
CHFF
JEAN...

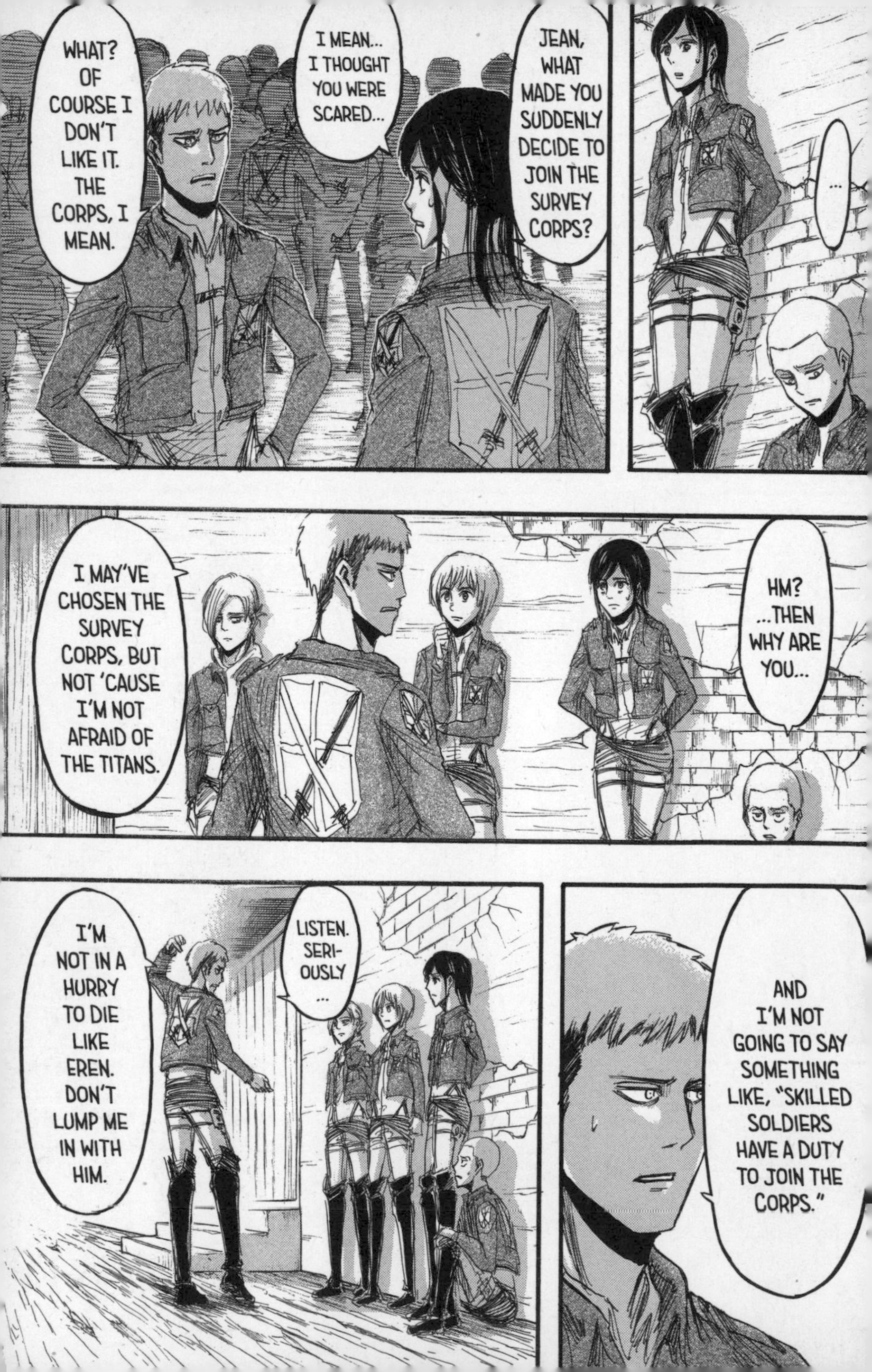
...
JEAN, WHAT MADE YOU SUDDENLY DECIDE TO JOIN THE SURVEY CORPS?
I MEAN... I THOUGHT YOU WERE SCARED...
WHAT? OF COURSE I DON'T LIKE IT. THE CORPS, I MEAN.
HM? ...THEN WHY ARE YOU...
I MAY'VE CHOSEN THE SURVEY CORPS, BUT NOT 'CAUSE I'M NOT AFRAID OF THE TITANS.
AND I'M NOT GOING TO SAY SOMETHING LIKE, "SKILLED SOLDIERS HAVE A DUTY TO JOIN THE CORPS."
LISTEN. SERIOUSLY...
I'M NOT IN A HURRY TO DIE LIKE EREN. DON'T LUMP ME IN WITH HIM.

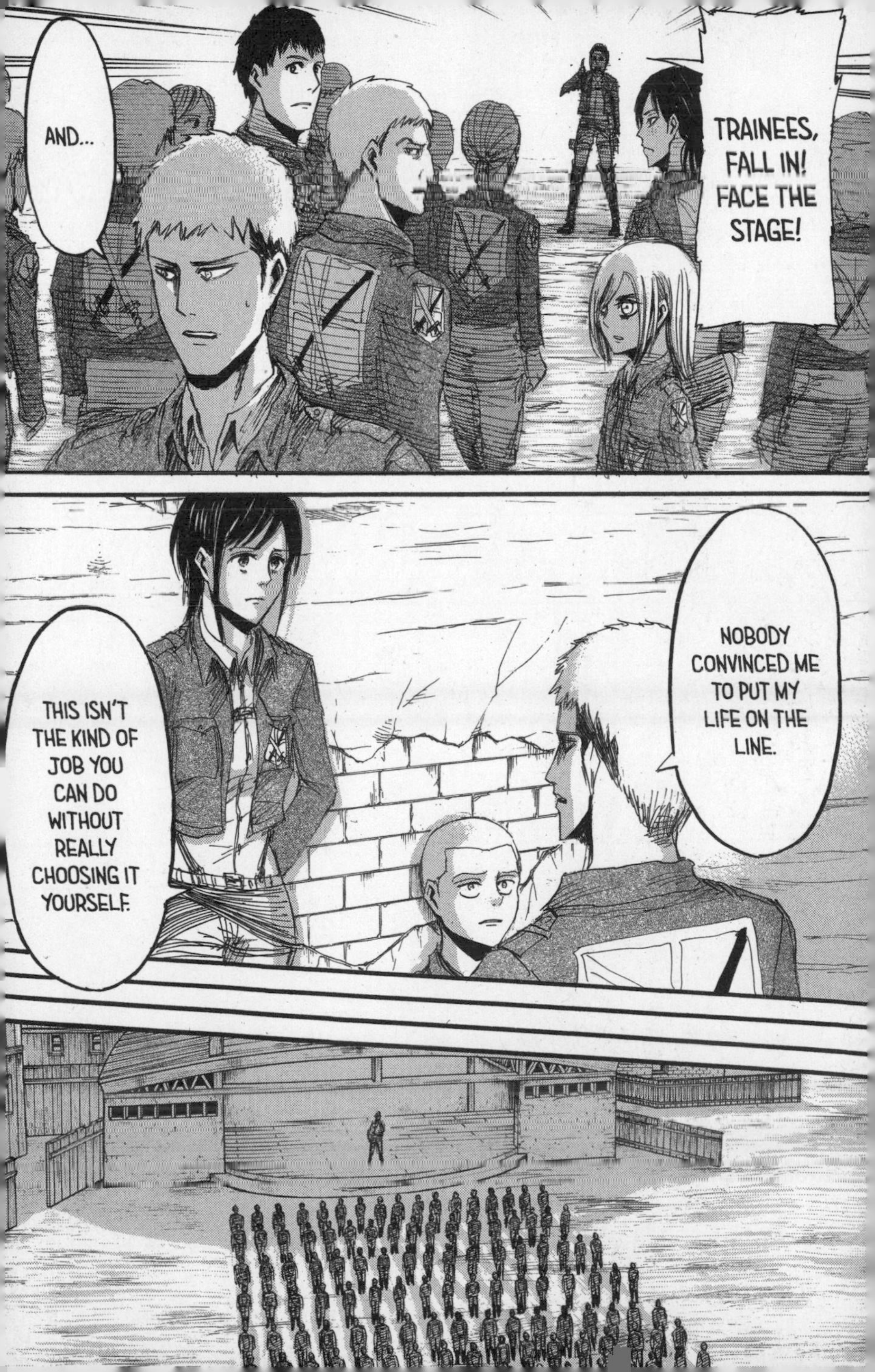
TRAINEES, FALL IN! FACE THE STAGE!
AND...
NOBODY CONVINCED ME TO PUT MY LIFE ON THE LINE.
THIS ISN'T THE KIND OF JOB YOU CAN DO WITHOUT REALLY CHOOSING IT YOURSELF.

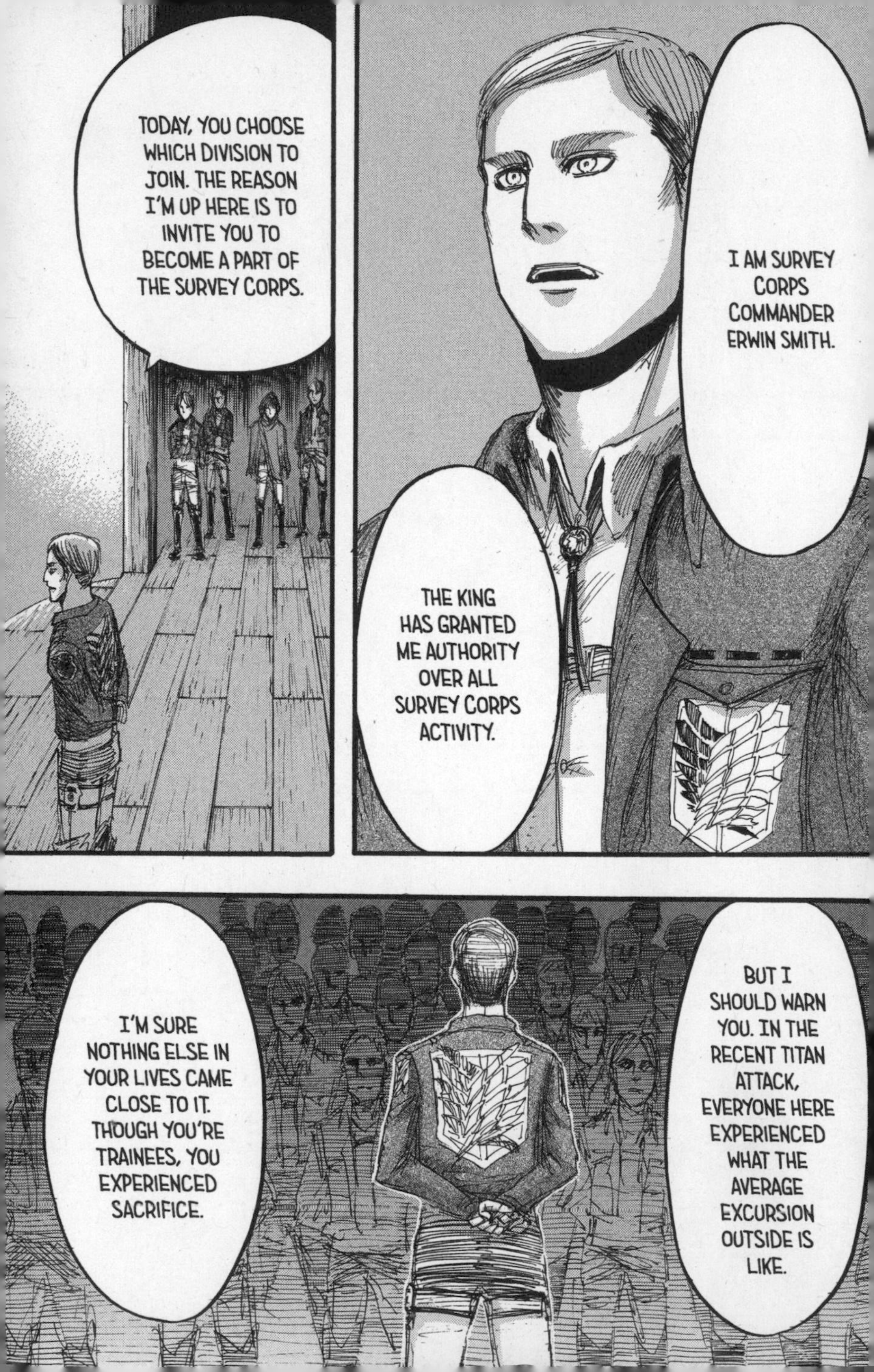
I AM SURVEY CORPS COMMANDER ERWIN SMITH.
THE KING HAS GRANTED ME AUTHORITY OVER ALL SURVEY CORPS ACTIVITY.
TODAY, YOU CHOOSE WHICH DIVISION TO JOIN. THE REASON I'M UP HERE IS TO INVITE YOU TO BECOME A PART OF THE SURVEY CORPS.
BUT I SHOULD WARN YOU. IN THE RECENT TITAN ATTACK, EVERYONE HERE EXPERIENCED WHAT THE AVERAGE EXCURSION OUTSIDE IS LIKE.
I'M SURE NOTHING ELSE IN YOUR LIVES CAME CLOSE TO IT. THOUGH YOU'RE TRAINEES, YOU EXPERIENCED SACRIFICE.

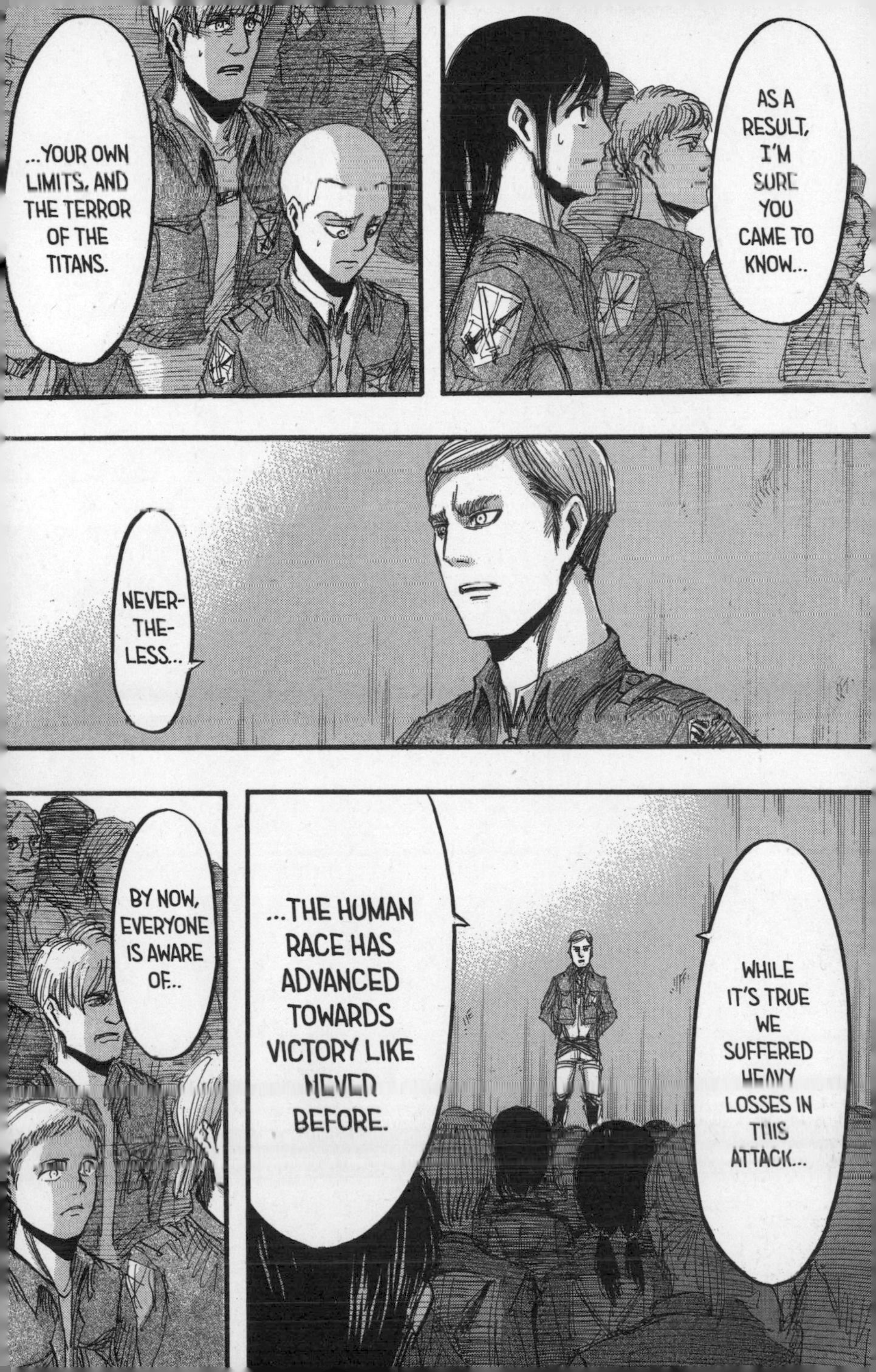
AS A RESULT, I'M SURE YOU CAME TO KNOW...
...YOUR OWN LIMITS, AND THE TERROR OF THE TITANS.
NEVER-THE-LESS...
WHILE IT'S TRUE WE SUFFERED HEAVY LOSSES IN THIS ATTACK...
...THE HUMAN RACE HAS ADVANCED TOWARDS VICTORY LIKE NEVER BEFORE.
BY NOW, EVERYONE IS AWARE OF...

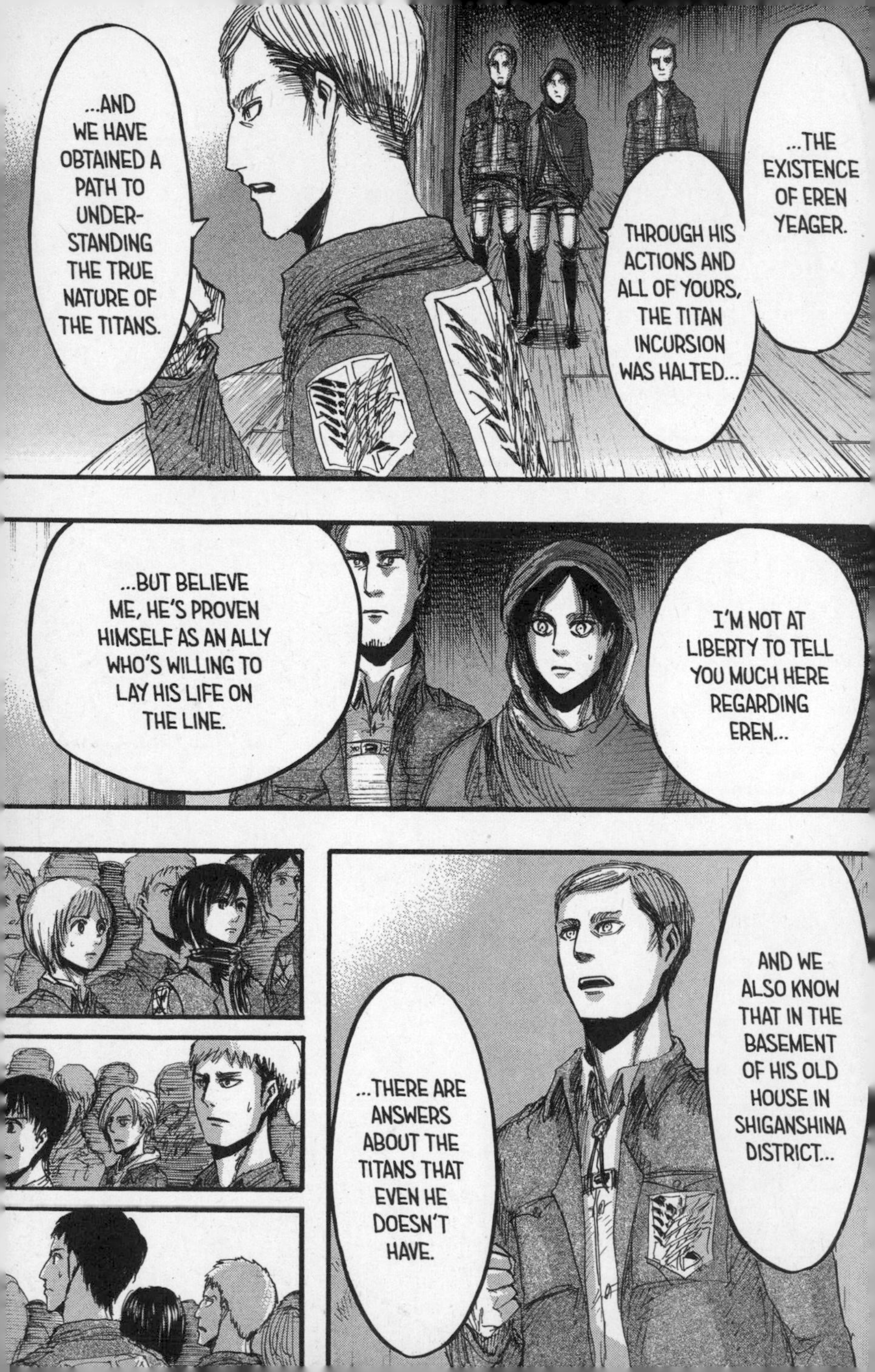
...THE EXISTENCE OF EREN YEAGER.
THROUGH HIS ACTIONS AND ALL OF YOURS, THE TITAN INCURSION WAS HALTED...
...AND WE HAVE OBTAINED A PATH TO UNDER-STANDING THE TRUE NATURE OF THE TITANS.
I'M NOT AT LIBERTY TO TELL YOU MUCH HERE REGARDING EREN...
...BUT BELIEVE ME, HE'S PROVEN HIMSELF AS AN ALLY WHO'S WILLING TO LAY HIS LIFE ON THE LINE.
AND WE ALSO KNOW THAT IN THE BASEMENT OF HIS OLD HOUSE IN SHIGANSHINA DISTRICT...
...THERE ARE ANSWERS ABOUT THE TITANS THAT EVEN HE DOESN'T HAVE.

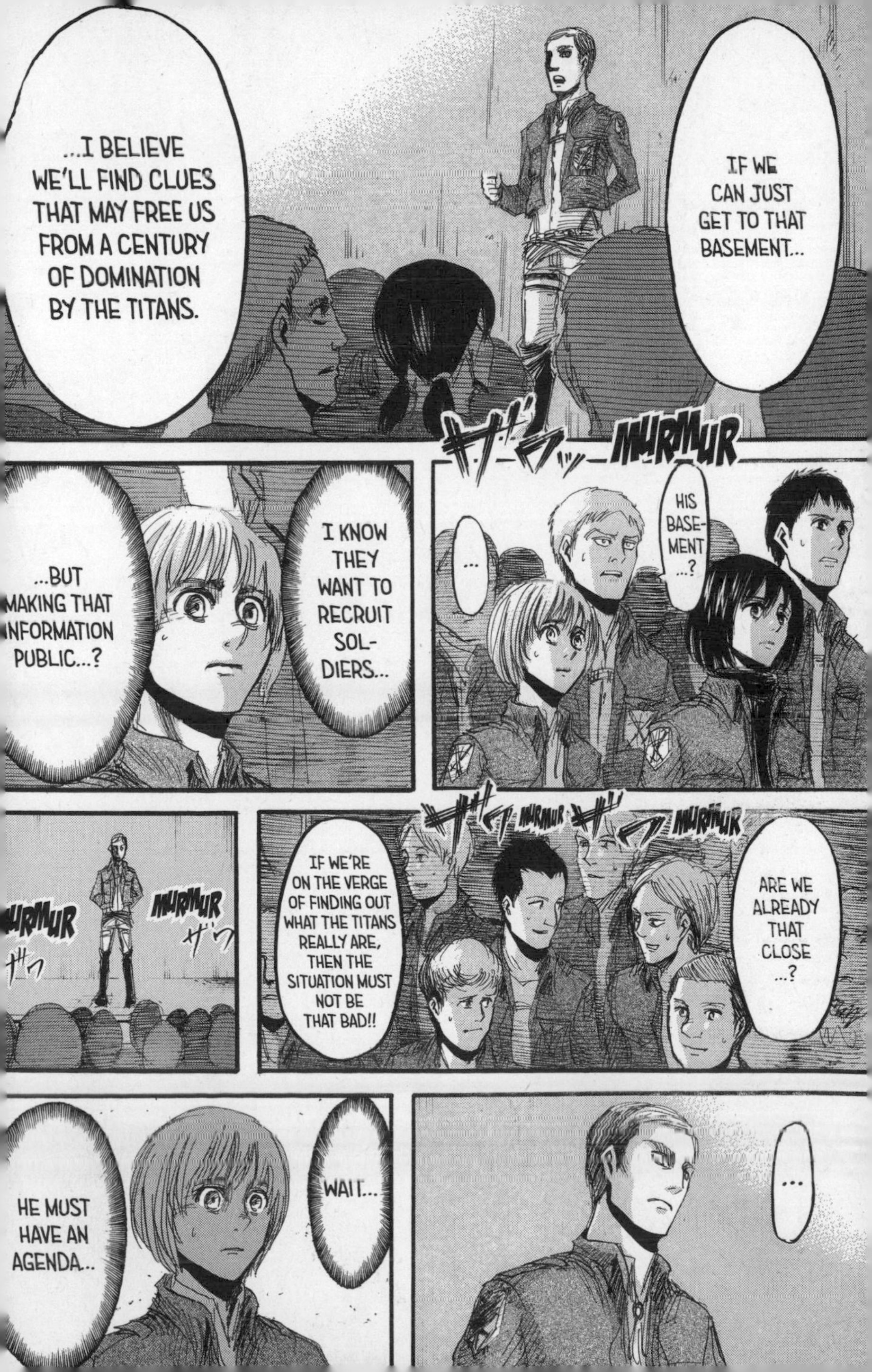
IF WE CAN JUST GET TO THAT BASEMENT...
...I BELIEVE WE'LL FIND CLUES THAT MAY FREE US FROM A CENTURY OF DOMINATION BY THE TITANS.
MURMUR
HIS BASE-MENT ...?
...
I KNOW THEY WANT TO RECRUIT SOL-DIERS...
...BUT MAKING THAT INFORMATION PUBLIC...?
MURMUR
MURMUR
ARE WE ALREADY THAT CLOSE ...?
IF WE'RE ON THE VERGE OF FINDING OUT WHAT THE TITANS REALLY ARE, THEN THE SITUATION MUST NOT BE THAT BAD!!
MURMUR
ザワ
MURMUR
...
WAIT...
HE MUST HAVE AN AGENDA...

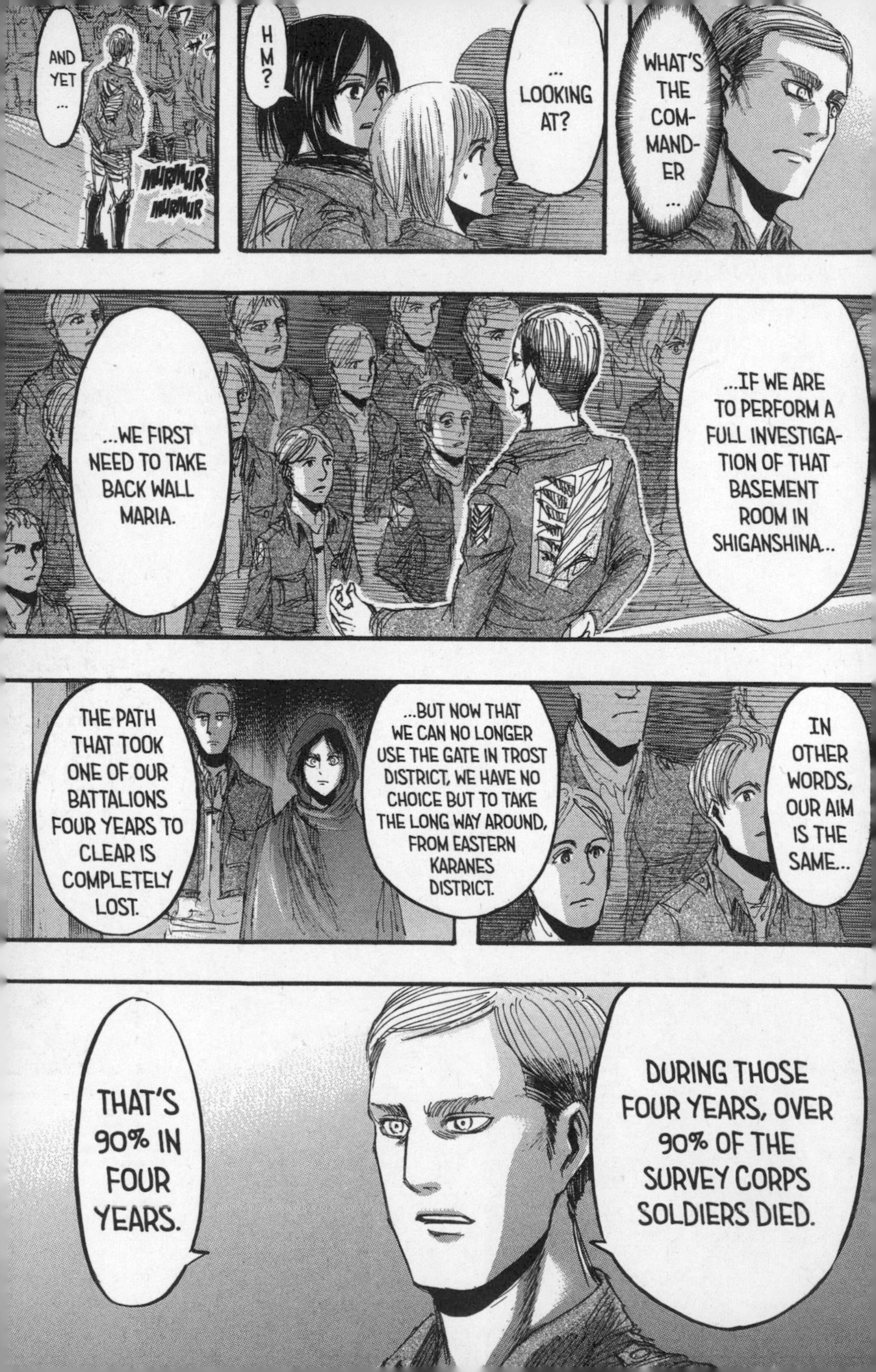
WHAT'S THE COMMANDER ...
... LOOKING AT?
HM?
AND YET ...
MURMUR MURMUR
...IF WE ARE TO PERFORM A FULL INVESTIGATION OF THAT BASEMENT ROOM IN SHIGANSHINA...
...WE FIRST NEED TO TAKE BACK WALL MARIA.
IN OTHER WORDS, OUR AIM IS THE SAME...
...BUT NOW THAT WE CAN NO LONGER USE THE GATE IN TROST DISTRICT, WE HAVE NO CHOICE BUT TO TAKE THE LONG WAY AROUND, FROM EASTERN KARANES DISTRICT.
THE PATH THAT TOOK ONE OF OUR BATTALIONS FOUR YEARS TO CLEAR IS COMPLETELY LOST.
DURING THOSE FOUR YEARS, OVER 90% OF THE SURVEY CORPS SOLDIERS DIED.
THAT'S 90% IN FOUR YEARS.

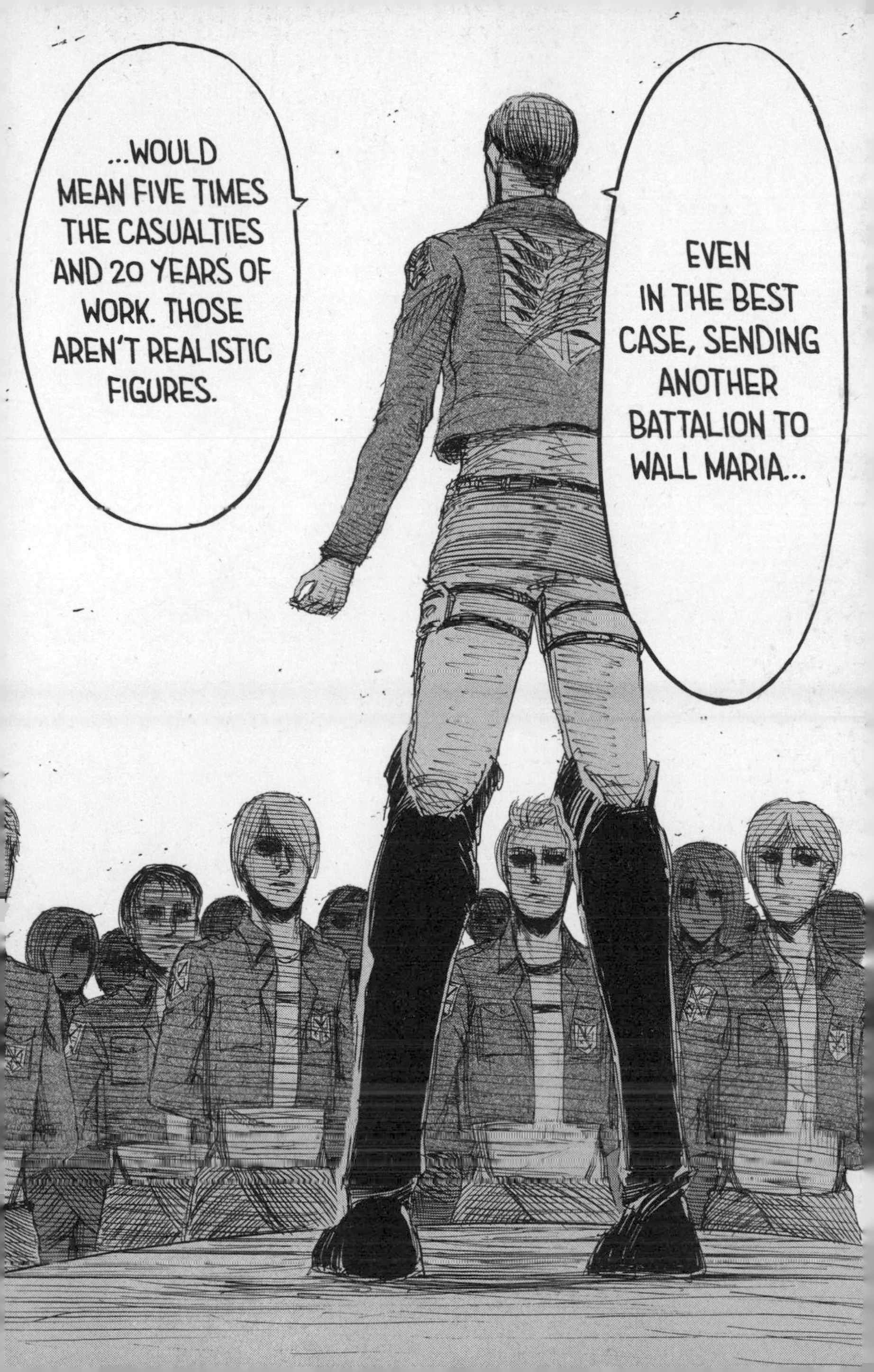
EVEN IN THE BEST CASE, SENDING ANOTHER BATTALION TO WALL MARIA...
...WOULD MEAN FIVE TIMES THE CASUALTIES AND 20 YEARS OF WORK. THOSE AREN'T REALISTIC FIGURES.

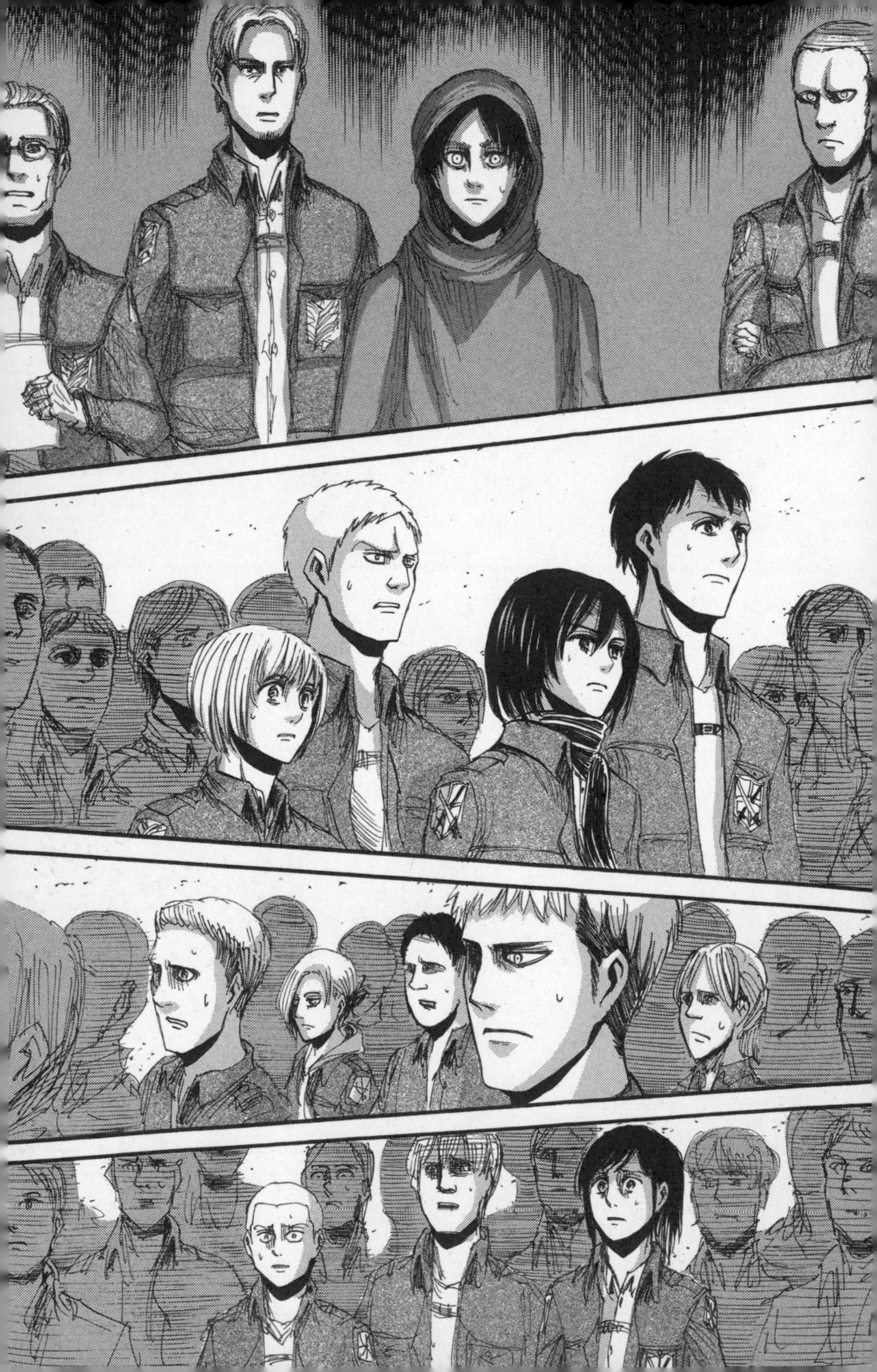

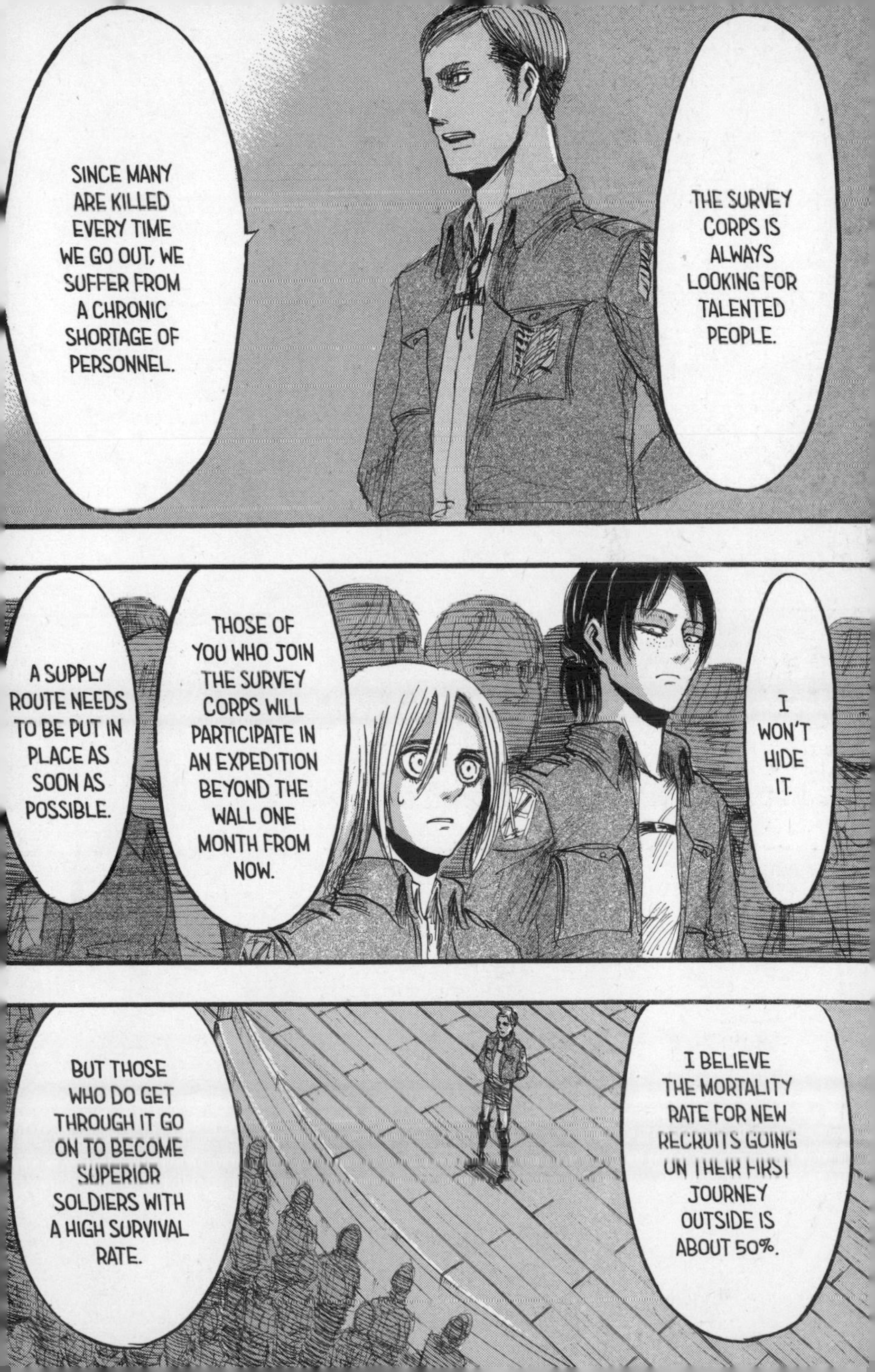
THE SURVEY CORPS IS ALWAYS LOOKING FOR TALENTED PEOPLE.
SINCE MANY ARE KILLED EVERY TIME WE GO OUT, WE SUFFER FROM A CHRONIC SHORTAGE OF PERSONNEL.
I WON'T HIDE IT.
THOSE OF YOU WHO JOIN THE SURVEY CORPS WILL PARTICIPATE IN AN EXPEDITION BEYOND THE WALL ONE MONTH FROM NOW.
A SUPPLY ROUTE NEEDS TO BE PUT IN PLACE AS SOON AS POSSIBLE.
I BELIEVE THE MORTALITY RATE FOR NEW RECRUITS GOING ON THEIR FIRST JOURNEY OUTSIDE IS ABOUT 50%.
BUT THOSE WHO DO GET THROUGH IT GO ON TO BECOME SUPERIOR SOLDIERS WITH A HIGH SURVIVAL RATE.

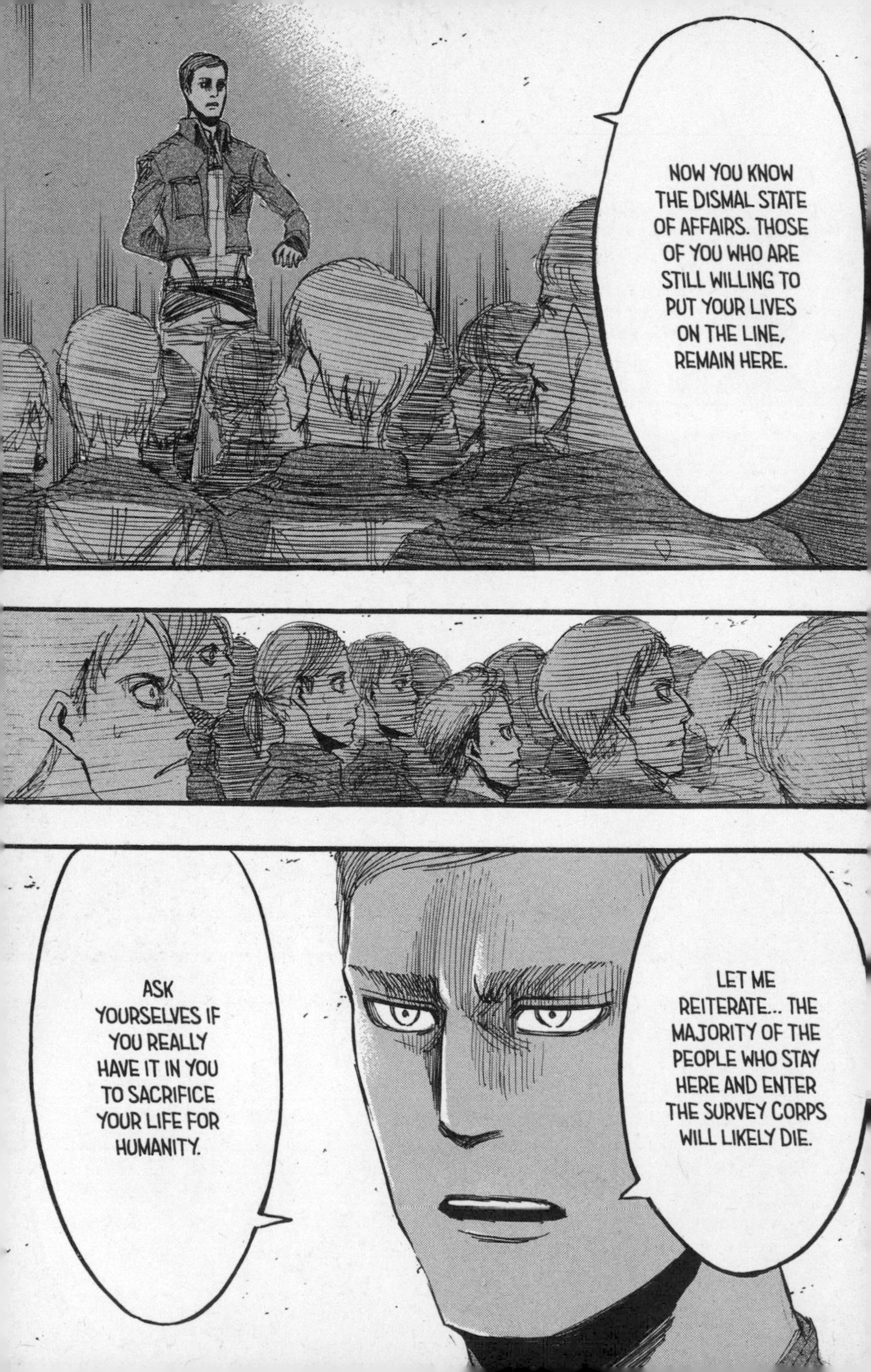
NOW YOU KNOW THE DISMAL STATE OF AFFAIRS. THOSE OF YOU WHO ARE STILL WILLING TO PUT YOUR LIVES ON THE LINE, REMAIN HERE.
LET ME REITERATE... THE MAJORITY OF THE PEOPLE WHO STAY HERE AND ENTER THE SURVEY CORPS WILL LIKELY DIE.
ASK YOURSELVES IF YOU REALLY HAVE IT IN YOU TO SACRIFICE YOUR LIFE FOR HUMANITY.

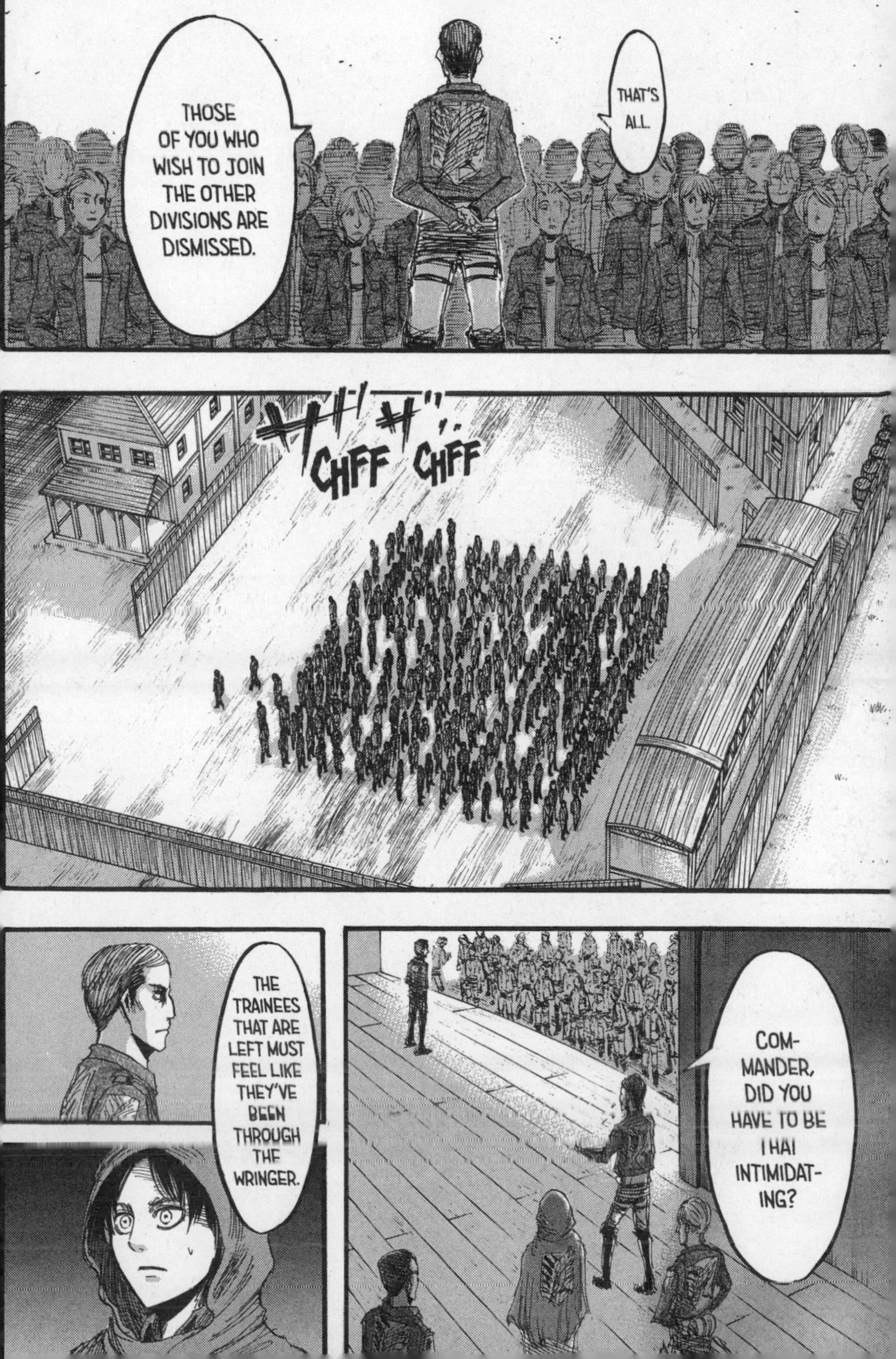
THAT'S ALL.
THOSE OF YOU WHO WISH TO JOIN THE OTHER DIVISIONS ARE DISMISSED.
CHFF CHFF
COM-MANDER, DID YOU HAVE TO BE THAT INTIMIDAT-ING?
THE TRAINEES THAT ARE LEFT MUST FEEL LIKE THEY'VE BEEN THROUGH THE WRINGER.

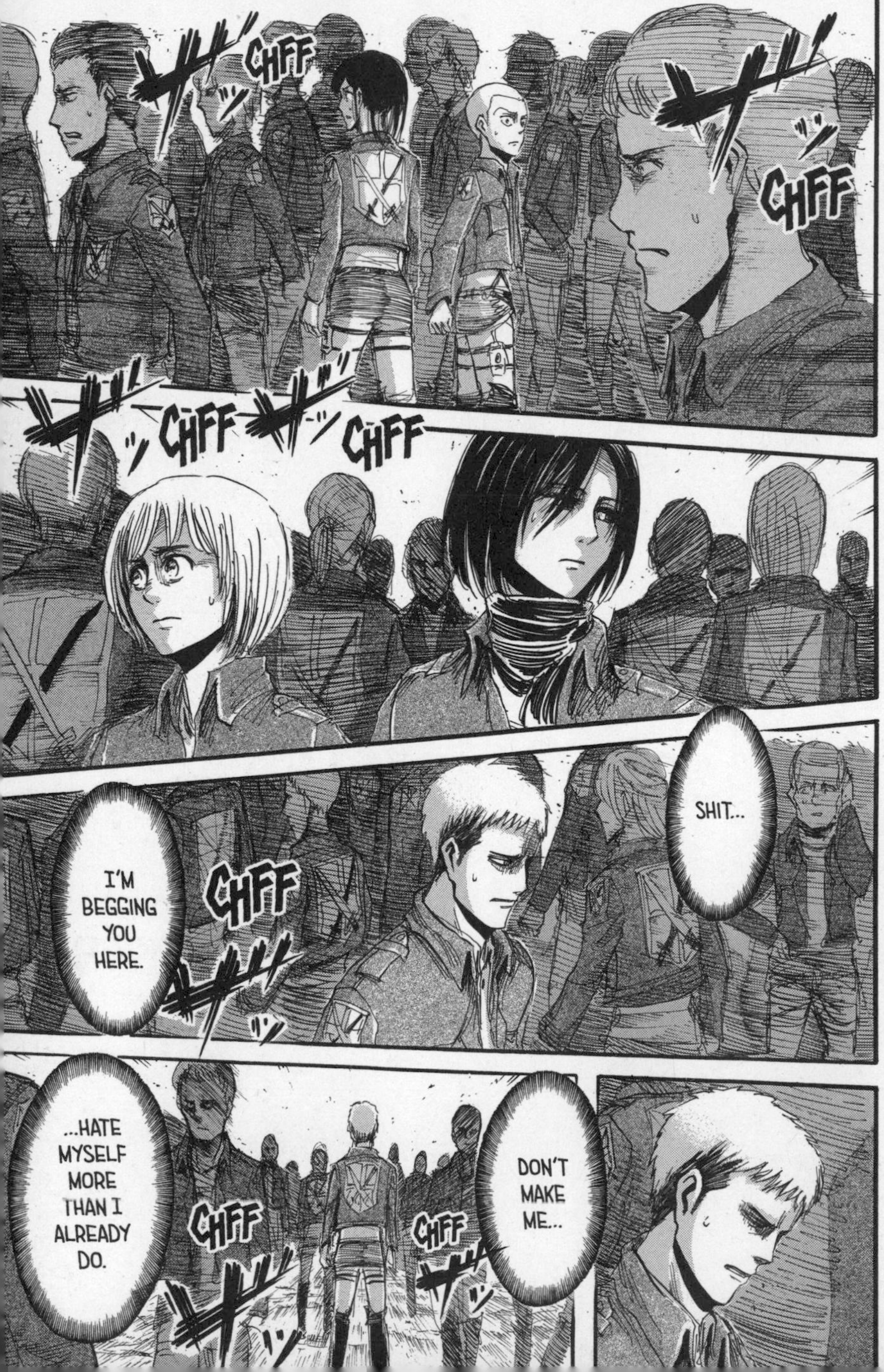
CHFF
CHFF
CHFF
CHFF
SHIT...
CHFF
I'M BEGGING YOU HERE.
DON'T MAKE ME...
CHFF
CHFF
...HATE MYSELF MORE THAN I ALREADY DO.

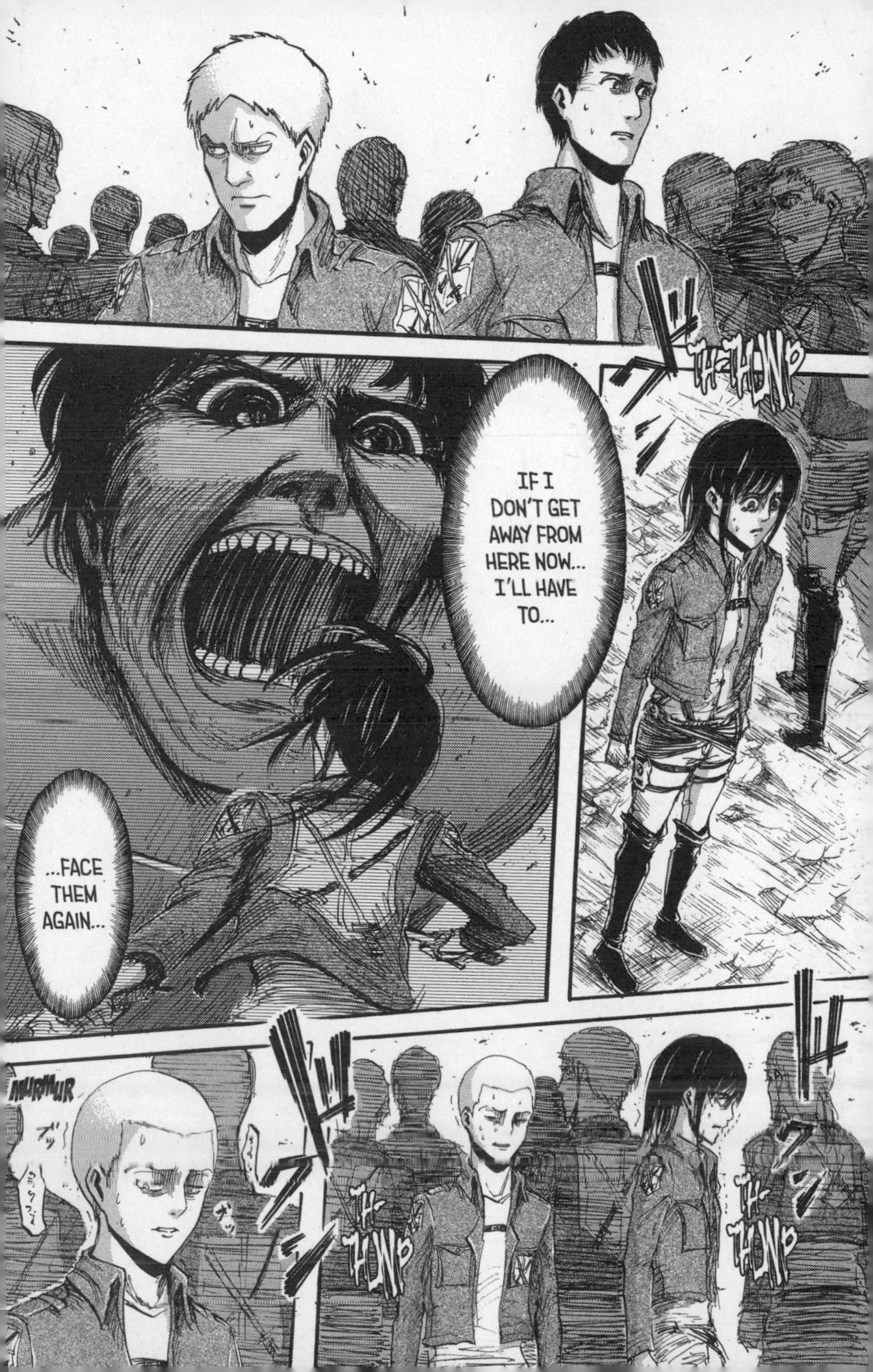
TH-THUMP
IF I DON'T GET AWAY FROM HERE NOW... I'LL HAVE TO...
...FACE THEM AGAIN...
TH-THUMP
TH-THUMP
MURMUR

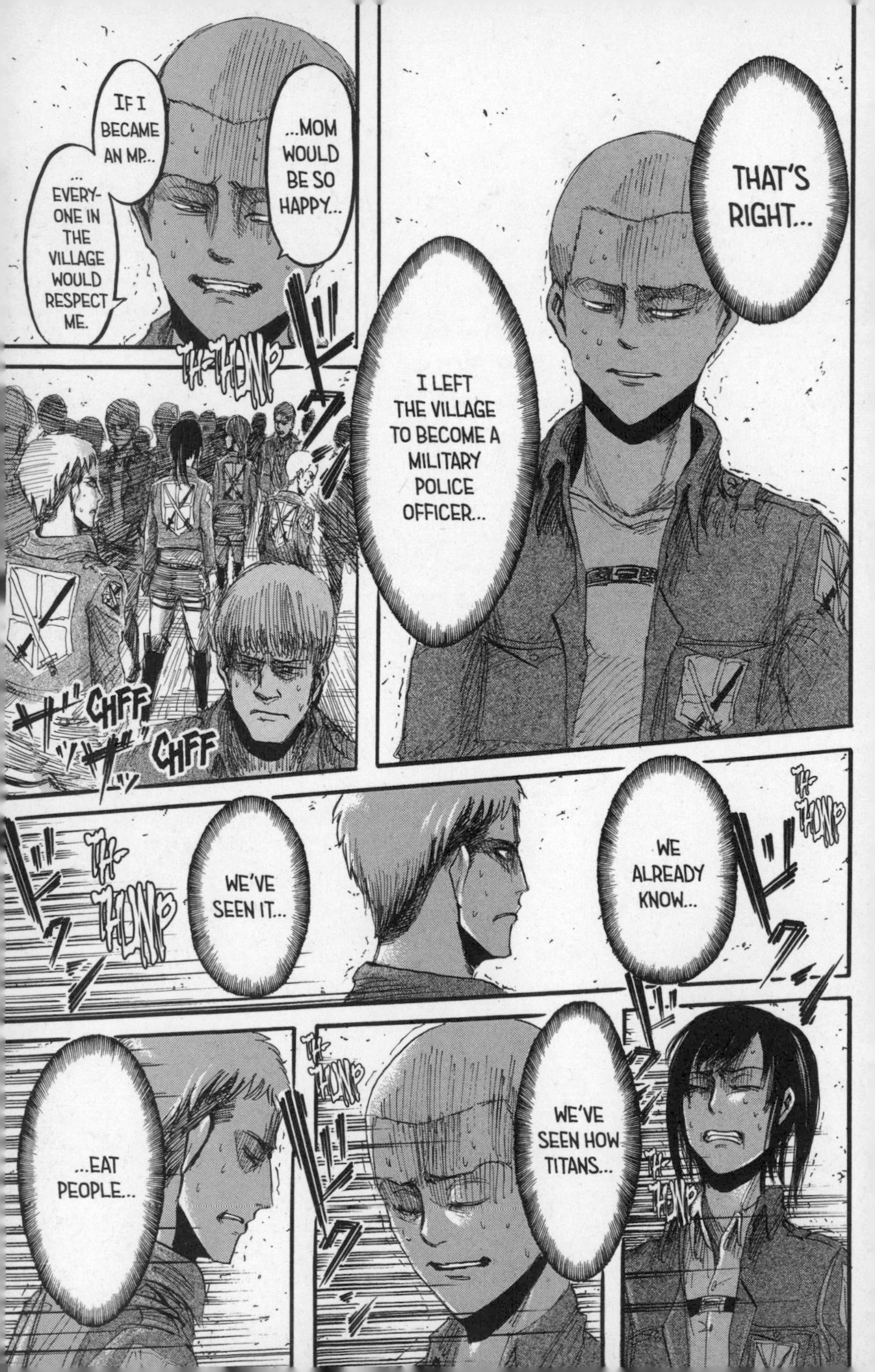
THAT'S RIGHT...
I LEFT THE VILLAGE TO BECOME A MILITARY POLICE OFFICER...
IF I BECAME AN MP...
...MOM WOULD BE SO HAPPY...
...EVERYONE IN THE VILLAGE WOULD RESPECT ME.
TH-THUMP
CHFF
CHFF
TH-THUMP
WE ALREADY KNOW...
TH-THUMP
WE'VE SEEN IT...
TH-THUMP
WE'VE SEEN HOW TITANS...
TH-THUMP
...EAT PEOPLE...

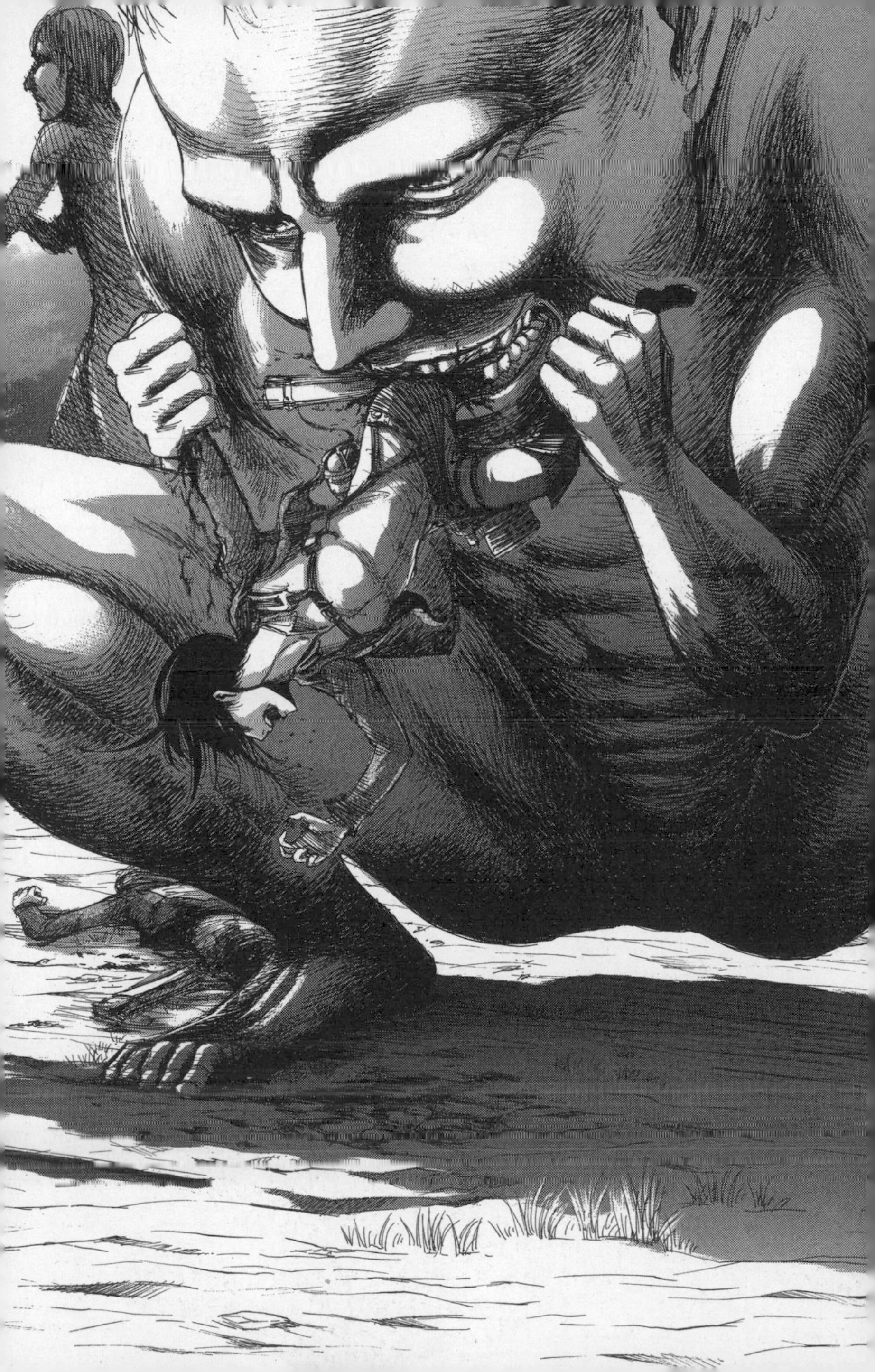

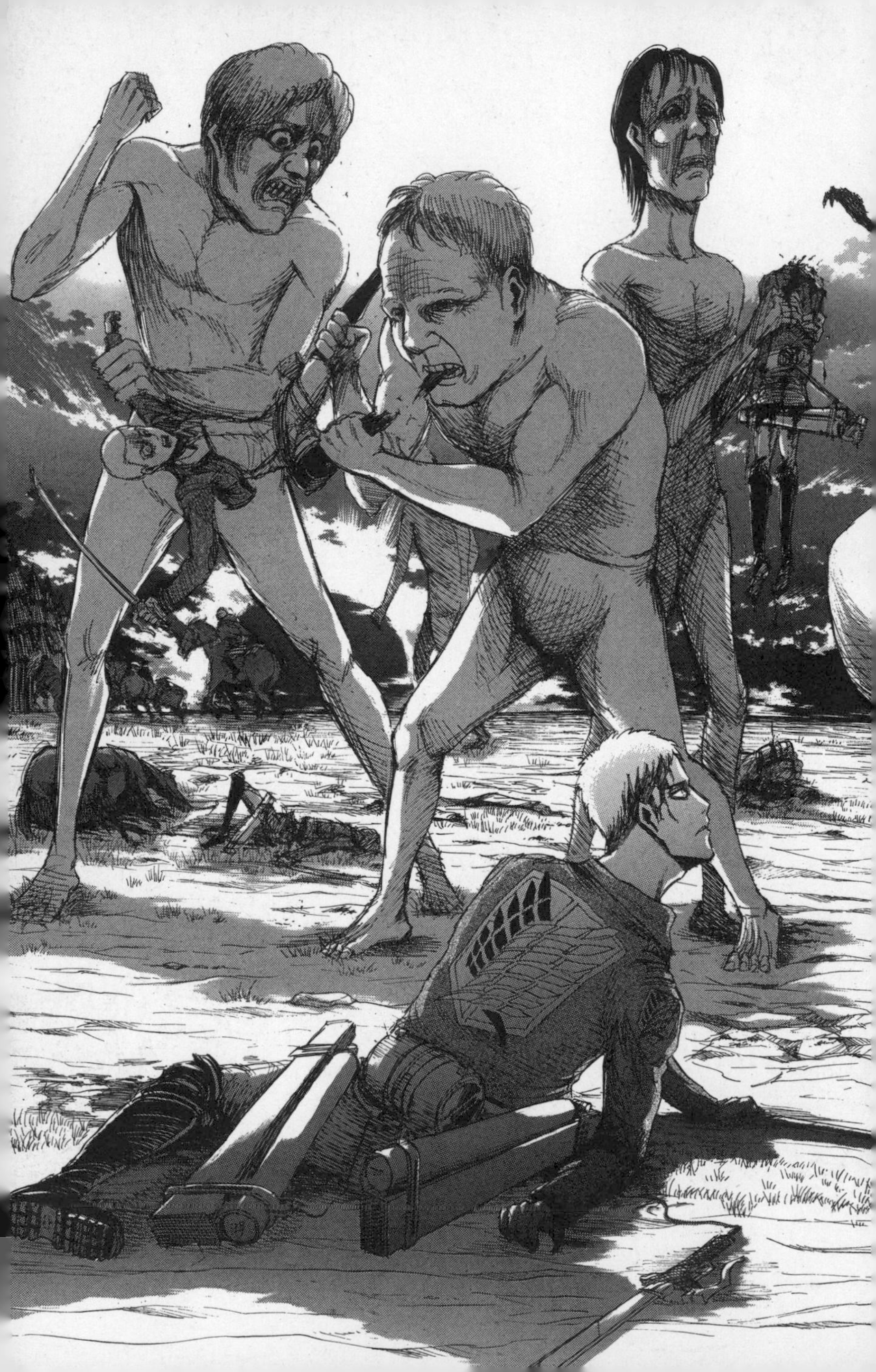

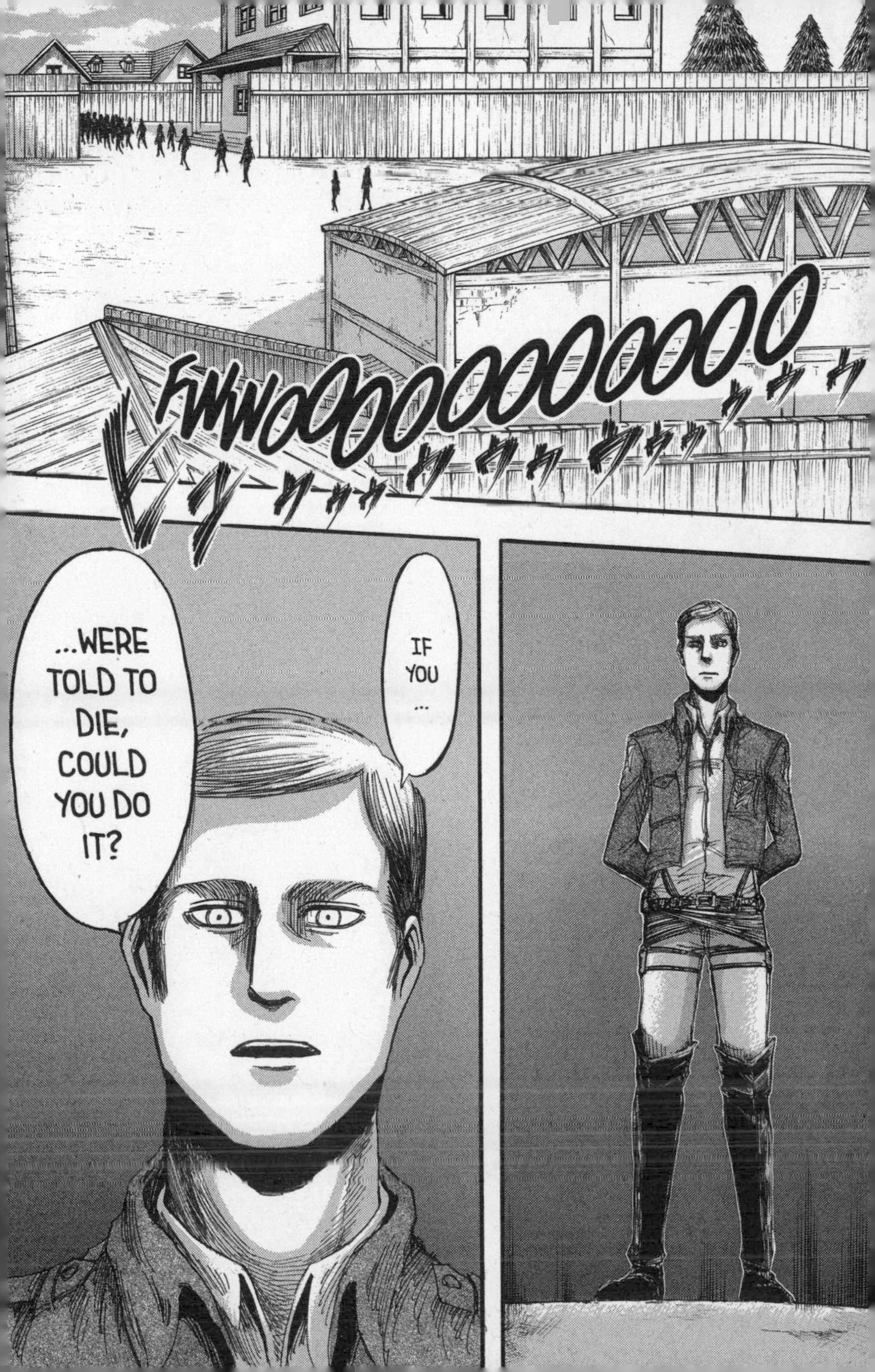
FWWOOOOOOOOOOOOOO
IF YOU ...
...WERE TOLD TO DIE, COULD YOU DO IT?

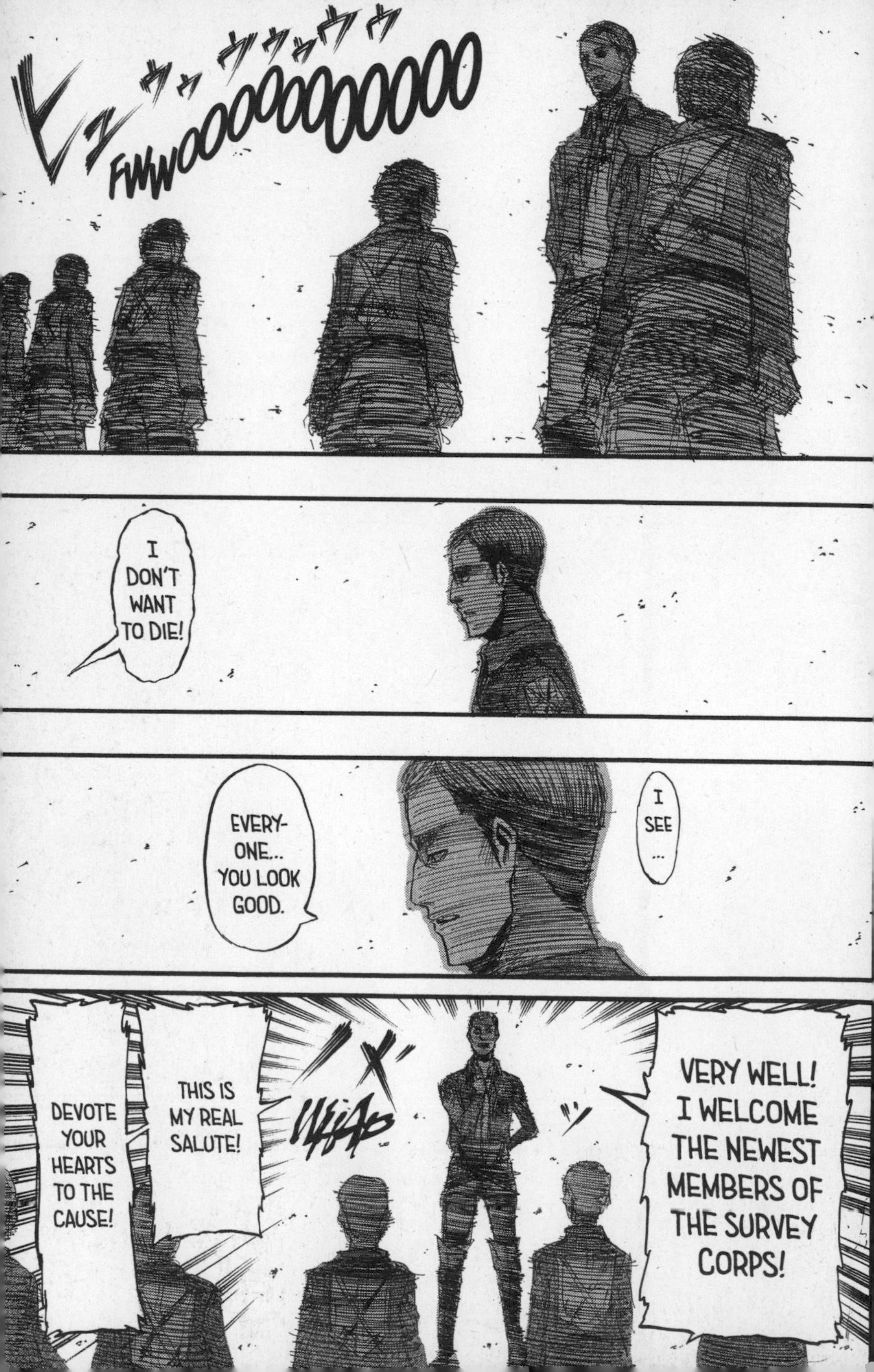
FWWOOOOOOOOOOO
I DON'T WANT TO DIE!
I SEE...
EVERYONE... YOU LOOK GOOD.
VERY WELL! I WELCOME THE NEWEST MEMBERS OF THE SURVEY CORPS!
THIS IS MY REAL SALUTE!
DEVOTE YOUR HEARTS TO THE CAUSE!

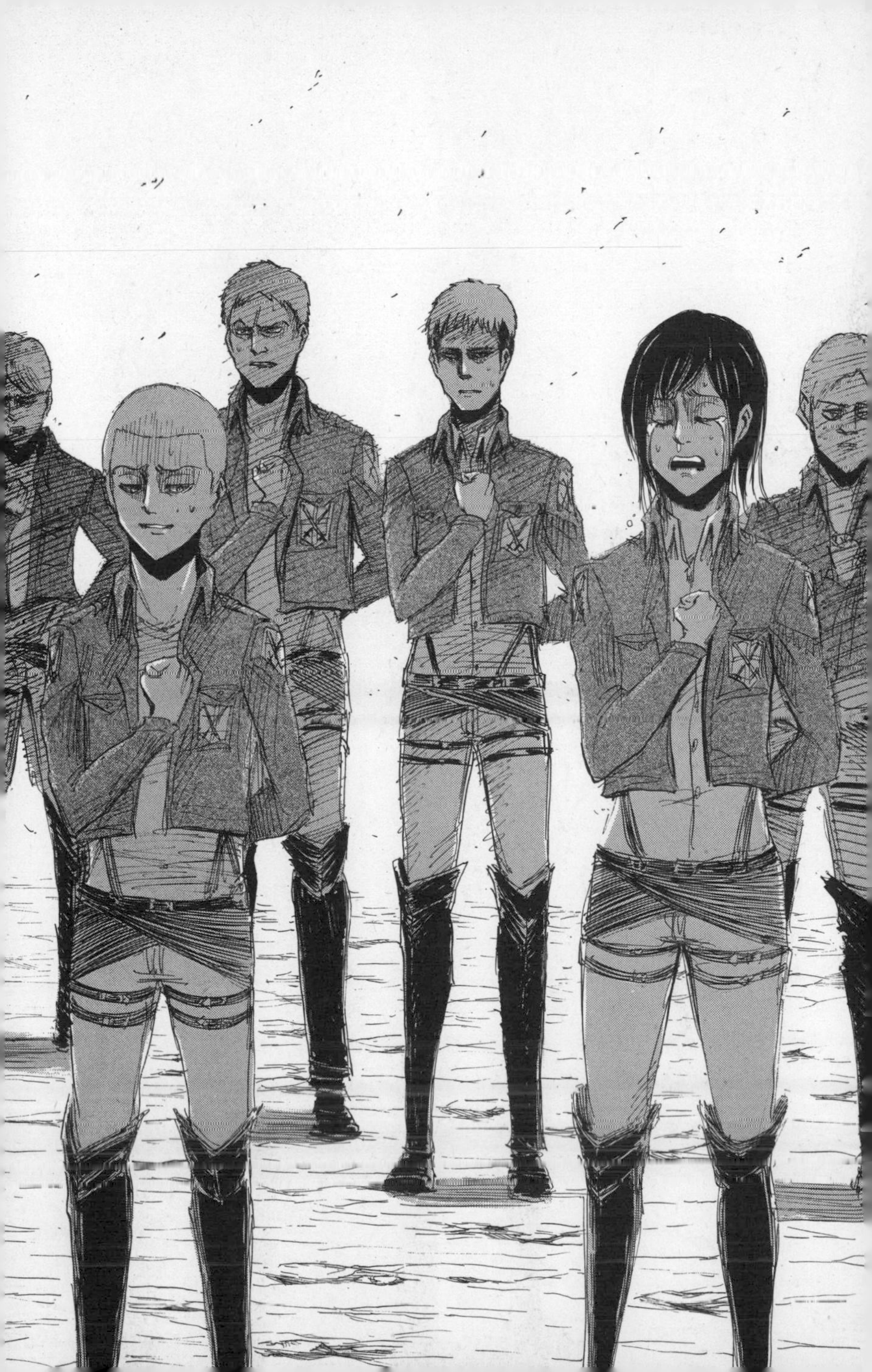

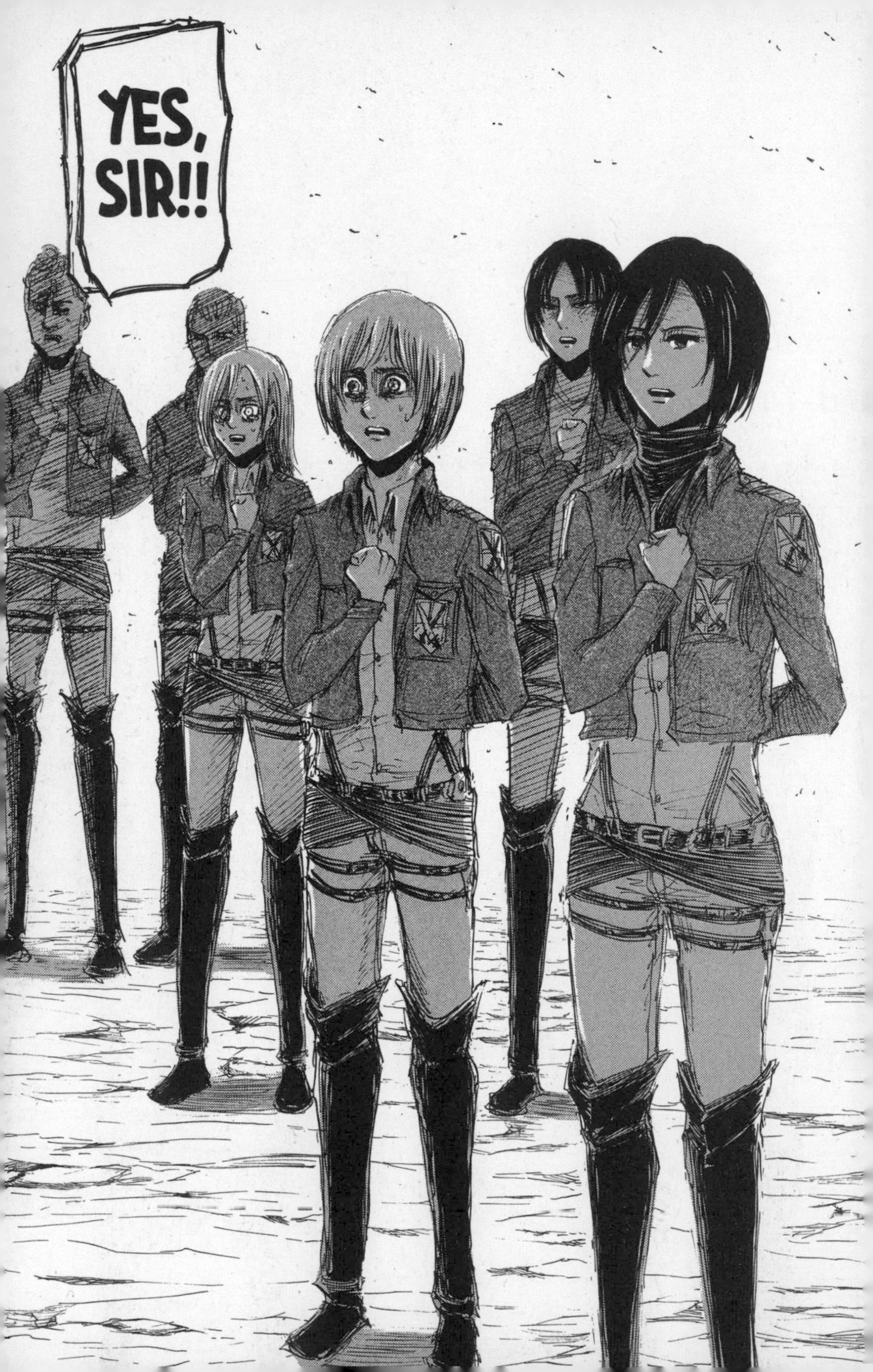
YES, SIR!!

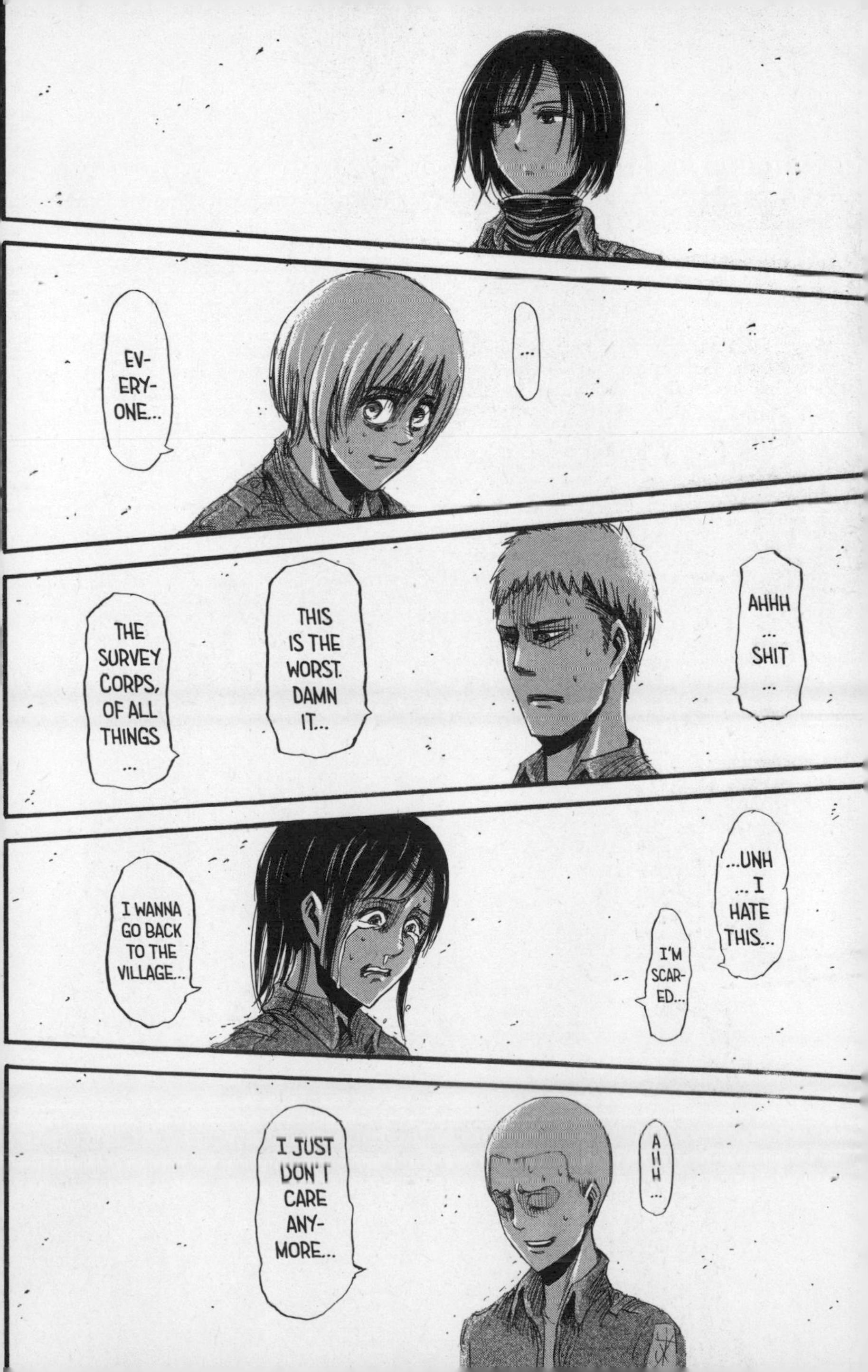
...
EV-ERY-ONE...
AHHH ... SHIT ...
THIS IS THE WORST. DAMN IT...
THE SURVEY CORPS, OF ALL THINGS ...
...UNH ... I HATE THIS...
I'M SCAR-ED...
I WANNA GO BACK TO THE VILLAGE...
A—H ...
I JUST DON'T CARE ANY-MORE...

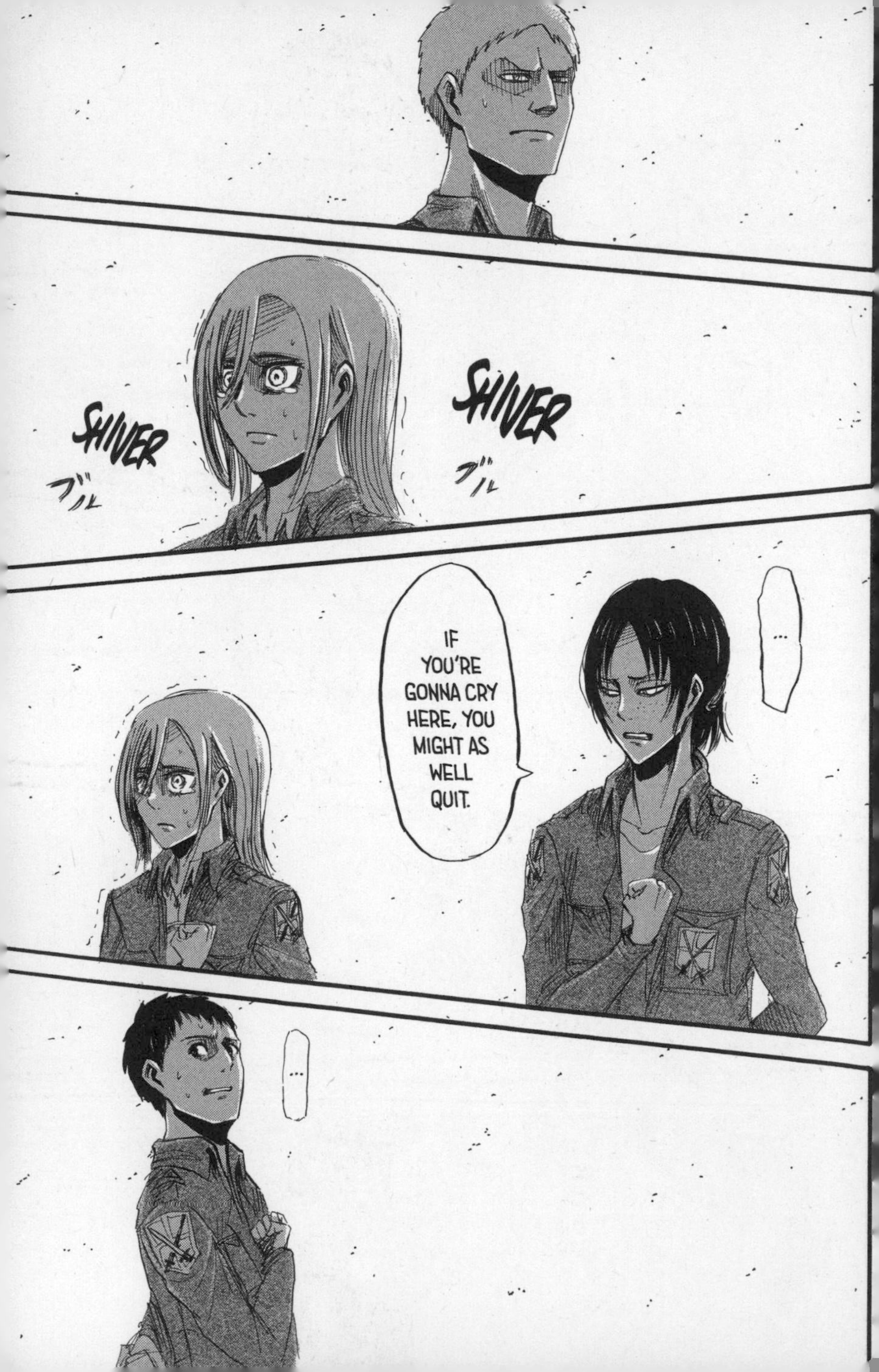
SHIVER
ブル
SHIVER
ブル
...
IF YOU'RE GONNA CRY HERE, YOU MIGHT AS WELL QUIT.
...

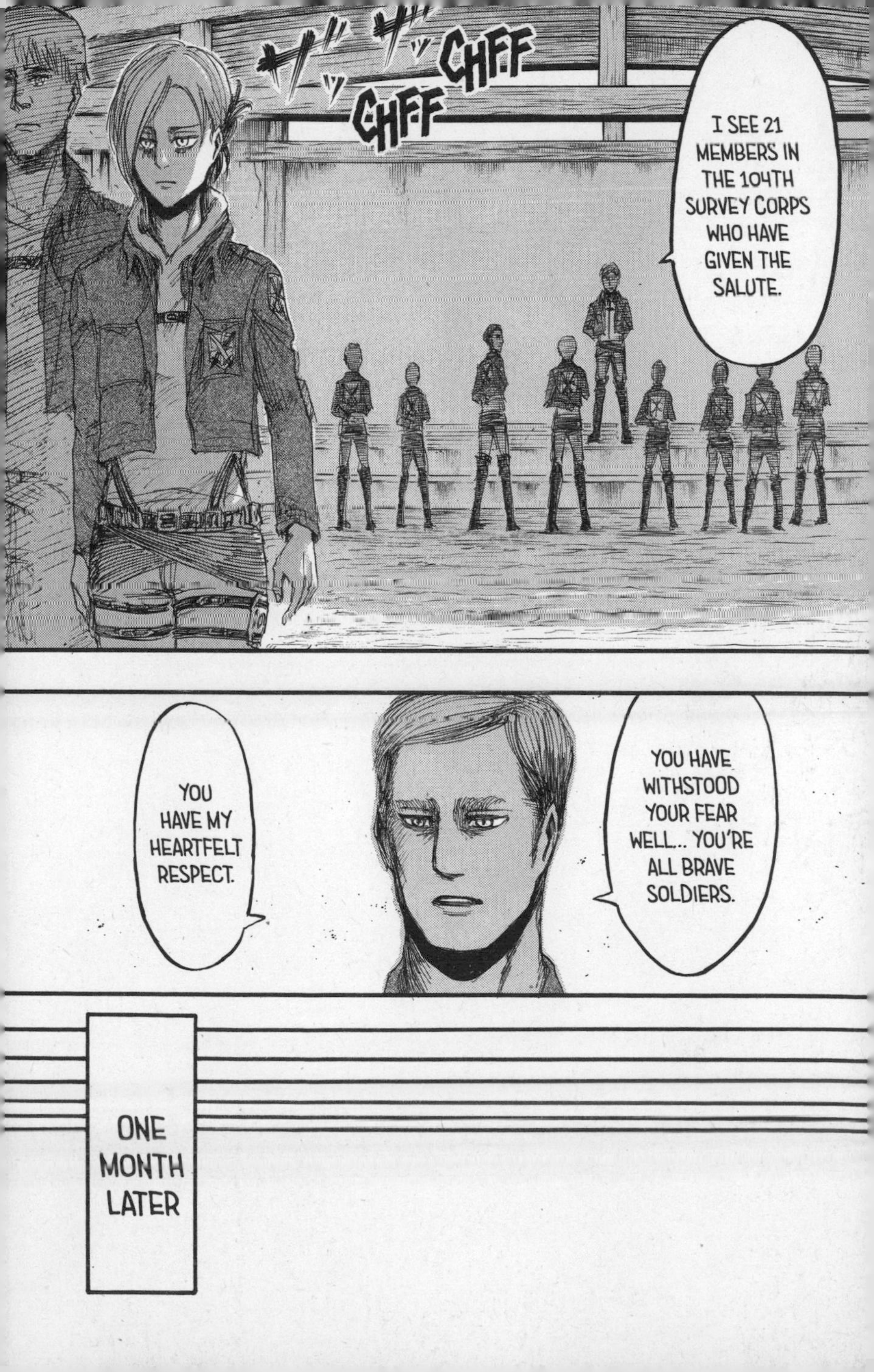
ザッ ザッ
CHFF CHFF
I SEE 21 MEMBERS IN THE 104TH SURVEY CORPS WHO HAVE GIVEN THE SALUTE.
YOU HAVE WITHSTOOD YOUR FEAR WELL... YOU'RE ALL BRAVE SOLDIERS.
YOU HAVE MY HEARTFELT RESPECT.
ONE MONTH LATER

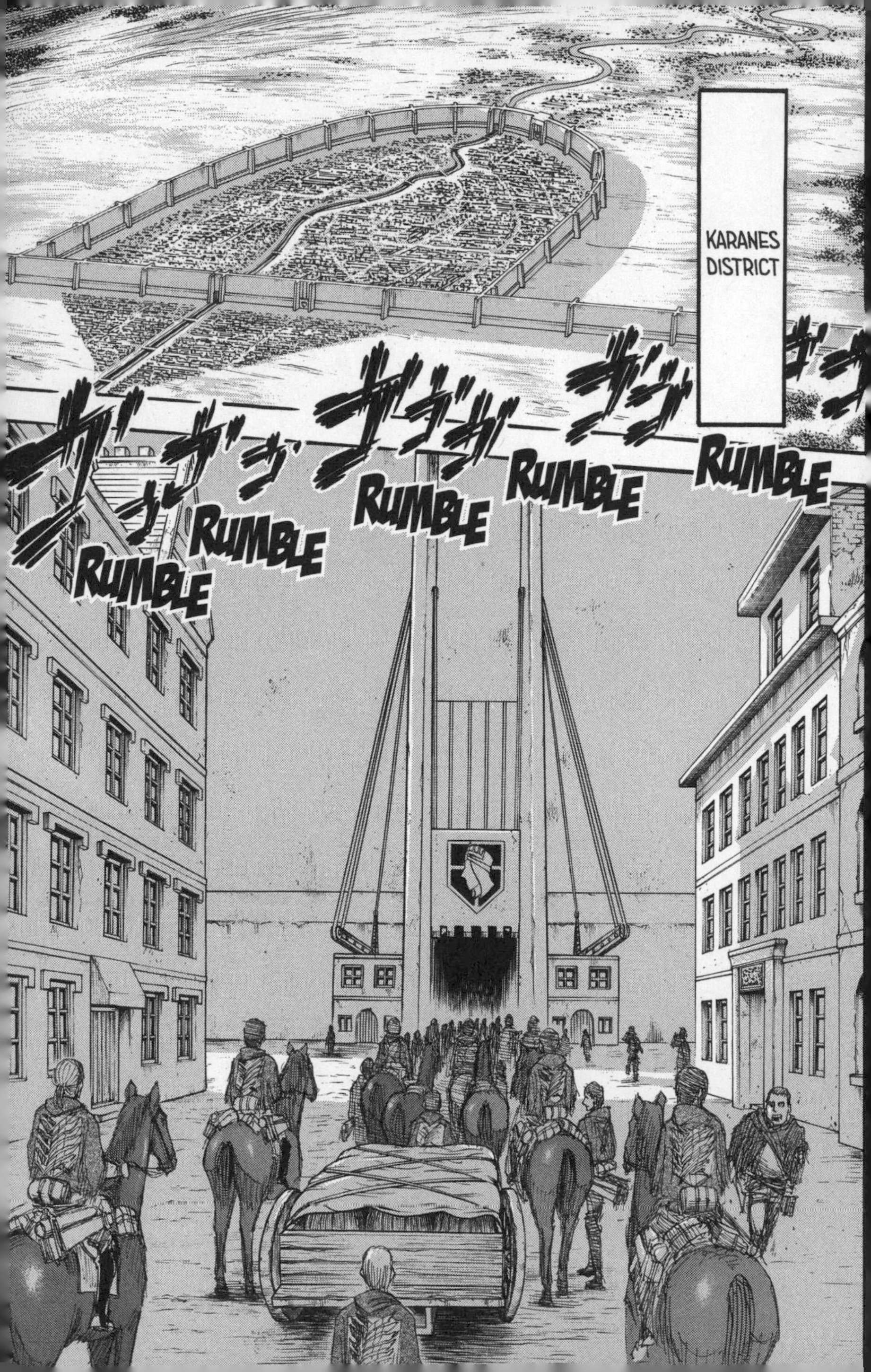
KARANES DISTRICT
RUMBLE
RUMBLE
RUMBLE
RUMBLE
RUMBLE

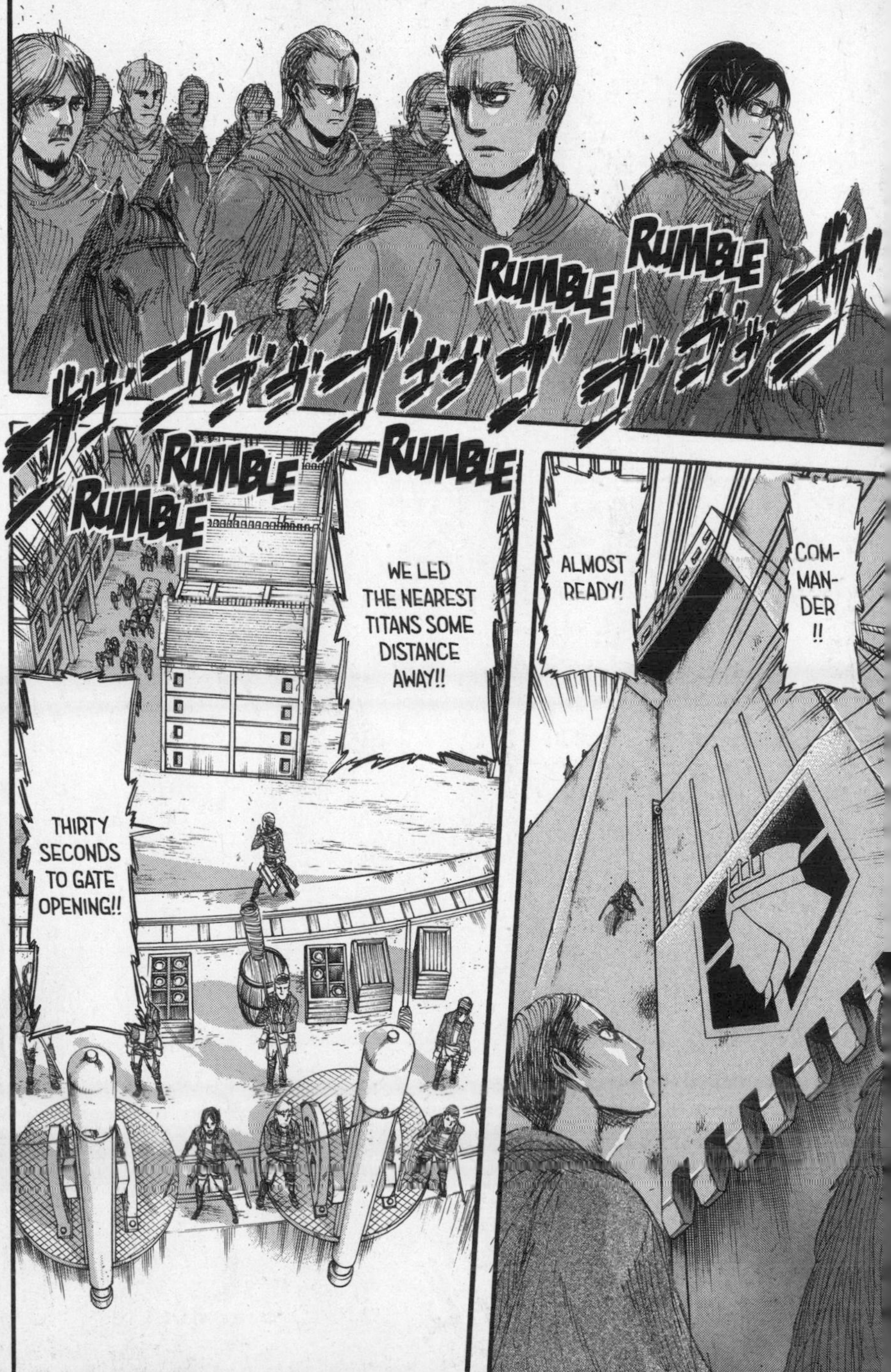
RUMBLE
RUMBLE
COM-MAN-DER !!
ALMOST READY!
RUMBLE
RUMBLE
RUMBLE
WE LED THE NEAREST TITANS SOME DISTANCE AWAY!!
THIRTY SECONDS TO GATE OPENING!!

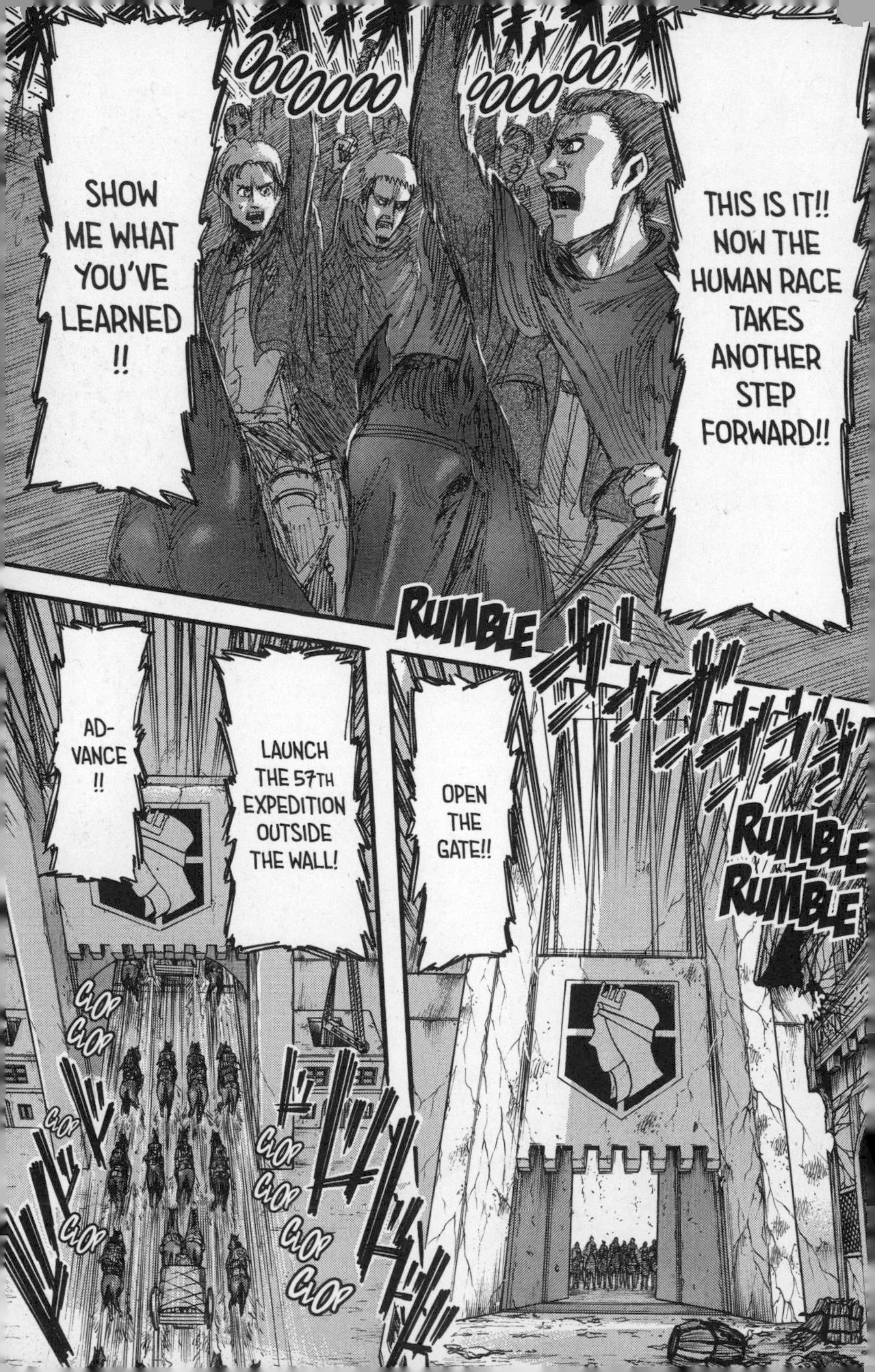
OOOOOO
OOOOOOO
THIS IS IT!! NOW THE HUMAN RACE TAKES ANOTHER STEP FORWARD!!
SHOW ME WHAT YOU'VE LEARNED !!
RUMBLE
OPEN THE GATE!!
RUMBLE RUMBLE
LAUNCH THE 57TH EXPEDITION OUTSIDE THE WALL!
AD-VANCE !!
CLOP CLOP
CLOP CLOP
CLOP CLOP
CLOP CLOP
CLOP

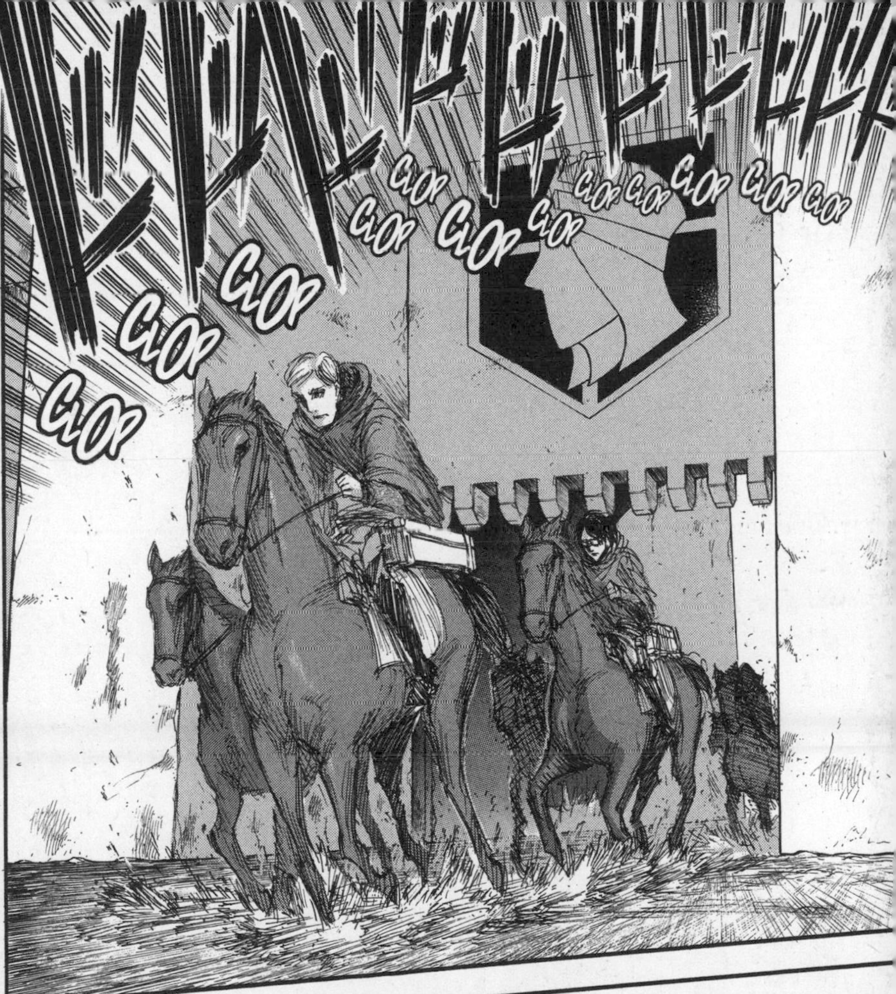
CLOP
CLOP
CLOP
CLOP
CLOP
CLOP
CLOP
CLOP
CLOP
CLOP
CLOP
CLOP

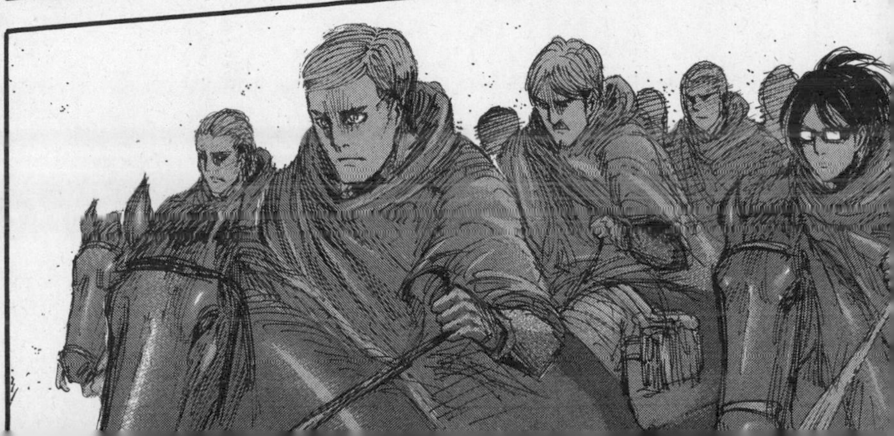

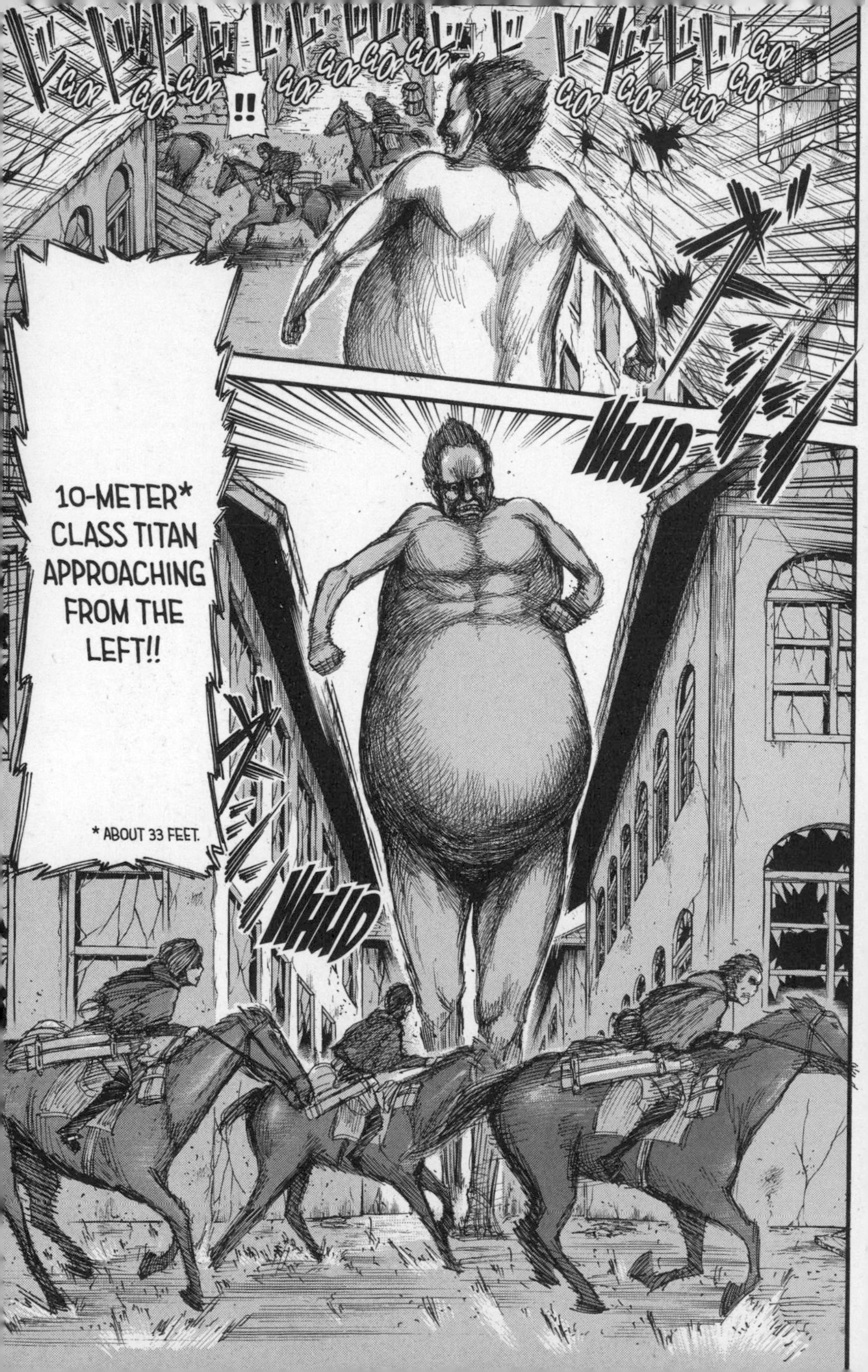
CLOP CLOP CLOP CLOP CLOP CLOP CLOP CLOP CLOP CLOP CLOP CLOP CLOP
!!
WHUD
10-METER* CLASS TITAN APPROACHING FROM THE LEFT!!
* ABOUT 33 FEET.
WHUD

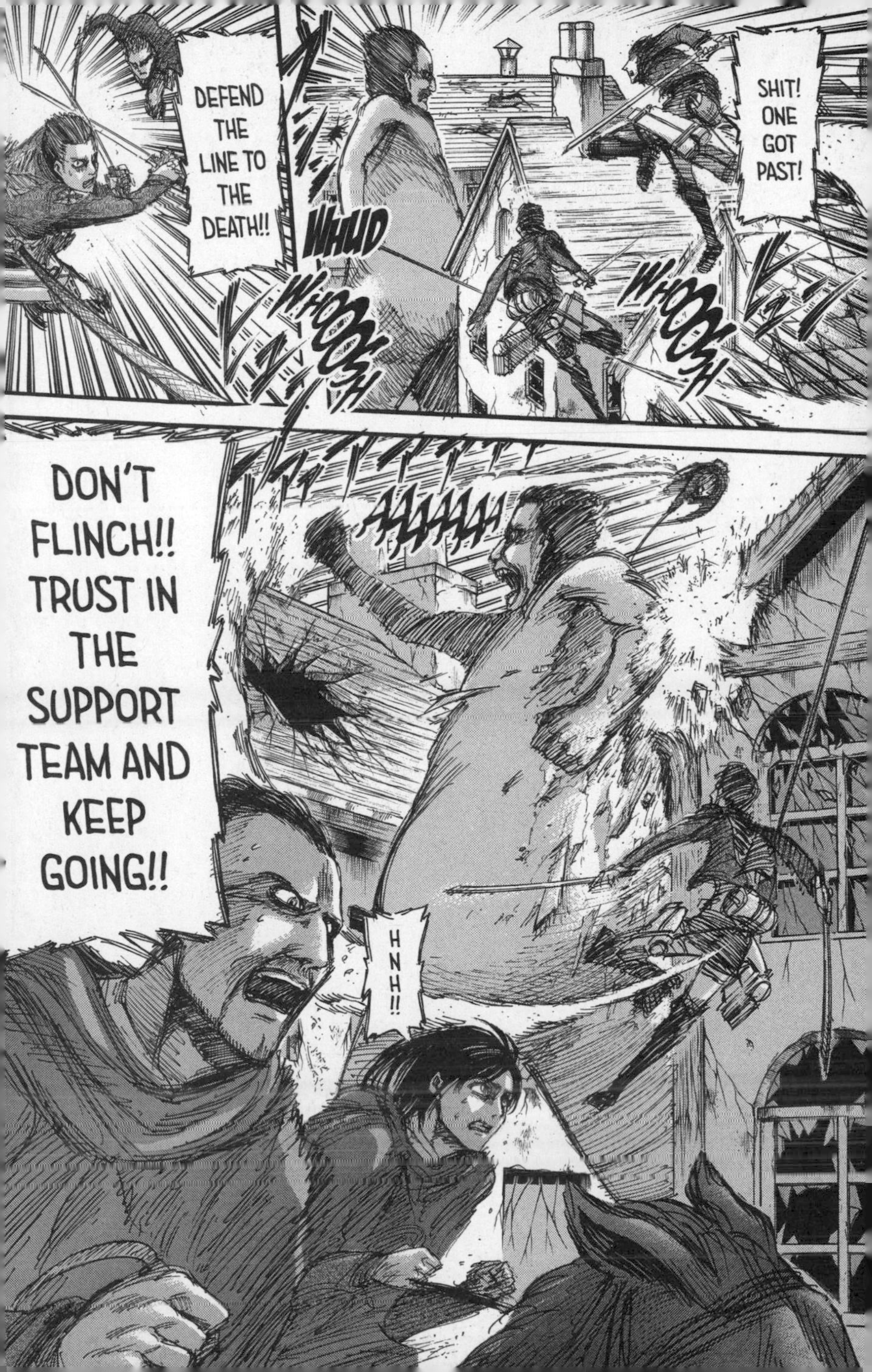

SHIT! ONE GOT PAST!
WHOOOSH
WHUD
WHOOOSH
DEFEND THE LINE TO THE DEATH!!
AAAAAAH
DON'T FLINCH!! TRUST IN THE SUPPORT TEAM AND KEEP GOING!!
HNH!!

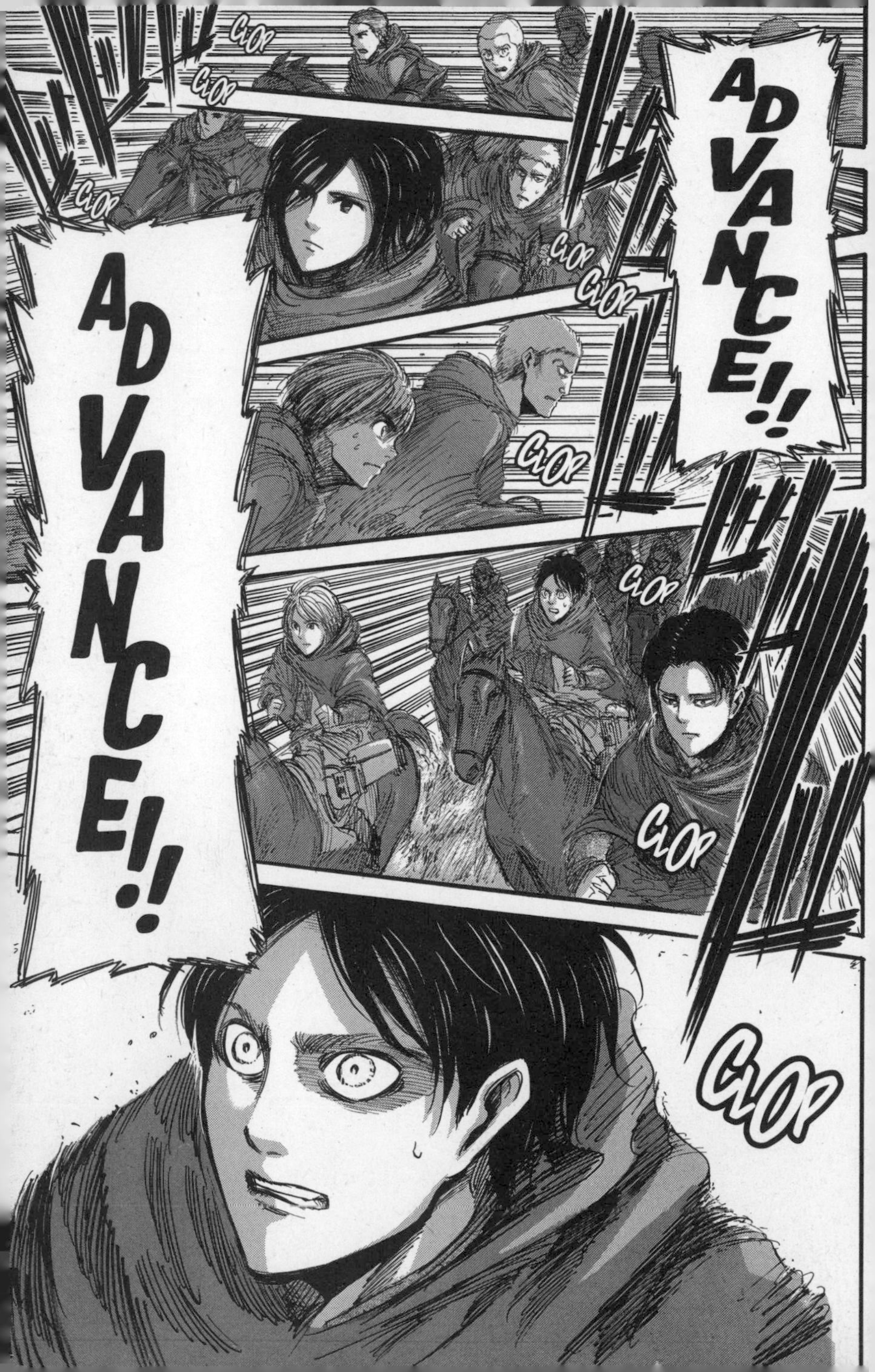
ADVANCE!!
CLOP
CLOP
CLOP
ADVANCE!!
CLOP
CLOP
CLOP
CLOP
CLOP
CLOP

10. Survey Corps Horses

THE STABLE HORSES USED BY THE SURVEY CORPS ARE SELECTIVELY BRED TO BE APPROXIMATELY 160 CM (5 FEET 3 INCHES) TALL AND 450-500 KG (990-1,100 LBS). THEY CAN GET BY ON A SIMPLE DIET AND TRAVEL FOR MANY HOURS WITHOUT COMPLAINING. THESE HORSES HAVE A MILD TEMPERAMENT AND RARELY PANIC, EVEN WHEN CONFRONTED WITH TITANS. THEIR TOP SPEED IS BETWEEN 75-80 KPH (46-50 MPH), AND THEY CAN MAINTAIN A SWIFT 35 KPH (22 MPH) GALLOP. THE HORSES ARE TENACIOUS, ABLE TO MAINTAIN A FINE SPEED OF 20 KPH (12 MPH) EVEN WHEN PULLING A CARRIAGE. THEY AREN'T THE TITANS' DIRECT GOAL AND ARE ABLE TO OUTRUN THE TITANS ON FOOT, MAKING THEM THE ONLY METHOD OF ESCAPE. THESE HORSES ARE EXTREMELY VALUABLE. IN MONETARY TERMS, ONE IS WORTH AN AVERAGE PERSON'S LIFETIME INCOME. (WITH THANKS TO UKYŌ KODACHI AND KIYOMUNE MIWA)

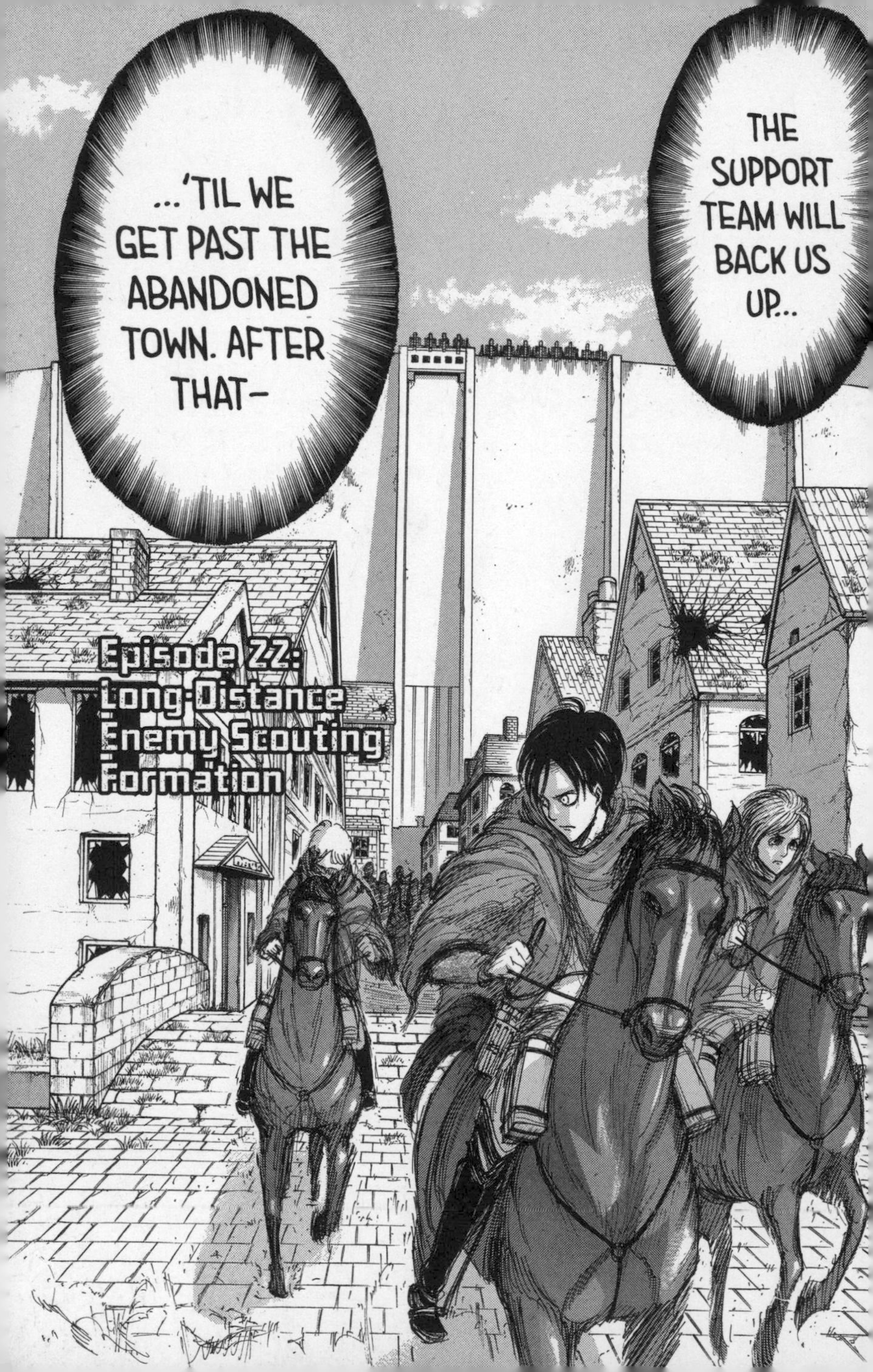
THE SUPPORT TEAM WILL BACK US UP...
...'TIL WE GET PAST THE ABANDONED TOWN. AFTER THAT–
Episode 22: Long-Distance Enemy Scouting Formation

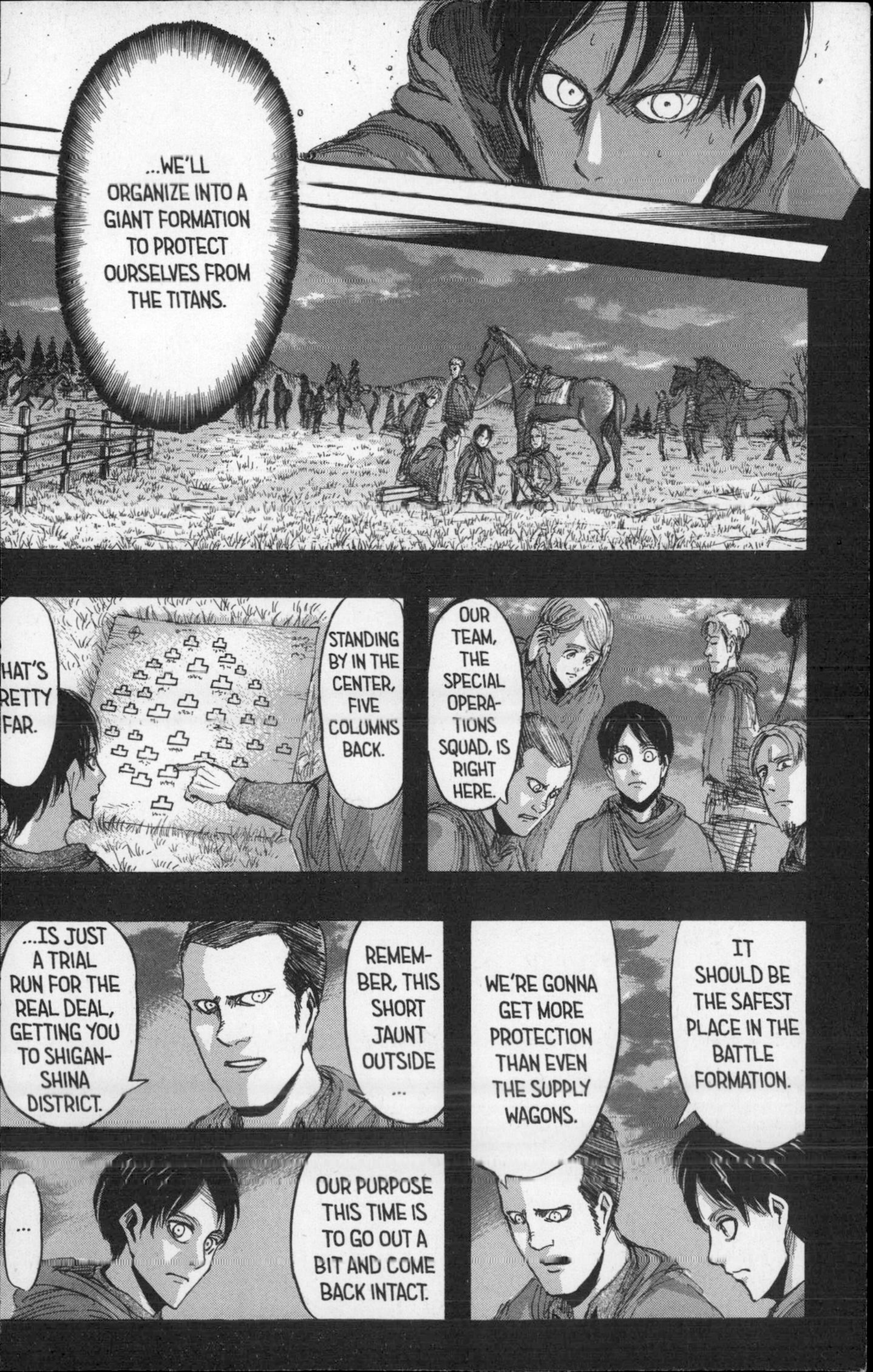
...WE'LL ORGANIZE INTO A GIANT FORMATION TO PROTECT OURSELVES FROM THE TITANS.
OUR TEAM, THE SPECIAL OPERA-TIONS SQUAD, IS RIGHT HERE.
STANDING BY IN THE CENTER, FIVE COLUMNS BACK.
HAT'S RETTY FAR.
IT SHOULD BE THE SAFEST PLACE IN THE BATTLE FORMATION.
WE'RE GONNA GET MORE PROTECTION THAN EVEN THE SUPPLY WAGONS.
REMEM-BER, THIS SHORT JAUNT OUTSIDE ...
...IS JUST A TRIAL RUN FOR THE REAL DEAL, GETTING YOU TO SHIGAN-SHINA DISTRICT.
OUR PURPOSE THIS TIME IS TO GO OUT A BIT AND COME BACK INTACT.
...

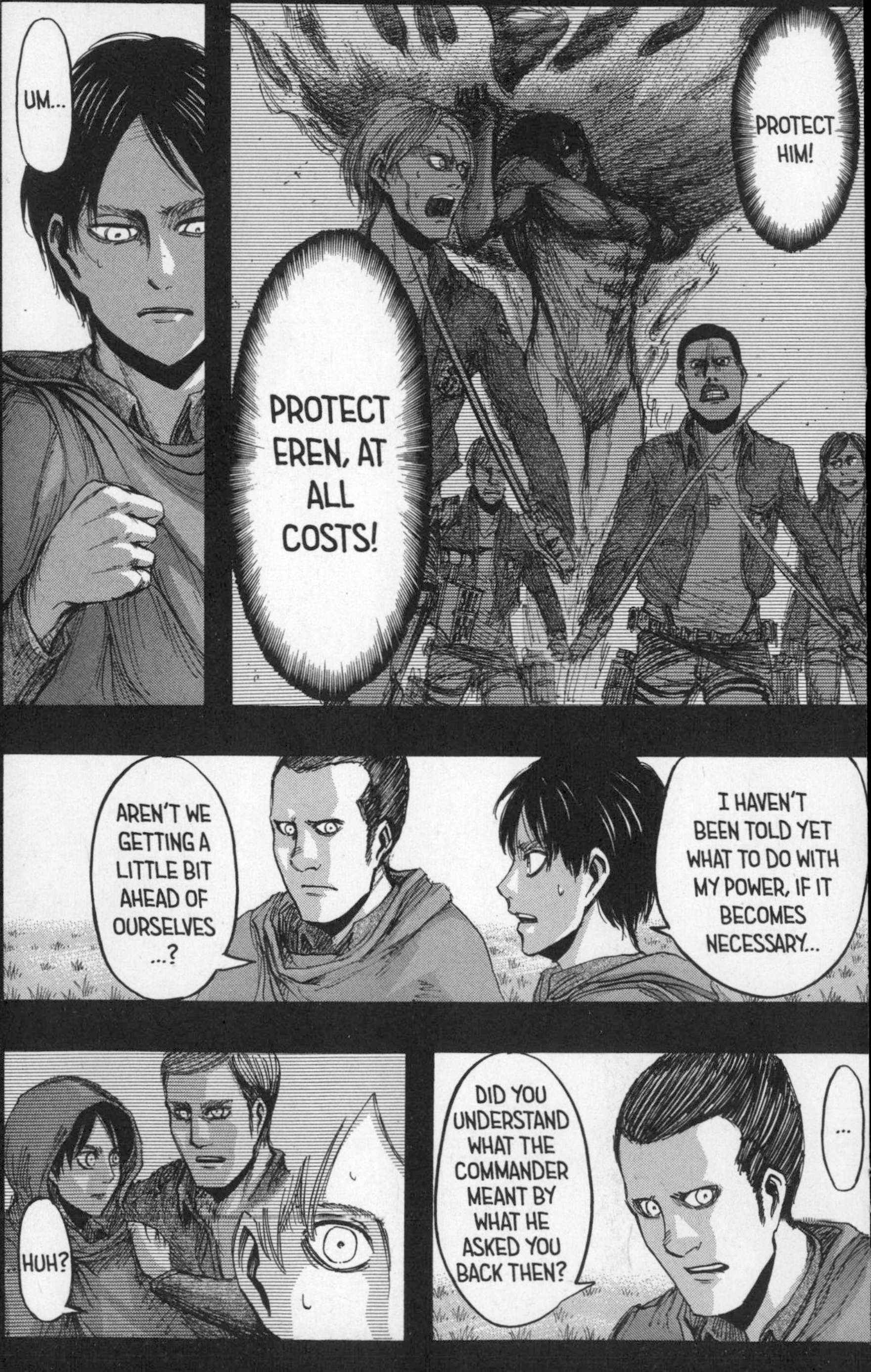
PROTECT HIM!
PROTECT EREN, AT ALL COSTS!
UM...
I HAVEN'T BEEN TOLD YET WHAT TO DO WITH MY POWER, IF IT BECOMES NECESSARY...
AREN'T WE GETTING A LITTLE BIT AHEAD OF OURSELVES ...?
...
DID YOU UNDERSTAND WHAT THE COMMANDER MEANT BY WHAT HE ASKED YOU BACK THEN?
HUH?

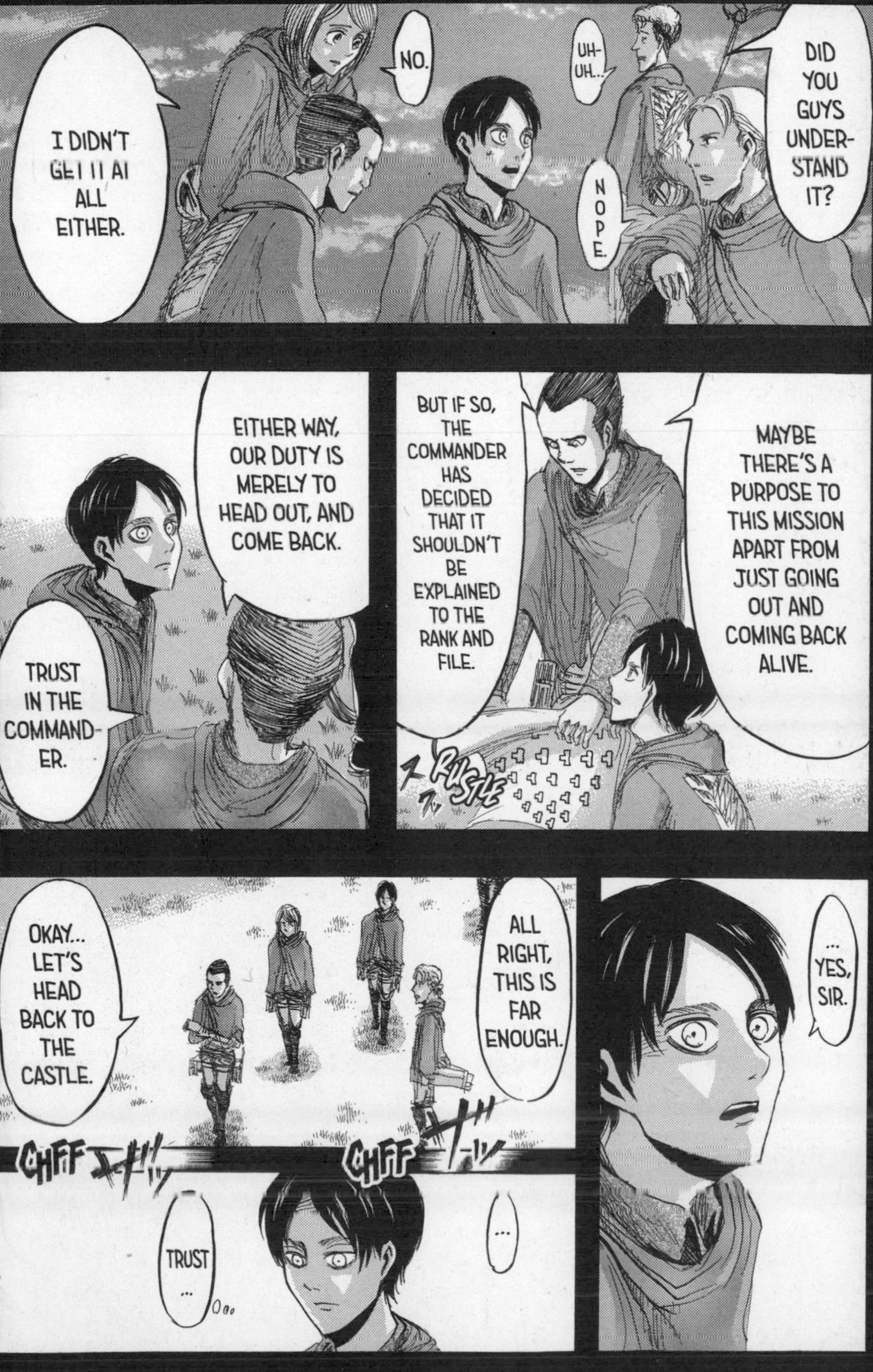

DID YOU GUYS UNDER-STAND IT?
NOPE.
UH-UH...
NO.
I DIDN'T GET IT AT ALL EITHER.
MAYBE THERE'S A PURPOSE TO THIS MISSION APART FROM JUST GOING OUT AND COMING BACK ALIVE.
BUT IF SO, THE COMMANDER HAS DECIDED THAT IT SHOULDN'T BE EXPLAINED TO THE RANK AND FILE.
RUSTLE
EITHER WAY, OUR DUTY IS MERELY TO HEAD OUT, AND COME BACK.
TRUST IN THE COMMAND-ER.
... YES, SIR.
ALL RIGHT, THIS IS FAR ENOUGH.
OKAY... LET'S HEAD BACK TO THE CASTLE.
CHFF
CHFF
...
TRUST ...

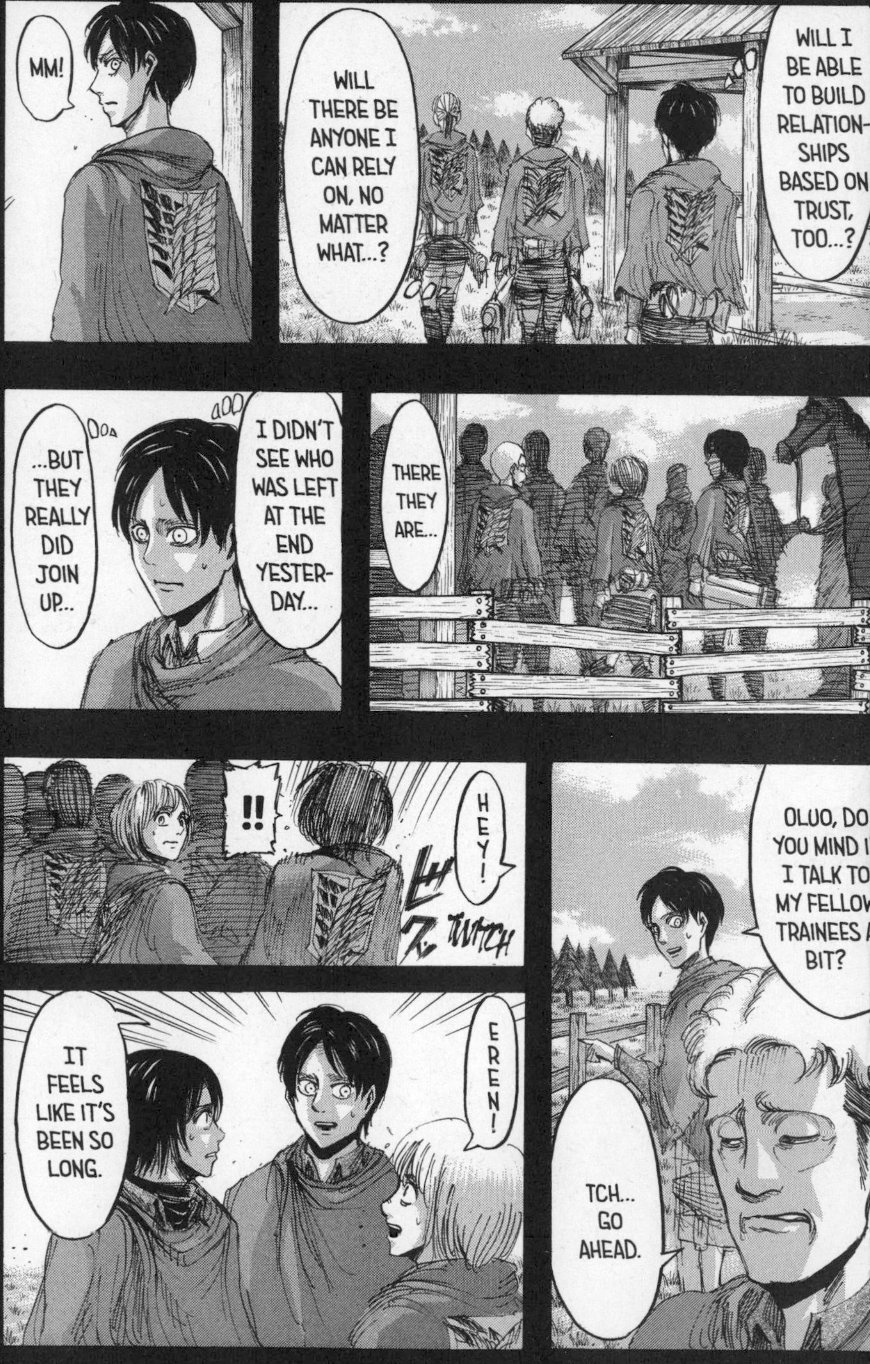
WILL I BE ABLE TO BUILD RELATION-SHIPS BASED ON TRUST, TOO...?
WILL THERE BE ANYONE I CAN RELY ON, NO MATTER WHAT...?
MM!
THERE THEY ARE...
I DIDN'T SEE WHO WAS LEFT AT THE END YESTER-DAY...
...BUT THEY REALLY DID JOIN UP...
OLUO, DO YOU MIND I I TALK TO MY FELLOW TRAINEES A BIT?
TCH... GO AHEAD.
HEY!
!!
TWITCH
EREN!
IT FEELS LIKE IT'S BEEN SO LONG.

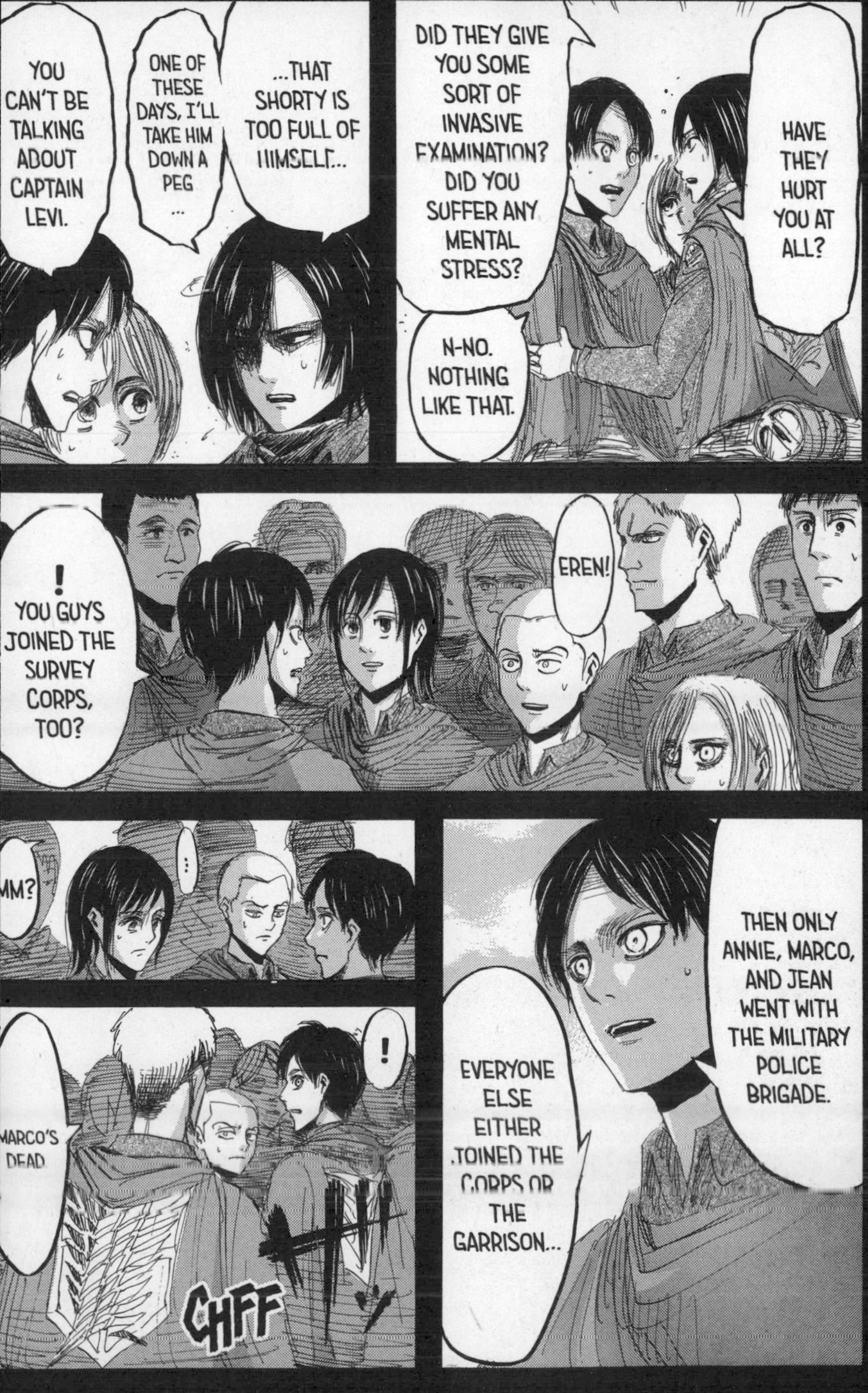

HAVE THEY HURT YOU AT ALL?
DID THEY GIVE YOU SOME SORT OF INVASIVE EXAMINATION? DID YOU SUFFER ANY MENTAL STRESS?
N-NO. NOTHING LIKE THAT.
...THAT SHORTY IS TOO FULL OF HIMSELF...
ONE OF THESE DAYS, I'LL TAKE HIM DOWN A PEG ...
YOU CAN'T BE TALKING ABOUT CAPTAIN LEVI.
EREN!
! YOU GUYS JOINED THE SURVEY CORPS, TOO?
THEN ONLY ANNIE, MARCO, AND JEAN WENT WITH THE MILITARY POLICE BRIGADE.
EVERYONE ELSE EITHER JOINED THE CORPS OR THE GARRISON...
...
MM?
!
MARCO'S DEAD.
CHFF

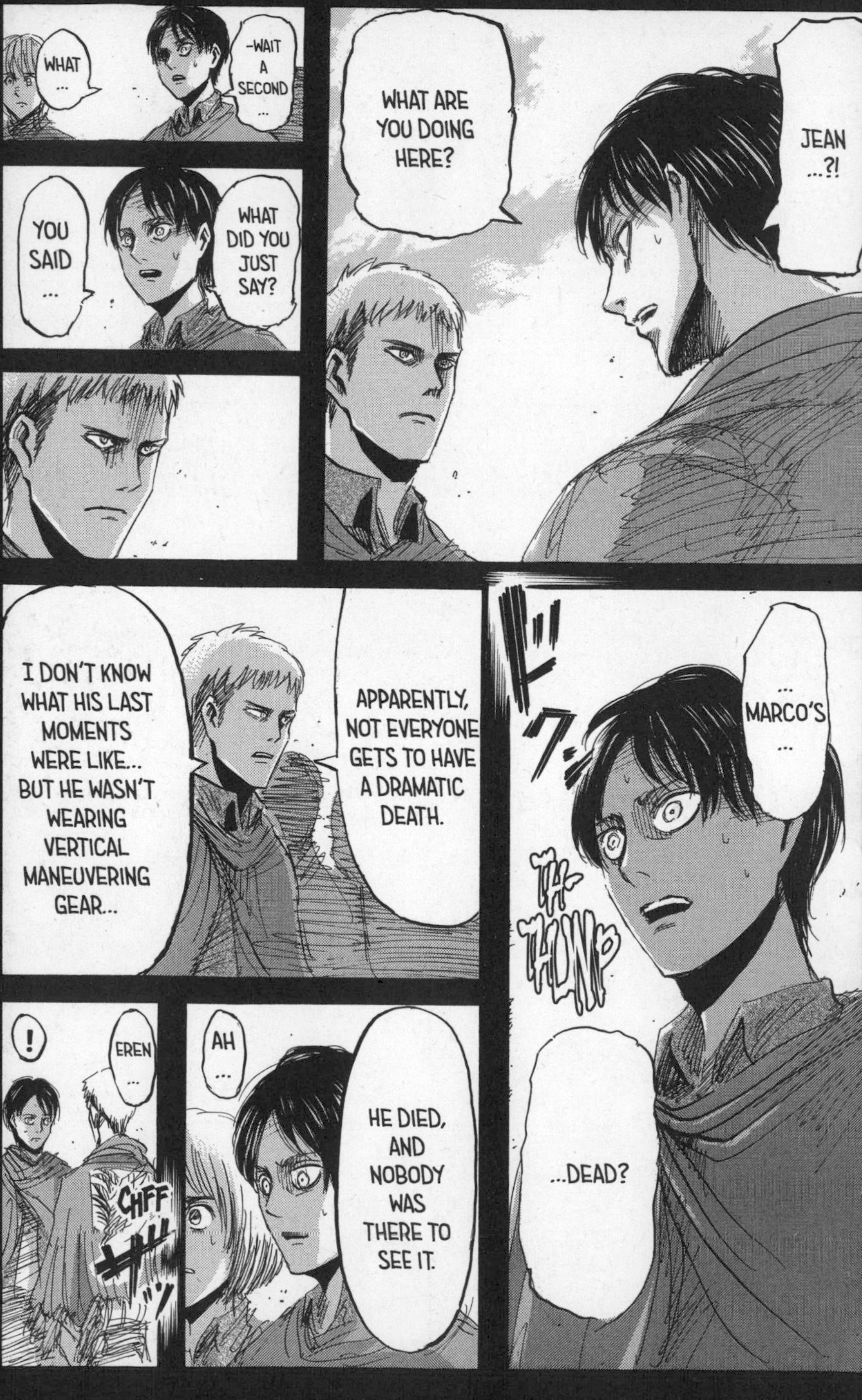
JEAN ...?!
WHAT ARE YOU DOING HERE?
-WAIT A SECOND ...
WHAT ...
WHAT DID YOU JUST SAY?
YOU SAID ...
... MARCO'S ...
THA THUMP
...DEAD?
APPARENTLY, NOT EVERYONE GETS TO HAVE A DRAMATIC DEATH.
I DON'T KNOW WHAT HIS LAST MOMENTS WERE LIKE... BUT HE WASN'T WEARING VERTICAL MANEUVERING GEAR...
HE DIED, AND NOBODY WAS THERE TO SEE IT.
AH ...
EREN ...
!
CHFF

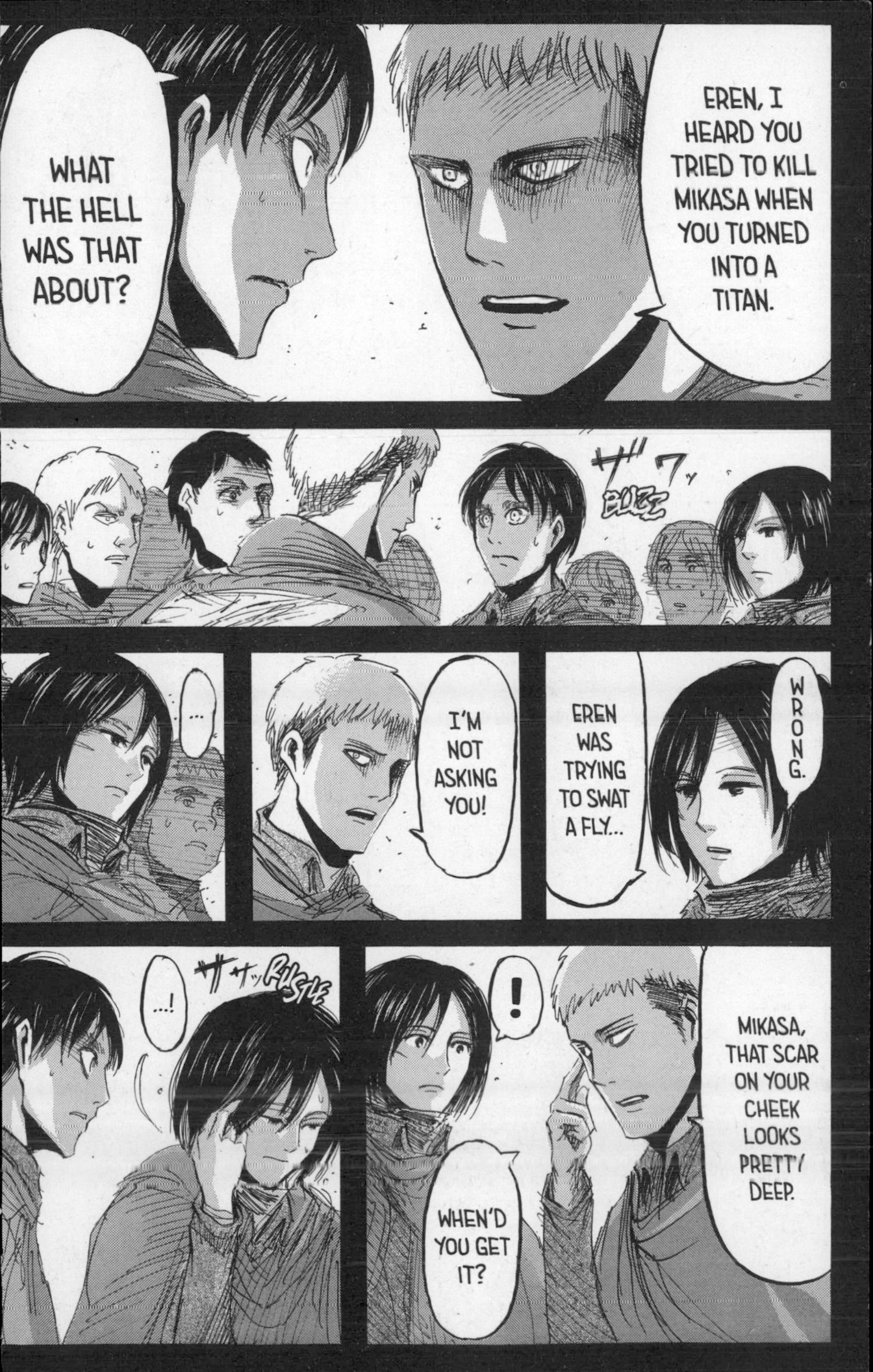
EREN, I HEARD YOU TRIED TO KILL MIKASA WHEN YOU TURNED INTO A TITAN.
WHAT THE HELL WAS THAT ABOUT?
BUZZ
WRONG.
EREN WAS TRYING TO SWAT A FLY...
I'M NOT ASKING YOU!
...
MIKASA, THAT SCAR ON YOUR CHEEK LOOKS PRETTY DEEP.
!
WHEN'D YOU GET IT?
RUSTLE
...!

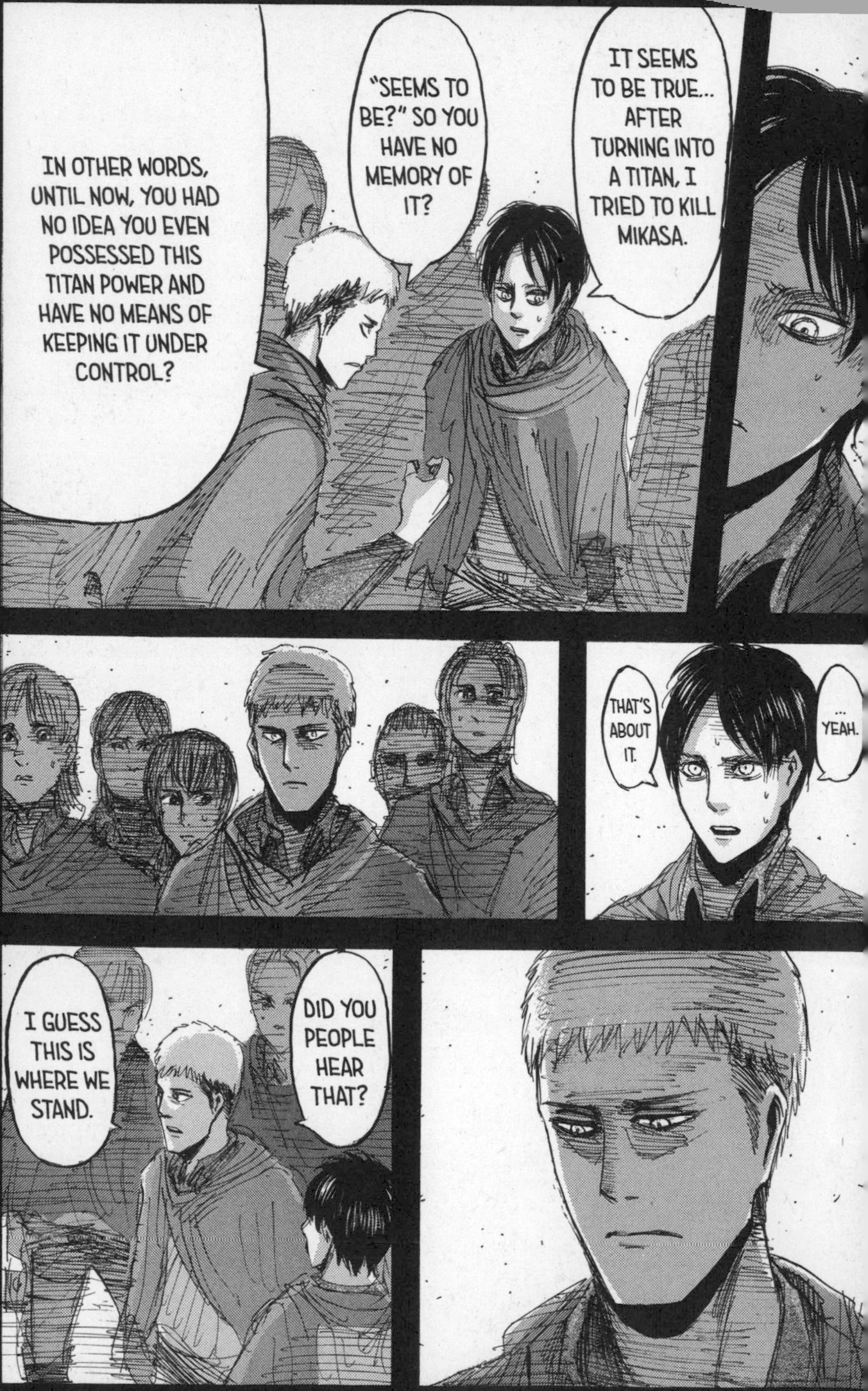
IT SEEMS TO BE TRUE... AFTER TURNING INTO A TITAN, I TRIED TO KILL MIKASA.
"SEEMS TO BE?" SO YOU HAVE NO MEMORY OF IT?
IN OTHER WORDS, UNTIL NOW, YOU HAD NO IDEA YOU EVEN POSSESSED THIS TITAN POWER AND HAVE NO MEANS OF KEEPING IT UNDER CONTROL?
... YEAH.
THAT'S ABOUT IT.
DID YOU PEOPLE HEAR THAT?
I GUESS THIS IS WHERE WE STAND.

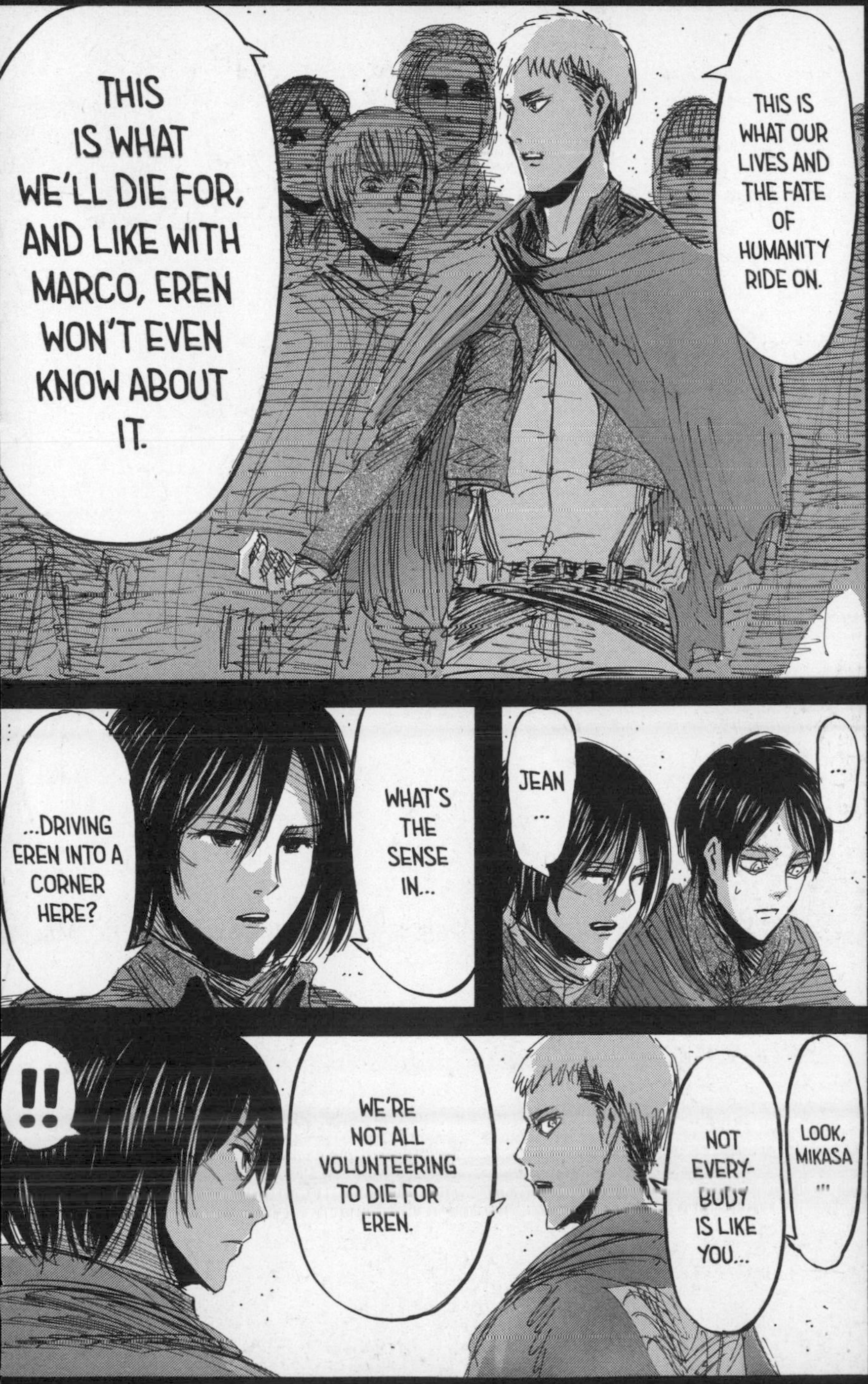

THIS IS WHAT OUR LIVES AND THE FATE OF HUMANITY RIDE ON.
THIS IS WHAT WE'LL DIE FOR, AND LIKE WITH MARCO, EREN WON'T EVEN KNOW ABOUT IT.
...
JEAN ...
WHAT'S THE SENSE IN...
...DRIVING EREN INTO A CORNER HERE?
LOOK, MIKASA ...
NOT EVERY-BODY IS LIKE YOU...
WE'RE NOT ALL VOLUNTEERING TO DIE FOR EREN.
!!

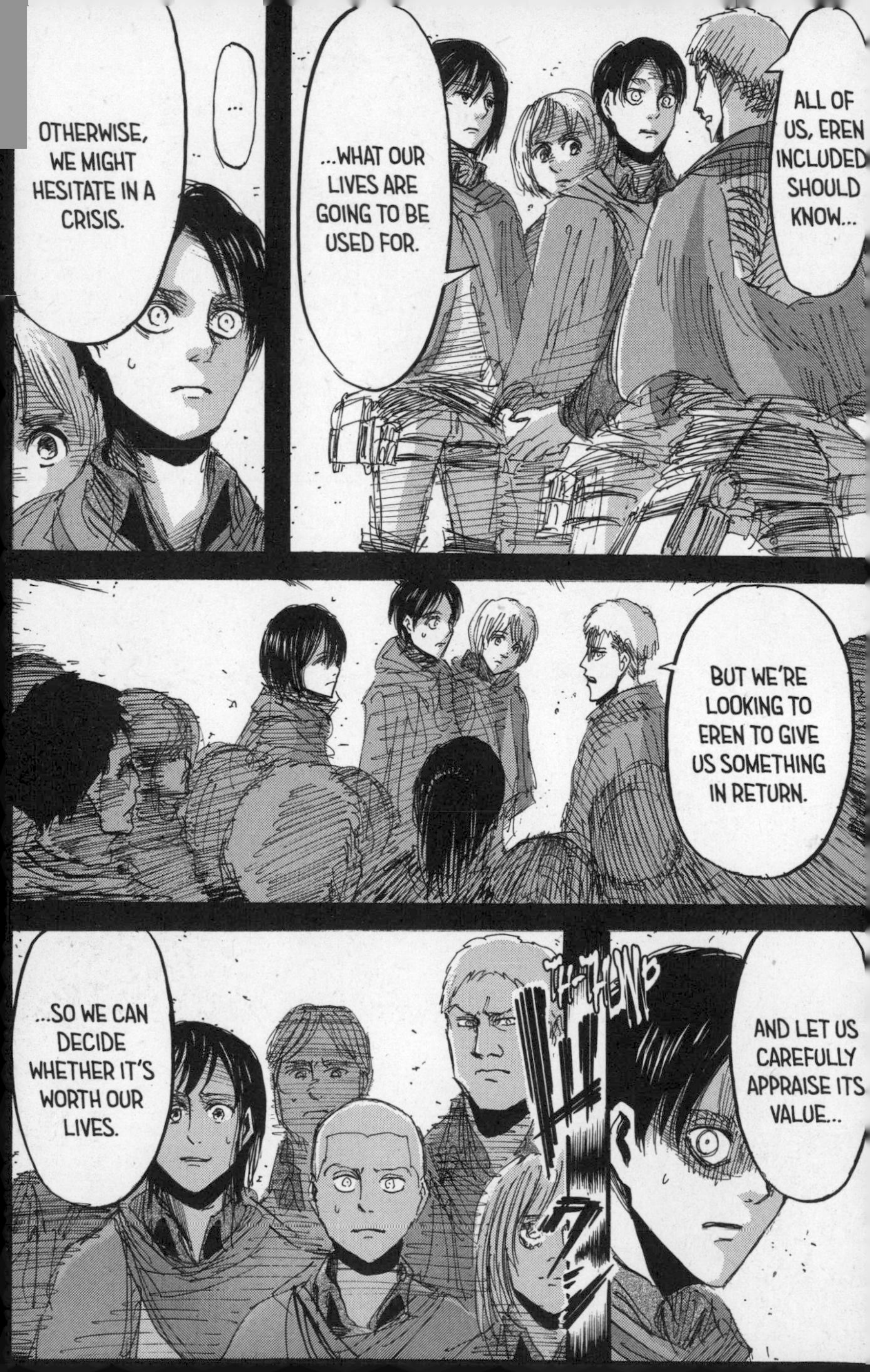
ALL OF US, EREN INCLUDED SHOULD KNOW...
...WHAT OUR LIVES ARE GOING TO BE USED FOR.
...
OTHERWISE, WE MIGHT HESITATE IN A CRISIS.
BUT WE'RE LOOKING TO EREN TO GIVE US SOMETHING IN RETURN.
AND LET US CAREFULLY APPRAISE ITS VALUE...
TH-THUMP
...SO WE CAN DECIDE WHETHER IT'S WORTH OUR LIVES.

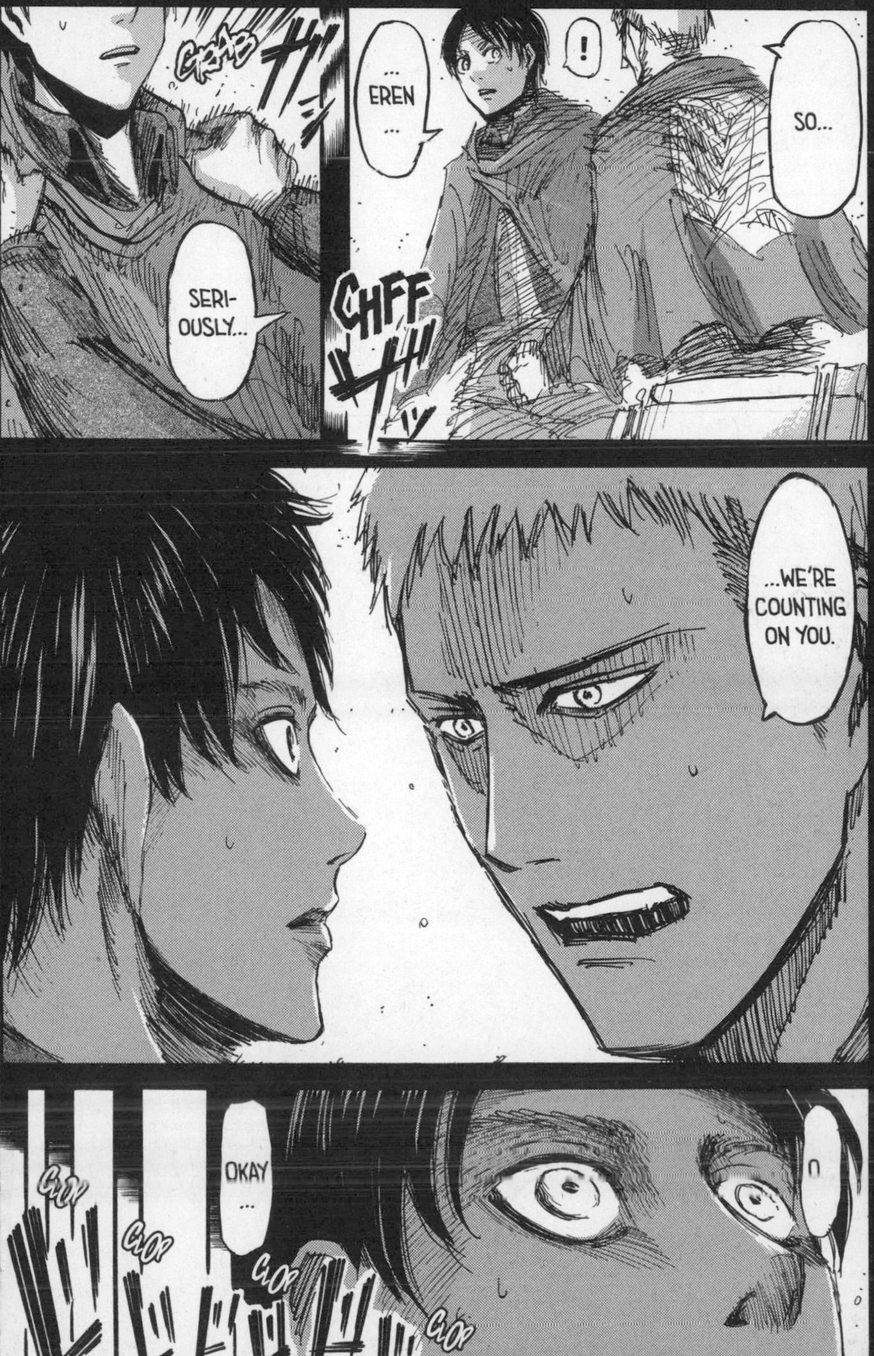
SO...
!
... EREN ...
CHFF
GRAB
SERI-OUSLY...
...WE'RE COUNTING ON YOU.
OKAY ...
CLOP
CLOP
CLOP
CLOP

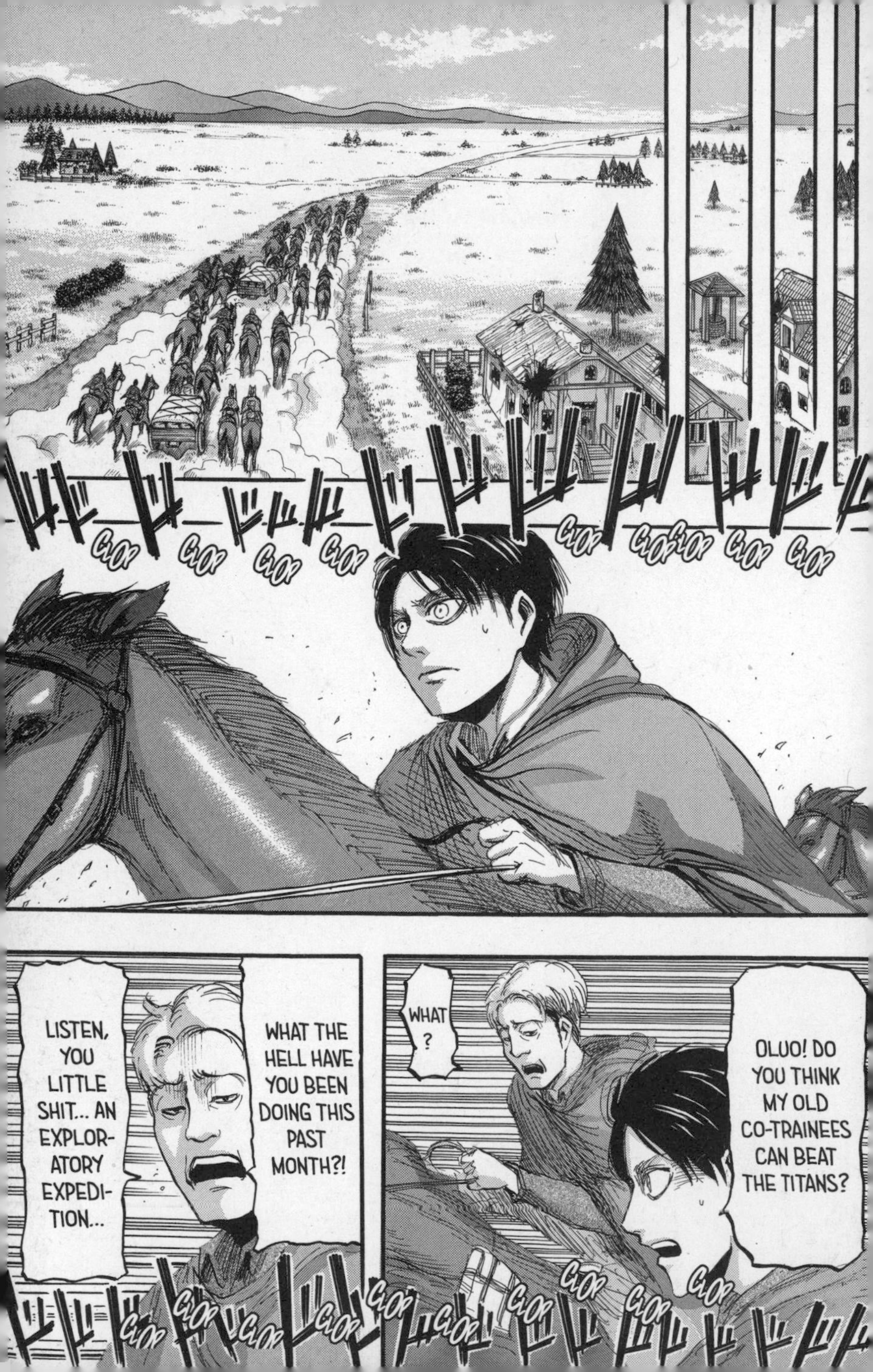

CLOP CLOP CLOP CLOP CLOP CLOP CLOP CLOP CLOP
OLUO! DO YOU THINK MY OLD CO-TRAINEES CAN BEAT THE TITANS?
WHAT ?
CLOP CLOP CLOP CLOP
WHAT THE HELL HAVE YOU BEEN DOING THIS PAST MONTH?!
LISTEN, YOU LITTLE SHIT... AN EXPLORATORY EXPEDITION...
CLOP CLOP CLOP CLOP

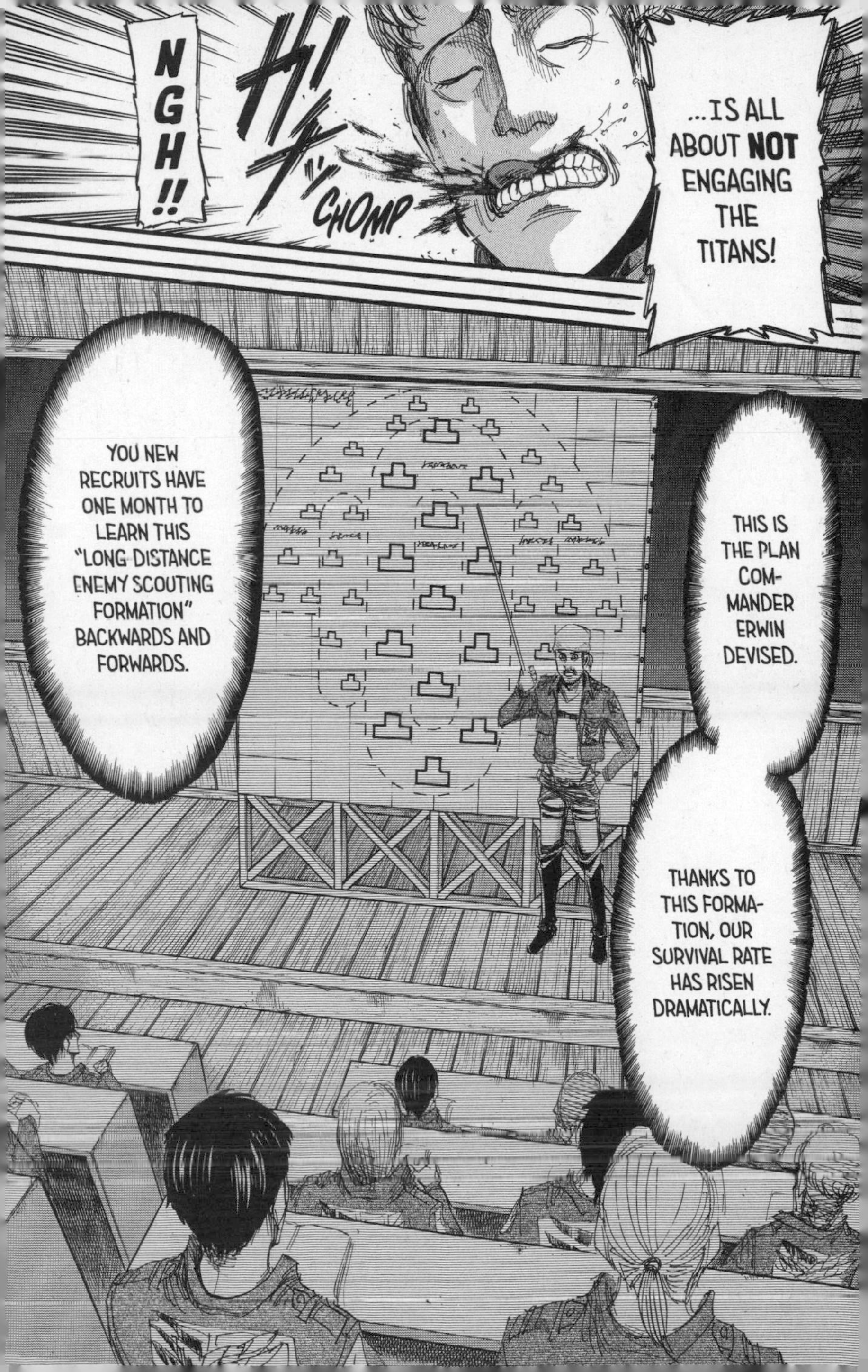
...IS ALL ABOUT NOT ENGAGING THE TITANS!
CHOMP
NGH!!
THIS IS THE PLAN COMMANDER ERWIN DEVISED.
THANKS TO THIS FORMATION, OUR SURVIVAL RATE HAS RISEN DRAMATICALLY.
YOU NEW RECRUITS HAVE ONE MONTH TO LEARN THIS "LONG DISTANCE ENEMY SCOUTING FORMATION" BACKWARDS AND FORWARDS.

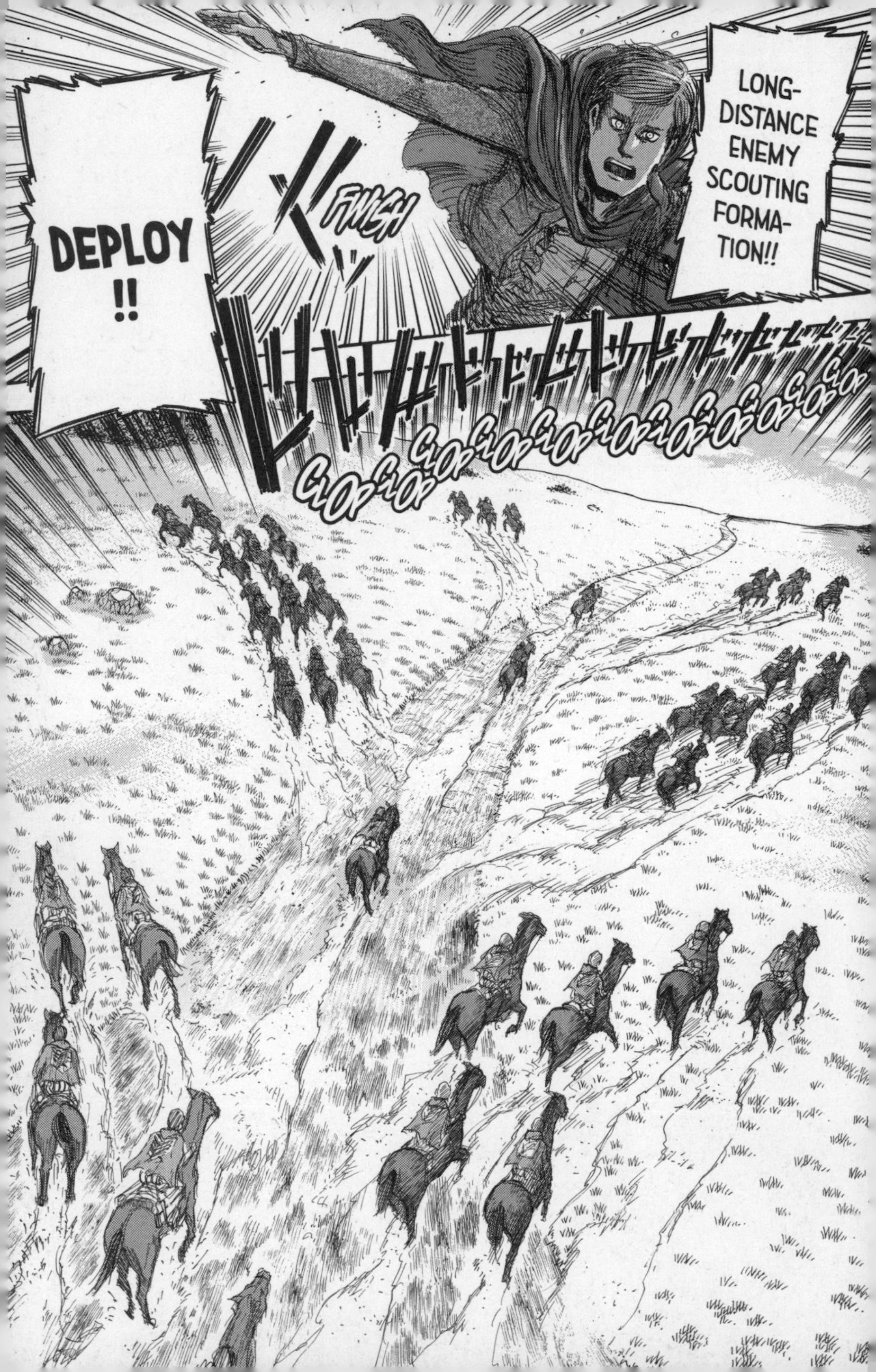
LONG-DISTANCE ENEMY SCOUTING FORMATION!!
DEPLOY!!
FWISH
CLOP CLOP CLOP CLOP CLOP CLOP CLOP CLOP CLOP CLOP CLOP CLOP CLOP

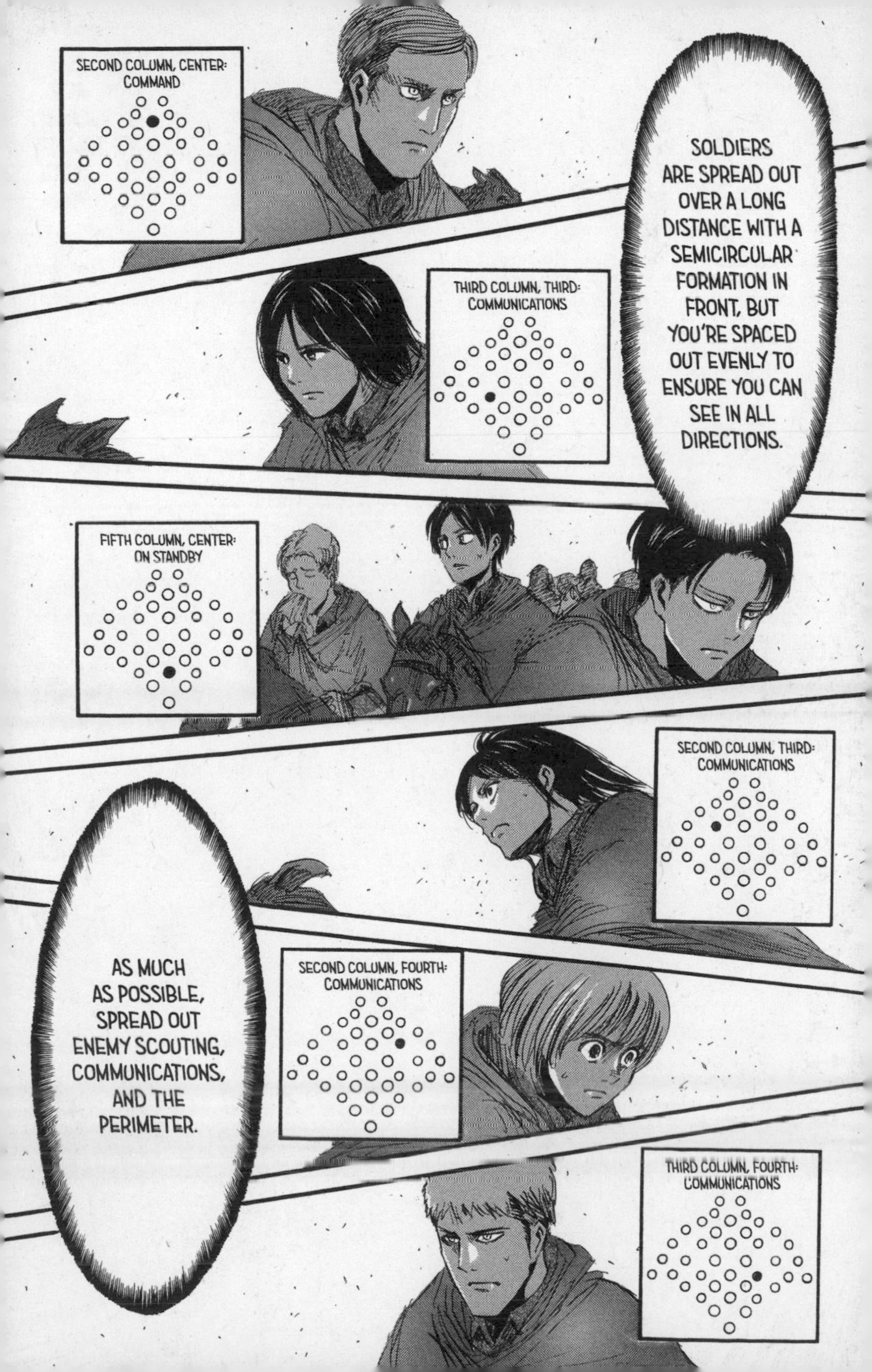
SOLDIERS ARE SPREAD OUT OVER A LONG DISTANCE WITH A SEMICIRCULAR FORMATION IN FRONT, BUT YOU'RE SPACED OUT EVENLY TO ENSURE YOU CAN SEE IN ALL DIRECTIONS.
SECOND COLUMN, CENTER: COMMAND
THIRD COLUMN, THIRD: COMMUNICATIONS
FIFTH COLUMN, CENTER: ON STANDBY
SECOND COLUMN, THIRD: COMMUNICATIONS
AS MUCH AS POSSIBLE, SPREAD OUT ENEMY SCOUTING, COMMUNICATIONS, AND THE PERIMETER.
SECOND COLUMN, FOURTH: COMMUNICATIONS
THIRD COLUMN, FOURTH: COMMUNICATIONS

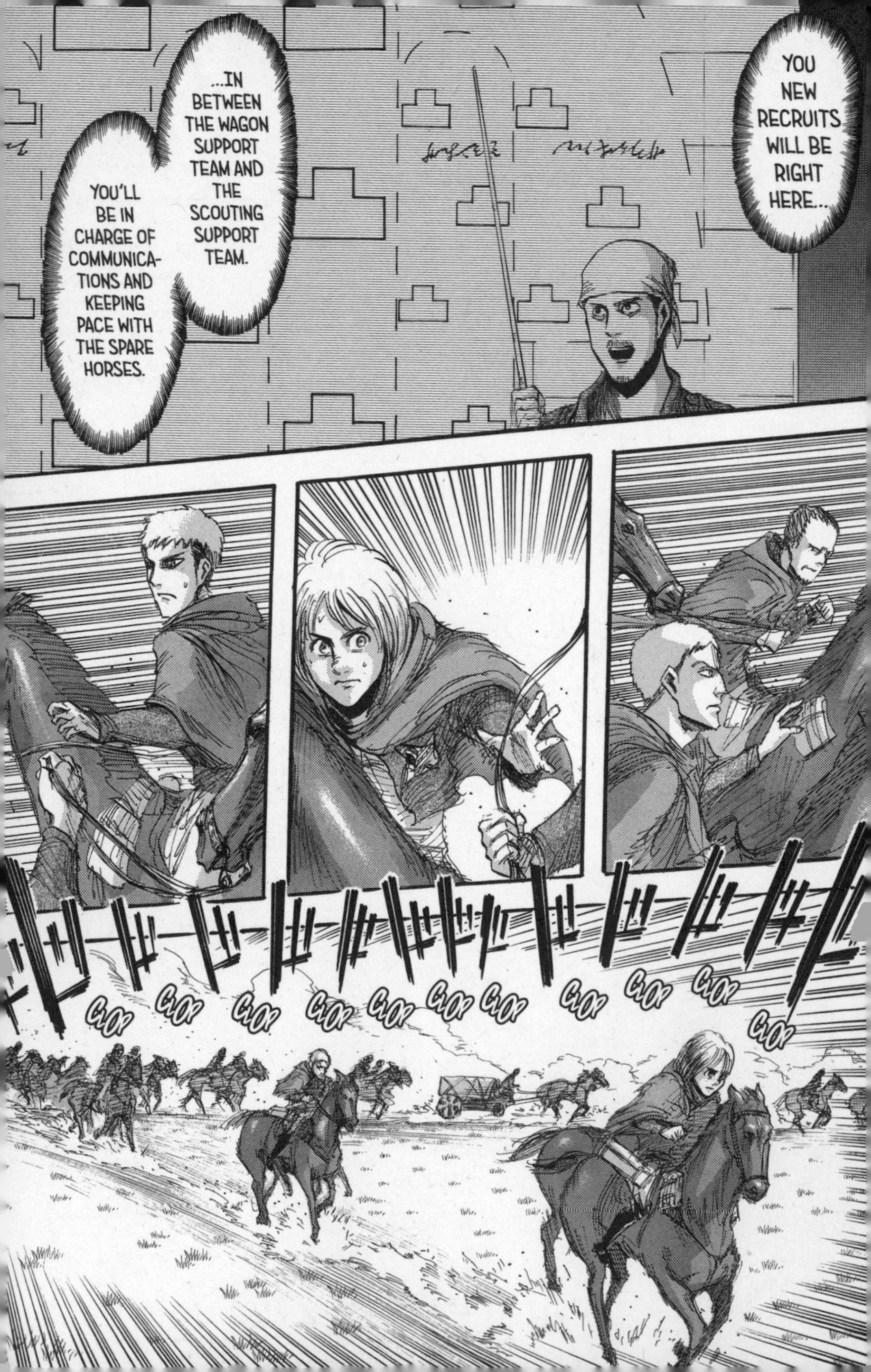
YOU NEW RECRUITS WILL BE RIGHT HERE...
...IN BETWEEN THE WAGON SUPPORT TEAM AND THE SCOUTING SUPPORT TEAM.
YOU'LL BE IN CHARGE OF COMMUNICATIONS AND KEEPING PACE WITH THE SPARE HORSES.
CLOP CLOP CLOP CLOP CLOP CLOP CLOP CLOP CLOP CLOP CLOP

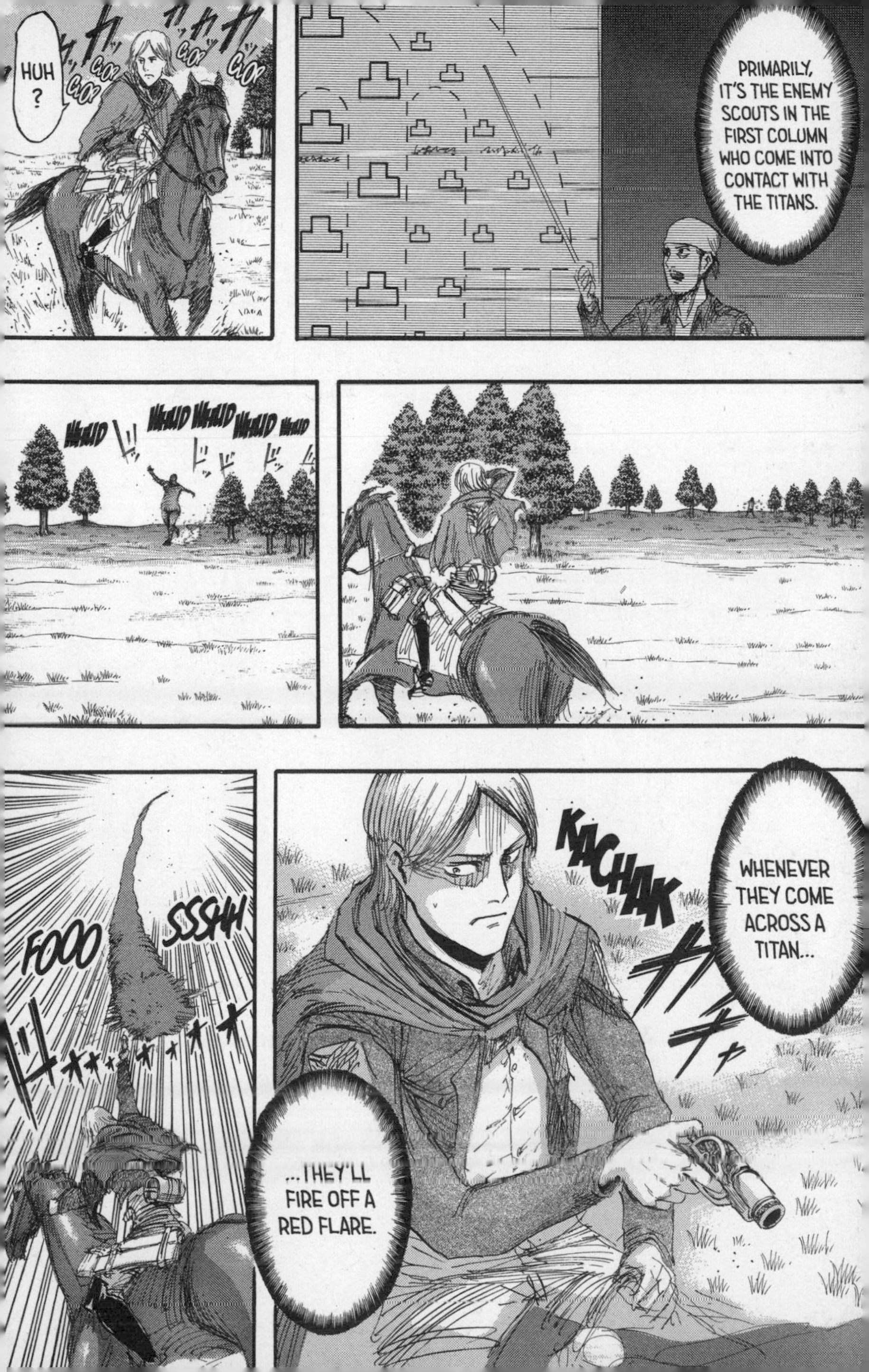
PRIMARILY, IT'S THE ENEMY SCOUTS IN THE FIRST COLUMN WHO COME INTO CONTACT WITH THE TITANS.
HUH ?
CLOP CLOP CLOP CLOP
WHUD WHUD WHUD WHUD WHUD
KACHAK
WHENEVER THEY COME ACROSS A TITAN...
...THEY'LL FIRE OFF A RED FLARE.
FOOO SSSHH

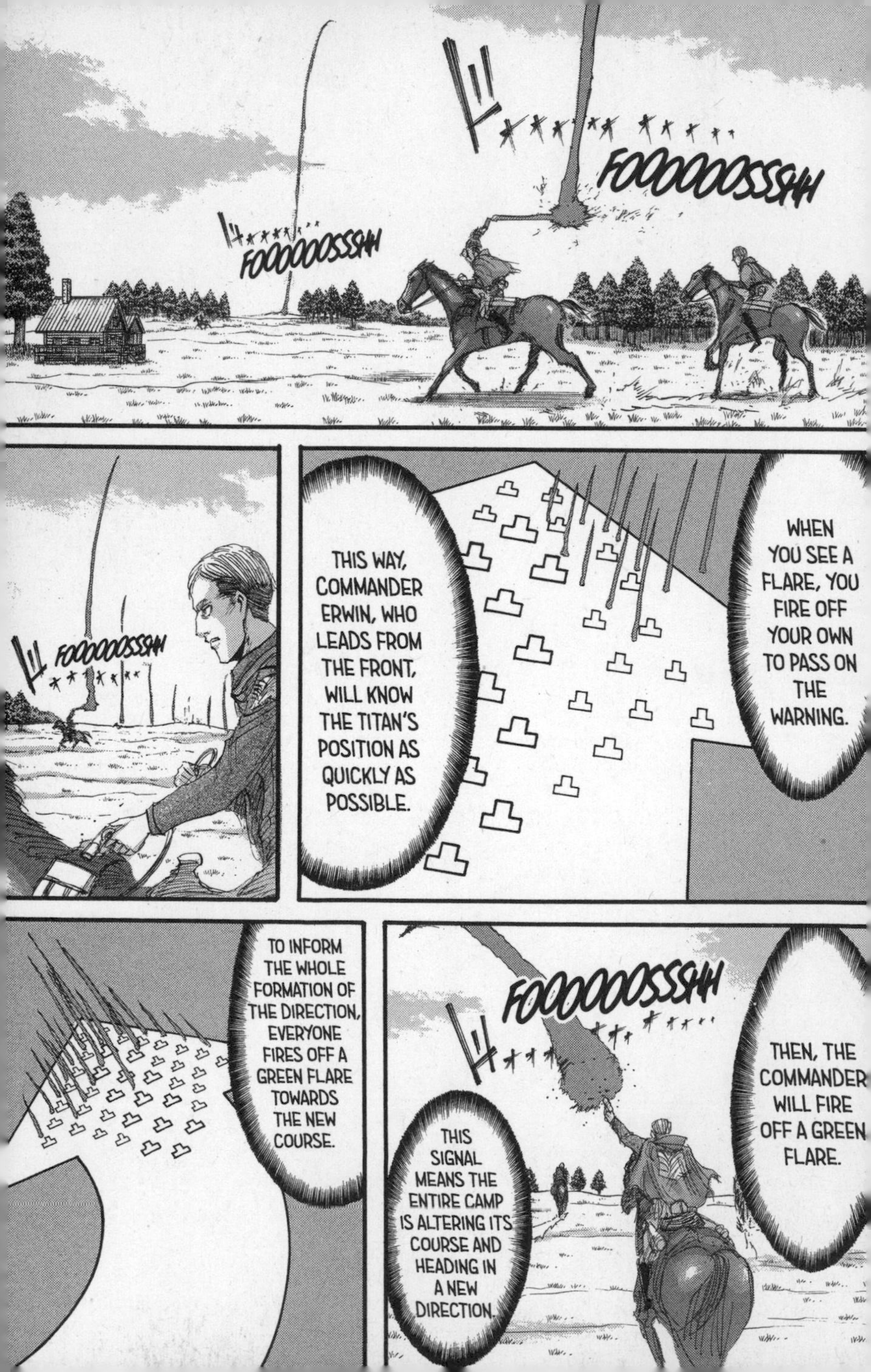
FOOOOOOOSSSHH
FOOOOOOSSHH
WHEN YOU SEE A FLARE, YOU FIRE OFF YOUR OWN TO PASS ON THE WARNING.
THIS WAY, COMMANDER ERWIN, WHO LEADS FROM THE FRONT, WILL KNOW THE TITAN'S POSITION AS QUICKLY AS POSSIBLE.
FOOOOOOOSSHH
THEN, THE COMMANDER WILL FIRE OFF A GREEN FLARE.
FOOOOOOOSSSHH
THIS SIGNAL MEANS THE ENTIRE CAMP IS ALTERING ITS COURSE AND HEADING IN A NEW DIRECTION.
TO INFORM THE WHOLE FORMATION OF THE DIRECTION, EVERYONE FIRES OFF A GREEN FLARE TOWARDS THE NEW COURSE.

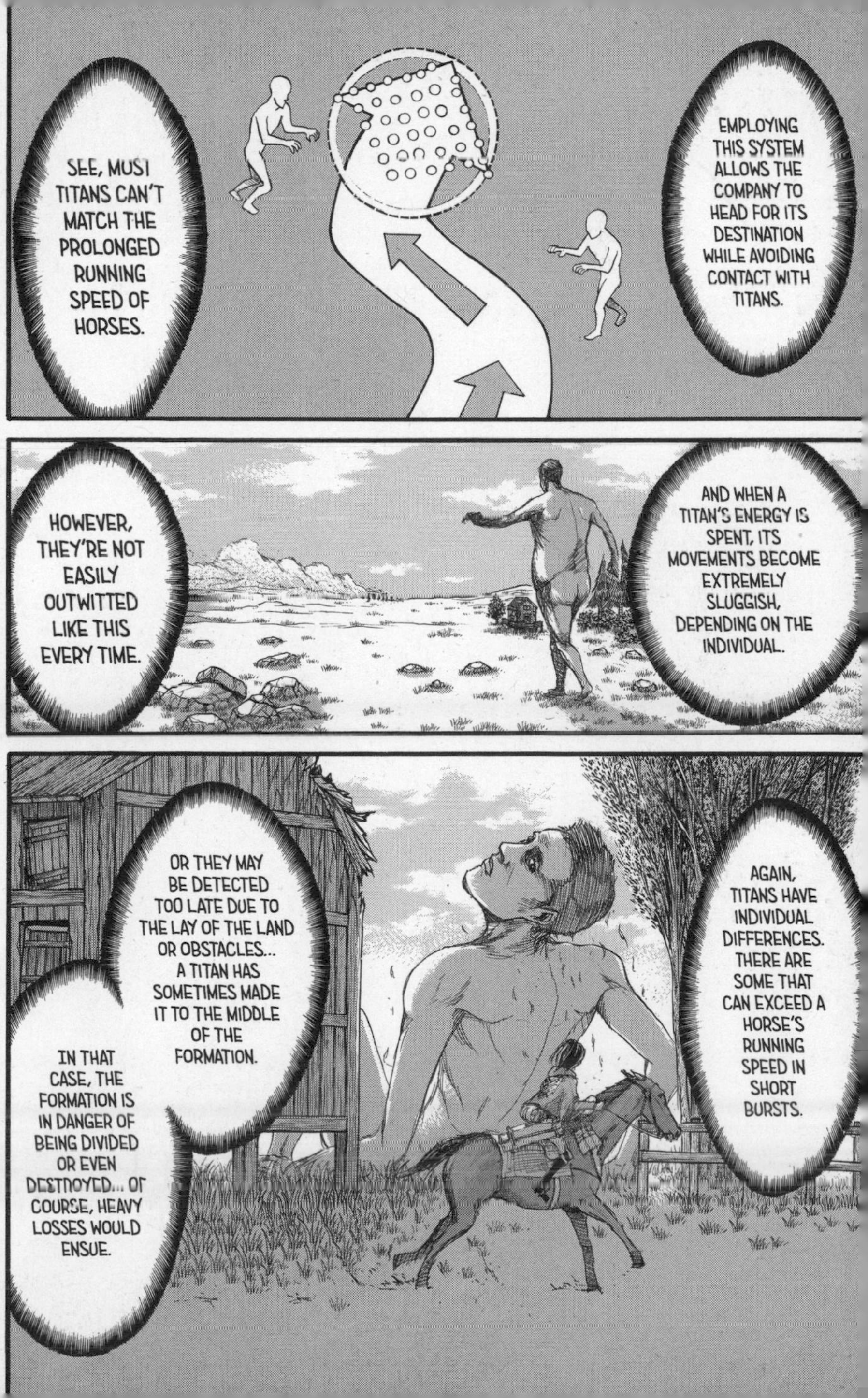
EMPLOYING THIS SYSTEM ALLOWS THE COMPANY TO HEAD FOR ITS DESTINATION WHILE AVOIDING CONTACT WITH TITANS.
SEE, MOST TITANS CAN'T MATCH THE PROLONGED RUNNING SPEED OF HORSES.
AND WHEN A TITAN'S ENERGY IS SPENT, ITS MOVEMENTS BECOME EXTREMELY SLUGGISH, DEPENDING ON THE INDIVIDUAL.
HOWEVER, THEY'RE NOT EASILY OUTWITTED LIKE THIS EVERY TIME.
AGAIN, TITANS HAVE INDIVIDUAL DIFFERENCES. THERE ARE SOME THAT CAN EXCEED A HORSE'S RUNNING SPEED IN SHORT BURSTS.
OR THEY MAY BE DETECTED TOO LATE DUE TO THE LAY OF THE LAND OR OBSTACLES... A TITAN HAS SOMETIMES MADE IT TO THE MIDDLE OF THE FORMATION.
IN THAT CASE, THE FORMATION IS IN DANGER OF BEING DIVIDED OR EVEN DESTROYED... OF COURSE, HEAVY LOSSES WOULD ENSUE.

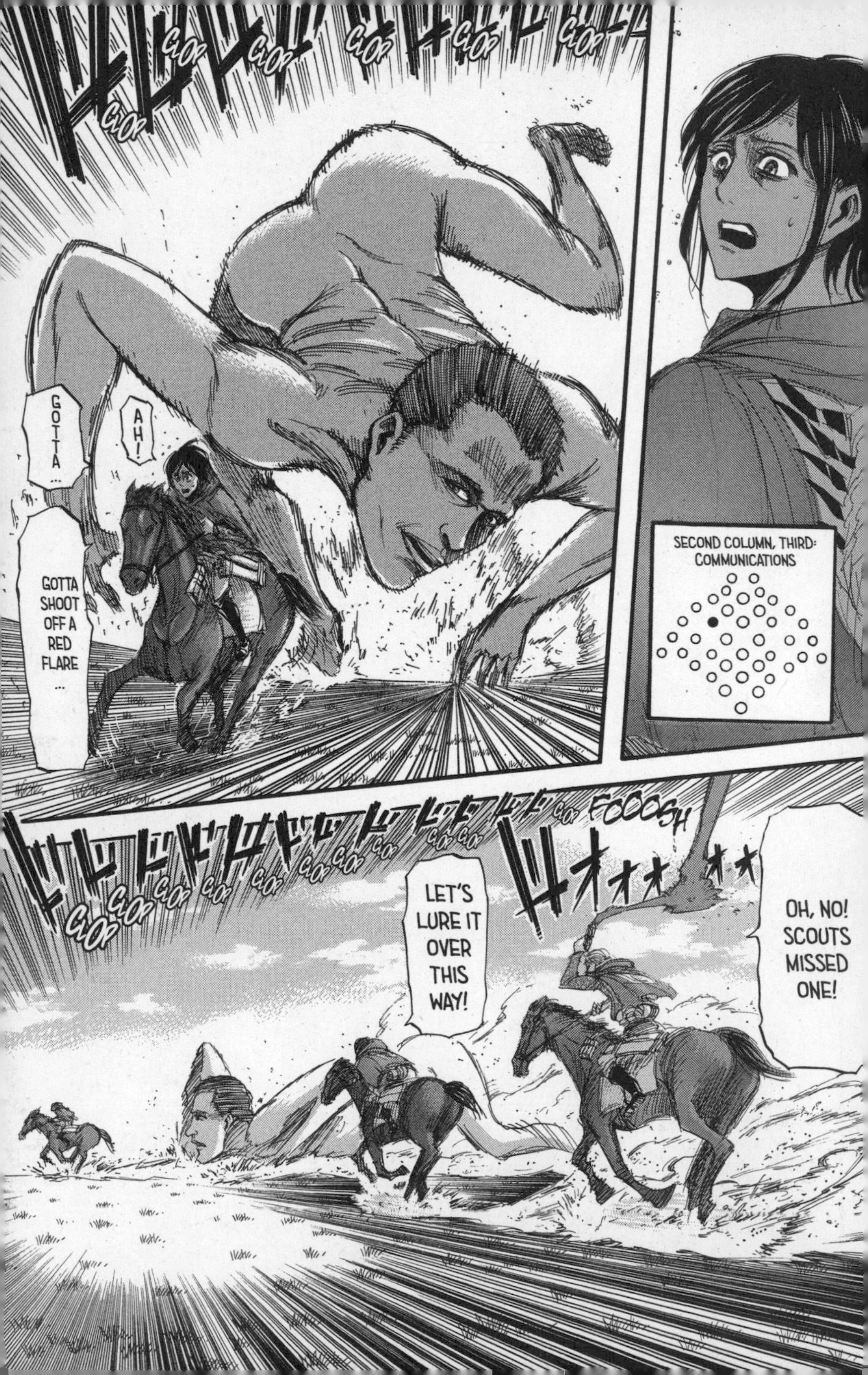
SECOND COLUMN, THIRD: COMMUNICATIONS
CLOP CLOP CLOP CLOP CLOP CLOP
AH!
GOTTA...
GOTTA SHOOT OFF A RED FLARE...
FOOOSH
CLOP CLOP CLOP CLOP CLOP CLOP CLOP CLOP CLOP CLOP CLOP CLOP
OH, NO! SCOUTS MISSED ONE!
LET'S LURE IT OVER THIS WAY!

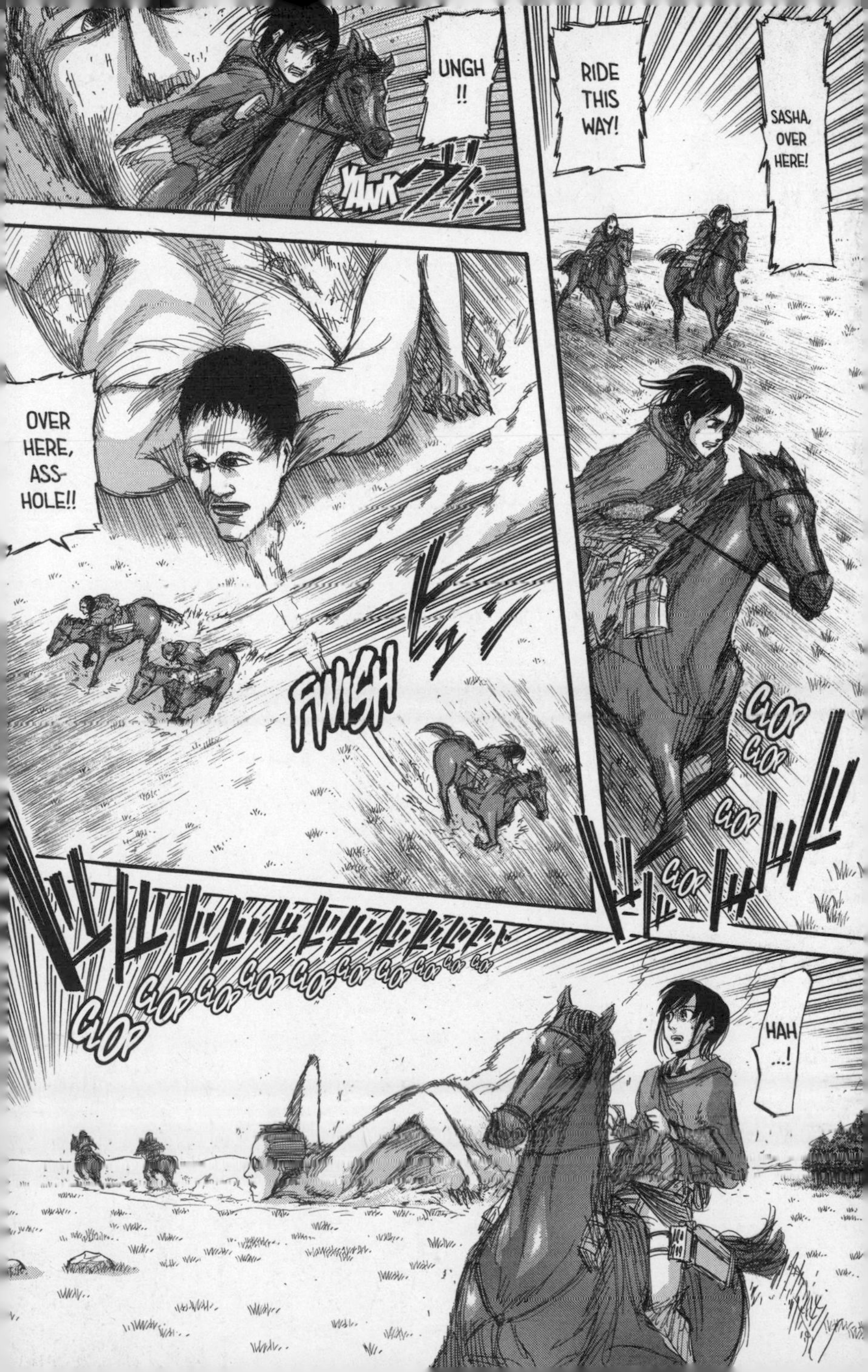
SASHA, OVER HERE!
RIDE THIS WAY!
CLOP CLOP
CLOP
CLOP
UNGH !!
YANK
OVER HERE, ASS-HOLE!!
FWISH
HAH ...!
CLOP CLOP CLOP CLOP CLOP CLOP CLOP CLOP CLOP CLOP

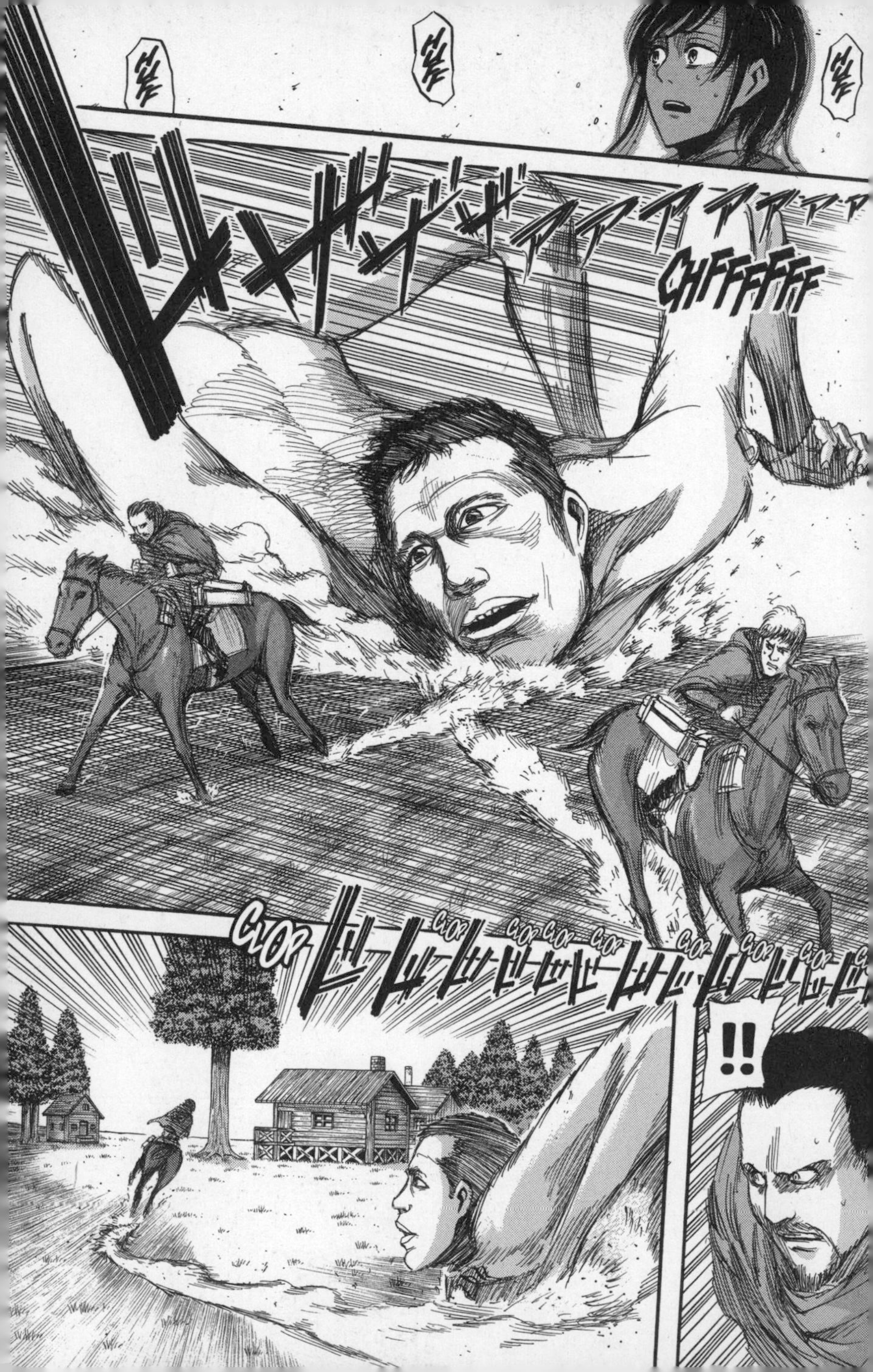
CHFFFFFF
!!
CLOP
CLOP
CLOP
CLOP
CLOP
CLOP
CLOP
CLOP

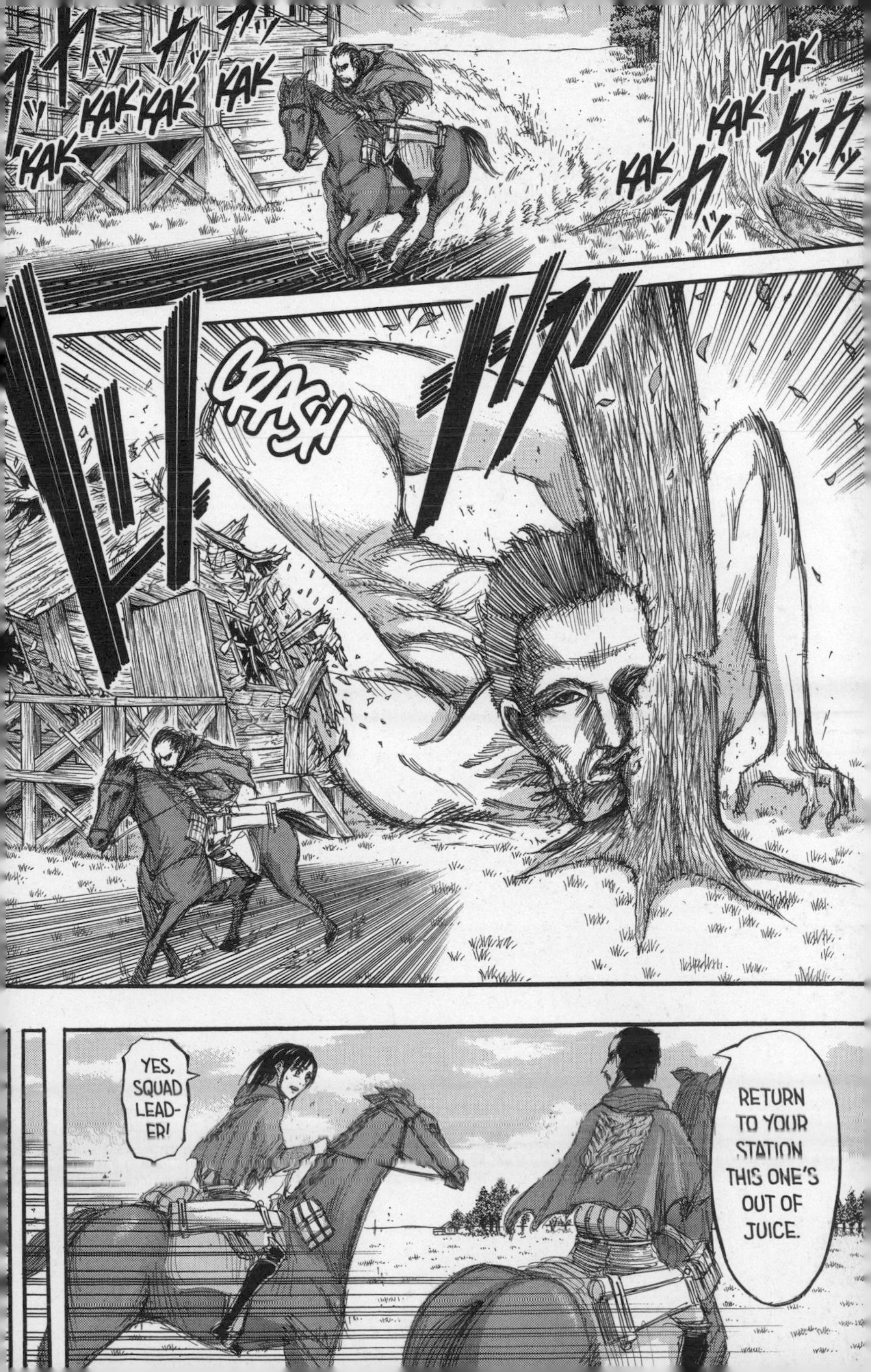
KAK KAK KAK
KAK KAK KAK KAK
CRASH
RETURN TO YOUR STATION THIS ONE'S OUT OF JUICE.
YES, SQUAD LEADER!

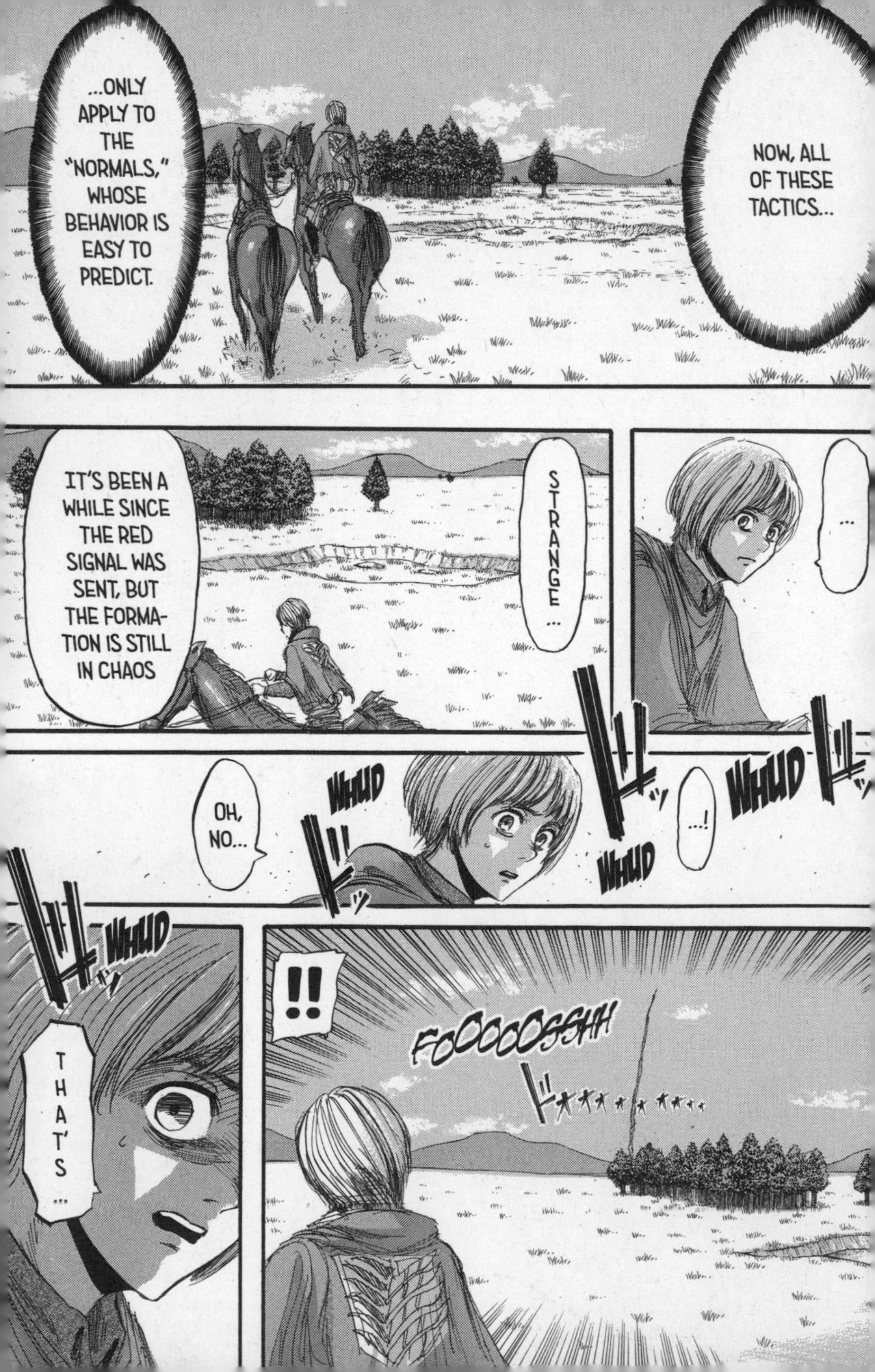
NOW, ALL OF THESE TACTICS...
...ONLY APPLY TO THE "NORMALS," WHOSE BEHAVIOR IS EASY TO PREDICT.
...
STRANGE...
IT'S BEEN A WHILE SINCE THE RED SIGNAL WAS SENT, BUT THE FORMATION IS STILL IN CHAOS
WHUD
...!
WHUD
WHUD
OH, NO...
!!
FOOOOOOSSHH
WHUD
THAT'S...

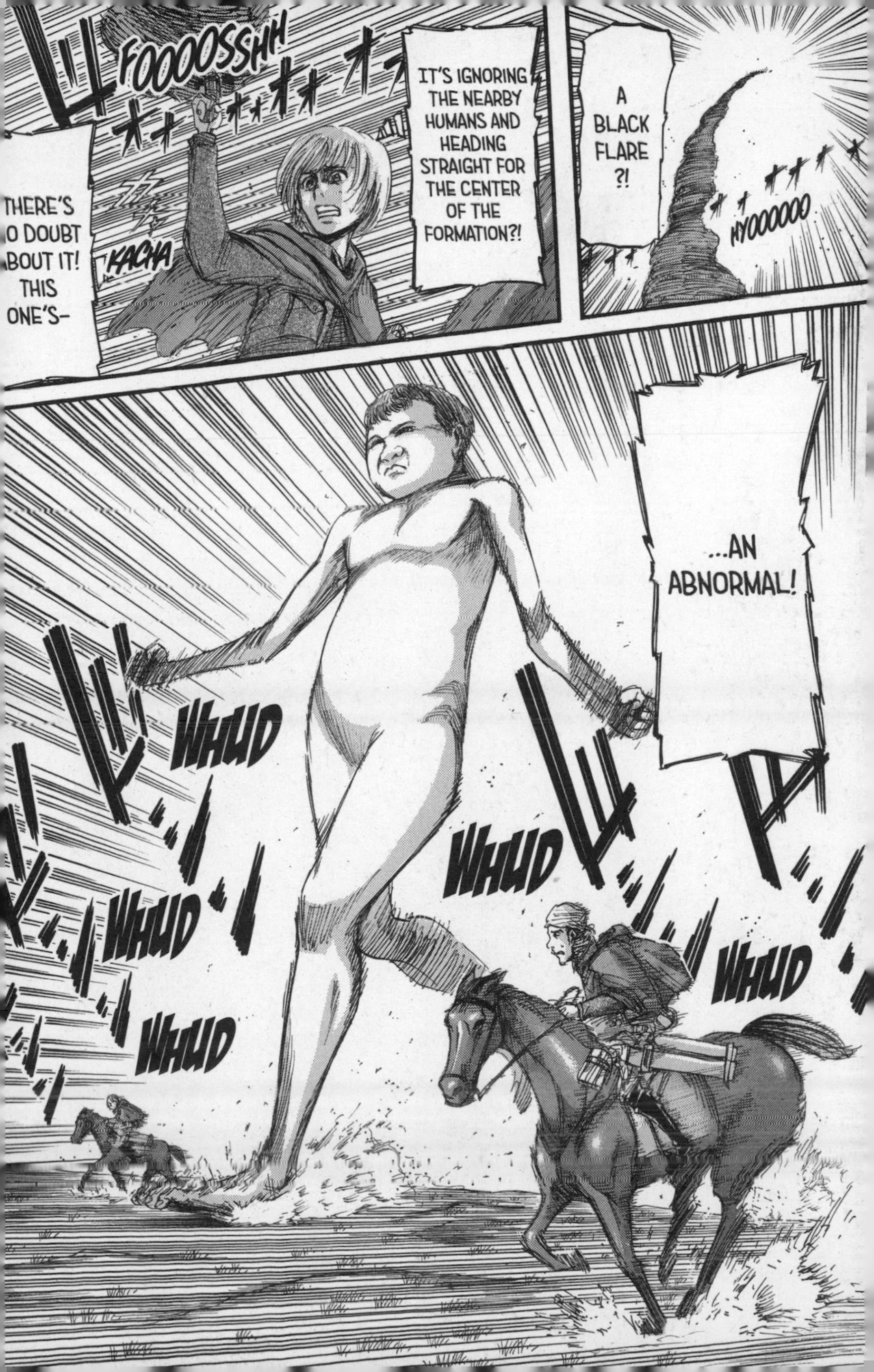
A BLACK FLARE?!
HYOOOOOO
IT'S IGNORING THE NEARBY HUMANS AND HEADING STRAIGHT FOR THE CENTER OF THE FORMATION?!
FOOOOOSSHH!
KACHA
THERE'S O DOUBT BOUT IT! THIS ONE'S-
...AN ABNORMAL!
WHUD
WHUD
WHUD
WHUD
WHUD

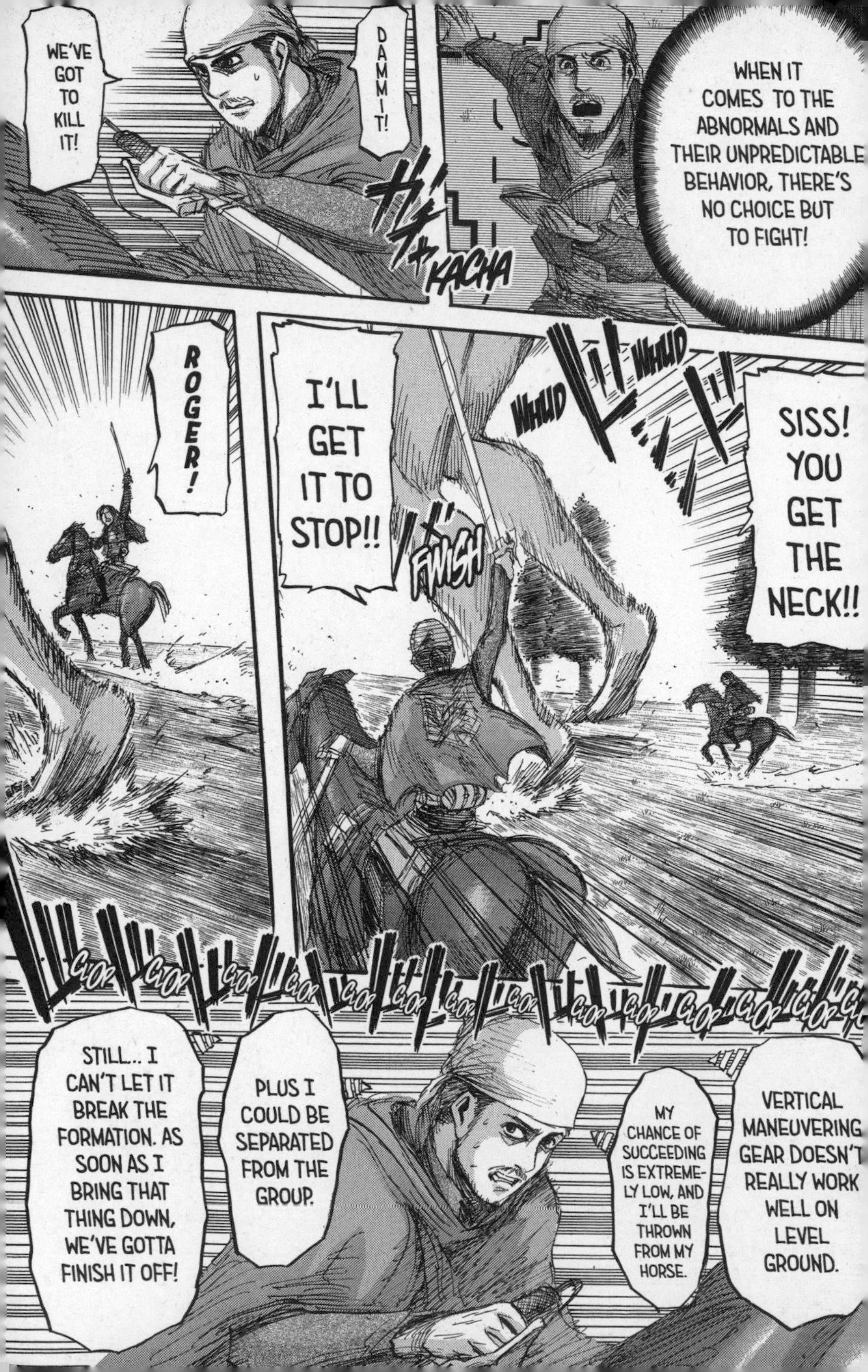
WHEN IT COMES TO THE ABNORMALS AND THEIR UNPREDICTABLE BEHAVIOR, THERE'S NO CHOICE BUT TO FIGHT!
DAMMIT!
WE'VE GOT TO KILL IT!
KACHA
SISS! YOU GET THE NECK!!
WHUD
WHUD
I'LL GET IT TO STOP!!
FWISH
ROGER!
CLOP CLOP CLOP CLOP CLOP CLOP CLOP CLOP CLOP CLOP CLOP CLOP CLOP CLOP
VERTICAL MANEUVERING GEAR DOESN'T REALLY WORK WELL ON LEVEL GROUND.
MY CHANCE OF SUCCEEDING IS EXTREMELY LOW, AND I'LL BE THROWN FROM MY HORSE.
PLUS I COULD BE SEPARATED FROM THE GROUP.
STILL... I CAN'T LET IT BREAK THE FORMATION. AS SOON AS I BRING THAT THING DOWN, WE'VE GOTTA FINISH IT OFF!

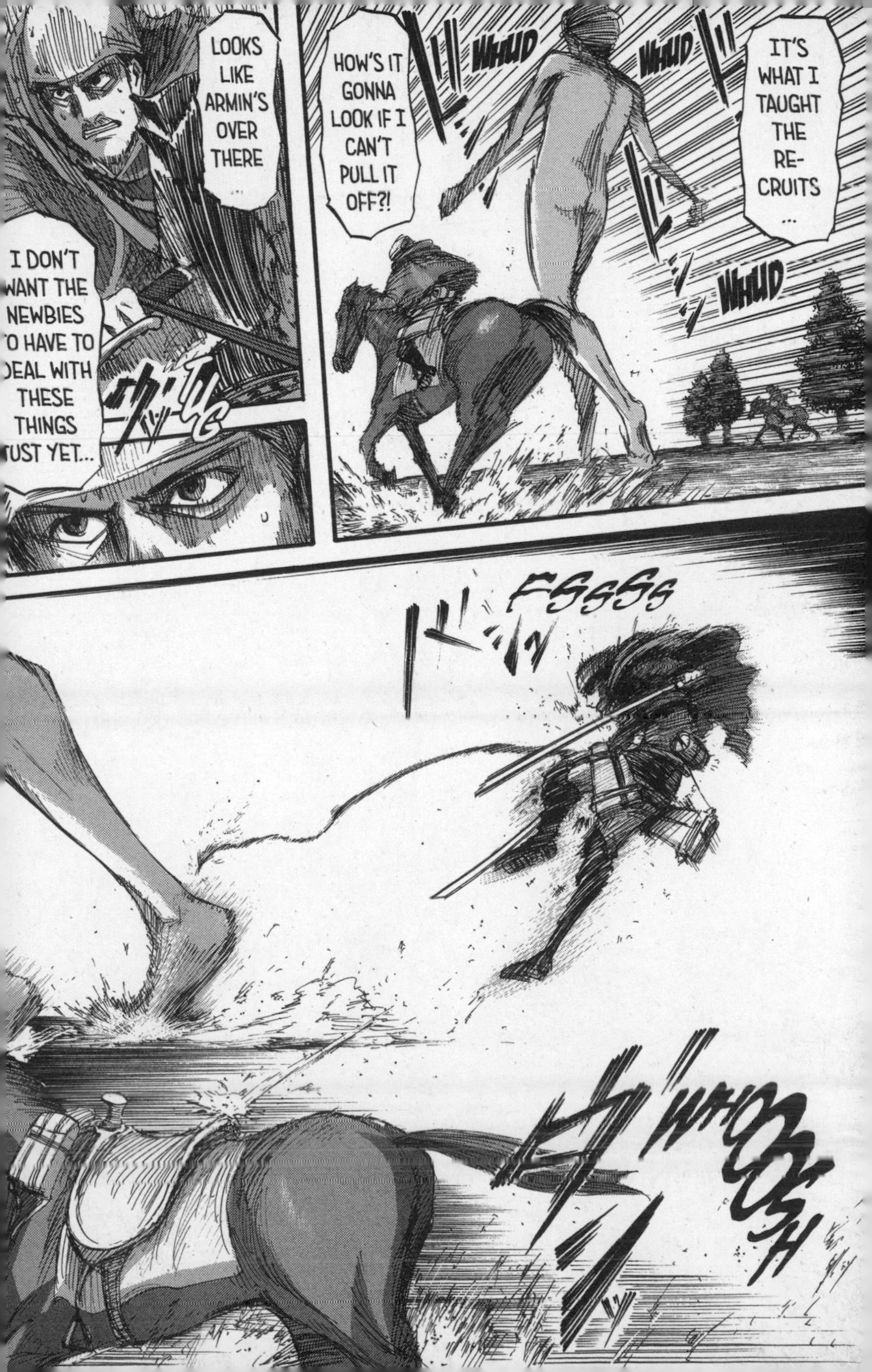
WHUD
WHUD
IT'S WHAT I TAUGHT THE RE-CRUITS ...
HOW'S IT GONNA LOOK IF I CAN'T PULL IT OFF?!
WHUD
LOOKS LIKE ARMIN'S OVER THERE ...
I DON'T WANT THE NEWBIES TO HAVE TO DEAL WITH THESE THINGS JUST YET...
TUG
FSSSS
WHOOSH

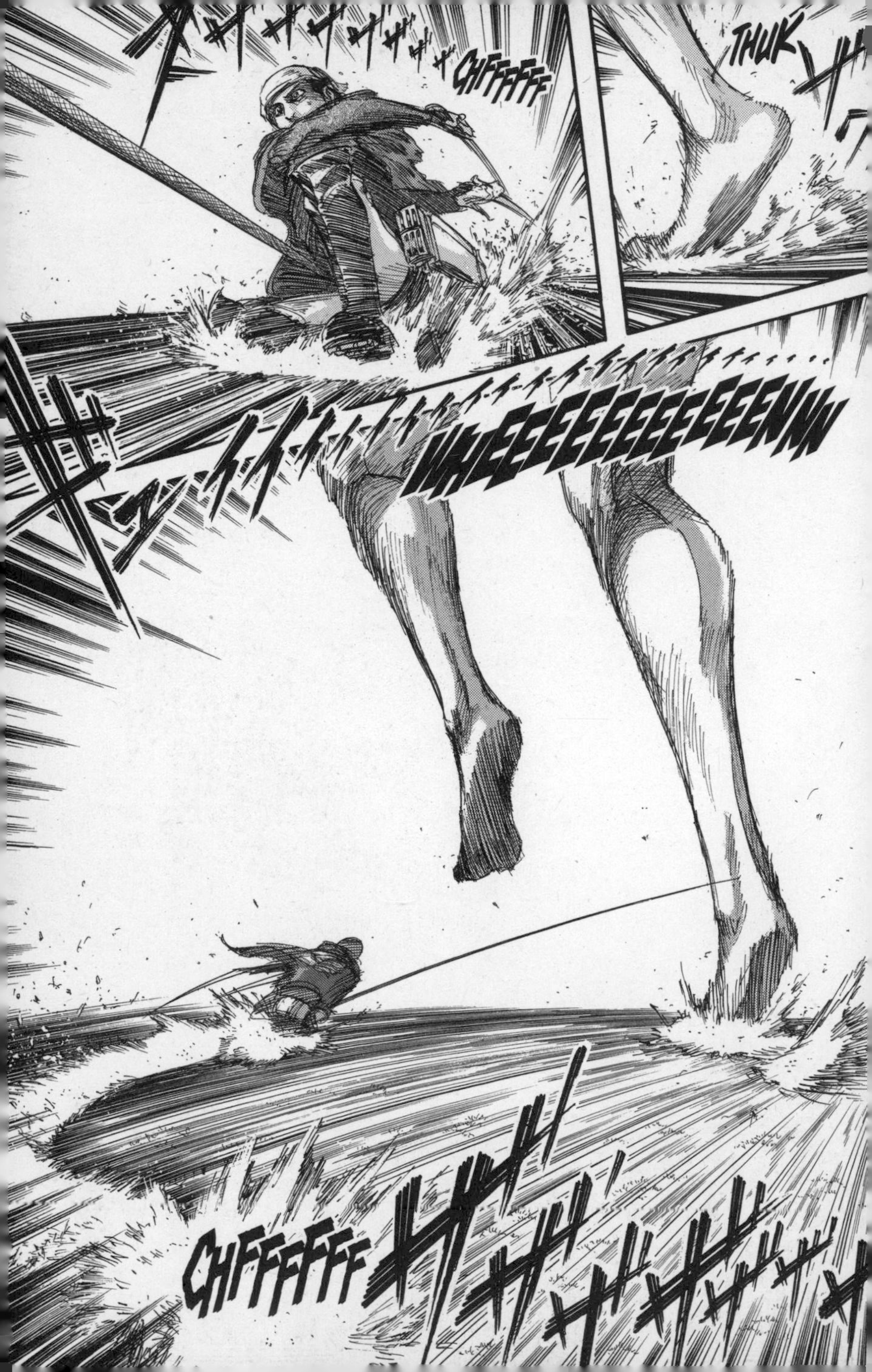
THUK
CHFFFFFF
WHEEEEEEEEEENNN
CHFFFFFF

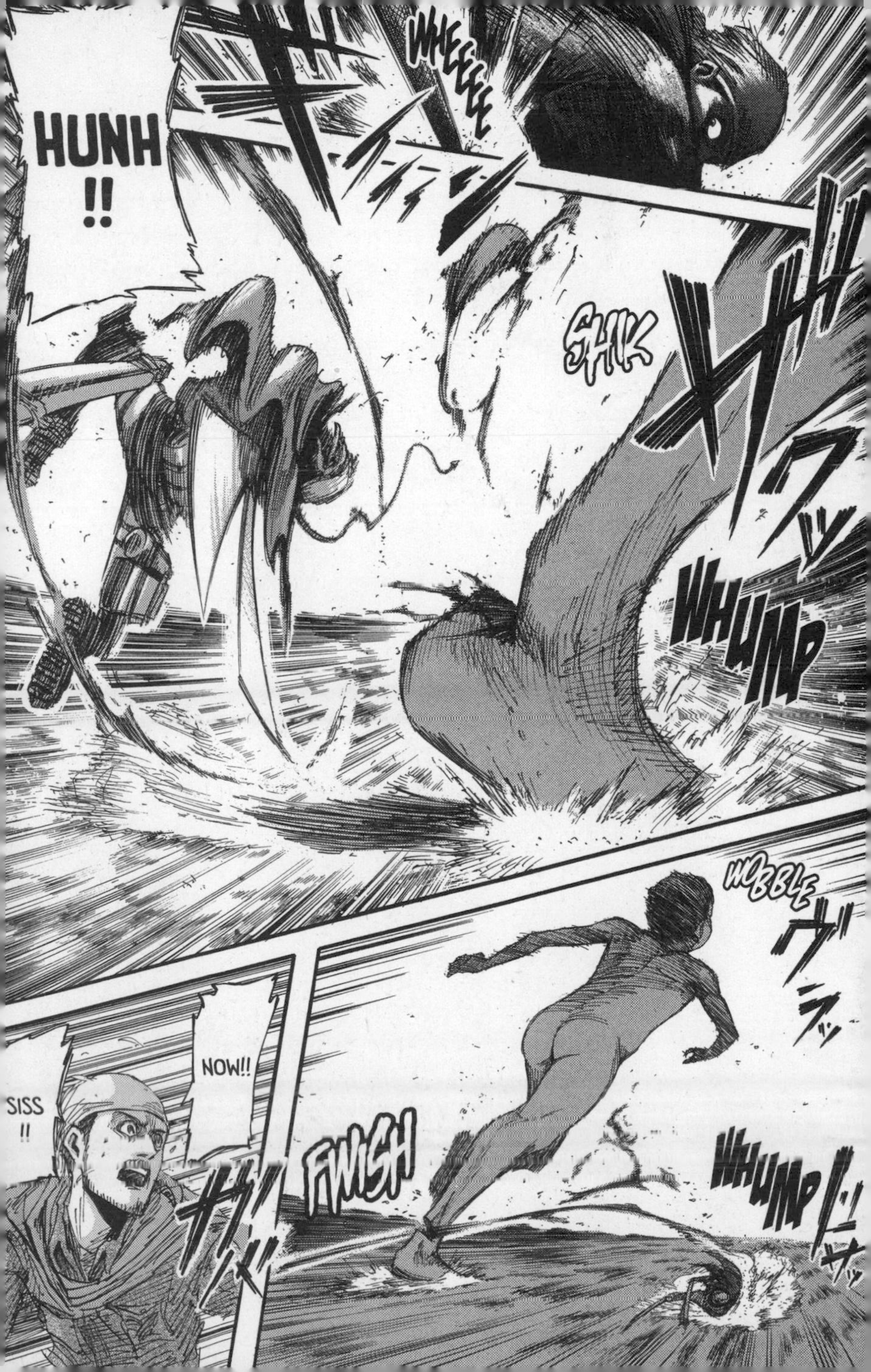
WHEEEEE
HUNH !!
SHINK
WHUMP
WOBBLE
FWISH
WHUMP!
NOW!!
SISS !!

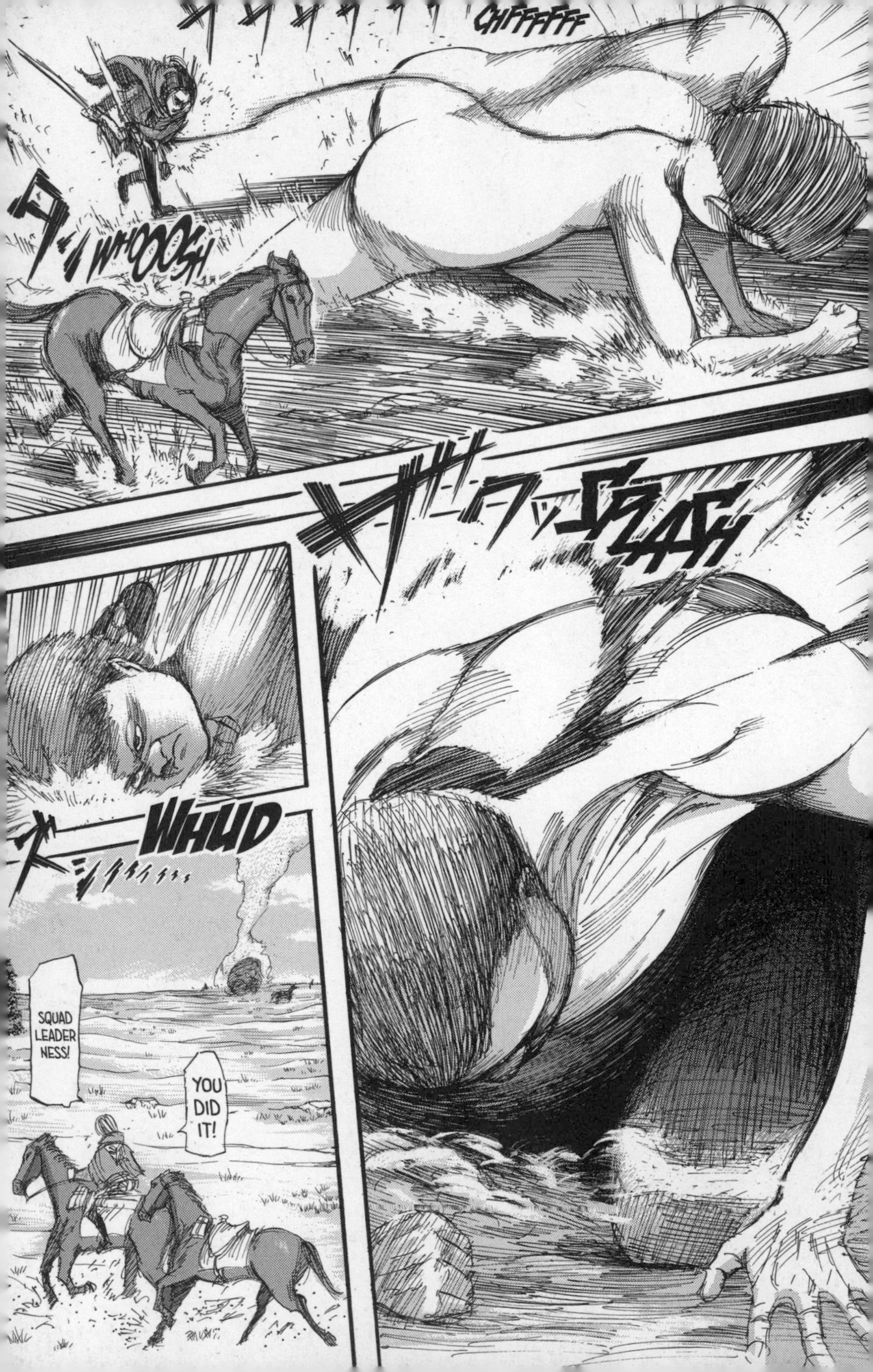
CHFFFFFF
WHOOOSH
SLASH
WHUD
SQUAD LEADER NESS!
YOU DID IT!

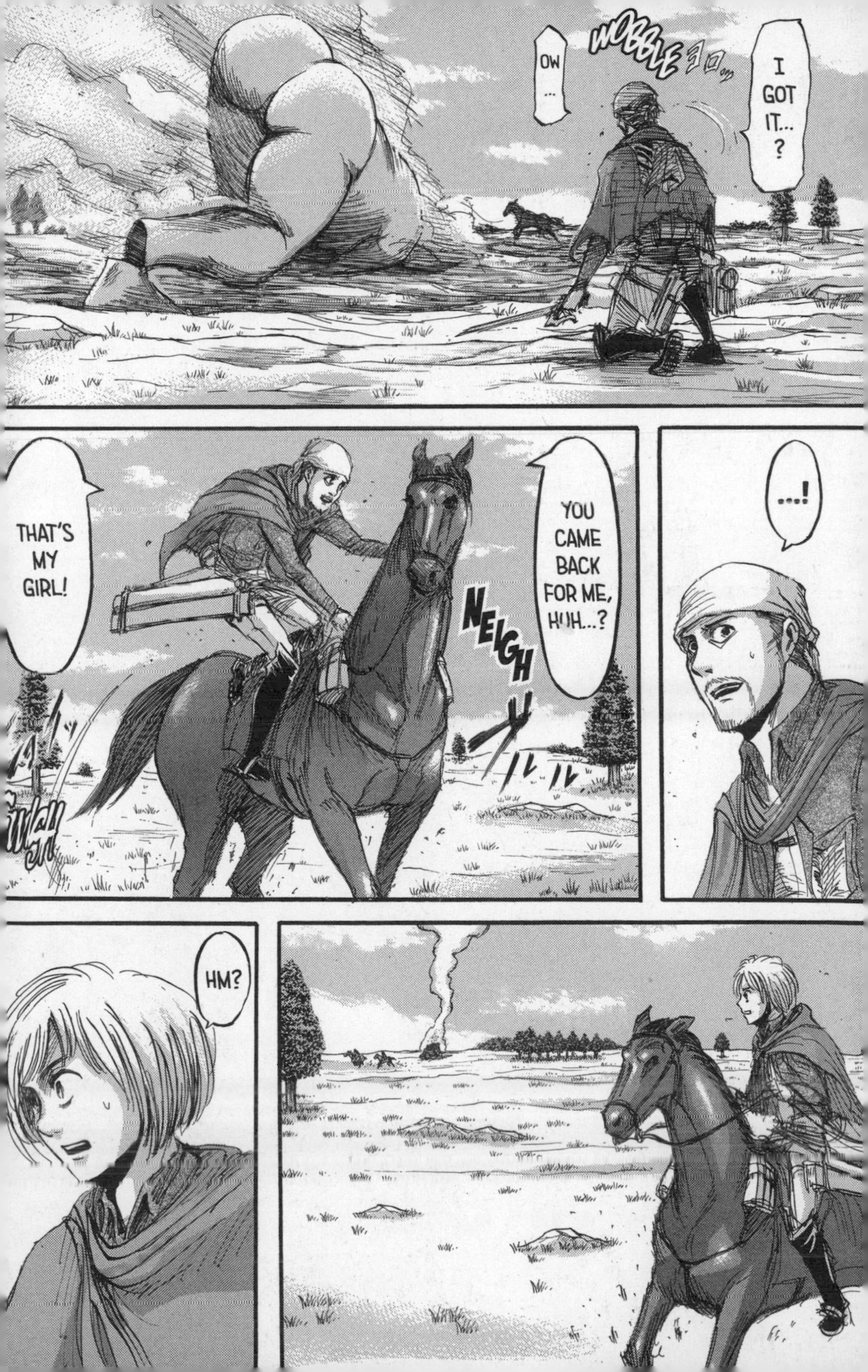
I GOT IT... ?
WOBBLE ヨロ
OW ...
...!
YOU CAME BACK FOR ME, HUH...?
NEIGH
THAT'S MY GIRL!
HM?

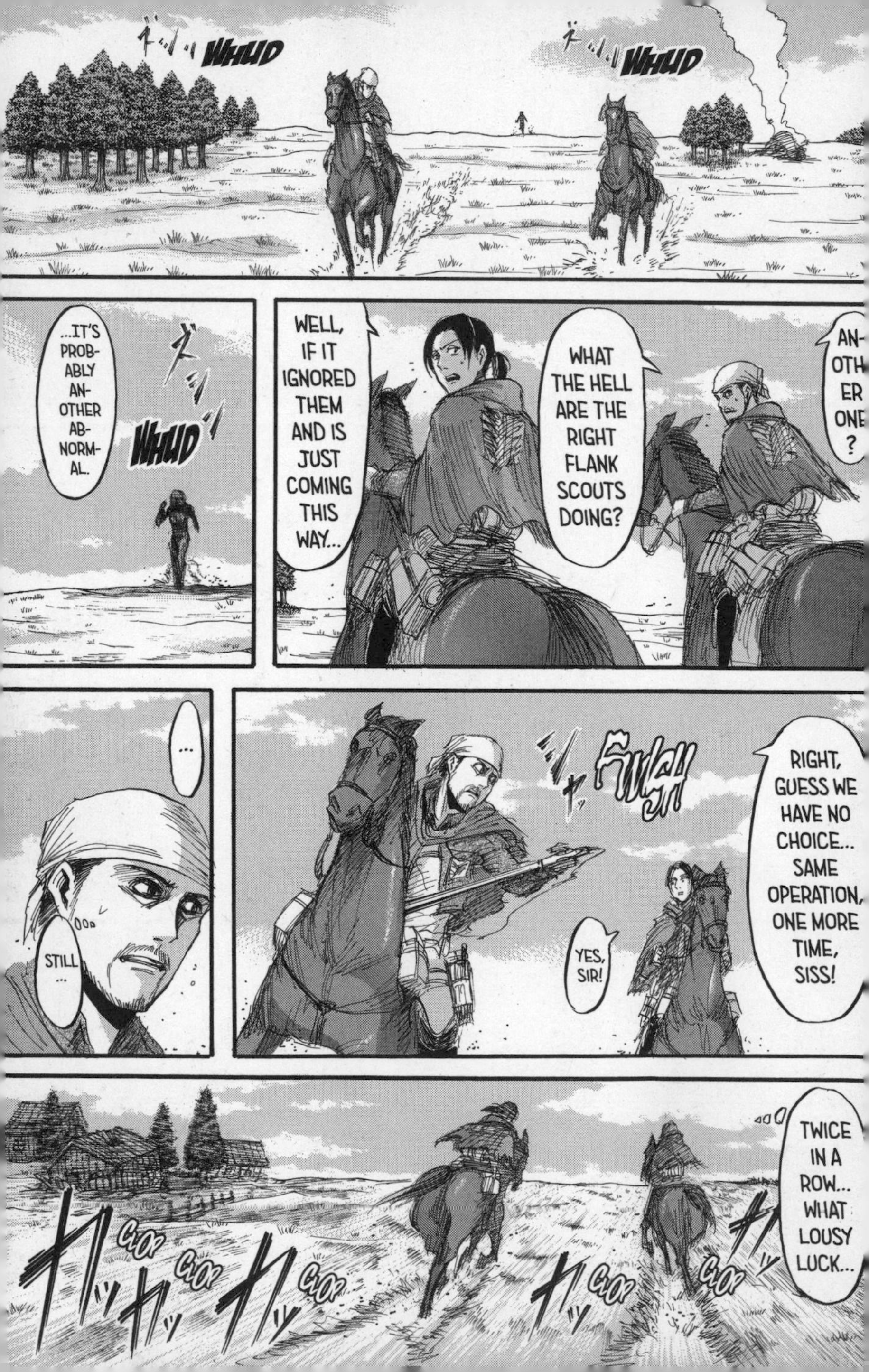
WHUD
WHUD
AN-OTHER ONE?
WHAT THE HELL ARE THE RIGHT FLANK SCOUTS DOING?
WELL, IF IT IGNORED THEM AND IS JUST COMING THIS WAY...
...IT'S PROBABLY AN-OTHER AB-NORM-AL.
WHUD
RIGHT, GUESS WE HAVE NO CHOICE... SAME OPERATION, ONE MORE TIME, SISS!
FWISH
YES, SIR!
...
STILL...
TWICE IN A ROW... WHAT LOUSY LUCK...
CLOP
CLOP
CLOP
CLOP
CLOP

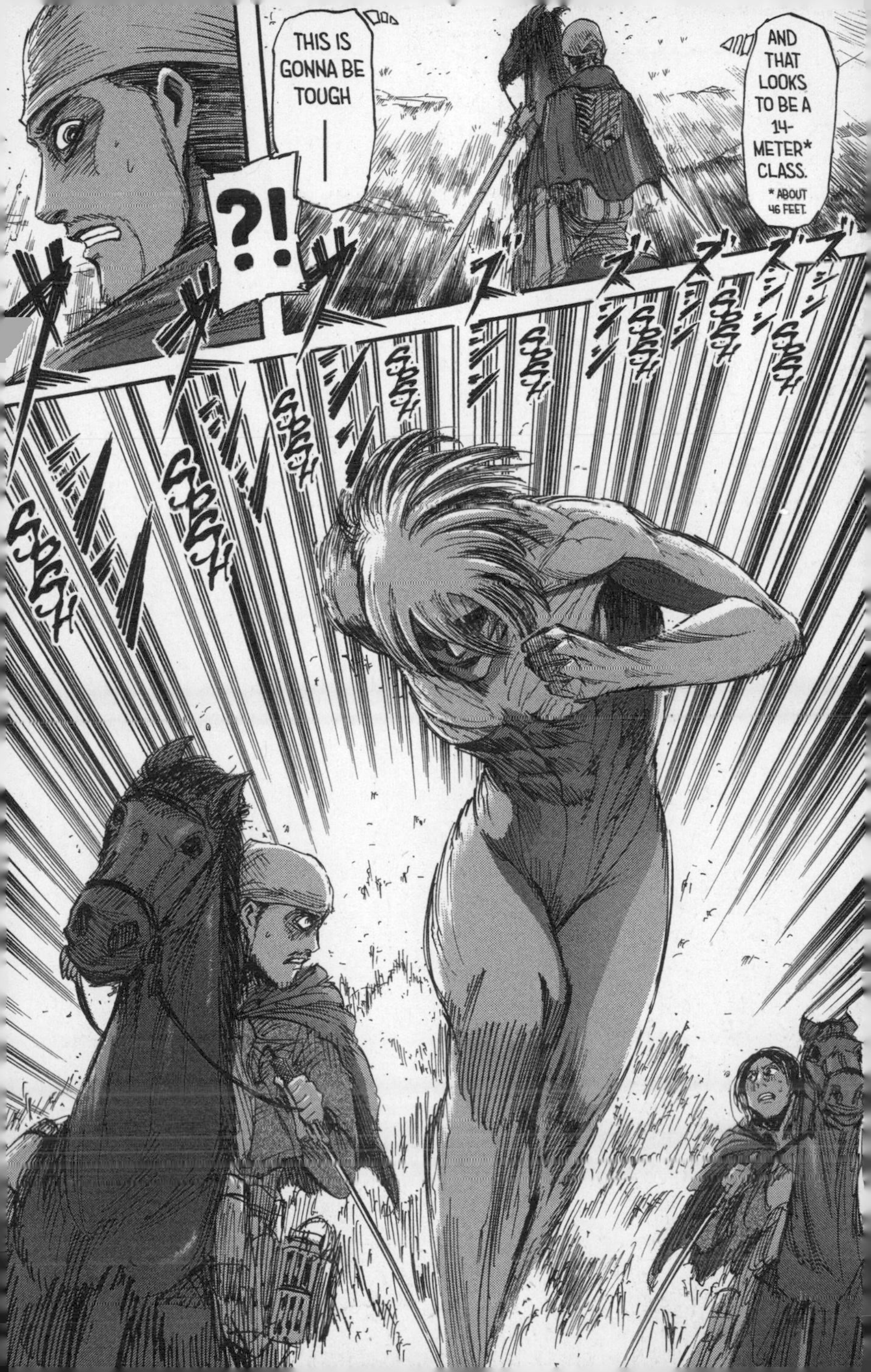
AND THAT LOOKS TO BE A 14-METER* CLASS.
* ABOUT 46 FEET.
THIS IS GONNA BE TOUGH —
?!
ズシン

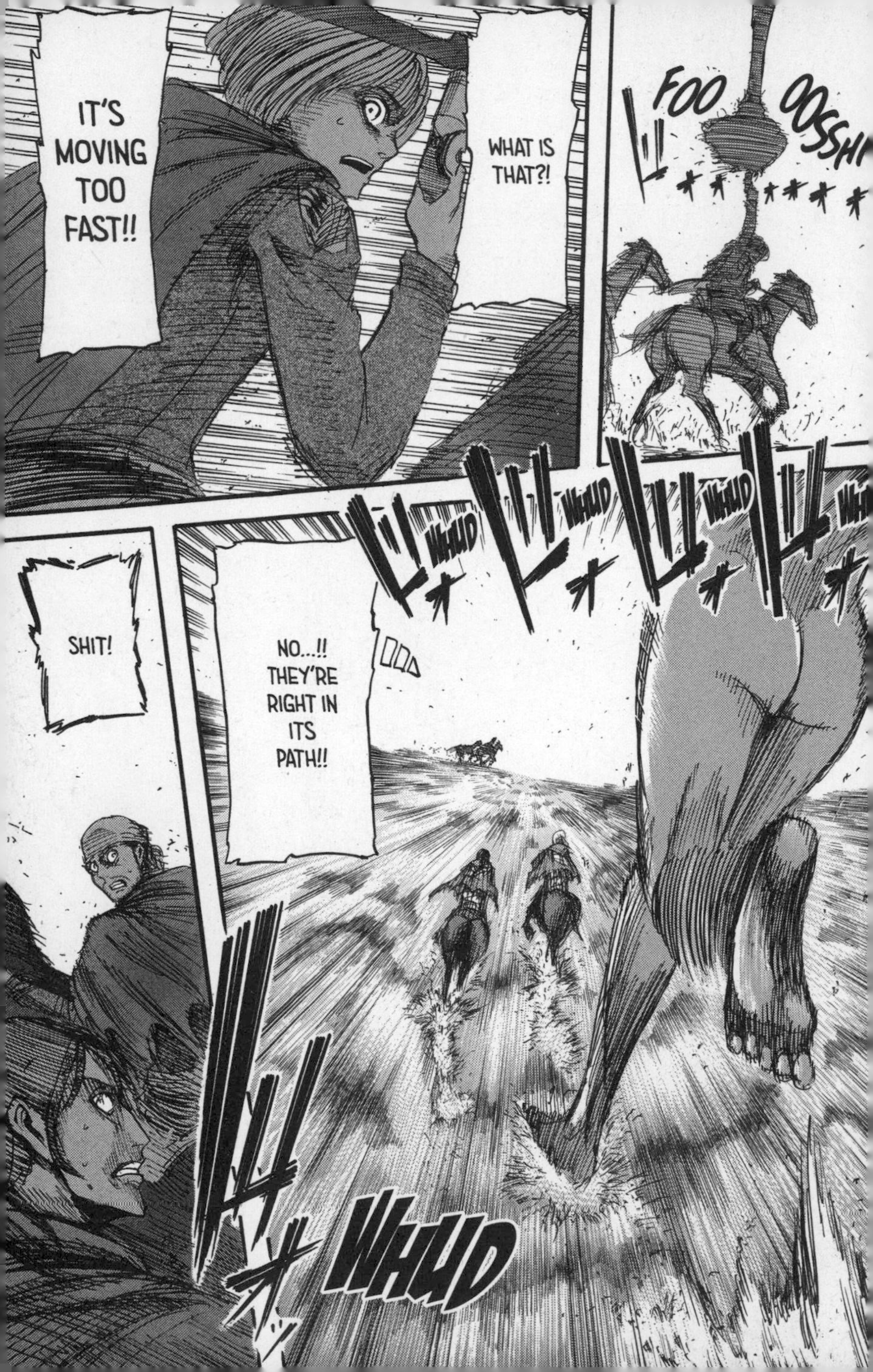
FOO
OOSSH
WHAT IS THAT?!
IT'S MOVING TOO FAST!!
WHUD
WHUD
WHUD
WHUD
NO...!! THEY'RE RIGHT IN ITS PATH!!
WHUD
SHIT!

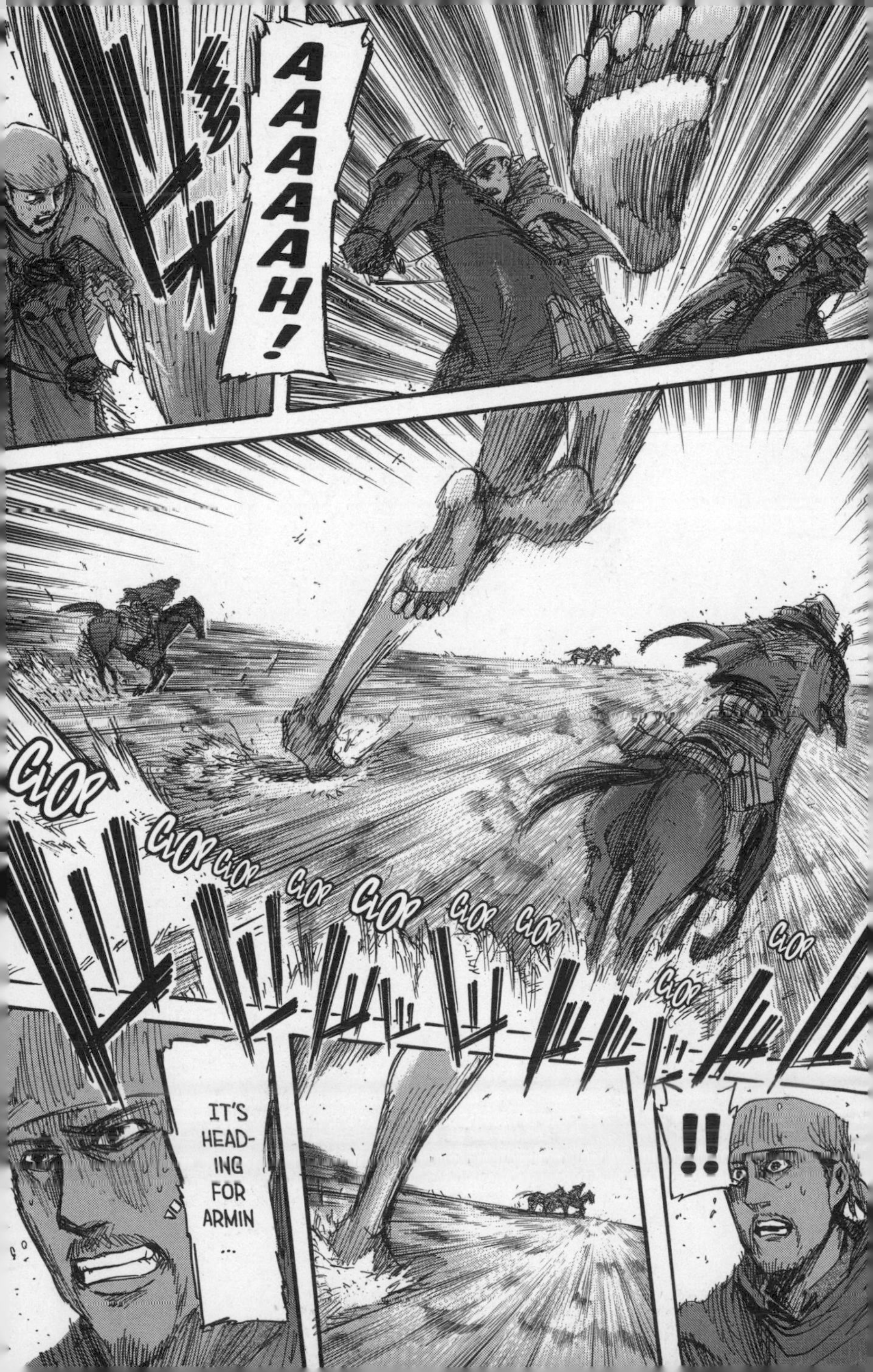
AAAAAAH!
CLOP
CLOP
CLOP
CLOP
CLOP
CLOP
CLOP
CLOP
CLOP
!!
IT'S HEADING FOR ARMIN ...

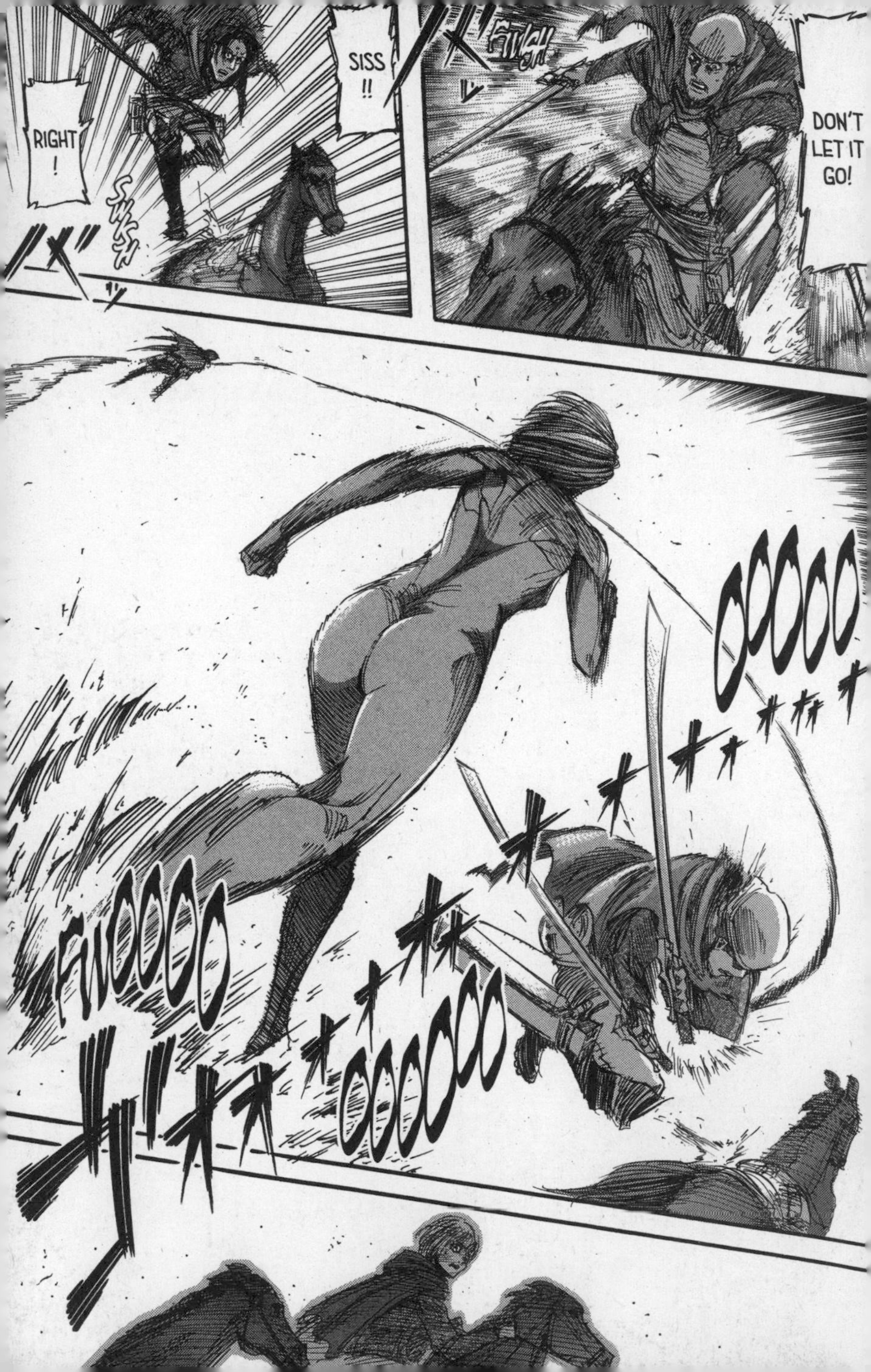
DON'T LET IT GO!
FWSH
SISS!!
RIGHT!
SWSH
OOOOO
FWOOOO
OOOOOO

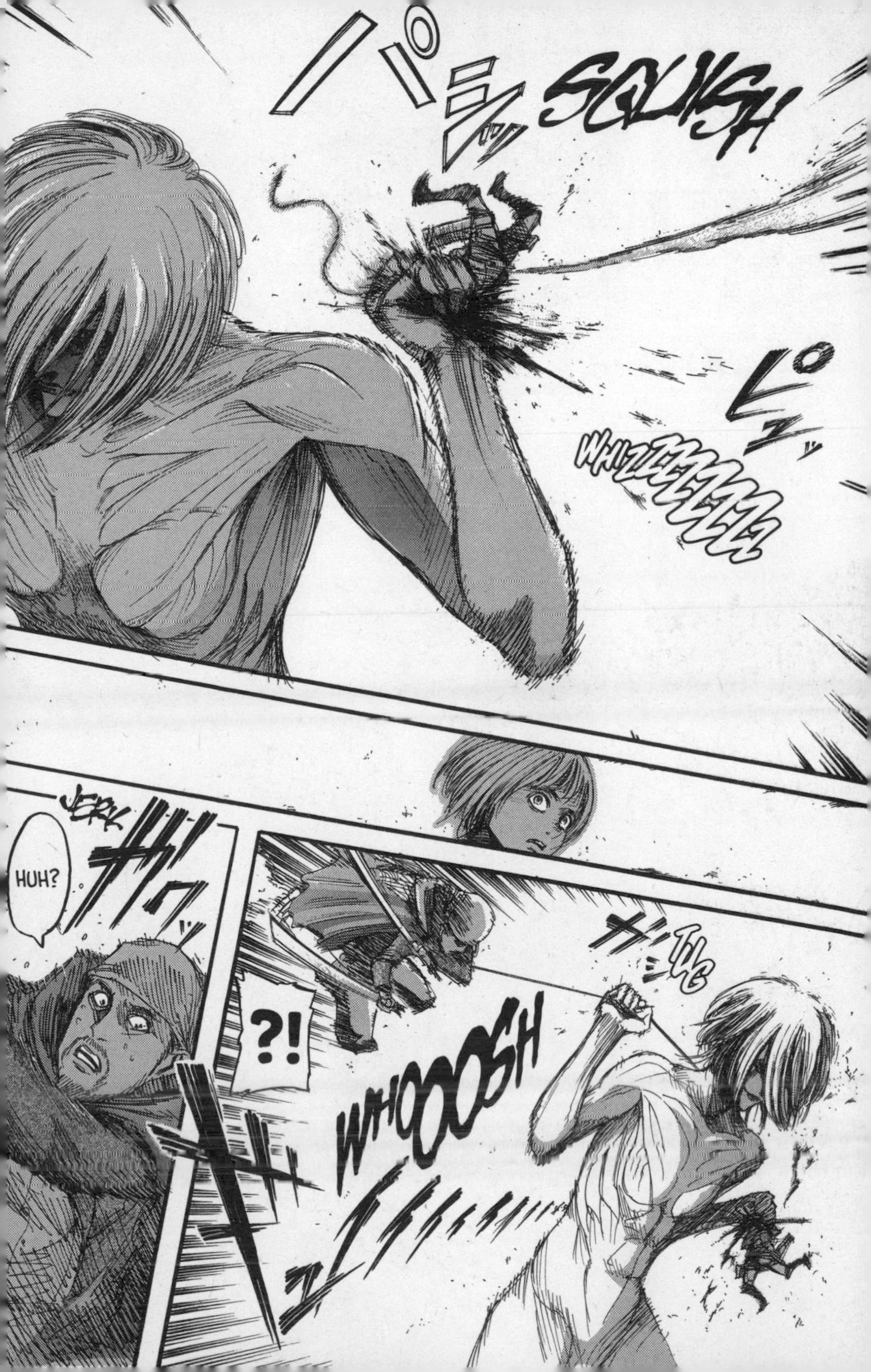
SQUISH
WHIZZZZZZZZ
TUG
WHOOOSH
?!
JERK
HUH?

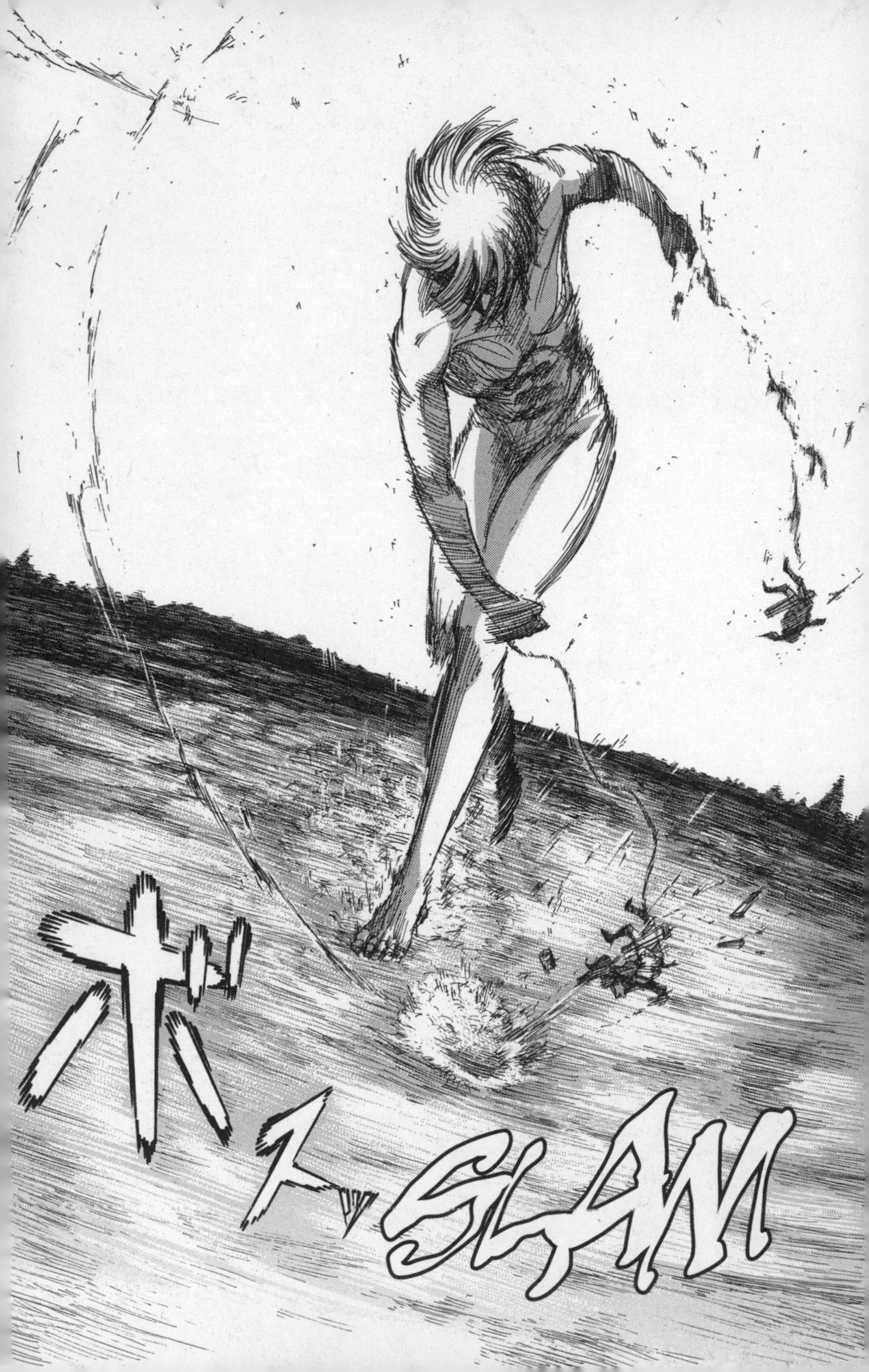
ボバッ
SLAM

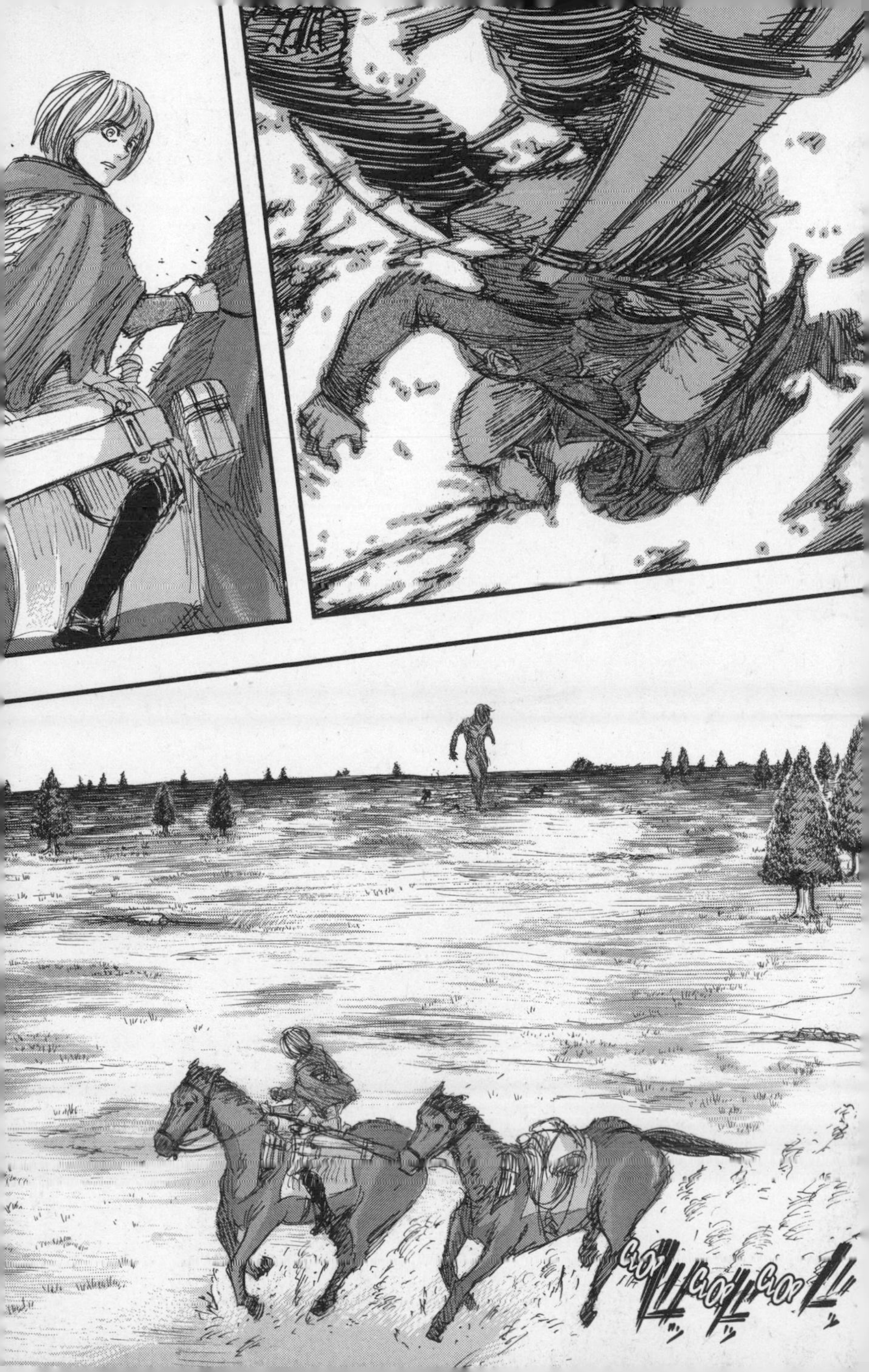
CLOP
CLOP
CLOP

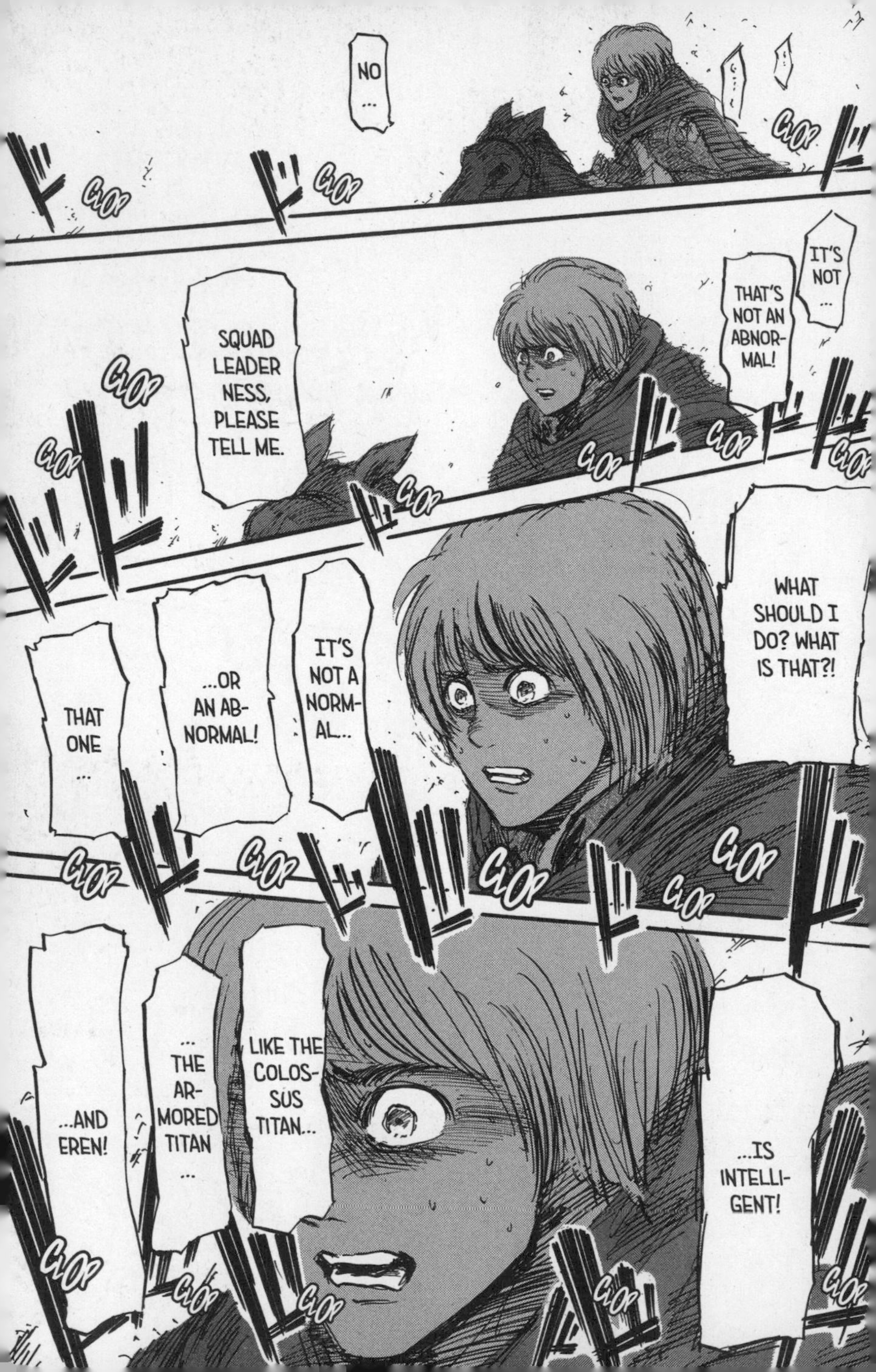
CLOP
NO ...
CLOP
CLOP
IT'S NOT ...
THAT'S NOT AN ABNORMAL!
SQUAD LEADER NESS, PLEASE TELL ME.
CLOP
CLOP
CLOP
CLOP
CLOP
WHAT SHOULD I DO? WHAT IS THAT?!
IT'S NOT A NORMAL...
...OR AN ABNORMAL!
THAT ONE ...
CLOP
CLOP
CLOP
CLOP
CLOP
...IS INTELLIGENT!
LIKE THE COLOSSUS TITAN...
... THE ARMORED TITAN ...
...AND EREN!
CLOP
CLOP
CLOP
CLOP
CLOP

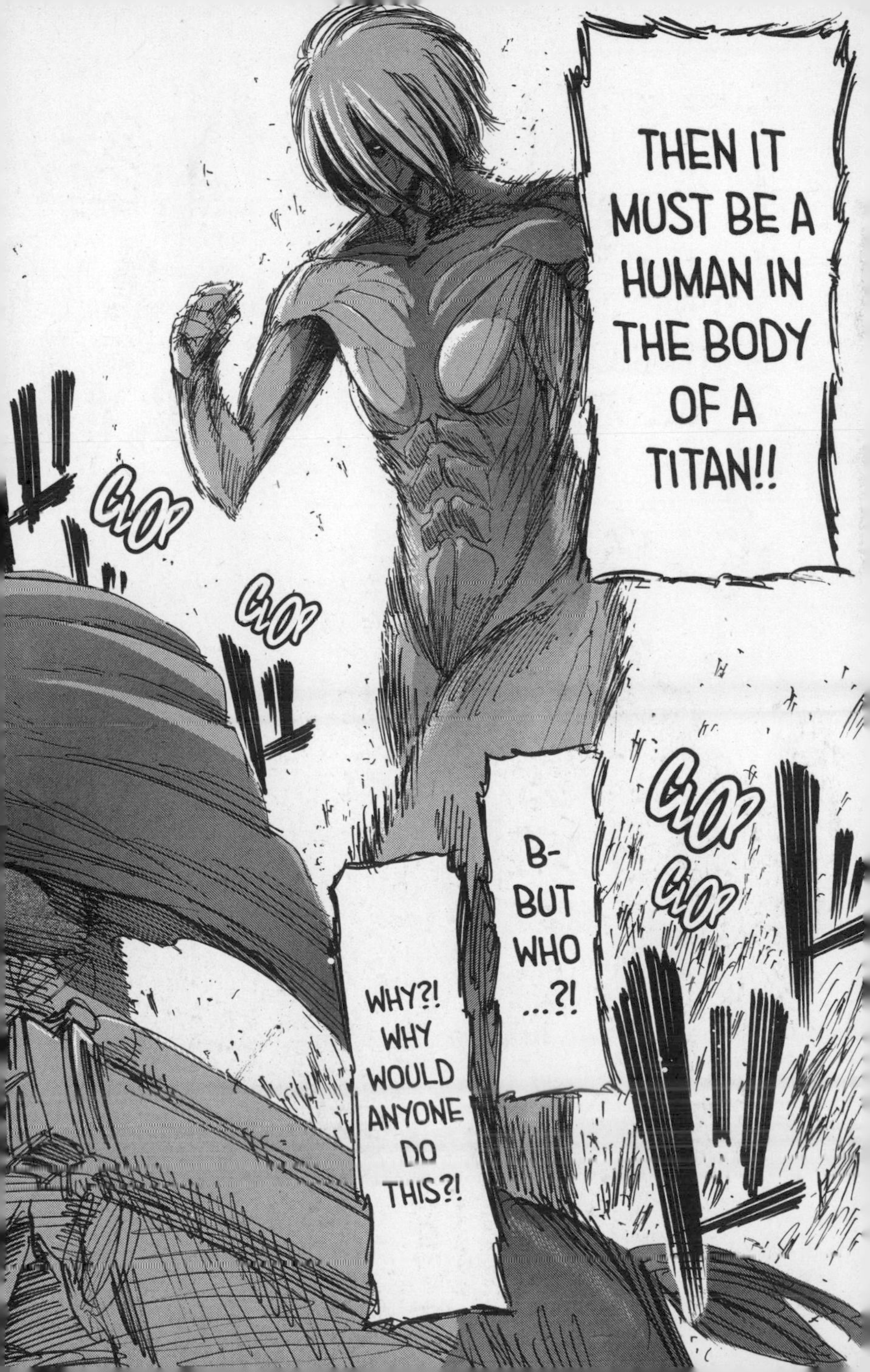
THEN IT MUST BE A HUMAN IN THE BODY OF A TITAN!!
CLOP
CLOP
CLOP
CLOP
B-BUT WHO ...?!
WHY?! WHY WOULD ANYONE DO THIS?!

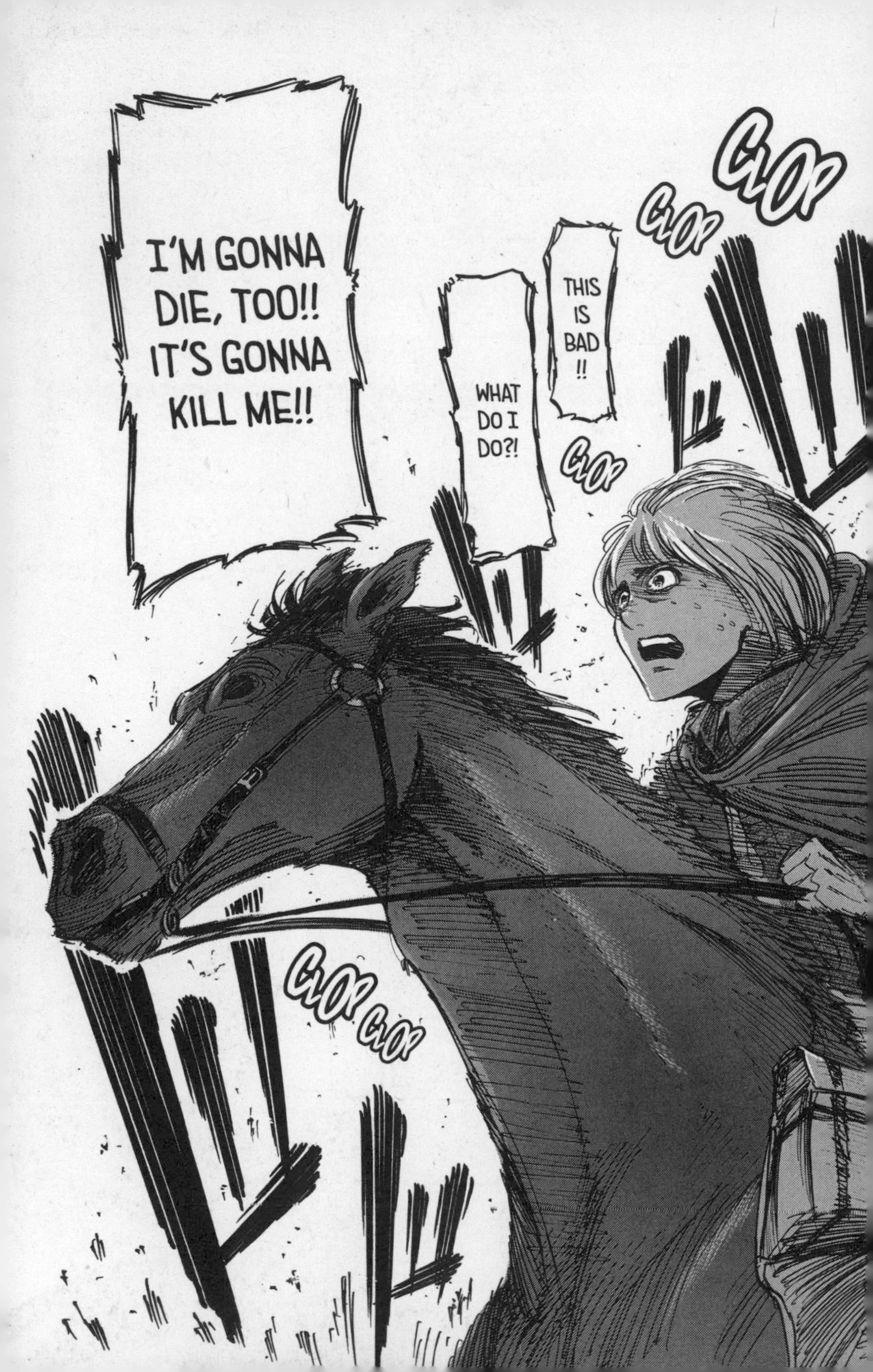
CLOP
CLOP
THIS IS BAD!!
WHAT DO I DO?!
CLOP
I'M GONNA DIE, TOO!! IT'S GONNA KILL ME!!
CLOP CLOP

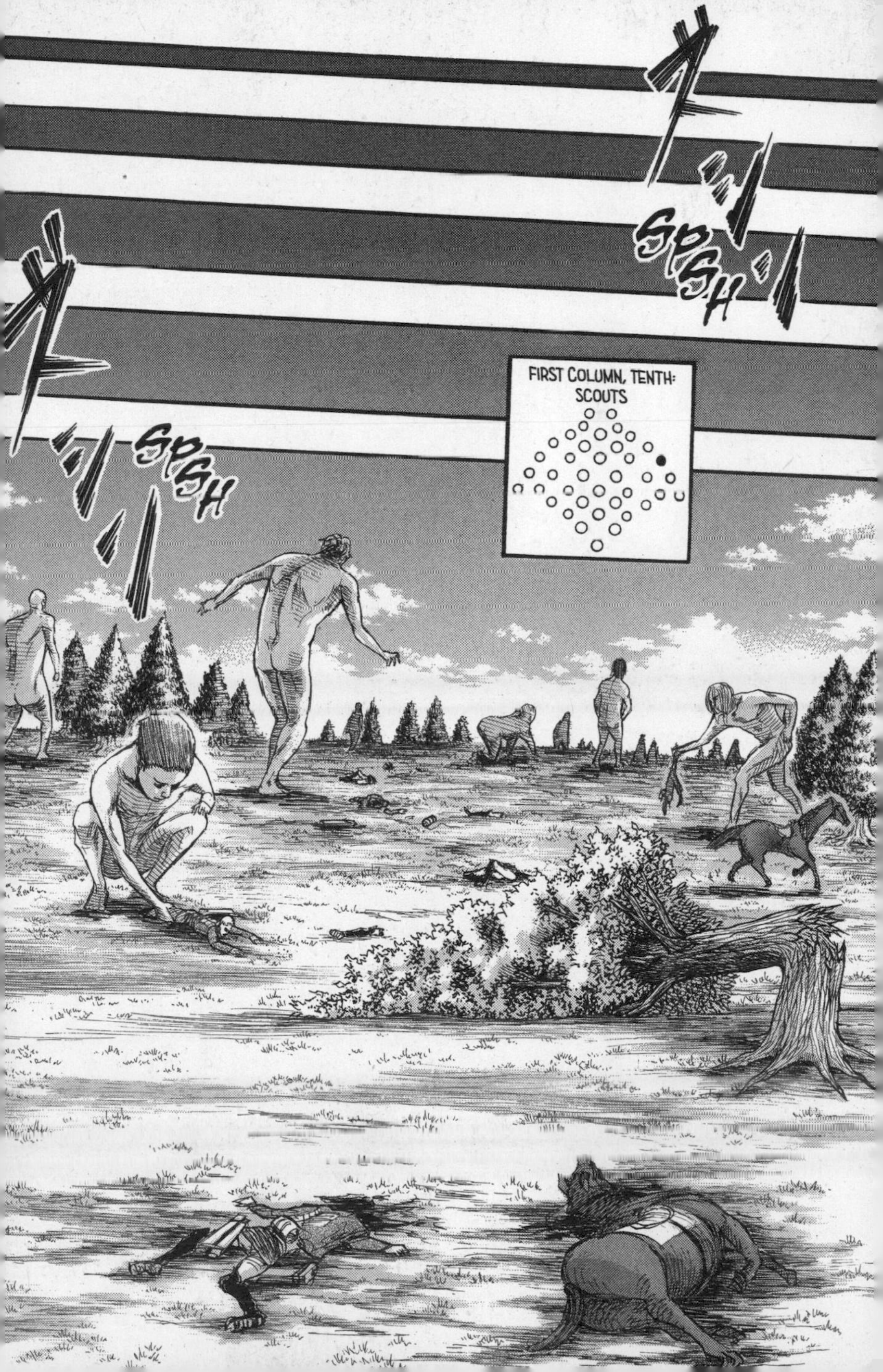
SPSH
FIRST COLUMN, TENTH:
SCOUTS
SPSH

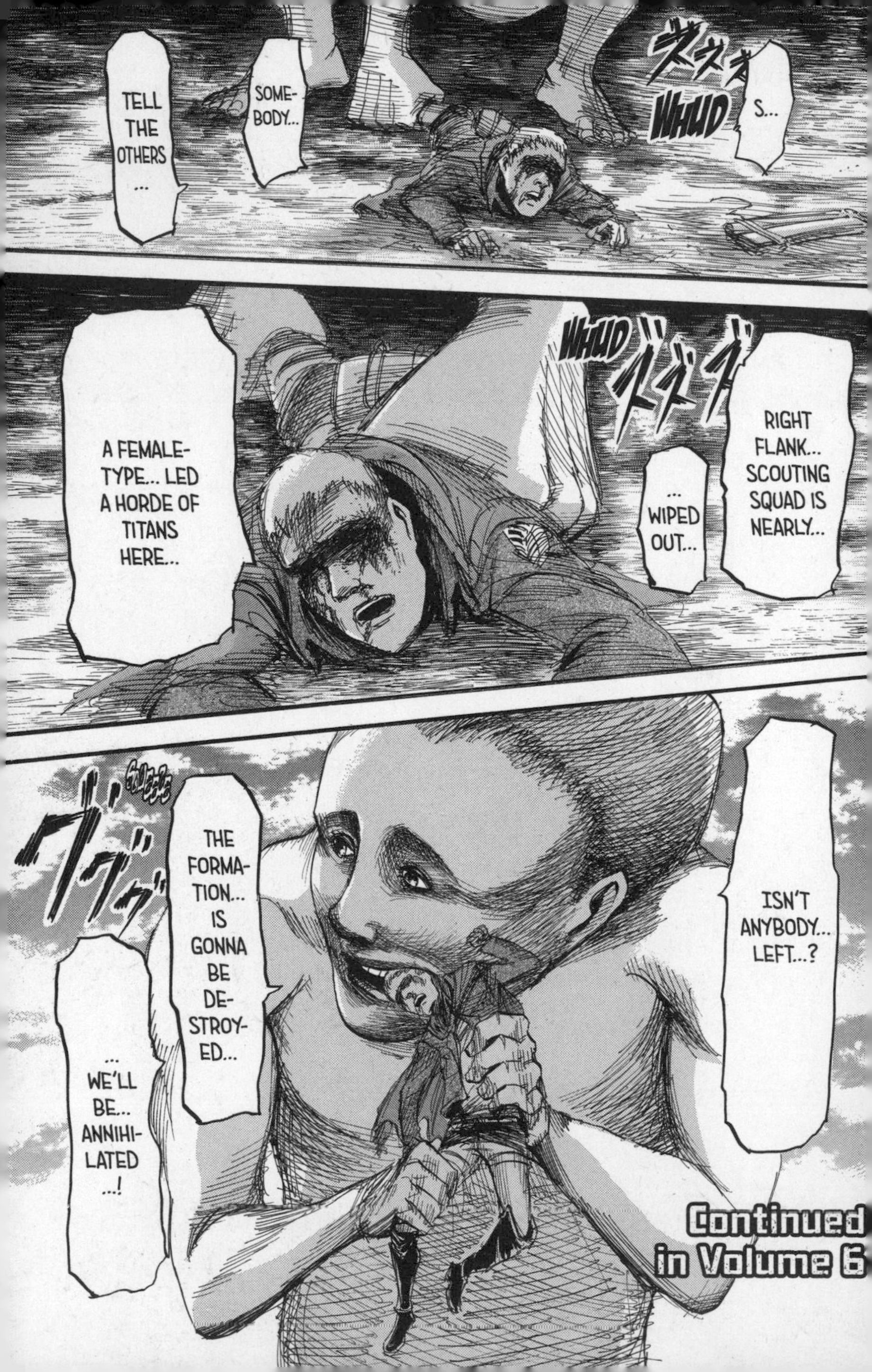
WHUD
S...
SOMEBODY...
TELL THE OTHERS ...
RIGHT FLANK... SCOUTING SQUAD IS NEARLY...
... WIPED OUT...
WHUD
A FEMALE-TYPE... LED A HORDE OF TITANS HERE...
ISN'T ANYBODY... LEFT...?
THE FORMATION... IS GONNA BE DESTROYED...
... WE'LL BE... ANNIHILATED ...!
Continued in Volume 6

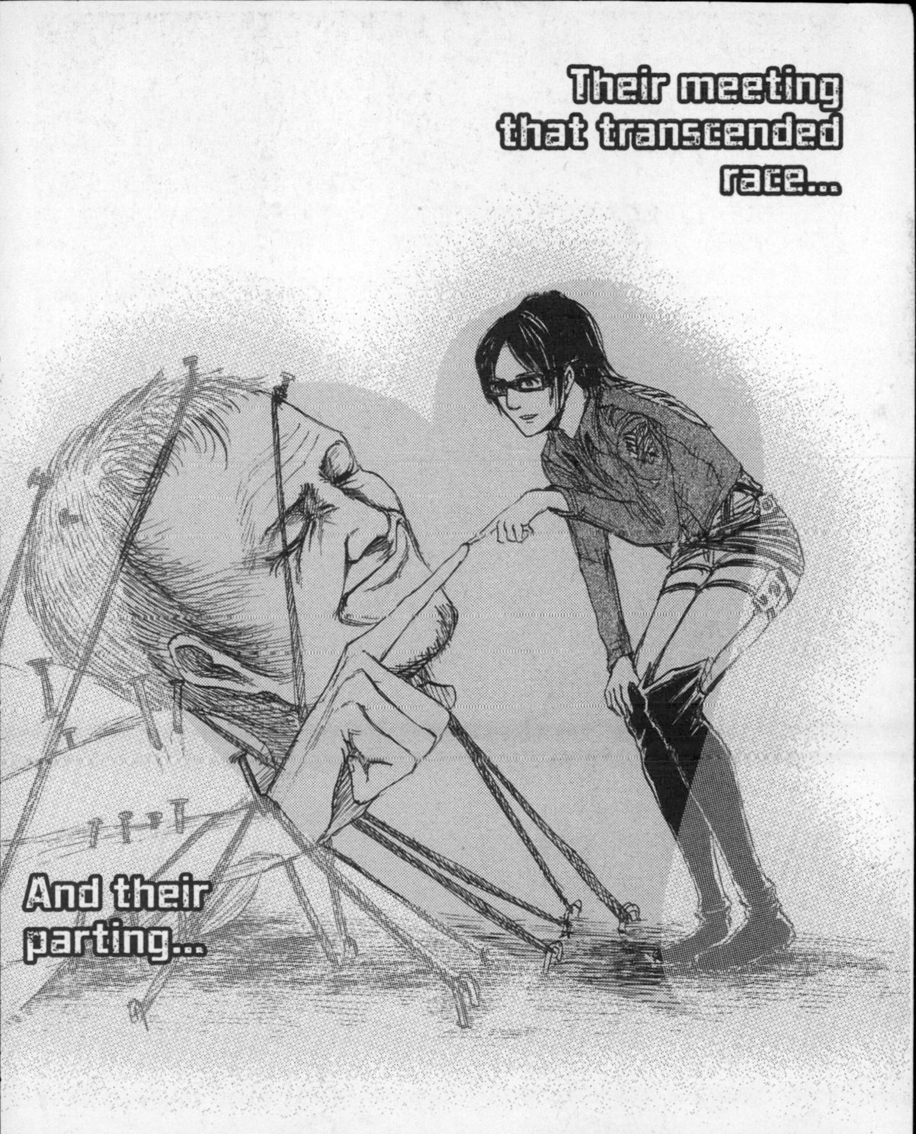
Their meeting that transcended race...
And their parting...

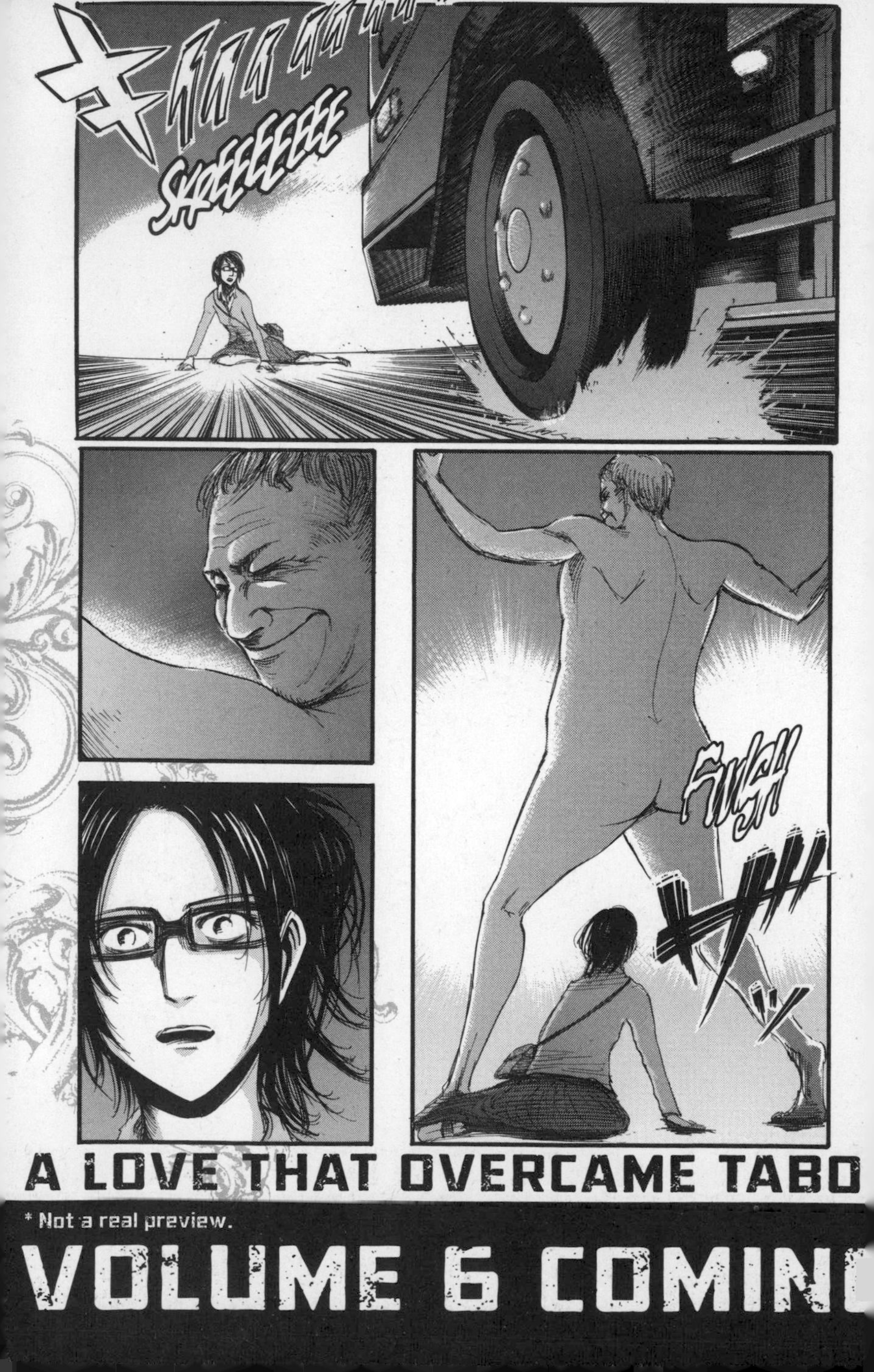
SKREEEEEEE
FWISH

A LOVE THAT OVERCAME TABO

* Not a real preview.

VOLUME 6 COMINC

Translation Notes

YMIR, PAGE 12 [12.5]

NO SPOILERS HERE, BUT IN NORSE MYTHOLOGY,
YMIR WAS THE PRIMEVAL GIANT SLAIN BY ODIN AND
HIS BROTHERS. THEY CREATED THE EARTH FROM
HIS BODY AND THE SEA FROM HIS BLOOD.